SO-BME-602

ARCHBISHOP ALEMANY LIB
DOMINICAN UNIVERSITY
SAN RAFAEL, CALIFORNIA 94901

HUMAN
RIGHTS
WATCH

WORLD REPORT

2009

EVENTS OF 2008

Copyright © 2009 Human Rights Watch
All rights reserved.
Printed in the United States of America

ISBN-13: 978-1-58322-858-6

Front cover photo: *A young man enters South Africa
on the Zimbabwe-South Africa border.*
© 2007 Dirk-Jan Visser

Cover and book design by Rafael Jiménez

Human Rights Watch

350 Fifth Avenue, 34th floor
New York, NY 10118-3299 USA
Tel: +1 212 290 4700
Fax: +1 212 736 1300
hrwnyc@hrw.org

1630 Connecticut Avenue, N.W.,
Suite 500
Washington, DC 20009 USA
Tel: +1 202 612 4321
Fax: +1 202 612 4333
hrwdc@hrw.org

2-12 Pentonville Road, 2nd Floor
London N1 9HF, UK
Tel: +44 20 7713 1995
Fax: +44 20 7713 1800
hrwuk@hrw.org

27 Rue de Lisbonne
75008 Paris, France
Tel: +33 (0) 1 43 59 55 35
Fax: +33 (0) 1 43 59 55 22
paris@hrw.org

Avenue des Gaulois, 7
1040 Brussels, Belgium
Tel: + 32 (2) 732 2009
Fax: + 32 (2) 732 0471
hrwbe@hrw.org

64-66 Rue de Lausanne
1201 Geneva, Switzerland
Tel: +41 22 738 0481
Fax: +41 22 738 1791
hrwgva@hrw.org

Poststraße 4-5
10178 Berlin, Germany
Tel: +49 30 2593 06-10
Fax: +49 30 2593 0629
berlin@hrw.org

www.hrw.org

Human Rights Watch is dedicated to protecting the human rights of people around the world.

We stand with victims and activists to prevent discrimination, to uphold political freedom, to protect people from inhumane conduct in wartime, and to bring offenders to justice.

We investigate and expose human rights violations and hold abusers accountable.

We challenge governments and those who hold power to end abusive practices and respect international human rights law.

We enlist the public and the international community to support the cause of human rights for all.

HUMAN RIGHTS WATCH

Human Rights Watch is one of the world's leading independent organizations dedicated to defending and protecting human rights. By focusing international attention where human rights are violated, we give voice to the oppressed and hold oppressors accountable for their crimes. Our rigorous, objective investigations and strategic, targeted advocacy build intense pressure for action and raise the cost of human rights abuse. For 30 years, Human Rights Watch has worked tenaciously to lay the legal and moral groundwork for deep-rooted change and has fought to bring greater justice and security to people around the world.

Human Rights Watch began in 1978 with the founding of its Europe and Central Asia division (then known as Helsinki Watch). Today, it also includes divisions covering Africa, the Americas, Asia, and the Middle East and North Africa; a United States program; thematic divisions or programs on arms, business and human rights, children's rights, HIV/AIDS and human rights, international justice, lesbian, gay, bisexual and transgender rights, refugees, terrorism/counterterrorism, and women's rights; and an emergencies program. It maintains offices in Berlin, Brussels, Chicago, Geneva, Johannesburg, London, Los Angeles, Moscow, New York, Paris, San Francisco, Tokyo, Toronto, and Washington DC, and field presences in around a dozen more locations globally. Human Rights Watch is an independent, nongovernmental organization, supported by contributions from private individuals and foundations worldwide. It accepts no government funds, directly or indirectly.

The staff includes Kenneth Roth, Executive Director; Michele Alexander, Development and Outreach Director; Clive Baldwin, Senior Legal Advisor; Carroll Bogert, Associate Director; Emma Daly, Communications Director; Ian Gorvin, Senior Program Officer; Barbara Guglielmo, Finance and Administration Director; Peggy Hicks, Global Advocacy Director; Iain Levine, Program Director; Andrew Mawson, Deputy Program Director; Suzanne Nossel, Chief Operating Officer; Dinah PoKempner, General Counsel; Aisling Reidy, Senior Legal Advisor; James Ross, Legal and Policy Director; Joseph Saunders, Deputy Program Director; and Minky Worden, Media Director.

The division directors of Human Rights Watch are Brad Adams, Asia; Joseph Amon, HIV/AIDS and Human Rights; John Biaggi, International Film Festival; Peter Bouckaert, Emergencies; Holly Cartner, Europe and Central Asia; Richard Dicker, International Justice; David Fathi, United States; Bill Frelick, Refugees; Georgette Gagnon, Africa; Arvind Ganesan, Business and Human Rights; Liesl Gerntholtz, Women's Rights; Steve Goose, Arms; Scott Long, Lesbian, Gay, Bisexual and Transgender Rights; Joanne Mariner, Terrorism/Counterterrorism; José Miguel Vivanco, Americas; Lois Whitman, Children's Rights; and Sarah Leah Whitson, Middle East and North Africa.

The advocacy directors of Human Rights Watch are Steve Crawshaw, United Nations–New York; Juliette De Rivero, United Nations–Geneva; Jean-Marie Fardeau, Paris; Marianne Heuwagen, Berlin; Lotte Leicht, European Union; Tom Porteous, London; and Tom Malinowski, Washington DC.

The members of the board of directors are Jane Olson, Chair, Bruce J. Klatsky, Vice Chair, Sid Sheinberg, Vice Chair, John J. Studzinski, Vice Chair, Louise Arbour, Lloyd Axworthy, Jorge Castañeda, Geoffrey Cowan, Tony Elliott, Hassan Elmasry, Michael G. Fisch, Michael E. Gellert, Richard J. Goldstone, James F. Hoge, Jr., Wendy Keys, Robert Kissane, Joanne Leedom-Ackerman, Susan Manilow, Kati Marton, Linda Mason, Barry Meyer, Pat Mitchell, Joel Motley, Catherine Powell, Sigrid Rausing, Victoria Riskin, Shelley Rubin, Kevin P. Ryan, Jean-Louis Servan-Schreiber, Darian W. Swig, John R. Taylor, Shibley Telhami, Catherine Zennström.

Emeritus board members are Robert L. Bernstein, Founding Chair, 1979-1997, Jonathan F. Fanton, Chair, 1998-2003, Lisa Anderson, David M. Brown, William D. Carmichael, Dorothy Cullman, Adrian W. DeWind, Edith Everett, Vartan Gregorian, Alice H. Henkin, Stephen L. Kass, Marina Pinto Kaufman, Josh Mailman, Samuel K. Murumba, Peter Osnos, Kathleen Peratis, Bruce Rabb, Orville Schell, Gary Sick, and Malcolm B. Smith.

Acknowledgments

A compilation of this magnitude requires contribution from a large number of people, including most of the Human Rights Watch staff. The contributors were:

Fred Abrahams, Pema Abrahams, Brad Adams, Paola Adriazola, Chris Albin-Lackey, Susie Alegre, Henrik Alffram, Nada Ali, Joseph Amon, Leeam Azulay-Yagev, Laurie Ball, Nadia Barhoum, Clarisa Bencomo, Andrea Berg, Helene Blary, Jackie Bornstein, Sebastian Brett, Selena Brewer, Cynthia Brown, Jane Buchanan, David Buchbinder, Maria Burnett, Elizabeth Calvin, Juliana Cano Nieto, Holly Cartner, Haleh Chahrokh, Grace Choi, Jonathan Cohen, Sara Colm, Tanya Cooper, Steve Crawshaw, Kiran D'Amico, Sara Darehshori, Jennifer Daskal, Juliette De Rivero, Farida Deif, Fernando Delgado, Rachel Denber, Alison Des Forges, Thodleen Dessources, Richard Dicker, Corinne Dufka, Andrej Dynko, Dahlia El Zein, Elizabeth Evenson, Jean-Marie Fardeau, Alice Farmer, David Fathi, Jamie Fellner, Conor Fortune, Bill Frelick, Chloë Fussell, Georgette Gagnon, Arvind Ganesan, Meenakshi Ganguly, Liesl Gerntholtz, Neela Ghoshal, Brent Giannotta, Thomas Gilchrist, Allison Gill, Sebastian Gillioz, Giorgi Gogia, Eric Goldstein, Veronika Szente Goldston, Steve Goose, Ian Gorvin, Brian Griffey, Eric Guttschuss, Julia Hall, Ali Hasan Dayan, Leslie Haskell, Angela Heimburger, Jehanne Henry, Marianne Heuwagen, Peggy Hicks, Nadim Houry, Claire Ivers, Pamela Jao, Rafael Jiménez, Tiseke Kasambala, Elise Keppler, Carolyn Kindelan, Juliane Kippenberg, Kennji Kizuka, Sonya Kleshik, Kathryn Koonce, Charu Lata Hogg, Leslie Lefkow, Lotte Leicht, Iain Levine, Maria Lisitsyna, Joseph Logan, Tanya Lokshina, Scott Long, Anna Lopriore, Tom Malinowski, Joanne Mariner, Abigail Marshak, Sarah Mathewson, David Mathieson, Veronica Matushaj, Andrew Mawson, Maria McFarland, Megan McLemore, Omid Memarian, Rikky Minyuku, Lisa Misol, Marianne Møllmann, Ashoka Mukpo, Jim Murphy, Zama Coursen Neff, Stephanie Neider, Carolyn Norris, Alison Parker, Elaine Pearson, Sasha Petrov, Sunai Phasuk, Carol Pier, Tom Porteous, McKenzie Price, Mia Psorn, Ayla Qadeer, Ben Rawlence, Meg Reber, Emina Redzic, Rachel Reid, Aisling Reidy, Meghan Rhoad, Sophie Richardson, Lisa Rimli, James Ross, Kenneth Roth, Joe Saunders, Ida Sawyer, Matthew Schaaf, Rebecca Schleifer, Kay Seok, Jeffrey Severson, Kavita Shah, Bede Sheppard, Emma Sinclair-Webb, Param-Preet Singh,

Ole Solvang, Alexandra South, Mickey Spiegel, Nik Steinberg, Joe Stork, Rania Suidan, Stacy Sullivan, Jude Sunderland, Tamara Taraciuk, Sarah Tofte, Geoff Traugh, Simone Troller, Wanda Troszczynska-van Genderen, Bill Van Esveld, Anneke Van Woudenberg, Nisha Varia, Jose Miguel Vivanco, Igor Vorontsov, Benjamin Ward, Lois Whitman, Sarah Leah Whitson, Christoph Wilcke, Daniel Wilkinson, Nicholas Wood, Kreshnik Zhega, Iwona Zielinska.

Ian Gorvin edited the report with assistance from Iain Levine, Andrew Mawson, and Joe Saunders. Dahlia El Zein coordinated the editing process. Layout and production were coordinated by Grace Choi and Rafael Jiménez, with assistance from Anna Lopriore, Veronica Matushaj, and Jim Murphy.

Leeam Azulay-Yagev, Jonathan Cohen, Dahlia El Zein, Conor Fortune, Chloë Fussell, Thomas Gilchrist, Brian Griffey, Carolyn Kindelan, Kennji Kizuka, Kathryn Koonce, Mignon Lamia, Abigail Marshak, Ashoka Mukpo, Stephanie Neider, McKenzie Price, and Alexandra South proofread the report.

For a full list of Human Rights Watch staff, please go to our website: www.hrw.org/about/info/staff.html.

Table of Contents

Taking Back the Initiative from the Human Rights Spoilers

By Kenneth Roth

A government's respect for human rights must be measured not only by how it treats its own people but also by how it protects rights in its relations with other countries. As we commemorate the sixtieth anniversary of the Universal Declaration of Human Rights, the response of governments to the plight of people abroad is often anemic. Indeed, it is a sad fact that when it comes to this international protection of rights, the governments with the clearest vision and strategy are often those that seek to undermine enforcement. The days are past when one would look to Washington, Brussels, or other Western capitals for the initiative in intergovernmental discussions of human rights. Today, those conducting the most energetic diplomacy on human rights are likely to reside in such places as Algiers, Cairo, or Islamabad, with backing from Beijing and Moscow. The problem is that they are pushing in the wrong direction.

These human rights opponents defend the prerogative of governments to do what they want to their people. They hide behind the principles of sovereignty, non-interference, and Southern solidarity, but their real aim is to curb criticism of their own human rights abuses or those of their allies and friends. The activities of these "spoilers" have come to dominate intergovernmental discussions of human rights. For example, they have ended United Nations scrutiny of severe repression in Uzbekistan, Iran, and the Democratic Republic of Congo. They have mounted intense challenges to criticism of the Burmese military and possible prosecution of Sudanese President Omar al-Bashir. And they have deeply compromised the new UN Human Rights Council.

The reason for their success lies less in the attractiveness of their vision than in the often weak and inconsistent commitment of governments that traditionally stood for the defense of human rights. It is not as if the people of the world are suddenly enamored of dictatorship and repression. Their desire for basic rights remains unchanged, whether in the displaced persons camps of Darfur, the tribal areas of Pakistan, or the prisons of Egypt. Rather, the vigor of the anti-human rights campaign is, ironically, a testament to the power of the human rights ideal.

The spoilers would hardly bother if the stigma of being labeled a human rights violator did not carry such sting.

Shifts in global power have emboldened spoiler governments in international forums to challenge human rights as a "Western" or "imperialist" imposition. The force of China's authoritarian example and the oil-fueled muscle of Russia have made it easier to reject human rights principles. The moral standing of a country like South Africa by virtue of its own dark past means that its challenge to the international human rights agenda is influential.

Nevertheless, governments that care about human rights worldwide retain enough clout to build a broad coalition to fight repression—if they are willing to use it. Instead, these governments have largely abandoned the field. Succumbing to competing interests and credibility problems of their own making, they have let themselves be outmaneuvered and sidelined in UN venues such as the Security Council and the Human Rights Council, and in the policy debates that shape multilateral diplomacy toward Burma, Darfur, Sri Lanka, Zimbabwe, and other trouble spots.

For the United States, that withdrawal is the logical consequence of the Bush administration's decision to combat terrorism without regard to the basic rights not to be subjected to torture, "disappearance," or detention without trial. Against that backdrop, Washington's periodic efforts to discuss rights have been undercut by justifiable accusations of hypocrisy. Reversing that ugly record must be a first priority for the new administration of Barack Obama if the US government is to assume a credible leadership role on human rights.

Washington's frequent abdication has often forced the European Union to act on its own. Sometimes it has done so admirably, such as after the Russia-Georgia conflict, when its deployment of monitors eased tensions and helped protect civilians, or in eastern Chad, where it sent 3,300 troops as part of a UN civilian protection mission. But the EU did a poor job of projecting its influence more broadly, to places like Burma, Somalia, or the Democratic Republic of Congo. It often sought to avoid the political fallout of doing nothing by hiding behind a cumbersome EU decision-making process that favors inaction. Moreover, its frequent reluctance to stand up to the Bush administration in protest against abusive counterterrorism policies opened the EU to charges of double standards that poisoned the global debate on human rights and made it easier for spoilers to prevail.

The US and the EU are not the only ones promoting human rights abroad. Increasingly, some governments in Latin America, Africa, and Asia can be looked to for support on international rights initiatives. Those that stand out include Argentina, Chile, Costa Rica, Mexico, and Uruguay in Latin America, and Botswana, Ghana, Liberia, and Zambia in Africa. In Asia, Japan and South Korea tend to be sympathetic to rights but are generally reluctant to take strong public positions.

Yet forced to act without the firm and consistent backing of the major Western democracies, these important voices are rarely able to mount on their own a major international diplomatic effort to address serious human rights abuses. Even the best-intentioned middle-sized powers cannot forge a solution to the world's most repressive situations without the partnership of the larger Western powers that still dominate the United Nations, have large and active diplomatic corps, and can deploy substantial military and economic resources.

So by default, those often setting the human rights agenda in international forums are opponents of human rights enforcement—governments of nations such as Algeria, China, Egypt, India, Pakistan, and Russia. They want to return to an era when the defense of human rights was left to the discretion of each government, and violations carried little international cost.

To resist that aspiration will take a determination that too often has been lacking. First, because the most effective human rights advocacy is by example, governments hoping to defend human rights elsewhere must commit themselves to respect those rights in their own conduct. As described in more detail below, that means, in the counterterrorism realm, a definitive end to such abuses as the use of torture and other coercive interrogation techniques, the "disappearance" of suspects in secret detention facilities, and the long-term detention of suspects without trial—as well as a willingness to speak out immediately if any government, including a close ally, resumes these practices. It also means addressing such persistent abuses as racism in the criminal justice system, mistreatment of migrants, or use of the death penalty.

Second, as in the case of any serious human rights violation, offenders must be held to account. For example, only by investigating, acknowledging, and repudiating the wrongdoing that has occurred, prosecuting serious crimes, and taking remedial steps to ensure that these abuses never recur, will Washington begin to build credibility as a government that practices what it preaches in the human rights realm.

Third, serious efforts must be undertaken to build a broad global coalition in support of human rights. In the case of the United States, it should seek to rejoin multilateral institutions such as the UN Human Rights Council and ratify key treaties such as those on women's and children's rights, enforced disappearances, cluster munitions, and antipersonnel landmines. It should adopt a policy of embracing the rule of law by re-signing the International Criminal Court treaty, actively supporting the court, and initiating a process for ultimate ratification. And it should actively support—politically, financially, and militarily—multilateral efforts to protect civilians from mass atrocities.

In the case of both the European Union and the United States, vigorous efforts should be made to reach out to governments of the global South, especially those that largely respect human rights at home but continue to resist the defense of human rights in their foreign policy. That requires addressing issues of particular concern to Southern governments, such as economic and social rights, racism, and the rights of migrants. It also requires avoiding double standards and remaining open to dialogue and appropriate political compromise.

Governments of the global South, in turn, must reconsider their reflexive stand shoulder to shoulder with the oppressors of the world rather than their victims. This misguided solidarity is particularly disappointing in the case of governments such as India and South Africa, which today are democracies that on balance respect the rights of their own people but pursue a foreign policy suggesting that others do not deserve similar rights. Bloc solidarity should not become a substitute for embracing the more fundamental values of human rights.

Finally, the new Obama administration must abandon the Bush administration's policy of hyper-sovereignty. It is music to the ears of the governments of China, Russia, and India to hear Washington deflect human rights criticism on sovereignty grounds. That approach effectively pushes back the clock to an era before the Universal Declaration of Human Rights and the many legal and institutional mechanisms it has spawned. A radical reappraisal of US policy is urgently needed. President Obama has promised such changes, and none too soon. The test will be whether he can resist pressures to sustain the Bush-led status quo.

A Callous Solidarity

Today, 60 years after the Universal Declaration of Human Rights, it is not tenable simply to deny the worthiness of the human rights ideal. As a result, the spoilers that are intent on undermining the international human rights regime rarely describe their intentions in those terms. Instead, these governments tend to say that they support human rights in principle, but oppose only the way that rights are allegedly twisted, used, or perverted by more powerful nations. They mimic the language of anti-imperialism, anti-colonialism, or solidarity with the downtrodden, but in fact, the spoilers are no friends of the persecuted. They find common cause with the dictators and tyrants of the world, not with the ordinary people facing oppression. They invoke Southern solidarity, but behind the lofty rhetoric, the solidarity they have in mind is with repressive governments, not their Southern victims.

There are many different reasons why some governments choose to play negative or indifferent roles with respect to human rights. Certain serious offenders, such as Belarus, Sudan, and Zimbabwe, push back against any human rights scrutiny to forestall international consideration of their own abuses. They are not leaders in international forums but they do speak up and vote. They seek to avoid any external constraint on how they treat their people. Sovereignty, not rights, is their watchword.

Other states play more of a leadership role in trying to limit human rights scrutiny.

They include the governments of nations with poor human rights records, such as Algeria, China, Egypt, Pakistan, and Russia. They also include certain democracies from the developing world, such as India and South Africa, which boast strong institutional guarantees protecting rights despite committing some ongoing violations. Some of these governments also want to avoid scrutiny of their domestic rights practices, but they are motivated as well by a rejection of what they see as a US-led imperialist vision of international politics and development. In addition, some members of the Organization of the Islamic Conference resist what they perceive as a war against Islam waged by the United States and other Western powers.

The governments seeking to subvert human rights articulate a litany of excuses for their actions. They cite Western double standards in promoting rights—a deplorable reality, but irrelevant to the plight of the victim. There is no question that Western governments are at times responsible for committing, supporting, or ignoring serious human rights violations, and they deserve criticism for those transgressions. But few people facing slaughter, rape, or arbitrary detention would forsake rescue simply because someone else's suffering is being ignored. Nor should they be forced to by the spoilers' ideology of convenience.

The same is true of the spoilers' invocation of the colonialist heritage of some nations that want to end human rights abuses. Yes, the West has a history, often ruthless, of colonial exploitation. But few people facing repression today would reject help simply because those who might lend a hand had ancestors who themselves were repressive. The spoilers should not block that help for these victims.

A disappointing illustration of this hostility to the international protection of human rights is the South African government's response to the crisis in Zimbabwe. The African National Congress built a broad international coalition in its struggle against apartheid. Where Western governments failed them, they found willing allies in the global human rights movement. During Nelson Mandela's presidency, South Africa seemed to embrace the human rights cause, establishing a model constitutional democracy with strong legal guarantees of individual rights. But under President Thabo Mbeki, rather than join a global movement to apply pressure on the Zimbabwean government to stop its repression, Pretoria refused to speak out. It justified that softer approach to itself by interpreting the anti-apartheid struggle as primarily a fight against imperialism, and by casting Robert Mugabe as the legitimate heir to that mantle. As a result, the South African government was seen as backing a repressive leader rather than his suffering victims.

Indulging a short memory of its own struggle, the South African government also turned its back on the people of Burma. International pressure helped to end the apartheid regime. But today, Pretoria opposes action by the UN Security Council on behalf of the people of Burma because severe military repression supposedly falls outside the Security Council's mandate. South Africa says it prefers more democratic UN institutions, such as the General Assembly or the Human Rights Council, but it has hardly been a vigorous promoter of human rights for Burma there, either.

The new government in Pakistan also has yet to translate its own struggle against dictatorship into support for similar efforts elsewhere. The elected, civilian government of President Asif Ali Zardari is a direct beneficiary of interventions by the international human rights community. Over the past two years, human rights groups placed enormous pressure on Gen. Pervez Musharraf and his military to release pro-democracy jurists from detention, restore ousted judges, and permit free and fair parliamentary elections. Now that Musharraf has resigned under threat of impeachment, there are some signs that the Zardari government is reconsidering Pakistan's traditional hostility to international human rights initiatives. It signed the Convention Against Torture and the International Covenant on Civil and Political Rights, and its ambassador to the Human Rights Council has toned down Pakistan's usual attacks on the UN high commissioner for human rights and graciously accepted comments by nongovernmental organizations on Pakistan's human rights record. But Pakistani diplomats at the UN still often push an anti-human rights agenda, as if Musharraf were still in power. For example, they have been at the forefront of efforts to limit NGO comments on the rights records of governments undergoing the new "universal periodic review" at the Human Rights Council.

The spoilers should not be equated with the global South as a whole. Many Southern governments today are at the forefront of efforts to enforce human rights. In Latin America, for example, the governments of Argentina, Chile, Costa Rica, and Uruguay have consistently supported human rights initiatives, from the

International Criminal Court to the Human Rights Council. Mexico has played an important role at the Human Rights Council (actively engaging in the examination of all countries undergoing universal periodic review), the UN General Assembly (defending the independence of the high commissioner for human rights and her program) and as a prospective member of the UN Security Council (stating its belief that major human rights issues should be on the agenda). Unfortunately, Mexico has been slow to address severe and persistent human rights problems at home, resisting human rights conditionality on US assistance to fight drug trafficking known as the Merida Initiative, and pressing for removal of the representative of the UN high commissioner for his critical comments about Mexico's domestic human rights record. Brazil in recent years has actively supported the human rights mechanisms of the Organization of American States, but at other times it has shown sympathy for the sovereignty-trumps-human-rights views of the spoilers, such as in the negotiations for a treaty banning cluster munitions. Meanwhile, Cuba—still the one closed society in the Americas after the transfer of power from Fidel Castro to his brother Raúl—has toned down its leadership role among the spoilers, though with the tacit understanding that the Human Rights Council not revive critical resolutions on Havana.

In Africa, a number of governments have bucked the unhelpful lead of Algeria, Egypt, and South Africa. For example, Botswana, Liberia, Nigeria, Sierra Leone, and Zambia tried to press the African Union to stand up to Robert Mugabe in Zimbabwe. Nigeria is also well represented in Geneva by its ambassador who presides over the Human Rights Council and has shown a commitment to depolarizing it. Numerous African governments have provided troops to peacekeeping efforts in Burundi, Darfur, Somalia, and the Democratic Republic of Congo, where the main task is to protect civilians. Morocco played a constructive role at negotiations for a new treaty against enforced disappearances. Even South Africa, after failing to support a special session of the Human Rights Council on Burma, finally spoke out against Burmese repression once the session took place. But these positive examples are often overshadowed by the aggressively destructive efforts of the spoilers.

Resisting International Justice

The spoilers were recently roused to action by the request of the prosecutor of the International Criminal Court (ICC) for an arrest warrant for Sudanese President Omar al-Bashir, on charges of genocide, war crimes, and crimes against humanity in Darfur. Sudan sought to convince the Security Council to suspend the prosecution. The ensuing political battle pitted a government that is responsible for mass murder, rape, and displacement against the victims and their quest for justice. One would have hoped that African governments would join hands with the victims. But in the name of African solidarity, South Africa, along with Algeria, Egypt, and Libya, backed a campaign to stop the prosecution of the accused mass murderer—Bashir. Clearly these governments did not have the suffering of ordinary African people in mind. To their disgrace, the African Union, the Arab League, the Non-Aligned Movement, and the Organization of Islamic Conference joined the campaign.

Some African governments complain that the ICC has unfairly singled out Africa. Although the four countries where the ICC has initiated prosecutions are indeed African, none was selected solely by the ICC. Three African governments (Uganda, the Central African Republic, and the Democratic Republic of Congo) petitioned the court to take cases in their countries, and the Security Council referred the fourth (Sudan) to the court for its atrocities in Darfur. The criticism also ignores the larger international justice effort. For example, the International Criminal Tribunal for the former Yugoslavia has prosecuted far more suspects than the ICC. This past year, it took custody of former Bosnian Serb political leader Radovan Karadzic to try him for genocide.

Some of those who denounce international justice most vigorously are leaders who fear that they or those whom they have commanded might be held to account for criminal conduct. Rwandan President Paul Kagame, for example, seeks to prevent independent prosecution of soldiers of the Rwanda Patriotic Front (RPF), a rebel group he once headed, for war crimes committed during and after the Rwandan genocide, including the killing of at least 30,000 people. The International Criminal Tribunal for Rwanda (ICTR) is mandated to prosecute such crimes, but rather than see it try RPF soldiers, the Rwandan government arranged to have the one remaining case under ICTR investigation transferred to its own court where it could more easily determine, and limit, the outcome.

When the families of French and Spanish victims killed by RPF soldiers sought justice through their national courts, the judges charged with investigating these crimes issued arrest warrants for Rwandan officials whom they wished to interrogate. Rwanda retaliated by whipping up African sentiment against this supposed "clear violation of sovereignty and territorial integrity." Taking up the mantle of anti-colonialism, Rwanda also denounced universal jurisdiction (the power of any government to prosecute the most heinous crimes wherever they occurred) as an affront to Africa. But that claim ignored the fact that Rwanda itself has benefited more than any other country from universal jurisdiction—in holding to account many of those responsible for the genocide. The claim also overlooks the long history of universal jurisdiction being used against non-African perpetrators, such as the agents of the "dirty wars" of the 1970s and 1980s in Latin America including former Chilean President Augusto Pinochet as well as individuals involved in genocide in Bosnia and war crimes in Afghanistan.

The UN Human Rights Council

Showing far more initiative and clarity of vision than traditional supporters of human rights, the spoilers have taken numerous steps to defang the new Human Rights Council, the UN's leading governmental body on human rights, because of its potential to hold them or their allies to account. Most notably, and tellingly, they resist critical resolutions about particular countries—unless the resolution could be watered down so much that the country in question would actually consent to it.

The spoilers in Geneva have included, at various times, Algeria, China, Egypt, India, Pakistan, Russia, and South Africa. Algeria and Egypt have played formal roles at the Human Rights Council as leaders of the African group. In the past year or two, a loose version of this coalition has:

- successfully sponsored a resolution ending the mandate of the independent expert for the Democratic Republic of Congo despite ongoing mass atrocities there. Egypt, claiming to act on behalf of the African Union, led the charge.

- ended the review of the human rights records of Iran and Uzbekistan.

- opposed or abstained on a critical resolution on North Korea, although it was adopted anyway.

- generally failed to support a special session on Darfur and thoroughly failed to sponsor one on Burma.

The only exception to this campaign against country resolutions has been the spoilers' enthusiastic support for criticism of Israel for its conduct in the West Bank and Gaza and its war in Lebanon. Israel deserves criticism, but these condemnations lose much of their punch because of the spoilers', and hence the council's, reluctance to criticize anyone else.

The spoilers justify their opposition to most country resolutions by asserting that the council should seek only to cooperate and engage in dialogue with governments, never to pressure them. But that falsely assumes that all governments have a good-faith desire to respect human rights, and commit abuses only because of a lack of technical capacity which cooperative assistance might remedy. In fact, governments often commit abuses deliberately. The only appropriate response in such cases is to ratchet up pressure, through such responses as critical UN resolutions, until they stop.

As the spoilers have been able to cobble together majorities among the 47 governmental members of the Human Rights Council, they have sought to cement control by limiting the influence of independent voices. These voices—the UN high commissioner for human rights and her staff, the special rapporteurs and independent experts, as well as NGOs—serve as an important antidote to the politicized debates among governments that tend to dominate the council. The spoilers have tried to silence them.

For example, the biggest problem facing the experts, rapporteurs, and other independent observers from the UN system is a lack of cooperation from governments. Illustrative of the problem, Angola—a country with growing influence within the Africa group—closed the local office of the UN high commissioner for human rights only one year after pledging to increase cooperation with the office as part of its campaign to be elected to the Human Rights Council. But the spoilers promote the fiction that the problem is misconduct by these observers themselves, and that the solution lies in more state control of them. So the spoilers, led by Algeria, have increased governments' role in selecting the experts and rapporteurs, and restrained them with a new, intrusive "code of conduct."

The spoilers have also tried to tame the universal periodic review of governments' human rights record by insisting that it be based primarily on information provided by the government under review rather than by experts and human rights groups. Furthermore, they are now arguing for increased council oversight of the high commissioner for human rights.

At the UN General Assembly

Most of the spoilers' UN activity has been at the Human Rights Council, but they have also sought to undermine human rights initiatives in the General Assembly. There, however, they tended to have less success. For example:

- Claiming to be speaking on behalf of the African group, South Africa opposed a General Assembly resolution condemning rape as a war crime. Its rationale: the resolution would be "an imposition on African nations." Fortunately, a majority of governments rejected that cold-hearted excuse.

- Algeria, Egypt, Libya, Sudan, and Zimbabwe opposed a General Assembly resolution criticizing Burma for detaining and using violence against peaceful demonstrators. That was too much even for the majority of states, including most African ones, which either abstained or voted in favor of the resolution, leading to its adoption.

China: A Spoiler May Be Evolving

Having long rejected any international criticism of its own rights record, China traditionally has been reluctant to criticize abuses by others. It thus frequently joins with the spoilers. In recent years, however, there have been exceptions. In Darfur, for example, China at times has used its influence as Sudan's largest oil purchaser and arms provider to nudge Khartoum toward accepting in principle the deployment of international peacekeepers. For the most part, however, the Chinese government remains hostile to human rights enforcement. It especially resists imposing sanctions, making its aid relationships more transparent, or acting upon the "responsibility to protect" doctrine that was adopted at a global summit in 2005. In some of the worst situations, its insistence that international intervention is unlikely to succeed masks an actual indifference to the welfare of the victims.

For example, China, along with Russia, vetoed a Security Council resolution that would have tightened sanctions on Zimbabwe in response to President Mugabe's violent refusal to accept the electoral victory of his opponent, Morgan Tsvangirai. In addition, at the height of Mugabe's repression, including widespread violence against peaceful opposition supporters, China sent a boatload of arms to the Zimbabwean military. The South African government would have delivered the arms to Harare but for a protest by South African dock workers.

Similarly, Beijing may have exerted some behind-the-scenes pressure on the Burmese military to allow humanitarian aid into the country following the devastating Cyclone Nargis, but it blocked Security Council action to address the problem. It also tried to prevent the Security Council from even discussing Burma's use of child soldiers, let alone imposing a wider arms embargo for that pervasive abuse, even though China had just ratified the child soldiers treaty ban.

Despite its endless rhetoric about being a good citizen at the United Nations, China snubbed not only the UN high commissioner for human rights but also five UN special rapporteurs who wanted to visit Tibet following violence there in March 2008. China also put pressure on Nepal to crack down on Tibetans who were demonstrating in Kathmandu against Chinese repression in their homeland.

13

Russia

While formally endorsing respect for human rights, Russia often joins with the spoilers in UN forums to protect its allies and ward off potential scrutiny of its increasingly repressive practices at home. It affirms that national sovereignty should override action on human rights, and stresses the importance of avoiding double standards and the imposition of "borrowed value systems." At the Security Council, for example, it tends to oppose consideration of human rights. It has deployed its veto or the threat of its use to block critical resolutions on Burma and Zimbabwe. Russia eventually supported the deployment of international peacekeepers in Darfur, but resisted moves for increased pressure on the Sudanese government.

Russia also uses its membership in various European human rights bodies to undermine them. For example, Russia is alone among Council of Europe states in blocking reform of the European Court of Human Rights that would enable the court to reduce its huge backlog. One of the apparent reasons is that the court has repeatedly ruled against Russia in cases of extrajudicial executions and "disappearances" in Chechnya. Russia also has failed to implement structural reforms ordered by the court.

In addition, Russia has successfully curtailed scrutiny of its own conduct, especially in Chechnya, and bullied other European governments to largely refrain from protest. For more than a year it prevented the Council of Europe's Parliamentary Assembly from carrying out on-site monitoring of human rights in Chechnya and holding public debates on the topic. It also continues to block publication of reports on Chechnya by the Council of Europe's Committee for the Prevention of Torture.

Russia also plays a negative role in the Organization for Security and Co-operation in Europe (OSCE). It has threatened, so far unsuccessfully, to "reform" the OSCE's Office for Democratic Institutions and Human Rights (ODIHR). Moscow sought to subject the ODIHR's election observation reports to consensus approval by all OSCE states, thereby enabling every state (including Russia) to veto criticisms and greatly weakening the ODIHR's work. Russia also tried to limit participation at OSCE meetings to those NGOs that were registered in their home country and approved by their country delegation—providing another way for abusive governments to silence their critics.

India

As the world's most populous democracy, India might be expected to be at the forefront of global efforts to promote human rights. In the past, India sometimes took a leadership role in defending rights, such as by opposing apartheid in South Africa and supporting the 1988 democracy movement in Burma. However, its current foreign policy often would make a confirmed dictator proud.

There are several reasons for this disappointing performance. First, despite strong legal protections and an independent justice system, the Indian government still commits serious abuses—for example, in Kashmir and in Manipur, in its repression of Naxalite insurgents and their alleged supporters, and in its treatment of Dalits—so it tends to oppose international action on rights, fearing a precedent that might be used against it. Second, as an emerging and globalizing economy, India increasingly prioritizes its economic and strategic interests over the promotion of human rights, particularly as it tries (often unsuccessfully) to minimize Chinese influence in South Asia and to compete with China in countries like Burma.

Finally, like South Africa, the Indian government subscribes to a misplaced Southern solidarity. Both the government and the bureaucracy, which has significant sway over policy-making, harbor a deeply ingrained world view that conflates international rights protection with colonialism. India has every right to remind Western powers of their earlier sins, but it is wrong to subordinate the needs of people suffering abuses today to a policy that is fixated on the past. Sadly, too many Indian officials seem to feel no responsibility for seeing that the people of other countries enjoy the same rights as most Indians.

There have been exceptions. At an important moment in Nepal, for example, India helped ease the way for the establishment of an office of the UN high commissioner for human rights (in part because of fears over a common Maoist movement), although it is now trying to ease out the UN's political mission. With respect to Burma, India appears to have suspended military aid in response to

15

Burma's 2007 crackdown against peaceful demonstrators and the restrictions on international assistance to the survivors of Cyclone Nargis in 2008, but its private diplomacy achieved at best uncertain results.

More typically, however, India is hostile to the international protection of human rights, usually voting against country-specific resolutions at the Human Rights Council. For example, it voted in favor of blocking any debate on Sudan, abstained on a resolution criticizing North Korea, voted against a resolution on Cuba, and endorsed a "no action" motion on Belarus. To justify this hostility to the defense of human rights, India typically parrots the rationale about believing in private engagement on human rights rather than public pressure. Privately, officials say that such enforcement is almost always targeted at poorer countries while powerful nations get away with egregious abuses—an injustice but, as noted, not a legitimate excuse for inaction on behalf of poorer victims.

India also remains sensitive to any public discussion of its own rights record. It often opposes visits to India by UN human rights investigators, permitting visits only by special rapporteurs on the right to food in 2005, on violence against women in 2000, and on freedom of religion or belief in 1996. Meanwhile, it has ignored requests to visit by the special rapporteurs on torture and extrajudicial execution since 1993, as well as more recent requests by UN investigators on racism, toxic waste, human rights defenders, and arbitrary detentions.

The Disastrous Bush Years

As noted, the rise of the spoilers would have had less impact without an abdication of leadership by governments that traditionally hold themselves forth as defenders of human rights. No government bears greater blame for this abdication than the United States under President George W. Bush. As is widely known, the Bush administration chose to respond to the serious security challenge of terrorism by ignoring the most basic requirements of international human rights law. Its decision, made not by low-level "bad apples" but at the highest levels of government, was to "disappear" suspects into secret detention facilities run by the Central Intelligence Agency (CIA) where their detention was unacknowledged, subject them to torture and other abusive interrogation including "waterboarding" (mock execution by drowning) and various "stress" techniques, and detain them for years on end without charge or trial at Guantanamo. The consequences have been disastrous. This flouting of international human rights law generated resentment that was a boon to terrorist recruiters, and discouraged international cooperation with law-enforcement efforts, particularly in countries that are most likely to identify with the victims and to learn of suspicious activity.

The Bush administration's misconduct profoundly undermined US influence on human rights. Sometimes Washington could still productively promote human rights: when the issue was the right to free speech or association, which is still widely respected in the United States; when the US government enjoyed the added leverage of a major funding relationship with the government in question; or when the atrocities were so massive, such as widespread ethnic or political slaughter, that the United States could oppose them without facing accusations of hypocrisy.

More typically, however, when the issue was human rights abuses that the Bush administration practiced itself, the United States was forced to cede the field. Nowhere was this more visible than at the Human Rights Council. Washington rightly criticized the many shortcomings of this new institution, but as explained in more detail below, it is far from a lost cause. Rather than work to realize its considerable potential, the Bush administration abandoned it from the start.

In part that may have been a concession to reality, since given the Bush administration's human rights record, the United States would have had a hard time getting elected. But a good part of the motivation seems to have been the Bush administration's arrogant approach to multilateral institutions. Instead of undertaking the difficult but essential task of building a broad global coalition for human rights, Washington tended to throw rhetorical grenades from the sidelines when it did not get its way. With one of the human rights movement's most powerful traditional allies having given up without a fight, it is no surprise that those allies who remain on the council face an uphill struggle.

The Failure to Seize the Initiative

As noted, the spoilers have taken center stage on global policy debates about human rights in part because the major rights-respecting democracies have chosen to hide in the wings. Of course, many of those democracies have never been consistent defenders of human rights, with their long history of closing their eyes to, and sometimes sponsoring, abuses by allies and strategic partners. But the hopes that the new century would usher in foreign policies built on a consistent and principled defense of human rights have been dashed by compromises made in the fight against terrorism and by a disappointing lack of commitment. Recent years have seen a particularly feeble performance. Increasingly, these governments seem to consign the promotion of human rights to relations with pariahs and adversaries.

In some cases of bilateral ineffectiveness, the United States bore principal responsibility. For example:

• Washington provided massive assistance to the Pakistani military while doing little to rein in its Inter-Services Intelligence's use of torture and the "disappearance" of suspects. Indeed, the CIA worked closely with Pakistani intelligence forces, taking custody of suspected terrorists and interrogating them in secret prisons. The Pakistani judiciary's principled insistence on probing into these enforced disappearances, as well as its apparent unwillingness to bless General Musharraf's election as president while still a member of the army, is what led Musharraf to depose the chief justice, Iftikhar Chaudhry, and other high court judges. Washington did little to press for their restoration or to call on Musharraf to subject himself to the rule of law. Musharraf ultimately resigned under domestic pressure, but efforts to hold him accountable for his lawlessness were stymied by Washington's paramount concern that its close ally not be humiliated.

• Ethiopia has among the worst human rights records in Africa. Its troops have used scorched-earth counterinsurgency policies, including strangling people and burning villages, to displace rural villagers in the ethnic Somali Ogaden region. In Somalia, Ethiopian forces have indiscriminately shelled densely populated urban areas and tortured and executed alleged supporters of insurgent groups. Meanwhile, the Ethiopian government has used violence and arbitrary detention to suppress peaceful dissent at home. Yet as an important regional ally in the fight against terrorism, Ethiopia is the beneficiary of some US$700 million annually from the

US government—and of a notable public silence from Washington about these atrocities.

- Washington in 2005 briefly demonstrated its ability to gain human rights concessions from the Egyptian government, but it backed off its push for reform when parliamentary elections gave the Muslim Brotherhood big wins. With the restoration of unconditional support—Egypt remains the world's second largest recipient of US aid—the government has reverted to arresting and beating democracy activists, including thousands of members of the Muslim Brotherhood; prosecuting journalists, publishers, and writers who have called for free elections or even commented on President Hosni Mubarak's health; committing widespread torture; mistreating refugees by forcibly returning many to Eritrea and Sudan; and murdering since 2007 at least 32 migrants trying to cross into Israel.

In other cases, the European Union or its member states were most at fault for a weak response to serious human rights abuses:

- The EU imposed sanctions—an arms embargo and visa restrictions for select senior officials—on Uzbekistan following the 2005 massacre of demonstrators in the town of Andijan. Since then, the EU's Uzbekistan policy has been a case study in capitulation. Initially EU sanctions were conditioned on Tashkent's agreement to an independent international investigation of the slaughter. The Uzbek government refused and, instead, arrested witnesses to the killings and forced them to exculpate the government. Nevertheless, the EU gradually weakened the sanctions, justifying its moves as "constructive gestures" to encourage the Uzbek government to undertake necessary reforms. To its credit, the EU tied the sanctions to the release of all imprisoned human rights defenders. But when Tashkent refused, the EU shrugged its shoulders and lifted the sanctions anyway. Among the examples of "progress" cited to justify this surrender was that Tashkent had released some political prisoners even as it imprisoned others, and had held a seminar on media freedom despite the lack of any actual media freedom in Uzbekistan.

- When the International Criminal Court's prosecutor sought an arrest warrant for Sudanese President Omar al-Bashir, Bashir tacitly threatened all manner of harm to civilians, humanitarian workers, and international peacekeepers unless the Security Council suspended the prosecution. Instead of condemning and rejecting this blackmail, Britain and France began negotiating terms (all the while denying that they were negotiating, as opposed to suggesting ways in which the issue could be resolved). The conditions they set were rigorous, and Bashir quickly showed he had no intention of meeting them, but the dangerous message implicitly delivered was that there might be a reward for following mass atrocities with a threat of more mass atrocities.

- As the forces of rebel leader Laurent Nkunda attacked and threatened civilians in the eastern region of the Democratic Republic of Congo, the British and French governments took the lead, dispatching their foreign ministers to the area, but their declarations of concern were not matched by substantially reinforced protection for the civilians of eastern Congo. Instead of urgently sending a modest European peacekeeping force, the EU dawdled during critical weeks. The Security Council authorized a slight expansion of the UN peacekeeping force in eastern Congo but without committing, as of late November 2008, to the improvements in the quality and capacity of the force needed to protect civilians. Notably, the EU expressed reluctance to deploy the two 1,500-troop "battle groups" that it had created in 2007 just for such situations, making one wonder when, if ever, these protective forces would be used.

- The EU lifted a travel ban on Belarus President Alexander Lukashenka despite a lack of discernible improvement in Minsk's dismal human rights record. The decision was motivated by the EU's worsening relations with Russia, and European governments' hope to bring Belarus closer to the West.

Quite apart from responding to abuses by others, Britain threatened to itself become complicit in abuse by continuing to insist on the right to send terrorist suspects to governments that torture. To do so, it would rely on flimsy diplomatic assurances of humane treatment from governments that routinely flout their treaty obligations not to torture. Britain's efforts to develop a common EU position endorsing this practice have so far been unsuccessful, but its bad example has helped to inspire other governments –including Denmark, Italy, Kyrgyzstan, Russia, Spain, and Switzerland – thereby weakening the global torture ban. Britain also sought to hollow out an exception to the prohibition of sending people to places where they risk ill-treatment short of torture by promoting a new rule that would allow such deportation if the suspect's continued presence in the sending country posed too much of a security threat. The European Court of Human Rights unanimously rejected that proposal.

Especially in the Middle East, all Western governments seemed to share equally in the failure to promote human rights:

- Because of Saudi Arabia's oil production and its position as a counterterrorism ally, no Western government mounted any serious challenge to its virtual lack of political freedoms and civil society, or its severe restrictions on the rights of women and migrants. Indeed, the United States and Britain praised and promised to study and learn from a Saudi program that keeps thousands of terrorism suspects detained without charge or trial, offering "reeducation" instead.

- The West actively sought improved relations with Libya with little criticism of its deplorable human rights records. In return for Libya giving up plans for weapons of mass destruction and compensating the victims of the Lockerbie bombing, the West has rewarded it handsomely with the resumption of diplomatic visits and renewed economic activity. But Western governments have had little to say about the virtual absence of any civil and political freedom in the country.

- Israel repeatedly closed off Gaza, blocking the import of fuel, food, medicine, and essential supplies. It sought to justify this collective punishment against the civilian population as retaliation for indiscriminate rocket attacks by Gazan armed groups into civilian areas of Israel. Western governments offered occasional public condemnations, but did not condition their massive economic assistance to Israel on change. Nor did Israel suffer consequences for its illegal settlement expansion and construction of the wall/barrier within the West Bank.

Elsewhere, Australia, Britain, Canada, France, Germany, and the Netherlands sought, at least at first, to undermine an absolute ban on cluster munitions by seeking exceptions for certain types that they tended to have stockpiled in their arsenals. An absolute ban was important because, as in the case of the land-mines treaty, certain major powers such as the United States, Russia, and China could be expected to reject the treaty, but an absolute ban, by stigmatizing the weapon system, would make it politically difficult for them to use it anyway. A coalition led by Austria, Ireland, Mexico, Norway, and New Zealand overcame this resistance and achieved a total ban.

Similarly, the 1990 Convention on the Rights of Migrant Workers and Members of their Families has not been ratified by any EU member state, or by Australia, Canada, Japan, or the United States. To date, only governments that send migrant workers have embraced the treaty, greatly undermining its capacity to protect a large and vulnerable population.

Some of the major democracies did occasionally show positive leadership on human rights:

- British Prime Minister Gordon Brown refused to attend a summit between the European Union and the African Union because of the presence of Zimbabwean President Robert Mugabe.

- Douglas Alexander, the British international development secretary, suggested he would link aid to Ethiopia to an end to its abuses in the Ogaden region. This marked a possible shift from Britain's traditional silence on Ethiopian abuses while providing substantial financial support to the government.

- To protest Rwanda's support for the abusive forces of its ally, rebel leader Laurent Nkunda, in eastern Congo, the Netherlands redirected its development aid from Rwanda to eastern Congo.

- The United States, Australia, and the European Union imposed sanctions against Burma for its brutal crackdown against peaceful demonstrators despite countervailing pressure from China and the governments of the Association of Southeast Asian Nations (ASEAN).

- German Chancellor Angela Merkel boycotted the opening ceremonies of the Beijing Olympics to protest China's crackdown in Tibet.

- The Bush administration, despite its opposition to the International Criminal Court, took the lead in fending off efforts to suspend the ICC's efforts to prosecute Sudanese President Bashir.

However, these positive examples were not repeated regularly enough to build momentum for the defense of human rights and thus to effectively deflect destructive pressure from the spoilers.

The EU and the UN Human Rights Council

The weakness of the EU's support for human rights was especially evident in multilateral settings such as the Human Rights Council. As noted, the Bush administration did not even try to make the council work, leaving the task to others. The EU has made some effort to assume the leadership mantle in Geneva, but talking to EU diplomats there is often a depressing lesson in defeatism.

Much of the reason lies in the influence-sapping procedures that the EU follows for building a consensus around a common policy. The council is divided roughly evenly among governments that tend to support human rights initiatives, governments that tend to oppose them, and swing votes—governments that have tended to join the spoilers but could be moved in a more pro-human rights direction. By giving broad strategic direction, the EU might have empowered its diplomats to act creatively and boldly to forge a multi-regional, pro-human rights majority from among the swing votes.

Instead, the EU let the process of building an internal consensus become an exercise in micromanagement. EU diplomats spend so much time negotiating a minutely detailed consensus among themselves, typically consisting of

23

word-for-word approval of any proposed resolution, that by the time they reach agreement among all 27 member states, they are exhausted, with no energy or flexibility to fashion a consensus among other potential allies. To avoid restarting the painstaking process of building a new EU consensus, European diplomats must avoid genuine give-and-take and instead try to convince others to accept the agreed-upon EU position without amendment. Needless to say, that is not an effective negotiating posture.

This approach tends to worsen the already-poisonous West-versus-rest atmosphere that frequently prevails at the UN. This polarization and "bloc mentality" makes it more difficult for moderate states to separate themselves from the spoilers such as Algeria, Egypt, and South Africa that tend to dominate African Union deliberations, and thus harder to build a cross-regional, pro-human rights majority.

Even when the EU has wanted to act, its reluctance to criticize Washington for abusive counterterrorism policies has left it open to charges of selectivity and double standards. For example, by refusing to endorse a Cuba-backed effort at the Human Rights Council to criticize Guantanamo (even though the proposed resolution was deliberately written in the exact same language as the Council of Europe had previously used in its own resolution), the EU contributed to the protect-your-own mentality that now plagues the Human Rights Council. Similarly, by agreeing to end UN scrutiny of Iraq and Afghanistan after the US invasions, the EU made it easier for others to oppose country resolutions aimed at their own friends.

Unable for these reasons to build a pro-human rights majority at the council, the EU tends to resign itself to watered-down consensus resolutions, such as on Sudan, or to outright defeat, such as on the decisions to end the work of an expert group on Darfur or to terminate scrutiny of Belarus and Cuba. Similarly, despite ongoing massive atrocities in the eastern Democratic Republic of Congo, the EU acquiesced in a "compromise" resolution sponsored by Egypt ending the mandate of the UN independent expert on Congo; the EU accepted the fig-leaf of scheduling another discussion of Congo a year later.

Taking Back the Initiative

That the initiative on human rights has been captured by governments that do not wish international protection well should generate not despair but resolve. The new Obama administration in Washington offers the hope of a US government that can assume a place of leadership in promoting human rights. If the European Union can generate the political will and surmount its self-imposed procedural paralysis, it will be in a position to help build a genuine global coalition for human rights that can seize the initiative from the spoilers.

Governments that purport to promote human rights should abide by certain basic rules to be effective. First, they should ensure their own scrupulous respect for human rights—because international law obliges them to do so, because it will set a positive example, and because compliance will help silence charges of hypocrisy. They should also abandon efforts to undermine human rights standards, such as the prohibition of torture in the context of fighting terrorism, or refugee protection in the rush to develop a common asylum policy. When these governments face criticism for violating human rights, they should accept it as legitimate discourse rather than an affront to be reflexively rejected.

In their foreign policy, these governments should promote human rights as even-handedly as possible. That means criticizing not only pariah states but also friends when they commit serious rights violations. They should also elevate the importance of human rights in their relations with other governments, assigning the issue to senior officials, insisting on human rights occupying a prominent place on the agenda during bilateral discussions, and establishing clear benchmarks for change with specific consequences for indifference or retrenchment.

In multilateral settings, these governments should make it a major priority to build a pro-human rights majority by encouraging rights-respecting states from all regions to speak out on human rights. With respect to the Human Rights Council, for example, rights-respecting states should be encouraged to offer their candidacy, while the candidacies of the spoilers and their allies should be actively opposed. The defeat in recent years of the candidacies of Belarus and Sri Lanka illustrates what must be done more regularly.

Efforts should also be made to ensure that governments obstructing the defense of human rights pay a political price at home. Democratic governments with vibrant civil societies such as India and South Africa are able to get away with negative positions on human rights because few people in those countries track their voting records in intergovernmental forums and their national media rarely report on their conduct there. So when they vote to protect Burma, Sudan, or Zimbabwe, they do not face the criticism that they surely would encounter were they to adopt similarly regressive domestic policies. Helping journalists and civil society representatives visit New York, Geneva, and regional capitals to monitor and lobby their governments would be a useful first step.

It is also important to recognize that many governments from the South have legitimate grievances about the behavior of Western governments. These grievances do not justify their hostility to human rights, but they clearly affect their perspective. Expanding the number of Southern governments willing to promote human rights will require addressing their sense that Western concern for human rights varies with the level of strategic interest, that powerful countries are allowed to get away with bad behavior, and that richer parts of the world are insufficiently concerned with economic and social rights in the global South, such as the right to food in the context of rising prices or the right to basic health care in the midst of a declining economy. A genuine commitment to recognizing these concerns would help to engage with states such as Ghana, Zambia, Mexico, Peru, Indonesia, and the Philippines that ought to be exerting greater human rights leadership in international and regional forums.

Finally, there is a need to break the bloc mentality that leads so many governments to vote—almost by default—with their regional groups even when their own views are more progressive. Moderate states need encouragement to distance themselves from the spoilers that tend to dominate bloc voting. Thus in Africa, Ghana and Zambia should be encouraged to part company with Algeria and Egypt. In Asia, the Philippines and Thailand should be weaned from Burma and Vietnam. Success will require a strategy and vision, engagement and diplomacy— all designed to reach out to moderate states, take their concerns seriously, and bring them into the pro-human rights fold.

A New Direction in Washington

The success of any effort to retake the initiative from the spoilers will depend to a large degree on Washington. The Obama administration must undo the enormous damage caused by the Bush administration and begin to restore the US government's reputation and effectiveness as a human rights defender. Changing US policy on how to fight terrorism is an essential place to start. Among the steps that President Obama should take would be to:

- Close the CIA's secret detention centers permanently. Bush suggested he had emptied them only temporarily.

- Apply to the CIA the US military's new rules (revised in the wake of the Abu Ghraib scandal) prohibiting coercive interrogation. Congress had tried to legislate that step, but Bush vetoed the bill, and Congress lacked the votes to override the veto.

- Close the Guantanamo detention center without effectively moving it on-shore by permitting detention without trial in the United States. That means repatriating or prosecuting all detainees, and ensuring that prosecutions are conducted in regular courts, not the substandard military commissions, which allow criminal convictions based on coerced confessions, or any other "special" tribunal that compromises basic due process. It also means abandoning the radical theory that terrorist suspects arrested anywhere in the world, even far from any recognizable battlefield, can be detained as enemy combatants without regard to the protections of human rights law.

- Launch a nonpartisan, professionally staffed investigative commission, with subpoena power, to examine who authorized these serious abuses, how they should be held accountable, and what steps should be taken to ensure that this ugly episode in US history never recurs. That process of exposure, acknowledgment, and repudiation is important so that the Bush administration's abuses do not stand as a precedent to be followed in future periods of security threat.

The Obama administration should also signal that, from now on, the US government will submit to the requirements of international human rights law and reengage with international institutions for the enforcement of that law. President Obama should:

- Offer the United States as a candidate for the UN Human Rights Council with the purpose of making it an effective institution for promoting human rights. While a candidacy under Bush might well have failed, a candidacy under Obama is likely to prevail.

- Signal an intention to reengage constructively with the International Criminal Court by re-signing the ICC treaty, repealing the American Service-Members' Protection Act (which cuts aid to governments that will not foreswear ever surrendering a US citizen for trial and authorizes invading The Hague to liberate any imprisoned American), and supporting the ICC politically and practically. The new administration should also begin the domestic political work needed for the United States to ratify the ICC treaty.

- Ratify other key human rights treaties, such as the new convention against enforced disappearances (as a sign of commitment never to resort to this despicable practice again), the long-ignored treaties on women's and children's rights (which the United States stands virtually alone in not having ratified), the treaty on economic, social, and cultural rights (to secure a safety net at home while helping to build a broader, cross-regional alliance for human rights abroad), the First Additional Protocol to the Geneva Conventions (setting forth standards for the conduct of warfare that the US already largely accepts as a matter of customary law), and the more recent, life-saving treaties banning cluster munitions and antipersonnel landmines (weapons that, because they have become so stigmatized, the US military would have a hard time using anyway).

Finally, President Obama should reassess US bilateral relations with certain governments whose significance as strategic or counterterrorism allies led the Bush administration to overlook their abuses. The United States should use its substantial economic leverage to push for an end to abuses by close allies, such as

Ethiopian atrocities in the Ogaden and Somalia, the Pakistani military's use of torture and "disappearances," Egypt's stifling of political opposition, Israel's use of collective punishment to respond to Palestinian rocket attacks on civilians, and Colombia's obstruction of investigations into links between senior government officials and murderous paramilitary forces.

Conclusion

Like other global endeavors, the effective promotion of human rights cannot ignore shifts in global power. The traditional role of the West in promoting human rights is not enough. New coalitions must be built by reaching out to other democracies that largely respect human rights at home and could be convinced to join efforts to promote human rights around the world. But such coalitions cannot be built without significant shifts in the policy and approach of the world's leading democracies.

Today, the effective defense of human rights requires new commitments—to studiously respect human rights in one's own conduct, to insist on accountability for serious abuses regardless of the perpetrator, to promote human rights consistently without favoritism for allies or strategic partners, and to reach out to potential new allies with an openness to addressing their human rights concerns. None of this is impossible. Those who believe that global shifts in power will sound the death knell of human rights enforcement are confusing the leading democracies' current poor performance with immutable reality.

But the successful defense of human rights will require serious self-examination on the part of these democracies and a willingness to change course. The arrival of the Obama administration in Washington with its seeming determination to end the disastrous abuses of the Bush years provides an ideal opportunity. The task facing the human rights community is to convince the supporters of human rights—both traditional allies and potentially new ones—to seize this opportunity. That would truly be something to celebrate in this sixtieth anniversary year of the Universal Declaration of Human Rights.

This Report

This report is Human Rights Watch's nineteenth annual review of human rights practices around the globe. It summarizes key human rights issues in more than 90 countries and territories worldwide, drawing on events through November 2008.

Each country entry identifies significant human rights issues, examines the freedom of local human rights defenders to conduct their work, and surveys the response of key international actors, such as the United Nations, European Union, Japan, the United States, and various regional and international organizations and institutions.

This report reflects extensive investigative work undertaken in 2008 by the Human Rights Watch research staff, usually in close partnership with human rights activists in the country in question. It also reflects the work of our advocacy team, which monitors policy developments and strives to persuade governments and international institutions to curb abuses and promote human rights. Human Rights Watch publications, issued throughout the year, contain more detailed accounts of many of the issues addressed in the brief summaries collected in this volume. They can be found on the Human Rights Watch website, www.hrw.org.

As in past years, this report does not include a chapter on every country where Human Rights Watch works, nor does it discuss every issue of importance. The failure to include a particular country or issue often reflects no more than staffing limitations and should not be taken as commentary on the significance of the problem. There are many serious human rights violations that Human Rights Watch simply lacks the capacity to address.

The factors we considered in determining the focus of our work in 2008 (and hence the content of this volume) include the number of people affected and the severity of abuse, access to the country and the availability of information about it, the susceptibility of abusive actors to influence, and the importance of addressing certain thematic concerns and of reinforcing the work of local rights organizations.

The World Report does not have separate chapters addressing our thematic work but instead incorporates such material directly into the country entries. Please consult the Human Rights Watch website for more detailed treatment of our work on children's rights, women's rights, arms and military issues, business and human rights, HIV/AIDS and human rights, international justice, terrorism and counterterrorism, refugees and displaced people, and lesbian, gay, bisexual, and transgender people's rights, and for information about our international film festivals.

Kenneth Roth is executive director of Human Rights Watch.

Ballots to Bullets

Organized Political Violence and Kenya's Crisis of Governance

**HUMAN
RIGHTS
WATCH**

HUMAN
RIGHTS
WATCH

WORLD REPORT
2009

AFRICA

ANGOLA

Angola held legislative elections in September 2008, the first since 1992. The ruling party, the Popular Movement for the Liberation of Angola (MPLA)—in power since 1975—substantially increased its majority, winning 191 out of 220 parliamentary seats. The main opposition party, the National Union for the Independence of Angola (UNITA), had held 70 seats but retained only 16.

The elections were generally peaceful during the campaign and on polling day, yet fell short of international and regional standards. The playing field for political parties was uneven, with unequal access to state resources and the media, and the MPLA dominating state institutions and the election oversight body. The landslide victory gives the MPLA the opportunity to reinforce its grip on the state, the economy, the media, and civil society; it can now revise the constitution without opposition support. Presidential elections are scheduled to take place during 2009.

Elections

In the months before the elections, intimidation and sporadic incidents of violence in rural areas restricted campaigning by opposition parties. During the official electoral campaign period and on polling day, the police provided even-handed security.

The National Electoral Commission (CNE), with a majority of members MPLA-aligned, was not able or willing to fulfill its role as an oversight body. A governmental body, the Inter-ministerial Commission for the Electoral Process (CIPE) retained almost exclusive control of voter registration. The CNE failed to address major violations of electoral laws, including unequal access of parties to the public media and ruling-party abuse of state resources and facilities. Moreover, the CNE obstructed accreditation of more than half of the independent national civil society election observers for polling day, giving preference to government-funded observers.

Polling day was marred by numerous logistical and procedural problems and irregularities, forcing the extension of voting by another day in Luanda, home to one-third of the electorate. Observers were not allowed to monitor the tabulation process. UNITA challenged electoral results in Luanda, and four other parties challenged the distribution of seats, but the recently inaugurated Constitutional Court rejected complaints for lack of evidence. The commission set up by CNE to investigate alleged irregularities lacked credibility, as it was totally made up of CNE members.

Cabinda

Since 1975 rebels in the oil-rich enclave of Cabinda have been fighting for independence. A 2006 peace agreement was meant to end the conflict. However, many local people reject it as they felt excluded from peace talks. Sporadic armed clashes continue in the interior. During the elections, international electoral observers remained near the provincial capital for security reasons. European Parliament observers publicly reported massive irregularities during the vote.

Freedom of association and expression in Cabinda continues to be particularly restrictive. The police regularly and arbitrarily arrest members of catholic groups critical of the terms of the peace agreement and of the new bishop appointed in 2005. In 2008, at least 14 civilians were accused of "crimes against the security of the state," and some have reportedly been mistreated in military detention. On September 16, the Military Court in Cabinda sentenced former Voice of America reporter Fernando Lelo to 12 years in imprison for armed rebellion and "crimes against the security of the state." Though a civilian, he was arrested in November 2007 and tried before a Military Court in a hearing at which no evidence was produced to sustain the accusations against him. According to defense lawyers, the Angolan Armed Forces (FAA) soldiers convicted with Lelo were tortured while in military detention. The arbitrary nature of these detentions, the alleged torture, and lack of a fair trial suggest the convictions were intended to intimidate people and discourage criticism of the peace agreement.

Freedom of Expression

Since late 2007 the media environment has deteriorated in Angola. Legislation required to implement crucial parts of a press law enacted in May 2006, which would bring improvements to the legal protection of freedom of expression and access to information, was not passed. Private radio stations cannot broadcast nationwide and there is no independent scrutiny of the public media, which remains biased in favor of the ruling party. During 2008 several state media journalists were suspended because they had criticized the government in public debates.

Defamation remains a criminal offence. Many of the legal provisions to protect media freedom and access to information are vaguely formulated, which can intimidate journalists and hamper their ability to criticize the government.

Since late 2007 courts accelerated legal proceedings in pending criminal prosecutions against private media journalists. For example, in June 2008 a court sentenced the editor of the private weekly *Semánario Angolense*, Felisberto Graça Campos, to six months in jail and ordered him to pay US$ 90,000 in damages, following conviction in three separate libel cases filed by government officials, years ago. At this writing, Graça Campos is awaiting the outcome of his appeal.

Housing Rights and Forced Evictions

The government has announced plans to allocate more resources for social housing over the next five years. However, the legal framework for housing rights in Angola—including the Land Law and the Law on Urban Management—does not protect from forced evictions and fulfill the right to adequate housing. Despite the fact that many people forcibly evicted in recent years continue to await compensation and alternative housing, UN Habitat chose Luanda to hold celebrations for UN Habitat Day on October 6, 2008.

Human Rights Defenders

The environment in Angola for civil society organizations has worsened since 2007. In July 2007, the head of the government's Technical Unit for the Coordination of Humanitarian Aid (UTCAH), Pedro Walipi Kalenga, accused several national and international civil society organizations of illegal activities. In previous statements, he had threatened some active human rights organizations with closure. Such statements amounted to harassment and intimidation of human rights groups ahead of the elections.

On September 4, 2008—the eve of polling—the Constitutional Court told the human rights organization Association Justice Peace and Democracy (AJPD) that it had 15 days to challenge proceedings banning it. A legal complaint against AJPD had been lodged by the attorney general in 2003 on the grounds that the organization's statutes did not conform to the law. Article 8 of the Law on Associations limits the possibility for civil society organizations to influence policy making. Members of the AJPD regularly criticized the government in the course of the electoral process for bias in the public media and violations of electoral laws. AJPD is awaiting the outcome of its appeal.

The Constitutional Law grants freedom of association, but the Law on Associations enacted in 1991 and a decree-law on NGOs enacted in 2003, which regulate the activity of civil society organizations, include a number of provisions that limit freedom of association. Ever since the end of the humanitarian emergency in 2004, the government has pursued a policy of controlling and restricting space for civil society organizations. The government has been revising the legal framework for civil society organizations since 2007, but the process was stalled before the elections.

Key International Actors

Angola's increasingly important strategic role as the biggest Sub-Saharan oil producer (due to assume the chair of OPEC in 2009), one of the fastest-growing world economies, and a regional military power has greatly reduced leverage of partners and international organizations that have pushed for good governance and human rights. Commercial partners remain reluctant to criticize the government, in order to protect economic interests.

The European Union has in the past approached the government regarding harassment of human rights defenders, but has not done so publicly. However, the EU sent an important election observer mission—the only one with long-term observers—and reported critically on the elections.

Most international observer missions to September's elections, including the Southern African Development Community (SADC), the Pan-African Parliament, the African Union, and the Community of Portuguese-Speaking Countries, came shortly before the polls and left shortly afterwards. SADC, in which Angola plays an important role as a member of the Troika, declared the elections "free and fair," even though the elections did not comply with its own Guidelines and Principles Governing Democratic Elections.

The government retains an uneasy relationship with the United Nations, which was not invited to observe the elections. In March 2008 the government ordered the UN Office of the High Commissioner for Human Rights (OHCHR) to leave the county by the end of May—three months before the elections. The government alleged that the Office had never acquired legal status in the country and its role to promote human rights had been fulfilled. This decision was a rejection of international human rights scrutiny in the run-up to the elections, and of a commitment to increase cooperation with the OHCHR that Angola made at the UN General Assembly before its May 2007 election to the Human Rights Council.

BURUNDI

Efforts to resolve conflict between the government and the last active rebel group, the Party for the Liberation of the Hutu People-National Liberation Forces (Palipehutu-FNL), made halting progress. Preliminary talks in early 2008 on renewed negotiations soon deadlocked. In April, FNL forces attacked the capital, Bujumbura. Tanzania, longtime host of the Palipehutu-FNL leadership, expelled them in May. Combined with combat losses, this brought the group back to the table, signing a new ceasefire on May 25. However, as of November, Palipehutu-FNL refused to enter the political process unless it could retain its name, although the constitution prohibits ethnically based political parties.

Rebels, security forces, and armed civilians linked to the ruling party carried out extrajudicial executions of opponents. Meanwhile, President Pierre Nkurunziza's National Council for the Defense of Democracy—Forces for the Defense of Democracy (CNDD-FDD) intimidated rival parties and civil society.

Progress in Peace Negotiations and Demobilization

Progress toward resuming peace talks deadlocked in April over Palipehutu-FNL demands for "provisional immunity" from prosecution, leading to combat that displaced thousands of civilians. Once talks resumed in May, FNL combatants refused to enter assembly sites, recruited new members, and continued pillaging civilians. Police killed an FNL member in August, raising fear of renewed violence. Talks continued under strong international pressure.

In addition to the matter of Palipehutu-FNL's name, the fate of a group claiming to be former FNL combatants was a sticking point. The Palipehutu-FNL charged the group was created by the government as an alternative negotiating partner, and the World Bank refused to fund its demobilization.

Some 230 children from this group were demobilized in May, but UN observers reported difficulties in reintegration. Human rights groups estimate that hundreds of children remain in the ranks of Palipehutu-FNL.

Political Violence

In early 2008 killings on both sides of the political divide raised concerns about violence as politicians began preparing for the 2010 elections. At least five persons linked to the FNL and three persons linked to the Front for Burundian Democracy (Frodebu), a political party, were murdered. Witnesses accused police, National Intelligence Service (SNR) agents, local officials, and members of the CNDD-FDD youth league. In March grenades were thrown at the homes of five politicians opposed to the CNDD-FDD, recalling similar attacks in mid-2007.

Five CNDD-FDD officials and a police informant linked to the CNDD-FDD were killed in early 2008, and attempts were made on the lives of two intelligence agents and two other CNDD-FDD officials. In at least three cases, witnesses attributed attacks to Palipehutu-FNL, while two other victims had been repeatedly threatened by FNL members.

Police arrested three suspects for the grenade attacks, but a magistrate released them due to lack of evidence. As of November, there had been no trials for any of these attacks.

Following the resumption of combat in April, police, soldiers, and intelligence agents arrested hundreds of suspected Palipehutu-FNL members, detaining many for weeks without charge, beating some. Police and intelligence agents frequently used former FDD combatants to harass, assault, and illegally arrest Palipehutu-FNL members and others.

Repression of Political Opposition

In April former CNDD-FDD president Hussein Radjabu was sentenced to 13 years in prison after being convicted with five others of threatening state security. Radjabu was arrested in April 2007 after he lost his post in political in-fighting. He had been detained for months in conditions that violated Burundian law. The convictions are under appeal.

Twenty-one CNDD-FDD deputies including 19 loyal to Radjabu left the party in 2007. Another was expelled in early 2008, leading to deadlock in the National Assembly. In June the CNDD-FDD president of the assembly asked the

Constitutional Court to declare the seats empty. He did not seek a ruling on the situation of deputies who had left the opposition Frodebu party. In a much-criticized, hastily issued decision, the court held that the seats of the CNDD-FDD defectors were occupied unconstitutionally, allowing the party to fill them with loyalists. The decision did not enable Frodebu also to replace defectors. Three defecting CNDD-FDD deputies were subsequently arrested; as of November two remained in pre-trial detention on charges of threatening state security.

In late 2007, at least 71 members of opposition parties and movements, mostly from the Union for Peace and Democracy (UPD-Zigamibanga) and the Movement for Security and Democracy (MSD), were arrested. MSD chairperson Alexis Sinduhije was arrested in November on charges of "insulting the president", based on documents seized in an illegal search at his headquarters.

Addressing Impunity

On October 23, a military tribunal convicted 15 soldiers for the killing of 31 civilians in Muyinga in 2006; a year after the Nkurunziza government took power. Although this was an important blow against impunity, no civilian officials implicated in the case, including local administrators and intelligence agents, were prosecuted. The primary Muyinga suspect, Colonel Vital Bangirinama, sentenced to death in absentia, had fled Burundi in January after learning he was to be arrested. A new criminal code before the National Assembly would eliminate the death penalty.

Impunity continued for crimes from the war years and other more recent human rights violations. Progress was slow in the trials of intelligence officers responsible for killing four civilians in Kinama in 2006 and of police officers accused of beating at least 20 civilians in Muramvya in 2007. Officers accused of abuses failed to appear in court in September because the court failed to send them subpoenas, and unknown individuals attempted to bribe and intimidate witnesses not to testify.

Transitional Justice

A committee including representatives of government, the United Nations, and civil society was formed in November 2007 to guide popular consultations on the establishment of a truth and reconciliation commission and a special tribunal. Although the UN Peacebuilding Fund, established by the UN Peacebuilding Commission, contributed US$1 million, the committee did not organize consultations, now scheduled for 2009. President Nkurunziza wrested control of the process from the first vice president, contravening an agreement with the UN, and was rebuked by the UN secretary-general. The government continued to urge amnesty for war crimes, crimes against humanity, and genocide, despite UN opposition.

Human Rights Defenders and Journalists

After three journalists held for allegedly threatening state security were freed in 2007, several months of relative press freedom followed. In August 2008, however, judicial authorities interrogated representatives from the Burundian human rights organization Ligue Iteka and a Burundian consultant for International Crisis Group about sources of information critical of the government they had allegedly passed to journalists. Gabriel Rufyiri, head of L'Observatoire de Lutte contre la Corruption et les Malversations Economiques (OLUCOME), detained for four months in 2006 for criticizing official corruption, was interrogated twice in 2008, once after criticizing the state budget.

In August, Jean Claude Kavumbagu, editor of the web-based Net Press, was imprisoned on defamation charges after publishing a report that the president had spent US$100,000 on a trip to China. Union activist Juvenal Rududura was imprisoned for "false declarations" after he accused the minister of justice of corruption. In September the director of Radio Publique Africaine (RPA) was interrogated after the station criticized officials. Pressured by the National Communications Council to apologize, the station expressed regret for some "journalistic errors," but otherwise stood by its reporting.

Violence against Women

In January the UN Committee on the Elimination of Discrimination against Women expressed concern over domestic and sexual violence in Burundi. The government took some measures to combat violence against women. A proposed new criminal code, currently before the National Assembly, explicitly defines the crimes of rape and sexual violence, and provides stiffer penalties.

Key International Actors

The UN Human Rights Council renewed the mandate for the independent expert on the situation of human rights in Burundi after the Burundian government, encouraged by local human rights groups and EU diplomats dropped its opposition. The government agreed to extend the mandate until a proposed national human rights commission begins operating.

Human rights officers of the United Nations Integrated Office in Burundi (BINUB), successor to the ONUB peacekeeping mission, monitored and denounced human rights abuses, although other sections of BINUB hesitated to criticize governmental actions.

The UN Peacebuilding Fund began disbursing US$35 million pledged to Burundi, including US$500,000 for the intelligence agency known for many abuses.

International donors supported police training and renovation of courts and prisons, projects important to assuring human rights. The EU defended press freedom, and the EU, UK, and US issued statements condemning the arrest of Sinduhije. But they were silent on the expulsion of the 22 deputies, and failed to send a proposed joint letter to the government expressing concerns about impunity.

A new political directorate including South Africa and the EU facilitated peace talks between the government and Palipehutu-FNL. An African Union force of South African troops provided security to Palipehutu-FNL leaders upon their return to Burundi, but planned to pull out after a December 31 deadline for a peace agreement.

Burundi is due to be reviewed under the Universal Periodic Review mechanism of the UN Human Rights Council in December 2008.

CENTRAL AFRICAN REPUBLIC (CAR)

Civilians continue to suffer serious human rights abuses at the hands of multiple armed groups active in the north of Central African Republic, which has been an area of antigovernment insurgency since 2004. Loosely organized criminal gangs known as *zaraguinas* that are not party to the conflict in CAR have also been responsible for criminal abuse.

The CAR government and the major rebel groups signed a peace agreement in June, but disagreements between rebels and the government over an amnesty law passed by parliament in September threatened to derail the peace process. Rebel leaders contended that the amnesty insulated government officials from responsibility for war crimes.

Abuses in the North

Government security forces were responsible for the majority of human rights violations in the northwest of CAR from 2005 to 2007. Abuses by government forces, however, have diminished since most of the elite Presidential Guard (GP) forces, which committed the most serious abuses, were withdrawn from the region in mid-2007, in response to international concern. Taking the place of the GP in the north were Central African Armed Forces (FACA) units, with well-trained commanders installed in a deliberate effort to address indiscipline.

Although FACA soldiers were responsible for thefts and harassment of civilians in 2008, particularly at roadblocks and checkpoints along roads in the northwest, violent abuses against civilians by FACA elements appeared to be isolated incidents rather than systematic. In September the CAR government established an office for international humanitarian law within the FACA that is responsible for conveying the laws of war to members of the army.

However, civilians in the north continue to face violence and harassment at the hands of multiple armed groups, and the government is failing to provide them with protection. The FACA has yet to plug a security vacuum created by the withdrawal of the GP, and rebel factions and criminal gangs have taken advantage of this to commit abuses with complete impunity. In the northwest, rebel fighters from the Popular Army for the Restoration of the Republic and Democracy (APRD) were responsible for unlawful killings, rapes and property thefts. APRD abuses increased in 2008, with a high incidence of abuses in areas where none had been reported one year earlier, thanks to the relative absence of government security forces. Since January the Chadian National Army (ANT) has launched cross-border raids on villages in northwestern CAR, killing civilians, burning villages, and stealing cattle.

Lawlessness and the *Zaraguinas*

The past year has seen a sharp increase in the number, scope, and frequency of attacks perpetrated by loosely organized criminal gangs known as *zaraguinas*, which have come to constitute the single greatest threat to civilians in the north of CAR. *Zaraguinas* are not parties to conflict in CAR but have goals that are purely criminal and engage in tactics that include hostage-taking. *Zaraguinas* have killed hostages when ransom demands were not met.

In July the United Nations estimated that 197,200 people in the north of the country had been displaced due to insecurity, in many cases *zaraguina* attacks. *Zaraguina* activities have had a deleterious impact on humanitarian operations in the north of the country, with private transporters contracted by the UN to deliver aid supplies frequently fired upon.

Lack of Accountability

The government has taken some steps to counter impunity in CAR by prosecuting individual members of the CAR security forces found to be responsible for crimes such as theft and assault, but for the most part the CAR government turned a blind eye to abuses committed by its forces. Senior GP commanders responsible for abuses in 2006-2007 that may have been at the level of war crimes have never been brought to trial or even disciplined. Diplomats in Bangui urged CAR President Francois Bozizé to institute judicial proceedings against Eugène Ngaïkosset, the commander of a GP unit that has been implicated in widespread atrocities in the northwest. Instead, Ngaïkosset was promoted to the rank of captain and placed in charge of a GP security brigade.

Activities of the International Criminal Court

On May 24, 2008, Belgian authorities arrested Jean-Pierre Bemba, leader of the Movement for the Liberation of Congo (MLC). He was transferred to The Hague, where the International Criminal Court (ICC) charged him with four counts of war crimes and two counts of crimes against humanity, all allegedly committed in the south of CAR between October 2002 and March 2003. In June 2008 the office of the prosecutor was permitted to include two additional counts, one of war crimes and one of crimes against humanity. In May 2007 the office of the prosecutor had announced that it would monitor more recent events to determine whether an investigation into crimes committed in the north of the country would warrant investigation. On June 10, 2008, ICC Prosecutor Luis Moreno-Ocampo addressed a letter to President Bozizé noting that acts of violence committed in the north of the country would require sustained attention.

Ocampo's letter resulted in a letter from President Bozizé to UN Secretary-General Ban-Ki Moon in August, wherein Bozizé asked the United Nations to intercede in any possible ICC investigations of crimes in the north of the country pursuant to article 16 of the Rome Statute of the ICC, which empowers the Security Council to suspend court proceedings for up to 12 months renewable if required to maintain international peace and security. Security Council intercession is highly unlikely given that the only ongoing ICC proceedings in CAR pertain to crimes committed in the south of the country in the 2002-2003 period, and there are no ICC investigations concerning northern CAR at this point.

Key International Actors

The United Nations Peace Building Support Office in the Central African Republic (BONUCA) has been present in Bangui since 2000 with a mandate to support peace efforts. BONUCA raises human rights cases with CAR government officials.

In September 2007 the UN Security Council approved a resolution to dispatch a European Union-United Nations hybrid civilian protection mission to Chad and the Central African Republic. The UN humanitarian component of the mission, the United Nations Mission in Central African Republic and Chad (MINURCAT), and the

EU military component, the European Union Force (EUFOR Tchad/RCA), established a base in Birao in northeast CAR in 2008.

In 2008, the Economic and Monetary Union of Central Africa (CEMAC) established the Mission for the Consolidation of Peace in Central Africa (MICOPAX), a peace-building mission incorporating combat troops, police, gendarmes and a civilian element mandated to help revive political dialogue in CAR. MICOPAX assumed operational responsibility in CAR from a predecessor force, the Multinational Force of the Central African Economic and Monetary Community (FOMUC), which was deployed by CEMAC in 2002 to support the regime of then-president Ange-Félix Patassé.

Although MINURCAT personnel have yet to deploy to Birao, the presence of EUFOR patrols has helped stabilize the fragile tri-border zone where CAR, Chad, and Sudan meet, and is reported by the UN to have deterred attacks against civilians. EUFOR troops airlifted nine humanitarian aid workers out of Ouandja, 120 kilometers south of Birao, following an exchange of gunfire between unidentified armed groups in November 2008.

The government of Chad wields a great deal of influence in CAR, especially since President Bozizé's ascension to the presidency in 2003. A significant number of the soldiers who helped Bozizé seize power in 2003 were Chadian nationals, many of them placed at Bozizé's disposal with the consent of Chadian President Idriss Déby Itno. The Chadian government maintains military forces in the north of CAR, and provides the 100 commandos that make up President Bozizé's personal security detail. President Bozizé cancelled a planned trip to Sudan in 2006 after Chad, which is engaged in a bitter proxy war with Sudan, threatened to withdraw military assistance.

French military intervention in December 2006 helped quash rebellion by the Union of Democratic Forces for Unity, allowing the government to regain control of the northeast. Both France and South Africa maintain defense cooperation agreements with Bangui.

CAR is due to be reviewed under the Universal Periodic Review mechanism of the UN Human Rights Council in May 2009.

Chad

Political violence continues to destabilize Chad and the human rights climate remains poor. More than 400,000 civilians live in refugee and displaced persons camps along Chad's eastern border with Sudan, at risk of rights abuses, including child recruitment and gender-based violence. Many conflict-affected civilians are situated in rural and remote parts of eastern Chad that insecurity puts off limits to humanitarian actors, including some areas under the control of Chadian rebel groups.

The past year saw a dramatic escalation in the three-year-old proxy conflict between Chad and Sudan. A February coup attempt by Chadian rebels backed by Sudan nearly toppled the government of Chadian President Idriss Deby Itno, and a raid in May by Sudanese rebels backed by Chad brought fighting to the streets of a suburb of Khartoum. Efforts by the African Union to mend relations between N'Djamena and Khartoum have proved fruitless.

February 2008 Coup Attempt

Chadian rebels backed by Sudan invaded Chad from bases in Darfur in January. By February 2, rebels and government forces were fighting gun battles in N'Djamena, Chad's capital. Government tanks and helicopters caused serious destruction to civilian installations, including the central market. More than 400 civilians were killed and over 1,000 wounded before the rebels retreated back to Darfur the next day. Spillover from the fighting left Chadian rebels in northern Cameroon, along with 30,000 Chadian refugees.

In the immediate aftermath of the attempted *coup d'etat*, three prominent opposition leaders were arrested. Two were subsequently released, but Ibni Oumar Mahamat Saleh, the spokesman for a coalition of opposition parties, "disappeared." Suspected rebel sympathizers were subject to arbitrary arrest by security forces, as were members of ethnic groups associated with rebel movements. While in detention, many civilians were tortured and most were denied due process.

In March the government convened a Commission of Inquiry to investigate crimes committed in the wake of the February coup attempt. The Commission issued a report in September that implicated President Deby's Presidential Guard in the disappearance of Ibni Oumar Mahamat Saleh and found that members of the Chadian security forces were responsible for crimes including arbitrary arrests, unlawful killings, torture, and rape. Chadian government helicopters were charged with indiscriminate attacks against civilians. The Commission's report represents an important step toward accountability, but did not identify specific perpetrators of abuses. A follow-up body established by the government to continue the work of the Commission is composed of 10 ministers and the prime minister—a lack of independence that suggests limited political willingness to push investigations forward.

EU-UN Civilian Protection Force

In September 2007 the UN Security Council approved a European Union-United Nations hybrid operation for the protection of refugees and internally displaced persons (IDPs) in eastern Chad. Deployment of the UN humanitarian component, the United Nations Mission in Central African Republic and Chad (MINURCAT), was subject to extensive delays, and its protection activities in refugee camps and displacement sites were negligible in 2008.

Deployment of the military component, the European Union Force (EUFOR Tchad/RCA), began in February 2008, and EUFOR's 3,300 troops have been successful in fostering a sense of security in some areas of eastern Chad, particularly in large towns, refugee camps, and IDP sites. However, IDPs and other conflict-affected civilians outside large towns received little protection from EUFOR, and attacks against humanitarian actors in eastern Chad increased despite EUFOR's presence in the field.

In December the UN Security Council is expected to expand the operation by adding up to 3,000 personnel and substituting European Union soldiers with UN peacekeeping troops.

Refugees and Internally Displaced Persons

Eastern Chad is host to over 220,000 refugees from Darfur and more than 180,000 IDPs. Most of the population is concentrated in official camps in the Chad-Sudan border zone, but thousands of IDPs live in remote "unofficial" sites.

Despite ongoing violence and insecurity, aid agencies reduced IDP food rations. Coupled with rising commodity prices, this put pressure on IDPs to return to their villages to cultivate. Camps for IDPs and refugees have become militarized. There is a high incidence of gender-based abuses in camps, including domestic violence, rape, early marriage, forced marriage, and child trafficking. Tasks, such as collecting firewood, expose women and girls to sexual violence. Threats and attacks against humanitarian aid workers have prompted many organizations to pull out of the region, leaving many civilians without access to aid.

The Use and Recruitment of Child Soldiers

The use and recruitment of child soldiers by government forces and allied paramilitary groups is ongoing. The recruitment of children into the Chadian National Army (ANT) is routine in internally displaced persons sites in the Goz Beida area of eastern Chad. Children in Sudanese refugee camps in eastern Chad are also subject to recruitment, primarily by the Justice and Equality Movement (JEM), a Sudanese rebel group that receives backing from the Chadian government.

The government reached a formal agreement with the United Nations Children's Fund to demobilize all children from the ANT in May 2007, but more than 93 percent of the 512 children released from the government army to date were former members of rebel factions that joined the ANT under the auspices of peace accords. Demobilization of child soldiers from the ANT itself has been negligible. In August 2008 the UN Security Council working group on children in armed conflict confirmed the continued use and recruitment of child soldiers by all parties. The working group noted that its recommendations issued in a September 2007 report had not been acted upon by the government.

51

World Bank Pipeline Project

In 1998 the World Bank loaned US$1.2 billion for a pipeline between oil fields in southern Chad and an offloading terminal in Cameroon, kick-starting Chad's petroleum industry. The World Bank's controversial Revenue Management Program obligated the government to devote the bulk of its oil revenues to priority sectors, such as health and education. In September, amid charges that government officials were unwilling to meet these terms, the Revenue Management Program was terminated. Citing the government's non-compliance with the loan terms, the World Bank secured the early repayment of the outstanding balance, ending the Bank's involvement in the pipeline project and freeing the government of its obligation to earmark revenues to poverty reduction. Government revenue over the lifetime of the World Bank project totaled at least US$2.5 billion.

Hissène Habré Trial

Senegal's parliament passed a constitutional amendment in July removing the final legal obstacle to judicial proceedings against former Chadian president Hissène Habré, who stands accused of crimes against humanity and torture during his 1982-1990 rule. The new legislation amended a 2007 law that permitted the prosecution of cases of genocide, crimes against humanity, war crimes and torture, including crimes committed outside of Senegal. The new law encompasses crimes committed prior to the enactment of the 2007 law.

Prosecutors are conducting interviews with victims and former officials of the Habré regime and are examining fourteen complaints filed in September, alongside documentary evidence from the files of the Bureau of Documentation and Security, Chad's former political police. Based on a review of the evidence, the prosecution will decide whether to file formal charges.

In August prosecutors in Chad accused Habré of providing support to rebel groups involved in the failed assault on N'Djamena in February, and sentenced him to death in absentia. Senegal's Justice Minister expressed concerns that the decision would interfere with Senegal's proceedings against Habré, but Chadian authorities insisted that the ruling pertained only to the events of February 2008.

Key International Actors

France has more than 1,000 troops permanently stationed in Chad and has provided military intelligence, logistical assistance, medical services, and ammunition to the Chadian military. During the attempted *coup d'etat* in February, French military advisors provided intelligence to their Chadian counterparts, and France arranged for the delivery of tank ammunition to the beleaguered government forces on the night of February 2. In the aftermath of the February events, pressure from France was instrumental in compelling the government to establish the Commission of Inquiry to investigate possible war crimes. France, with other international actors, will be pivotal in ensuring the follow-up commission is more appropriately composed than at the time of writing, and works rigorously and effectively.

The United States continues to train Chadian commandos in counterterrorism under the Trans-Saharan Counter-Terrorism Initiative. However, in 2008 security assistance to Chad came under scrutiny in the US Congress—in September Senator Richard J. Durbin wrote to US Secretary of State Condoleezza Rice questioning the provision of military assistance despite Chad's poor human rights record. The US Child Soldiers Accountability Act, which was signed into law in October, provides for the prosecution of any individual on US soil for the use and recruitment of child soldiers, even if the children were recruited or served as soldiers outside the US. Given the widespread use of child soldiers in Chadian government forces, the new US law could potentially be applied to Chadian government officials.

Chad is due to be reviewed under the Universal Periodic Review mechanism of the UN Human Rights Council in May 2009.

Côte d'Ivoire

At the end of 2008, hopes that a March 2007 peace accord would end the six-year political and military stalemate between government forces and northern-based rebels were dampened by insufficient progress in disarmament, elections preparations, and restoration of state authority in the north; an increase in criminal and political violence; and yet another postponement of the presidential election that was planned for November 2008.

Government forces and New Forces rebels continue to engage in predatory and abusive behavior, including widespread extortion at checkpoints and sexual violence against girls and women, with near-complete impunity. The increasingly entrenched culture of impunity led to serious concerns about prospects for peaceful elections and long-term stability.

Côte d'Ivoire's key partners, notably the United Nations, the European Union, France, and the Economic Community of West African States (ECOWAS), were reluctant to bring public pressure to bear on either the government or the rebels for the slow pace of election preparations, much less for the country's worrying human rights situation.

Efforts to End the Political-Military Stalemate

Since the crisis erupted, the UN, France, ECOWAS, and the African Union have all spearheaded initiatives to end the political-military stalemate in Côte d'Ivoire.

Following a series of unfulfilled peace agreements and the October 2005 expiry of the five-year constitutional mandate of President Laurent Gbagbo, the UN Security Council postponed elections for one year under resolution 1633 (2005). Then-prime minister Charles Konan Banny's efforts to implement a "roadmap" to elections soon deadlocked. In response, the Security Council adopted resolution 1721 (2006) extending the mandates of both Gbagbo and Banny for 12 more months, and granting sweeping powers to the prime minister. Soon after its adoption, however, President Gbagbo made clear that he would not accept key provisions of the resolution.

In March 2007 Gbagbo and rebel leader Guillaume Soro signed a peace accord negotiated with the help of Burkina Faso President Blaise Compaoré. The Ouagadougou Agreement, the first to have been directly negotiated by the country's belligerents, resulted in the appointment of Soro as prime minister in a unity government and set forth an ambitious 10-month timetable, which, if followed, would have led to a presidential election by early 2008.

Implementation of the Ouagadougou Agreement

Throughout the year target dates for completion of key provisions of the Ouagadougou Agreement—disarmament and reintegration of combatants, reunification of defense and security forces, restoration of state authority in the north, and voter registration—were missed and pushed further and further back.

At this writing, only 11,364 of some 35,000 rebels and 1,000 of approximately 24,000 militiamen have disarmed. Shockingly, only 10 serviceable weapons have been collected during the exercise. Observers blamed the delay on the lack of political will by both sides, disagreement over the number of high-ranking rebels to be integrated into the national army, and inadequate funding for reintegration programs. Meanwhile, violent demonstrations by disgruntled ex-combatants and militiamen caused instability in the north and west. Inadequate progress in disarmament in turn effectively stalled plans to reintegrate several thousand rebels into the national army and police force.

Attempts by the government to restore its authority throughout the north were largely unsuccessful. While some mayors and health and education workers managed to return, the redeployment of police, judicial, and corrections personnel was effectively blocked by rebel authorities.

The citizen identification process that ended in September 2008 resulted in the delivery of approximately 750,000 substitute birth certificates. However, the voter registration process that commenced on September 15 was interrupted several times due to attacks on registration offices by pro-government youth groups.

Politically Motivated Violence

There were several incidents of politically motivated violence by pro-government groups against real or perceived members of the political opposition. In western Côte d'Ivoire several citizens were prevented from attending citizenship hearings due to the presence of armed militiamen. In August 2008 pro-government youths stormed the hotel in which the secretary-general of the opposition Rally of Republicans (RDR) party was staying. And in October and November there were numerous attacks on voter registration centers in the commercial capital Abidjan and in the west during which youths harassed and threatened election workers and those standing in line, and stole computers and other registration materials. The attacks disrupted the process and, on one occasion, provoked a temporary suspension of voter registration.

However, with few exceptions, political leaders from all parties travelled the country unimpeded. In May President Gbagbo publicly called on a notorious pro-government student group implicated in committing violent acts in favor of the ruling party to refrain from such acts.

There were few instances of the vitriolic and xenophobic rhetoric that prevailed at the height of the crisis in 2002-2003. In August the National Assembly passed a law criminalizing racism, xenophobia, and tribalism, providing for sentences of up to 20 years if the infraction is committed in the media, during a political gathering, or by a government functionary. Critics noted that certain provisions of the law are written so broadly that they threaten freedom of expression.

Extortion and Racketeering

Countrywide, both rebels and members of the police, gendarmerie, army, and customs engaged in frequent acts of extortion, racketeering, intimidation, and physical assault at roadside checkpoints. Government efforts—including an open acknowledgment of and a parliamentary inquiry into the problem, sting operations, and limited efforts to prosecute alleged perpetrators—had at year's end failed to considerably reduce the level of these crimes. Racketeering was blamed for elevating already high food prices. UN efforts to dismantle numerous checkpoints were usually followed by the mounting of fresh barricades.

Criminality and the Rule of Law

Throughout the year, ordinary Ivorians were subjected to frequent acts of violent crime, including armed robbery, highway banditry, murder, torture, and sexual abuse, for which the perpetrators enjoyed near-total impunity. These incidents most frequently occurred in the west, in the rebel-held north, and within a buffer zone formerly occupied by international peacekeepers. Throughout 2008 neither the government nor the rebel leadership took significant steps to investigate or hold accountable those responsible.

In the government-controlled south, deficiencies in the judicial system, such as widespread corruption and lack of independence from the executive branch, pose a significant impediment to victims seeking justice and to rebuilding respect for the rule of law. Those unable to bribe judges and other officials are routinely denied justice.

Rebel leaders in the north appear to lack both capacity and will to hold accountable members of their increasingly fractured forces. Internecine struggles between commanders led to numerous acts of arbitrary detention, torture, forced disappearance, and murder by feuding rebel bands. Limited efforts at justice are meted out arbitrarily by zone commanders in complete disregard for even most basic due process. Extended pretrial detention is commonplace, including for those accused of petty crimes, and there are credible reports that members of the New Forces use beatings and torture to extract confessions.

The UN conducted numerous training sessions with police, judicial, and corrections personnel, and together with the EU rehabilitated court buildings and corrections facilities in the north that were destroyed during the 2002-2003 hostilities.

Inter-communal clashes over land rights in the west resulted in numerous deaths and other abuses and slowed the return of tens of thousands of people displaced during the 2002-2003 armed conflict.

Sexual Violence

There were frequent incidents of sexual violence against women and girls, including those committed during assaults by armed robbers on public transportation vehicles, and to a lesser extent at checkpoints manned by New Forces rebels and government security forces. In some cases, particularly in western Côte d'Ivoire, victims of sexual violence are targeted on the basis of their nationality or ethnic group. Survivors' access to health and legal services is extremely limited. Efforts to prosecute cases are hampered by deficiencies in the judicial system, particularly in the north, and the regular dismissal of cases due to out-of-court settlements between families of the victims and perpetrators.

Accountability for Past Abuses

The UN Security Council has still not made public the findings of the UN Commission of Inquiry into serious violations of human rights and international humanitarian law since September 2002, which was handed to the UN secretary-general in November 2004. In September 2003 the Ivorian government accepted the jurisdiction of the International Criminal Court (ICC) over serious crimes. However, as in previous years, the government consistently undermined a planned ICC mission to assess the possibility of opening an investigation into such crimes.

Key International Actors

Since 2004 the ruling party has effectively employed intimidation and political pressure to neutralize the criticism and minimize the influence of the UN, EU, and France. Throughout 2008 these key partners and ECOWAS remained reluctant to publicly criticize Ivorian actors for the slow implementation of the Ouagadougou Agreement, much less for their role in perpetuating serious human rights problems.

Since 2004 the UN has maintained a peacekeeping mission, the UN Operation in Côte d'Ivoire (UNOCI), which at year's end had 8,000 peacekeepers deployed countrywide, supported by some 1,800 French troops. In 2008 the UN

CÔTE D'IVOIRE

"The Best School"

Student Violence, Impunity, and the Crisis in Côte d'Ivoire

**H U M A N
R I G H T S
W A T C H**

Peacebuilding Fund and Support Office approved $5 million to support reintegration programs for ex-combatants and other programs.

Democratic Republic of Congo (DRC)

Violence, impunity, and horrific human rights abuses continue in the Democratic Republic of Congo, two years after historic elections were expected to bring stability. Early in 2008 a peace agreement brought hope to eastern Congo, but combat between government and rebel forces resumed in August. During the year, hundreds of civilians were killed, thousands of women and girls were raped, and a further 400,000 people fled their homes, pushing the total number of displaced persons in North and South Kivu to over 1.2 million.

In western Congo, state authorities used violence and intimidation against political opponents, killing over 200 protestors and others in Bas Congo and arresting scores of supposed opponents, many of them from Equateur province, on charges of plotting against the government. Officials harassed press and civil society critical of the government.

Violence in Eastern Congo

Hopes for peace soared in January when the government and 22 armed groups signed a ceasefire agreement and the government launched the Amani Program to coordinate peace efforts. But slow progress in implementing the agreement, plus frequent violations of the ceasefire, gave way in late August to serious fighting in North Kivu between the forces of rebel commander Laurent Nkunda's National Congress for the Defense of the People (CNDP) and the Congolese national army. In October the CNDP stopped just short of taking Goma and unilaterally declared a ceasefire, demanding talks with the government. The CNDP, claiming to protect people of Rwandan descent and particularly Tutsi, also fought the Coalition of Congolese Patriotic Resistance (PARECO), made up of other Congolese ethnic groups and the Democratic Forces for the Liberation of Rwanda (FDLR), a group including Congolese and Rwandan Hutu, some of whom had participated in the 1994 genocide in Rwanda.

All parties to the combat committed grave human rights abuses, including killing hundreds of civilians, forcibly recruiting children and adults for military service, and widespread looting. Sexual violence against women and girls continued at its previously horrifying rate with more than 2,200 cases of rape recorded from

January to June in North Kivu province alone, likely representing only a small portion of the total. Dozens of other women and girls were reported to have been raped following resumption of combat in August.

Violence in Bas Congo

In March police and other state agents used excessive force in quelling protests by the Bundu Dia Kongo (BDK), a political-religious group that promotes greater autonomy for Bas Congo province. Some protestors, armed with sticks and stones, used violence against police or officials. Police used disproportionate force, including grenades and machine guns against the protestors. As in operations in 2007, the police deliberately killed persons who were wounded, running away, or otherwise in no position to threaten them. Some 200 BDK supporters and others were killed, and BDK meeting places were destroyed. The police attempted to hide the extent of the carnage by dumping dozens of bodies in the Congo River and hastily burying others in mass graves. Police arrested over 150 persons suspected of supporting the BDK and tortured or ill-treated some of them. On March 21, the government revoked the authorization of the BDK to operate as a social and cultural organization, effectively making it illegal.

Political Repression

Security forces targeted political opponents, particularly those from Equateur province, the home region of former presidential candidate Jean-Pierre Bemba. They killed at least five and illegally detained scores of others, many of whom were tortured or ill-treated. At least a dozen detainees remain unaccounted for at this writing. Detainees were frequently accused of plotting a coup, but as of October 2008, no cases had been brought to trial.

On July 6, Republican Guards killed Daniel Boteti, the vice-president of the Kinshasa provincial assembly and a member of Bemba's Congolese Liberation Movement (MLC). In May and June security agents arrested at least 15 persons from Equateur. They were held incommunicado for several months before 12 of them were transferred to Makala central prison, some of them showing visible signs of torture. In July another eight people from Equateur were arrested, illegally detained, and brutally beaten. Government officials refused to answer questions from United Nations human rights monitors about the location of other detainees.

In July the government released 258 prisoners from Makala central prison, including many who had been illegally detained since March 2007. The decision was taken to resolve problems of overcrowding in the jail and did not appear to have been based on a judicial review of the cases. At this writing, at least 200 other political prisoners remain in detention without trial.

Threats to Journalists and Human Rights Defenders

On March 7, Nsimba Embete Ponte, editor of *L'Interprète,* was illegally detained at the National Intelligence Agency (ANR) prison in Kinshasa for writings critical of President Kabila. His colleague, Davin Ntondo Nzovuangu, was arrested several days later. After the private television station Global TV broadcast coverage of a press conference by opposition parliamentarian Ne Muanda Nsemi, the spiritual leader of the BDK, state agents raided its offices on September 12. They then arrested Global TV journalist Daudet Lukombo, charged him with inciting rebellion for his role in the broadcast, and confiscated essential broadcasting equipment. Two other journalists who covered the same press conference also reported receiving death threats.

In Ituri, northeastern Congo, activists working for the local human rights organization Justice Plus were threatened and fled the country after they called for justice for crimes committed in the district. In North Kivu a women's rights activist was threatened when she sought justice for an attack against her family by Congolese soldiers.

Justice and Accountability

Near total impunity for grave violations of international humanitarian law continues, with very few perpetrators arrested and prosecuted by national authorities. In a February 2008 report, the UN special rapporteur on violence against women concluded that "due to political interference and corruption, perpetrators, especially those who belong to the State security forces, go unpunished." In one exceptional case, a military court in Katanga continued proceedings against

Gedeon Kyungu Mutanga and 25 others accused of committing war crimes and crimes against humanity between 2004 and 2006, one of the largest war crimes trials in Congo's history.

The International Criminal Court (ICC) provided some hope for victims seeking justice. On February 6, the ICC took custody of Ituri warlord Mathieu Ngudjolo Chui, who was charged with war crimes and crimes against humanity. On September 26, the court confirmed the charges against Ngudjolo and Germain Katanga, another Ituri warlord arrested in 2007. The case is expected to go to trial in 2009. On April 28, the court unsealed an arrest warrant for Jean-Bosco Ntaganda, military chief of staff for Nkunda's CNDP, for crimes allegedly committed in Ituri. Procedural errors in the prosecution of Thomas Lubanga Dyilo, the first Congolese arrested by the court, delayed the proceedings and raised questions about the efficacy of ICC justice in the minds of some victims.

At the request of the ICC, Belgian authorities arrested Bemba in May to face charges of responsibility for war crimes and crimes allegedly carried out by his forces during the 2002-2003 conflict in the Central African Republic. The ICC was also investigating the conduct of Bemba's troops in Congo, but has not filed charges in that case.

Key International Actors

The escalating crisis in eastern Congo spurred diplomats from the European Union, African Union, United States, and UN to intervene to facilitate the January peace agreement and to assist in its implementation. After serious combat resumed and Nkunda's troops approached Goma in October, international leaders flocked to Congo and Rwanda, seeking an end to the fighting and the ensuing humanitarian crisis.

MONUC, the UN peacekeeping force, fulfilled its mandate of protecting civilians in some places, but its limited numbers and capacities prevented the force from providing effective protection in many situations. When confronted by violations to the ceasefire, MONUC troops attempted to halt advances by Nkunda's CNDP but not those of Congolese army soldiers, leading some Congolese to question the neutrality of MONUC. In some cases, angry civilians stoned UN troops whom they believed had taken sides in the conflict.

Human rights violations in western Congo received less attention than combat-related abuses in the east. Few international actors publicly criticized the excessive force used by the police in Bas Congo, or the illegal detention and torture of political opponents. In April the Belgian government raised some of these concerns. In protest, Congo recalled its ambassador from Belgium.

In March the UN Human Rights Council failed to renew the mandate of the independent expert on the human rights situation in the Congo despite the evident need for continued monitoring. Once the Congolese government made clear its opposition to a continued mandate, EU states failed to honor pledges to support the post. In September key donor nations agreed to establish the post of independent special advisor on human rights linked to the peace process in eastern Congo, but by November they had not named a person to the position.

Congo is due to be reviewed under the Universal Periodic Review mechanism of the UN Human Rights Council in December 2009.

Eritrea

In less than two decades of independence, the government of President Isayas Afewerki has established a totalitarian grip on Eritrea. Increasing numbers of citizens are fleeing oppression and seeking refuge in neighboring countries and beyond.

President Isayas's government controls all levers of power: political, economic, social, journalistic, and religious. A constitution approved by referendum in 1997 remains unimplemented. No national election has ever been held, and an interim parliament has not met since 2002. The judiciary exists only as an instrument of control. The press is entirely government-owned. No private civil society organizations are sanctioned; all are arms of the government or the sole political party, the People's Front for Democracy and Justice (PFDJ). International human rights organizations are denied entry.

Isayas uses Ethiopia's failure to permit demarcation of the border with Eritrea as the excuse to justify his repressive rule, claiming that the country must remain on a war footing. In 2008 he said that elections will not be held for decades because they polarize society "vertically." He declared he will remain in full control until Eritrea is secure, "as long as it takes."

Suppression of Free Expression

Dissent in any form has been ruthlessly suppressed since 11 PFDJ leaders were arrested in September 2001 for questioning the president's leadership. They remain detained without charge or trial in a remote maximum-security prison in solitary confinement. The independent press was destroyed in 2001 and its editors and publishers, except those who managed to flee, remain detained. In 2008 Reporters Without Borders ranked Eritrea last of 173 countries on its Press Freedom Index. An Asmara-based British reporter was expelled in 2008 after he refused a demand from the Ministry of Information for the names of sources for his report that veterans of the war of independence complained about life in Eritrea. More than 40 community leaders were detained in September 2008 for no apparent reason other than that they had complained about Isayas's economic policies at public meetings.

Prison Conditions and Torture

Detention conditions are harsh. There are generally no trials or terms of confinement; detention lasts as long as the government chooses. No independent monitoring organization has access to Eritrean prisons. Former detainees and guards report that prisoners are packed into unventilated cargo containers under extreme temperatures or are held in dark and cramped underground cells. Torture is common, as are indefinite solitary confinement, starvation rations, lack of sanitation and medical care, and hard labor. Of 31 political leaders and journalists arrested in 2001, nine are reported to have died. Other deaths in captivity have also been reported. For example, the family of a founder of the Eritrean Liberation Front—an armed pre-independence group—who was arrested in 2005, learned of his death in jail in 2008 only when called to collect his body.

Military Conscription and Arrests

Under a 1995 decree, all men between ages 18 and 50, and women between 18 and 27, must serve 18 months of military service. In fact, men serve indefinitely and boys under 18 years of age increasingly report being conscripted. In 2008 the World Bank estimated that 320,000 Eritreans are in the military. Conscripts are used as labor on infrastructure and projects benefitting military commanders. Working conditions are severe. Dozens of conscripts have died from intense heat, malnutrition, and lack of medical care; female conscripts are often victims of rape.

Eritreans flee the country by the thousands despite "shoot-to-kill" orders for anyone caught crossing the border. When Eritrea deployed troops to the border and clashed with Djiboutian forces in early 2008, at least 40 soldiers deserted. A refugee camp in northern Ethiopia became so cramped in 2008 that the United Nations High Commissioner for Refugees opened two new camps to accommodate new arrivals. Thousands of Eritreans escape through Sudan to Egypt and Libya despite efforts by Sudanese officials and Eritrean intelligence agents to return truckloads of people. Over 2,500 Eritreans arrived in Israel, mostly by way of Egypt, in the first nine months of 2008. In June 2008 Egypt forcibly returned about 1,200 refugees to Eritrea. Although women with children were soon released, single women and most men were incarcerated at Wi'a, a notorious military camp near the Red Sea.

In 2008, President Isayas claimed that international reports of increasing Eritrean refugees are deliberate distortions and that defections are caused by an "orchestrated, organized operation financed by the CIA."

Unable to staunch the flow of escapees, the government uses collective punishment to extort money. Once the government identifies those who have evaded or fled service, it fines their families at least 50,000 nakfa (US$3,300); if the family cannot pay, it imprisons family members or seizes their land. No law authorizes either practice.

Religious Persecution

The government permits members of only Orthodox Christian, Catholic, and Lutheran churches and traditional Islam to worship in Eritrea. Although four other denominations applied for registration in 2002, none has been registered. Members of unregistered churches, especially Protestant sects, are persecuted. Over 3,000 members of unregistered churches are incarcerated. Many are beaten and otherwise abused to compel them to renounce their faiths. Some are released after a month or two, but others are held indefinitely. Youths who protested confiscation of religious books at a military training school in 2008 were locked into shipping containers.

"Recognized" religious groups have not been spared. In 2006 the government removed the 81-year-old patriarch of the Eritrean Orthodox Church after he refused to interfere with a renewal movement within the church. He has been in solitary confinement since May 2007. Members of the renewal movement have been arrested and abused in the same fashion as members of non-recognized churches. In 2008 the regime revoked the exemption from military service of most Orthodox priests.

The government has also interfered with the Roman Catholic Church. It has taken over church schools, health clinics, and other social service facilities. Since November 2007 it expelled at least 14 foreign Catholic missionaries by refusing to extend their residency permits.

Relations with Neighboring Countries

Tensions with Ethiopia remain high. Ethiopia has not implemented the 2002 border demarcation recommended by the Border Commission established under an armistice agreement that Ethiopia and Eritrea signed at the end of their 1998-2000 war. The commission's decision was supposed to be binding, but Ethiopia refuses to permit demarcation to the extent that the demarcation awards the village of Badme, the flashpoint of the war, to Eritrea.

In July 2008 the United Nations disbanded a peacekeeping force that had been patrolling the border. Eritrea had heavily restricted the force's activities by denying it access to fuel and to large sections of the border, and the opportunity to engage in aerial observation. Heavily armed Ethiopian and Eritrean troops are now within meters of each other.

As in previous years, in 2008 a UN team monitoring an arms embargo on Somalia accused Eritrea of smuggling weapons to insurgents fighting the Somali transitional government and Ethiopian troops in Somalia. Eritrea hosts a faction of the Somali armed opposition led by Hassan Dahir Aweys, as well as several Ethiopian armed opposition groups, consistent with Eritrea's policy of supporting armed groups fighting the Ethiopian government.

In early 2008 Eritrea launched border incursions against Djibouti. On June 10, the Eritrean military opened fire on Djiboutian troops after Djibouti ignored an ultimatum to return Eritrean troops, including officers, who had deserted. The clash resulted in 35 deaths and dozens of wounded, according to a UN investigation. Although the UN did not receive access to Eritrea to investigate the incursions, it concluded that Eritrea was the aggressor.

Key International Actors

Eritrea depends heavily on remittances from Eritreans living abroad, including a 2 percent tax on foreign incomes. Because of Eritrea's repressive policies, remittances have fallen, from 41 percent of GDP in 2005, to 23 percent in 2007.

As a result, Eritrea still depends on substantial foreign aid despite Isayas's policy of self-sufficiency. In 2008, the European Union announced it will provide €115 million between 2008 and 2013. The World Bank announced US$29.5 million in grants for electrification and for early childhood health and education.

The United States provides no direct assistance partly because Isayas, angered by US support of Ethiopia, refuses its aid. Nevertheless, the US contributed US$3.1 million through UNICEF and other channels. The US did not in 2008 declare Eritrea a state sponsor of terrorism as it had earlier threatened to do because of Eritrea's support of Somali groups the US regards as "terrorists." However, in October the US government did ban arms sales to Eritrea on the basis that it is "not fully cooperating with anti-terrorism efforts."

Despite Eritrea's efforts to encourage financial assistance from Iran, China, and Middle Eastern countries, funding from those sources remains modest.

A 60 percent Canadian and 40 percent Eritrean government-owned gold-mining venture in Bisha, western Eritrea, is scheduled to begin in 2010.

Eritrea's human rights record is due to be reviewed under the Universal Periodic Review mechanism of the UN Human Rights Council in December 2009.

ETHIOPIA

The Ethiopian government's human rights record remains poor, marked by an ever-hardening intolerance towards meaningful political dissent or independent criticism. Ethiopian military forces have continued to commit war crimes and other serious abuses with impunity in the course of counterinsurgency campaigns in Ethiopia's eastern Somali Region and in neighboring Somalia.

Local-level elections in April 2008 provided a stark illustration of the extent to which the government has successfully crippled organized opposition of any kind—the ruling party and its affiliates won more than 99 percent of all constituencies, and the vast majority of seats were uncontested. In 2008 the government launched a direct assault on civil society by introducing legislation that would criminalize most independent human rights work and subject NGOs to pervasive interference and control.

Political Repression

The limited opening of political space that preceded Ethiopia's 2005 elections has been entirely reversed. Government opponents and ordinary citizens alike face repression that discourages and punishes free expression and political activity. Ethiopian government officials regularly subject government critics or perceived opponents to harassment, arrest, and even torture, often reflexively accusing them of membership in "anti-peace" or "anti-people" organizations. Farmers who criticize local leaders face threats of losing vital agricultural inputs such as fertilizer or the selective enforcement of debts owed to the state. The net result is that in most of Ethiopia, and especially in the rural areas where the overwhelming majority of the population lives, there is no organized opposition to the ruling Ethiopian People's Revolutionary Democratic Front (EPRDF).

The local-level elections in April 2008 were for *kebele* and *wereda* administrations, which provide essential government services and humanitarian assistance, and are often the institutions used to directly implement repressive government policies. In the vast majority of constituencies there were no opposition candidates at all, and candidates aligned with the EPRDF won more than 99 percent of all available seats.

Where opposition candidates did contest they faced abuse and improper procedural obstacles to registration. Candidates in Ethiopia's Oromia region were detained, threatened with violence by local officials, and accused of affiliation to the rebel Oromo Liberation Front (OLF). Oromia, Ethiopia's most populous region, has long suffered from heavy-handed government repression, with students, activists, or critics of rural administrations regularly accused of being OLF operatives. Such allegations often lead to arbitrary imprisonment and torture.

War Crimes and Other Abuses by Ethiopian Military Forces

Ethiopian National Defense Force (ENDF) personnel stationed in Mogadishu continued in 2008 to use mortars, artillery, and "Katyusha" rockets indiscriminately in response to insurgent attacks, devastating entire neighborhoods of the city. Insurgent attacks often originate in populated areas, prompting Ethiopian bombardment of civilian homes and public spaces, sometimes wiping out entire families. Many of these attacks constitute war crimes. In July ENDF forces bombarded part of the strategic town of Beletweyne after coming under attack by insurgent forces based there, displacing as many as 75,000 people.

2008 was also marked by the proliferation of other violations of the laws of war by ENDF personnel in Somalia. Until late 2007, Ethiopian forces were reportedly reasonably disciplined and restrained in their day-to-day interactions with Somali civilians in Mogadishu. However, throughout 2008 ENDF forces in Mogadishu participated in widespread acts of murder, rape, assault, and looting targeting ordinary residents of the city, often alongside forces allied to the Somali Transitional Federal Government. In an April raid on a Mogadishu mosque ENDF soldiers reportedly killed 21 people; seven of the dead had their throats cut.

ENDF forces have also increasingly fired indiscriminately on crowds of civilians when they come under attack. In August ENDF soldiers were hit by a roadside bomb near the town of Afgooye and responded by firing wildly; in the resulting bloodbath as many as 60 civilians were shot and killed, including the passengers of two crowded minibuses.

In Ethiopia itself, the ENDF continues to wage a counterinsurgency campaign against the rebel Ogaden National Liberation Front (ONLF) in the country's restive

Somali region. The scale and intensity of military operations seems to have declined from a peak in mid-2007, but arbitrary detentions, torture, and other abuses continue. Credible reports indicate that vital food aid to the drought-affected region has been diverted and misused as a weapon to starve out rebel-held areas. The military continues to severely restrict access to conflict-affected regions and the Ethiopian government has not reversed its decision to evict the International Committee of the Red Cross from the region in July 2007.

The Ethiopian government denies all allegations of abuses by its military and refuses to facilitate independent investigations. There have been no serious efforts to investigate or ensure accountability for war crimes and crimes against humanity committed in Somali Region and in neighboring Somalia in 2007 and 2008. Nor have ENDF officers or civilian officials been held accountable for crimes against humanity that ENDF forces carried out against ethnic Anuak communities during a counterinsurgency campaign in Gambella region in late 2003 and 2004.

Regional Renditions

In early 2007 at least 90 men, women, and children from 18 different countries fleeing conflict in Somalia were arrested in Kenya and subsequently deported to Somalia and then Ethiopia, where many were interrogated by US intelligence agents. An unknown number of people arrested by Ethiopian forces in Somalia were also directly transferred to Ethiopia. Many of the victims of these "regional renditions" were released in mid-2007 and early 2008, but at least two men, including a Kenyan and a Canadian national, remain in Ethiopian detention almost two years after their deportation from Kenya. The whereabouts and fate of at least 22 others rendered to Ethiopia, including Eritreans, Somalis, and Ethiopian Ogadeni and Oromo, is unknown.

Civil Society and Free Expression

The environment for civil society continues to deteriorate. In 2008 the government announced new legislation—the Charities and Societies Proclamation—which purports to provide greater oversight and transparency on civil society activities. In fact, the law would undermine the independence of civil society and criminalizes the work of many human rights organizations. At this writing, the law looked set to be introduced to parliament.

Alongside a complex and onerous system of government surveillance and control, the law would place sharp restrictions on the kinds of work permissible to foreign organizations and Ethiopian civil society groups that receive some foreign funding—barring such organizations from any kind of work touching on human rights issues. Individuals who fail to comply with the law's Byzantine provisions could face criminal prosecution.

A new media law passed in July promises to reform some of the most repressive aspects of the previous legal framework. Most notably, the law eliminates the practice of pretrial detention for journalists—although in August, the prominent editor of the Addis Ababa-based *Reporter* newspaper was imprisoned without charge for several days in connection with a story printed in the paper. In spite of its positive aspects, the law remains flawed—it grants the government significant leeway to restrain free speech, including by summarily impounding publications on grounds of national security or public order. The law also retains criminal penalties including prison terms for journalists found guilty of libel or defamation.

In March 2008 civil society activists Daniel Bekele and Netsanet Demissie were released from more than two years of incarceration, but only after the Ethiopian Federal High Court convicted them of "incitement" related to the 2005 elections.

Key International Actors

The United States and European donor states provide the Ethiopian government with large sums of bilateral assistance, including direct budgetary support from the United Kingdom and military assistance from the US. The US is Ethiopia's largest bilateral donor and has also provided logistical and political support for Ethiopia's protracted intervention in Somalia, and provides bilateral assistance to the Ethiopian military. Donor governments view Ethiopia as an important ally in an unstable region and, in the case of the US, in the "global war on terror."

The US, UK, and other key donors and political allies have consistently refused to publicly criticize widespread abuses or to demand meaningful improvements in

Ethiopia's human rights record. The sole exception in 2008 lay in donor government efforts to lobby against the repressive civil society legislation introduced by the government. No major donor made any significant effort to raise serious concerns about or demand a concrete response to war crimes and crimes against humanity in Ethiopia or ENDF atrocities in Somalia.

Ethiopia remains deadlocked over a boundary dispute with Eritrea dating from the two countries' 1998-2000 war. The war in Somalia is another source of tension between the two countries, with Eritrea backing and hosting one faction of the insurgency Ethiopian troops are fighting against in Somalia. Eritrea also plays host to other Ethiopian rebel movements, notably the OLF and ONLF, with the aim of destabilizing the Ethiopian government.

China's importance as a trading partner to Ethiopia grows year by year. According to official figures Chinese investment in Ethiopia totals more than US$350 million annually, up from just US$10 million in 2003.

Ethiopia is due to be reviewed under the Universal Periodic Review mechanism of the UN Human Rights Council in December 2009.

GUINEA

By the end of 2008, hope that nationwide protests in 2007 would improve governance and respect for human rights was replaced by growing concern over the human rights fall-out from Guinea's emergence as a major drug-trafficking hub. The chronic problems of endemic corruption, a fractious and abusive military, the rise of drug trafficking and the involvement of state agents in it, threaten to further erode the rule of law and the government's ability to meet the basic needs of its citizens.

Meanwhile, chronic state-sponsored violence by members of the security services, including torture, assault, and extortion, continues. Ordinary Guineans have scant hope for redress, as the government has taken no steps to tackle impunity for abuses committed by security forces. The National Commission of Inquiry, created to investigate the killings and abuses by security forces during the January and February 2007 strikes, is not yet operational due to inadequate government support. However, the newly appointed prime minister supported the creation of a National Observatory for Human Rights, which shows some promise if allowed to function independently.

International actors, most notably France and the European Union, are reluctant to bring public pressure to bear on the government, pinning their hopes for change on the legislative elections. However, in a further blow to good governance, in October these were postponed for a third time.

Insecurity and Abuses in Law Enforcement

In May grievances over pay and decreased rice subsidies within Guinea's military escalated to mutiny. Soldiers recklessly fired in the air killing or wounding dozens of civilians with stray bullets, kidnapped a senior officer, occupied the airport, and looted shops. Some weeks later, police and customs agents attempting a similar "strike" were violently put down by the military, resulting in the deaths of at least eight policemen. Meanwhile, several protests against spiraling food and fuel prices, electricity blackouts and water shortages were violently suppressed by security forces. In October soldiers responding to protests against mining companies killed two, including a thirteen-year-old boy, and raped three women. In

November at least four were killed and forty wounded when security forces in the capital Conakry opened fire on protesters demanding lower fuel prices.

Governance and Legislative Elections

The 2007 mass protests against widespread corruption, poor governance, and deteriorating economic conditions resulted in concessions by autocratic President Lansana Conté. Most notable was the appointment in February 2007 of a consensus prime minister, Lansana Kouyaté, who during his tenure managed to mitigate Guinea's spiraling inflation and restore the confidence of international donors. In May 2008 President Conté removed Kouyaté and replaced him with Ahmed Tidiane Souaré, dealing a serious blow to hopes that mass protest and "people power" could bring reform. However, since taking office, Prime Minister Souaré has appointed several reform-minded ministers to his cabinet. Nevertheless, given obstruction by President Conté and his highly influential family and inner circle, it remains unclear whether reforms proposed by Souaré will be implemented.

Legislative elections originally scheduled for June 2007 were postponed in October 2008 for a third time. They are now scheduled for the first quarter of 2009 at the earliest. The postponement is due to phenomenal shortcomings in preparations, a long delay in establishing the national electoral commission, and inadequate governmental support for the process. President Conté, age 74, is rumored to be gravely ill, and observers fear a military takeover should he die before his term ends in 2010.

Drug Trafficking

Reports about the involvement in drug trafficking of Guinean politicians, high-level members of the military, police, and presidential guard, and members of the president's family, generate considerable concern among Guinea's international partners. Efforts to combat the growing problem are undermined by widespread corruption within the judiciary and by rivalries between different security forces for control of the drug trade. In June the military ransacked the offices of Guinea's counter-narcotics unit, destroying records and office equipment. Prime Minister Souaré took some steps to address the scourge of drug trafficking, and following a visit by the executive director of the United Nations Office on Drugs and Crime in July, declared a "war" against it.

Commission of Inquiry for 2007 Strike-Related Abuses

The government showed limited interest in establishing a functioning commission of inquiry into the 2007 strike-related violence that left at least 137 dead and over 1,700 wounded. During the crackdown, security forces—particularly the presidential guard—fired directly into crowds of unarmed demonstrators. In May 2007 the National Assembly adopted legislation creating a national commission of inquiry into the violence and in September 2007, 19 commission members were sworn in. However, at this writing the commission has yet to receive funding or logistical support from the government. Although both France and the European Union promised financial support, they have conditioned disbursement on the government successfully establishing and supporting the commission.

National Observatory for Democracy and Human Rights

In late July Prime Minister Souaré supported the creation of a National Observatory for Human Rights to investigate human rights abuses and conduct human rights education, primarily within the security forces. At year's end, the Observatory has yet to become fully operational, and it is unclear to what extent the government would fund, support, and allow it to function independently.

Rule of Law

The judiciary in Guinea is plagued with deficiencies, including lack of independence from the executive branch, inadequate resources, corruption, poorly trained magistrates and other personnel, and insufficient numbers of attorneys. Many people are denied justice because they cannot afford to bribe judges, magistrates, and other officials.

In October the government for the first time acknowledged responsibility for the political violence committed during the 1958-1984 presidency of Ahmed Sekou Touré, but failed to reiterate an earlier commitment by Prime Minister Kouyaté to establish a truth commission into the thousands of Guineans—including ministers, ambassadors, judges, businessmen, and army officers—killed during Touré's regime.

Police Conduct

Guinean police continue to engage in unprofessional and often criminal conduct, including routine torture and mistreatment of criminal suspects, widespread extortion from citizens, involvement in drug trafficking and, in a few cases, sexual abuse of female detainees. During interrogation, suspects are frequently bound with cords, beaten, burned with cigarettes, and otherwise physically abused until they confess to the crime of which they are accused. Failure to prosecute perpetrators remains the largest single obstacle to ending these abuses.

Detention-Related Abuses

Prison and detention centers remain severely overcrowded and operate far below international standards. In 2008 the largest prison in Guinea housed nearly 900 prisoners in a facility designed for 300. Malnutrition and inadequate healthcare and sanitation led to the deaths of tens of detainees. Prison officials consistently fail to separate convicted and untried prisoners, and in some centers, children from adults. Unpaid prison guards regularly extort money from prisoners and their families, exacerbating problems of hunger and malnutrition.

Prolonged pretrial detention remains a serious human rights issue, although in 2008 local human rights organizations continued efforts to secure trials for prisoners and to free some who had spent more time awaiting trial than the maximum sentence for the crime of which they were accused. Nevertheless, over 80 percent of those held in Guinea's main prison in Conakry have not been brought to trial; some have been awaiting trial for more than five years.

Child Labor

Significant numbers of children continue to labor in gold and diamond mines and quarries where they perform dangerous work for little pay. Tens of thousands of girls—some trafficked from neighboring countries—work as domestic laborers, often in conditions akin to slavery. They are routinely denied education and

79

healthcare and are forced to work up to 18 hours a day. Beatings, sexual harassment, and rape at the hands of employers are frequent. The government took some steps to combat the problems of child labor and trafficking. In May parliament passed The Child Code that contains several enhanced protections for children, and throughout the year government and international organizations engaged in a public awareness campaign to combat trafficking. A special police unit to investigate child prostitution, trafficking, and other abuses resulted in a few arrests; however, there have been few prosecutions.

Key International Actors

Guinea remains averse to diplomatic efforts to improve human rights. Meanwhile, Guinea's key partners—France, the European Union, the United Nations, and the United States—are largely reluctant to publicly criticize the government on pressing human rights and governance issues.

In 2002, the International Monetary Fund, the World Bank, and the African Development Bank suspended economic assistance to Guinea because of poor economic and political governance. In 2005, the EU invoked article 96 of the Cotonou Agreement to suspend all but humanitarian assistance due to concerns over governance and human rights. While €86 million from the 9th European Development Fund was released in December 2006, renewed concerns about governance led to the postponement of funds due to be disbursed under the 10th EDF. The holding of free and fair parliamentary elections is widely viewed by Guinea's partners as the key strategy for improving governance and respect for human rights.

KENYA

Controversial presidential elections in December 2007 dominated events in 2008, exposing the longstanding lack of accountability in Kenyan political culture. Politicians on both sides of the political fence organized violence in the Rift Valley and western Kenya in January and February 2008, killing at least 1,133 people and displacing at least 300,000. International mediation produced a coalition government in March, returning a fragile stability to the country. Commissions established to investigate electoral fraud and post-election violence concluded that profound electoral reforms and a special tribunal to prosecute those most responsible for the violence were urgently needed.

Patterns of impunity by state security forces persist, with allegations of excessive use of force and extrajudicial killings shadowing the police. Military deployment in March to suppress a brutal insurgency in Mt. Elgon was characterized by mass arrests, detentions, disappearances, and systematic torture. Officials denied the military's responsibility for abuses.

Electoral Violence

Kenya is still reeling from the widespread violence following the presidential elections that saw President Mwai Kibaki returned to office. After the results were announced, youths allied to the opposition Orange Democratic Movement (ODM) began attacking Kikuyu and other tribes perceived to be supporters of the incumbent Party of National Unity (PNU) across the Rift Valley and in urban slums. Kikuyu gangs struck back, targeting Luo and other perceived opposition supporters, first in the Nairobi slums, and later, at the end of January, in the Rift Valley.

Some violence was prompted by spontaneous anger at the results, leading to the burning of cars and street protests. Police dispelled the crowds with live ammunition, killing over 400 people. However, the majority of the attacks on both sides were premeditated and coordinated by local leaders and politicians seeking to gain from the forced displacement of certain ethnic groups. According to the Waki Commission (see below), at least 1,133 people died and over 300,000 were displaced.

After several months of unrest, Kenyans pulled back from the brink when former UN Secretary-General Kofi Annan brokered a National Dialogue and Reconciliation Accord. The negotiations resulted in a government of national unity, agreement on the need for constitutional and land reforms, and the creation of commissions to investigate the crisis.

In September, the Independent Review Committee, chaired by South African judge Justice Kriegler to investigate electoral fraud, concluded that the electoral process had been so disrupted that it was impossible to tell who won the presidential poll. It recommended a series of reforms to the electoral law and procedures, including the replacement of the Electoral Commission.

In October, the Commission to Investigate the Post-Election Violence, chaired by Kenyan judge Justice Waki, published a damning report implicating senior politicians from both parties in organizing and encouraging the violence. The report also accused the police of excessive force. The commission recommended the creation of a special tribunal to investigate and prosecute those most responsible, along a strict timeline. In the event of non-compliance by the coalition government, the commission recommended that the Panel of Eminent African Personalities, headed by Kofi Annan, should forward a confidential list of individuals implicated in the violence, including ten senior politicians, to the International Criminal Court. The press and civil society strongly support the recommendations but the government, including both the president and the prime minister, has given mixed feedback.

Tens of thousands of people remain displaced. The government claimed at the end of October that 3,170 households remained in displaced persons camps. However, many have simply returned to "transit camps," with no reliable services and no government support to rebuild their homes. In November the UN estimated 113,761 people still to be in such camps. The UN, NGOs, and the Kenyan National Commission for Human Rights criticized the government for violating the UN Guiding Principles on Internally Displaced Persons, mismanaging resettlement programs and forcibly returning displaced people.

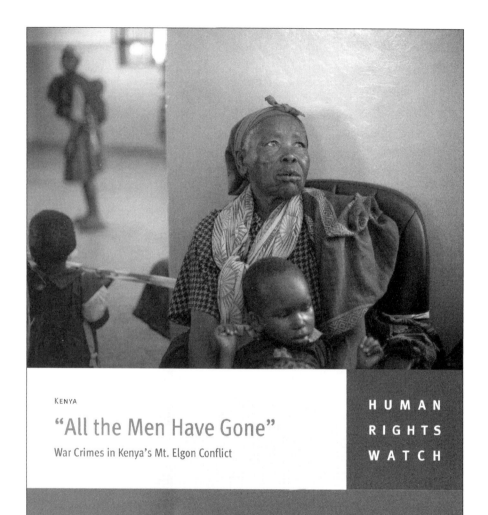

"All the Men Have Gone"

War Crimes in Kenya's Mt. Elgon Conflict

HUMAN
RIGHTS
WATCH

Atrocities in Mt. Elgon

The Kenyan government refuses to investigate and prosecute members of the police and army accused of committing systematic torture in Mt. Elgon. Security forces deployed in March 2008 in a joint operation to combat a two-year insurgency by the Sabaot Land Defence Force (SLDF), a militia allied to the local Member of Parliament, which had been terrorizing the district. Following the operation, the SLDF were much diminished and the extent of their crimes emerged: over 600 people killed since 2006; hundreds tortured, mutilated, and raped; and houses looted and destroyed.

However, members of the security forces also committed serious crimes, including extrajudicial killings and torture, in the course of counterinsurgency. Much of the male population was rounded up and beaten to force disclosure of the whereabouts of militia. Over 4,000 people were taken to military camps for "screening" where victims describe beatings, torture, and some deaths. More than 40 people are missing, last seen in military detention, and at least one grave containing seven bodies of people taken into military custody has been identified.

The United Kingdom and the United States have trained units of the 20th Parachute Regiment which was deployed in Mt. Elgon. Due to allegations of abuses, the UK announced in July 2008 that it was suspending training of 20 Para but resumed its military engagement two months later.

Police Impunity

Police were responsible for hundreds of deaths during the post-election violence and serious questions remain about the chain of command— who ordered the use of live rounds, and under what circumstances. The reluctance of the police to investigate its own conduct follows a well established pattern of impunity. Extrajudicial killings of members of the Mungiki criminal gang in Nairobi continued, adding to the more than 450 Mungiki linked killings last year. The Waki Commission recommended extensive reform of the police force, including the setting up of an independent agency to investigate police conduct.

Regional Renditions

In October, eight Kenyan nationals were repatriated from Ethiopia, some 21 months after they were first arrested in Kenya in 2007 and deported to Somalia and then Ethiopia, along with at least 90 other men, women, and children. Another Kenyan—Abdikadir Mohammed Adan—remains in incommunicado detention in Addis Ababa, some 15 months after he was first arrested, and the whereabouts of others who have claimed Kenyan citizenship remains unknown. Altogether in 2006 and 2007, the Kenyan government detained approximately 150 individuals fleeing Somalia, including women and children. The government did not take any steps to secure the release of its citizens until August 2008, and still disputes the Kenyan citizenship of Adan. Another Kenyan citizen, Mohammed Abdulmalik, disappeared for a month after he was arrested by Kenyan officials in February 2007, before ultimately ending up in Guantanamo Bay.

Women's, Children's, and LGBT Rights

The Kenyan government scaled up HIV/AIDS services across the country, though the drugs still did not reach an estimated 250,000 HIV-infected people in urgent need of antiretroviral treatment. Only about nine percent of those receiving treatment are children. Barriers for children include a reluctance of caregivers to test children, food insecurity, transport costs, unavailability of child treatment at local health facilities, and the neglect and abuse of AIDS orphans.

Following violent school strikes in June, there was debate in government whether to reintroduce corporal punishment in schools. Child rights groups protested vigorously.

Kenya's current abortion law criminalizes abortion except to save a woman's life. As a result, many women resort to clandestine, unsafe abortions that cause up to 40 percent of maternal deaths. The proposed Reproductive Health and Rights Bill 2008 would legalize abortion in some cases.

Article 162 of Kenya's criminal code, an inheritance from British colonialism, punishes consensual homosexual conduct with up to 14 years' imprisonment.

Human Rights Defenders and Journalists

During the violence in January and February, human rights defenders and journalists were threatened by individuals and groups affiliated with the incumbent PNU party. Journalists and human rights activists who criticized security force abuses in Mt. Elgon are still being threatened by the military and the police. Two were forced to leave the country for a short period after publishing a press release detailing abuses by the SLDF and the military in April 2008.

Key International Actors

Following the electoral violence, a spectrum of international actors including the United Nations, African Union, and the US secretary of state applied significant pressure on the government of Mwai Kibaki to compromise and share power with the opposition. The cooperation between Kenya's neighbors and donors in bringing Kenya back from the brink was unprecedented and demonstrated the potential of sustained diplomatic engagement in a crisis.

All Kenya's foreign partners and Kenyan civil society at large agree on the need for far-reaching reform of the justice sector, the constitution, land distribution and ownership, and major measures to stem corruption and impunity. Without major changes, including the prosecutions recommended by the Waki Commission, the risk of violence recurring remains high. The government will need significant sustained pressure from all sides to set up the special tribunal recommended by Waki and bring those responsible for political violence to justice. The International Criminal Court indicated that crimes committed in Kenya are under analysis by its prosecutor.

Due to their close relationship with the Kenyan military, the UK and the US have a particular responsibility and an opportunity to encourage an independent investigation into atrocities committed in Mt. Elgon.

LIBERIA

Throughout 2008 the government of President Ellen Johnson Sirleaf made tangible progress in addressing endemic corruption, creating the legislative framework for respect for human rights, and facilitating economic growth, but little headway in strengthening the rule of law. Numerous incidents of violent crime, mob and vigilante justice, and bloody land disputes claimed tens of lives and exposed the systemic and persistent weaknesses within the police, judiciary, and corrections sectors. The disappointing progress in these sectors, five years after the end of armed conflict, highlighted the fragility of the security situation and prompted calls for urgent action.

Disturbing witness accounts of atrocities at hearings of Liberia's Truth and Reconciliation Commission did more to generate controversy than to promote reconciliation, largely due to the lack of remorse or responsibility expressed by perpetrators who testified. Meanwhile, there have been few efforts to pursue justice for the egregious human rights violations committed during Liberia's 14 years of armed conflict that ended in 2003.

Ongoing Insecurity and Abuses in Law Enforcement

The internal security situation in Liberia worsened in 2008, characterized by frequent violent criminal acts, including armed robbery and rape, violent protests on rubber plantations, and deadly land disputes. Lack of public confidence in the police and judicial system led to mob attacks on police stations and courthouses to free or attack suspects; incidents of vigilante justice resulted in at least 10 deaths. United Nations peacekeepers deployed to Liberia since 2003 were, on several occasions, called in to restore calm.

Since 2004 the UN Mission in Liberia (UNMIL) has vetted and trained over 3,500 police officers, and together with donors, set up numerous police stations and barracks. Nonetheless, Liberian police continued to engage in unprofessional and sometimes criminal behavior, including extortion, bribery, and armed robbery; frequent absenteeism; and failing to adequately investigate and later freeing alleged criminals. Few of these infractions resulted in investigation, suspension, or arrest. Lack of funding for transportation, communications, and forensic equipment further undermined the effectiveness of the national police, especially in rural areas. These continued problems prompted an increase by 250 of UN police officers and generated concern about the need for a thorough re-vetting of the police force.

Performance of the Judiciary

Persistent deficiencies within the judiciary led to widespread abuses of the right to due process, undermined efforts to address impunity, and prompted calls for more leadership within the Justice Ministry and international support to strengthen the sector.

Weaknesses were attributable to insufficient judicial personnel, including prosecutors and public defenders, limited court infrastructure and logistics, archaic rules of procedure, and poor case management. Unprofessional, corrupt, and, in a few cases, criminal practices by judicial staff continued to lead to rights abuses and undermine progress.

Prisons and detention centers remain overcrowded and lack basic sanitation and healthcare for detainees. In 2008 hundreds of people were held in prolonged pre-trial detention; only ten percent of the some 1,000 individuals detained in Liberia's prisons had been convicted of a crime.

Some improvements were evident, including the continued renovation of court-houses and detention facilities, construction of separate blocks for female and juvenile detainees, revival of the Case File Management Committee, establishment of the Judicial Training Institute, and slight increases in the numbers of public prosecutions.

Legislative Developments

During 2008 the Liberian government made strides in creating the legislative framework for respect for human rights and good governance, with two important exceptions. Progress included the passage of the Freedom of Information Act, creation of the Anti-Corruption Commission and Governance Commission [mandated to conduct a much-needed constitutional review], and elaboration of the Poverty

Reduction Strategy. Disappointing was the failure to establish either the Law Reform Commission or the Independent National Commission on Human Rights, and the passage in July of a law that allowed for the death penalty for certain offenses. The legislation, passed in response to high rates of violent crime, contravened Liberia's obligations under the Second Optional Protocol to the International Covenant on Civil and Political Rights.

Harmful Traditional Practices

Serious abuses resulting from harmful traditional practices continued to occur in 2008, due in part to the absence or distrust of judicial authorities. These included the killing of alleged witches and "trials by ordeal," in which suspects are forced to swallow the poisonous sap of a tree or endure burning—their alleged guilt or innocence is determined by whether they survive. At least 16 people were tried, convicted and sentenced for administering the practice, but were months later granted clemency. Their release, conditional on community service, was part of a wider public education campaign by the government and UN to discourage the practice.

Sexual Violence

The incidence of rape of women and girls continued to be alarmingly high in 2008, despite positive efforts by the government and UNMIL, including a sustained nationwide anti-rape campaign and the establishment of a dedicated court for sexual violence. While police response to reports of rape improved somewhat, efforts to prosecute these cases are hampered by deficiencies in the justice system and the regular dismissal of cases due to out-of-court settlements between families of the victims and the perpetrators.

Corruption

The potential for corruption to undermine recent gains in establishing the rule of law and in providing the most vulnerable with basic services such as education, water, and healthcare received considerable attention by the government and Liberia's international partners.

Concrete steps to reduce corruption included the creation in September of Liberia's first Anti-Corruption Commission, the dismissal and arrest of a number of corrupt officials, the nullifying of contracts awarded without due adherence to the legal bidding process, and the continued trials of some 10 public officials from the 2003-2005 transitional government for the embezzlement of over US$5 million.

The Truth and Reconciliation Commission and Accountability

The Liberian Truth and Reconciliation Commission (TRC), which had since its creation in 2006 been plagued with leadership, transparency, and operational problems, showed significant improvement in 2008. Throughout 2008 the TRC conducted well-attended, countrywide hearings in which over 500 victims and some 35 former faction leaders testified. The victims recounted horrific accounts of war crimes committed by all sides, while perpetrators often failed to admit violations or ask forgiveness, and appeared to use the hearings to absolve perceptions of their guilt. TRC commissioners were praised for having brought the perpetrators to testify, but criticized for a lack of rigorous questioning to ensure a more accurate historical account.

In September, Charles "Chuckie" Taylor, Jr., the son of former Liberian president Charles Taylor, went on trial in the United States accused of torture while he headed Liberia's Anti-Terrorist Unit (ATU). On October 30, the jury found the defendant guilty on all counts. The case against Taylor, an American citizen, is the first brought under a US federal law that allows charges against a person accused of torture abroad if the accused is in the United States or is an American citizen. It is also the first prosecution for war crimes committed in Liberia.

The TRC hearings and the trial of "Chuckie" Taylor generated considerable public debate about the ongoing need to hold accountable perpetrators of war crimes and crimes against humanity committed during Liberia's wars. Questions remain about whether TRC commissioners would act on their power to recommend individuals for prosecution, as included in the commission's mandate; and whether the Liberian judicial system would be able and willing to try these cases.

Liberian Army

Since 2004 the US has led the recruitment and training of 2,100 soldiers for a new Liberian army, which, in contrast to the police, has been involved in few reports of abuse and indiscipline by its members. Recruits were vetted for past abuses by the American contractor DynCorp.

Disarmament of Former Combatants

Since the end of the war in 2003, 101,000 former combatants have been dis-armed. During 2008 the final group of some 7,250 former combatants received vocational training or education, but most remain unemployed. A joint program by the World Bank, UN, and Liberian government to offer short-term employment to some 60,000 was a welcome initiative. However, increases in global food prices and continuing high unemployment remain a serious concern for sustained peace.

Key International Actors

Liberia's post-war reconstruction needs remained high on the international agen-da in 2008, evidenced by visits by UN Secretary-General Ban Ki-moon and US President George Bush, and the receipt of considerable bi-lateral and multi-sec-toral aid.

The United States is Liberia's largest donor, and in fiscal year 2007-2008 con-tributed more than US$141 million to support democratization, security and reconstruction efforts. In January the US infused the Truth and Reconciliation Commission with $500,000, nearly doubling total US support for the TRC since its establishment.

From a high of US$4.7 billion in debt in June 2007, Liberia has set itself towards debt relief by clearing its arrears and securing an agreement in April 2008 with donor nations for 97 percent of Liberia's debt to be canceled.

In December 2007, the UN Security Council renewed for one year the arms and travel bans on associates of former President Charles Taylor. In 2008, Liberia was declared eligible for US$15 million in funds administered by the UN Peacebuilding Commission.

NIGERIA

The government of President Umaru Yar'Adua—now in its second year—has done little to address deeply-entrenched human rights problems. Despite record oil revenues in 2008, government corruption and mismanagement robbed Nigerians of their right to health and education. State security forces continued to commit extrajudicial killings, torture, and extortion. Intercommunal and political violence, often fomented by powerful politicians, claimed hundreds of lives.

Although many of these problems were inherited from the previous administration, the Yar'Adua administration has undermined fledgling anti-corruption efforts, taken inadequate steps to address poverty and violence in the Niger Delta, and failed to investigate or hold to account government officials and security forces responsible for serious human rights abuses. The National Assembly held public hearings into allegations of corruption but failed to pass progressive legislation including the Freedom of Information Bill.

Nonetheless, free speech in Nigeria remains robust and the judiciary continues to exercise a degree of independence. Nigeria's election tribunals annulled several of the 2007 state gubernatorial elections, but in February 2008 upheld the election of President Yar'Adua. Opposition candidates appealed the tribunals' decision in the presidential election petition, but at this writing, the Supreme Court had not yet ruled on the case.

Rising oil prices and disruptions in Nigeria's oil flow by militant violence focused the attention of Nigeria's international partners on the restive Niger Delta. However, foreign partners remained reluctant to publicly criticize those responsible for Nigeria's poor human rights record.

Violence and Poverty in the Niger Delta

In September 2008, the Movement for the Emancipation of the Niger Delta (MEND)—a loose umbrella network of armed groups—declared an "oil war" on government forces and the oil industry, resulting in the heaviest fighting in two years. MEND and other Niger Delta militant groups claim to be fighting for greater local control of the region's oil wealth, while simultaneously engaging in various forms of violent criminal activity, including attacks on oil facilities, kidnapping foreign and Nigerian oil workers, and the lucrative theft of crude oil.

In 2008 several dozen ordinary Nigerians were killed in clashes between security forces and gangs, and at least 130 Nigerians and oil-sector workers were kidnapped by militant groups. However, the security forces appear to have been more careful to avoid inflicting civilian casualties than in previous periods of Delta violence. In January 2008, seven ordinary citizens were reportedly killed in crossfire during an attack on a Port Harcourt police station. In July thousands of residents fled Bonny Island after gunmen killed several residents and allegedly threatened to behead anyone not originally from the area. In August the Nigerian military reportedly opened fire on a boat in Bayelsa State, killing three villagers.

Meanwhile, the government failed to address the poverty, embezzlement of revenues, and environmental degradation that underlie political discontent in the Delta. The government also failed to end impunity that fuels the violence.

Government Corruption

Efforts to fight corruption and graft suffered setbacks in 2008. In December 2007, Nuhu Ribadu, then-head of Nigeria's Economic and Financial Crimes Commission (EFCC), took the bold step of indicting the powerful former Delta State Governor James Ibori. Two weeks later, the inspector general of police ordered Mr. Ribadu to resign and attend a year-long training course. In February 2008 another senior EFCC official was attacked by armed thugs.

Following the controversial appointment of Farida Waziri as the new EFCC chair in May, the EFCC fired many of its top investigators. In August the former head of the EFCC unit investigating Mr. Ibori was arrested and held without charge for several weeks. Although Ms. Waziri has indicted several senior-level politicians on corruption charges, the high-profile cases initiated under Mr. Ribadu, including that of Mr. Ibori, have been effectively stalled.

Since 2004 Nigeria has taken significant steps towards complying with the Extractive Industries Transparency Initiative (EITI), including conducting comprehensive audits of the petroleum sector. However, efforts at improving transparency in federal government revenues have done little to reduce corruption and mismanagement, especially at state and local government levels; government budgets and expenditures remain shrouded in secrecy.

Intercommunal and Political Violence

More than 12,000 Nigerians have lost their lives in ethnic, religious, and political clashes since the end of military rule in 1999. In November, some 400 were killed in Plateau State when Christians and Muslims clashed over the result of a local election. This was the most serious episode of intercommunal violence since 2004. Meanwhile, clashes in Ebonyi, Enugu, and Benue states left at least 42 dead and hundreds displaced.

Nigeria's politicians have, for years, actively manipulated ethnic and religious tensions by sponsoring violence for personal political gain. The government has failed to investigate, much less criminally prosecute, those responsible for sponsoring or carrying out the election-related violence linked to the 2007 elections, which left 300 people dead. However, after taking up office, President Yar'Adua established an electoral reform committee that shows some promise.

Torture and Policing

Nigeria's poorly trained and under-resourced police force was in 2008 responsible for serious and persistent abuses, including extrajudicial killings of criminal suspects, torture, and extortion. In January 2006 the UN Special Rapporteur on Extrajudicial, Summary or Arbitrary Executions found that "the practice of summarily executing suspected criminals by the Nigerian Police is widespread and systematic." More than 10,000 Nigerians have been killed by the police since 2000.

The police routinely use torture as a tactic of interrogation and as a tool of extortion. Woefully under-equipped to carry out criminal investigations, the police often rely on confessions extracted by torture as the sole method of gathering evidence. Police also routinely extort bribes from ordinary Nigerians through the threat of arrest or violence, most commonly at checkpoints set up along Nigeria's roads. Meanwhile, thousands of people accused of common crimes continue to be detained without trial for months or even years in sub-standard conditions.

Lack of political will to hold the police to account remains the single biggest obstacle to ending abuses by the Nigerian police force.

Human Rights Concerns in the Context of Sharia

Twelve state governments in northern Nigeria have extended Sharia (Islamic law) to their criminal justice systems, including sentencing provisions that amount to cruel, inhuman, and degrading treatment—death sentences, amputations, and floggings. Sharia law as practiced in the north also includes the death penalty for consensual homosexual conduct between men. Although capital sentences have been thrown out on appeal or simply not carried out, Sharia courts continue to hand them down.

Serious due process concerns also exist in Sharia proceedings in Nigeria. Most defendants are sentenced without legal representation. Judges are inadequately trained and often rely on statements extracted under torture by police as the basis for convictions. The manner in which Sharia is applied also discriminates against women, particularly in adultery cases where standards of evidence differ based on the sex of the accused.

Sexual Orientation

Section 214 of the federal criminal code punishes homosexual conduct between men or between women with up to 14 years in prison. After a press campaign in September 2008 vilifying a Lagos church supportive of lesbian, gay, bisexual, and transgender people, police harassed several church members, detaining one for three days.

Freedom of Expression

Nigerian civil society and the country's independent press are generally free to criticize the government and its policies, allowing for vibrant public debate. However, journalists in Nigeria are at times subjected to arrest and detention. In September 2008 state security agents shut down Channels Television—one of Nigeria's largest private broadcasters—and arrested six journalists, including media executives, after the station reported that President Yar'Adua might resign

Politics as War

The Human Rights Impact and Causes of Post-Election
Violence in Rivers State, Nigeria

**H U M A N
R I G H T S
W A T C H**

from office due to health reasons. In October Nigerian security agents arrested and held without charge two US-based Nigerian online journalists who had published stories critical of the government. Local media outlets generally enjoy considerably less freedom than their national counterparts and are more often subjected to harassment and intimidation by government authorities. Government security forces continued to restrict journalists' access to the Niger Delta.

Sexual and Reproductive Rights

Nigeria continues to have some of the worst indicators for women's reproductive health worldwide. Maternal mortality rates and the number of pregnant women living with HIV are among the highest worldwide; in 2007 only seven percent of these women, and two percent of the children born to them, received antiretroviral therapy to prevent mother-to-child HIV transmission.

Key International Actors

Because of Nigeria's significance as a regional power and leading oil exporter, key governments—including the United Kingdom and the United States—and organizations such as the African Union were unwilling to publicly exert pressure on Nigeria over its human rights record. Private demarches by Nigeria's foreign partners were largely ignored by the government.

In fiscal year 2008, the UK increased development aid to Nigeria to £100 million and in July 2008, extended a controversial offer to train Nigeria's military forces operating in the Niger Delta.

As in past years, multinational oil companies operating in the Niger Delta did little to curb environmentally harmful gas flaring and oil spills caused by ageing and poorly-maintained infrastructure.

Nigeria is due to be reviewed under the Universal Periodic Review mechanism of the UN Human Rights Council in February 2009.

RWANDA

Fourteen years after the genocide that killed three-quarters of the Tutsi population in Rwanda, the government is moving towards ending genocide trials and redirecting attention to economic development. Conventional courts are operating more efficiently under reforms begun in 2004, but still lack independence and fair trial guarantees. In 2008 the government shifted thousands of the most serious genocide cases from conventional courts to community-based *gacaca* courts, while it stepped up efforts to persuade jurisdictions abroad to send Rwandans accused of genocide home for trial. Meanwhile, a Spanish judge issued arrest warrants for 40 officers of the current Rwandan army—the Rwandan Defense Force (RDF)—spurring Rwanda to mobilize other African governments against international justice.

Rwandan authorities exercise tight control over political space, civil society, and the media, often accusing dissenters of "genocide ideology." Legislative elections in September 2008 were peaceful, but marred by serious irregularities, and further strengthened the Rwandan Patriotic Front (RPF), the dominant political party since 1994. International donors, generally satisfied by the prospect of economic development, said little about election irregularities or human rights abuses.

Conventional Courts

Since reforms in 2004 Rwandan courts have operated with greater administrative autonomy. Judges, except those on the Supreme Court, once enjoyed life tenure. In June 2008, however, the legislature amended the constitution to limit judicial terms to four years, increasing the vulnerability of judges to pressure. The death penalty was abolished in 2007—a noteworthy achievement—but was replaced by life imprisonment in solitary confinement, a penalty that constitutes torture and violates international standards. In August 2008 the Rwandan Supreme Court found the penalty constitutional. In a more positive vein, the Supreme Court held that heavier penalties for women than for men convicted of adultery were unconstitutional.

Courts continued to be burdened by a backlog of thousands of ordinary criminal and civil cases, even after most genocide cases were transferred to *gacaca* jurisdictions. Former minister of justice Agnès Ntamabyaliro, the only minister from the previous government in Rwandan custody, incarcerated since 1997, was still being tried two years after her trial had begun.

In June 2008 Rwanda charged four Rwandan military officers with war crimes for the 1994 killing of 15 civilians, 13 of them clergy. Two of the officers confessed to the killing and were sentenced to eight years in prison. Two more senior officers were acquitted after a brief trial. The RPF had acknowledged the crime committed by its soldiers 14 years ago, but brought the accused to trial only after the International Criminal Tribunal for Rwanda (ICTR) prepared a case against them. Neither the Rwandan prosecutor's office nor the ICTR anticipate further such prosecutions, despite United Nations estimates that between 25,000 and 45,000 persons were killed by RPF soldiers in 1994.

Gacaca Jurisdictions

In June 2008 the legislature transferred the most serious genocide cases (category I) from conventional courts to community-based *gacaca* jurisdictions, created in 2001 in an effort to combine restorative and punitive justice. Nearly 90 percent of these 9,300 cases involve sexual violence and will be heard behind closed doors, a policy meant to protect victims but which also prevents monitoring the performance of judges, who are minimally trained and who can impose penalties up to life imprisonment in solitary confinement. Originally scheduled to end in 2007, *gacaca* jurisdictions will continue hearing cases until 2010.

Instances of faulty procedure, judicial corruption, and false accusations undermine trust in *gacaca* jurisdictions among victims as well as the accused. In February a *gacaca* appeals court sentenced former presidential candidate Dr. Théoneste Niyitegeka to 15 years in prison for genocide. Dr. Niyitegeka, who had cared for Tutsis in 1994, had been acquitted by a lower court because of the scanty, vague, and contradictory testimony against him. The appeals court gave no explanation for overturning the previous acquittal. In another case marred by grave procedural errors, an appeals court overturned the acquittal by a lower court of Jean Népomuscène Munyangabe, a Rwandan working for the UN in Chad, who voluntarily returned to Rwanda to contest charges against him.

The safety of witnesses in judicial proceedings continued to be a concern, with 17 genocide survivors killed in the first nine months of 2008, some in connection with testimony in *gacaca* proceedings.

International Justice

Rwanda intensified efforts to have persons accused of genocide sent back to Rwanda for trial, generally unsuccessfully. At the ICTR, where officials hoped to speed closure of the court by sending genocide cases to national jurisdictions, judges refused transfers to Rwanda, citing among other reasons difficulty in obtaining defense witness testimony and the possible imposition of a sentence of life in solitary confinement. The Rwandan legislature sought to remove one obstacle to transfers by adopting a law excluding imposition of this penalty on persons transferred from the ICTR.

The United Kingdom agreed to the extradition of four Rwandans, a decision being appealed. A French appeals court refused to extradite two Rwandans, as did a German court. More than a dozen requests are pending in other European countries and Belgium is pursuing further domestic prosecutions.

In February 2008 a Spanish judge issued arrest warrants for 40 Rwandan Defense Force officers for war crimes and crimes against humanity committed against Spanish, Rwandan, and Congolese citizens in the 1990s. The prosecution is based on both domestic law and universal jurisdiction, a doctrine which permits national courts to prosecute the most heinous crimes committed abroad. Rwandan authorities mobilized African governments against such judicial action, labeling it neo-colonialist.

In a similar situation in 2006, Rwanda broke relations with France after a judge issued warrants against nine RDF officers. In August 2008 Rwanda published a report charging French involvement in the genocide and announced possible prosecutions of French citizens. In November Germany arrested Rose Kabuye, one of the nine, on a French warrant. Rwanda immediately expelled the German ambassador and organized protest demonstrations in Rwanda and abroad.

"Genocide Ideology"

Authorities use prosecution, or the threat of prosecution, for "genocide ideology" to silence dissent of many kinds, including calls for justice for RPF war crimes. Prosecutors brought hundreds of cases involving this accusation before the charge was finally defined by law in June 2008. The current definition is vague, requires no link to any genocidal act, and prohibits speech protected by international conventions.

Elections

In the September legislative elections, RPF candidates won 79 percent of the vote in polling that was peaceful, but marred by numerous irregularities. While acknowledging some progress since the 2003 election, European Union observers faulted procedural irregularities in over half the polling stations, RPF dominance of the media, and the absence of political plurality, in due part to the fear of "genocide ideology" accusations. Women took 44 seats in the 80-seat assembly, making the Rwandan parliament the first in the world with a female majority. The Rwandan constitution provides that women must hold at least 30 percent of parliamentary seats.

Human Rights Defenders and Journalists

In late 2007 two activists from the Rwandan League for the Promotion and Defense of Human Rights (LIPRODHOR) were threatened and fled Rwanda following publication of a LIPRODHOR report documenting official abuses. LIPRODHOR as an organization was not allowed to monitor the 2008 elections and its members were excluded from joining other observer teams.

The Human Rights League of the Great Lakes (LDGL)—an umbrella group that includes Burundian, Congolese, and Rwandan organizations—monitored the elections, and in a balanced report identified many of the faults also noted by the EU observers. The chair of the National Election Commission attacked LDGL for the report, wrongly asserting that its Congolese president had changed an earlier version to make the report more critical.

RWANDA

Law and Reality

Progress in Judicial Reform in Rwanda

H U M A N
R I G H T S
W A T C H

Throughout the year, officials sought to limit reporting by critical journalists. Beginning in 2007 officials criticized the Voice of America and the BBC for favoring "genocide ideology" and in 2008 excluded their journalists from official events. In May 2008 reporters for three independent newspapers were excluded from an official celebration of World Press Day and were thereafter excluded from all government press conferences.

Journalist Dominique Makeli, jailed for 14 years on genocide charges, was acquitted in a *gacaca* trial, but the verdict has been appealed.

Key International Actors

Donors, including multilateral institutions, like the World Bank and the European Union, and bilateral donors, like the United Kingdom, the United States, Belgium, the Netherlands, Germany, and Sweden, provide generous support to Rwanda, citing its ambitious plans for economic growth and its achievement of internal stability. International actors rarely criticize the Rwandan human rights performance publicly, although some on occasion discreetly, and occasionally successfully, recommend changes in proposed legislation.

Even such generally supportive donors as the US criticized Rwanda for permitting the Congolese rebel commander Laurent Nkunda to obtain recruits and financial support from within Rwanda (see DRC chapter). Dutch parliamentarians, who attributed some responsibility to Rwanda for the Congolese crisis, proposed transferring Dutch general budget support from Rwanda to a Congolese emergency fund.

SIERRA LEONE

The government of President Ernest Bai Koroma, elected in 2007, made concerted efforts to address the issues which gave rise to the brutal 11-year armed conflict that ended in 2002—rampant corruption, gross public financial mismanagement, inadequate distribution of the country's natural resources, and weak rule of law. However, resistance to the reform agenda from some influential members of government threatened these efforts. Meanwhile, serious deficiencies in the police and judiciary continue to undermine fundamental human rights.

The discovery in July of a plane loaded with cocaine, and the subsequent arrest of several Latin Americans and Sierra Leonean officials allegedly involved in drug trafficking, focused Sierra Leone's key partners on the urgency of improving the rule of law, addressing extremely high rates of unemployment, and strengthening the security sector. Meanwhile, through the efforts of the UN-mandated Special Court for Sierra Leone, significant progress continues in achieving accountability for war crimes.

In 2007 and 2008 Sierra Leone ranked last in the UN's Human Development Index. At 1,800 deaths per 100,000 live births, the country has the highest maternal mortality rate in the world, largely due to lack of human resources and corruption in the healthcare sector.

Corruption

The government put the struggle against corruption at the top of the national agenda and took several meaningful steps to address a scourge that has for decades posed a major obstacle to human rights and development. In August parliament passed a bill expanding the powers of the existing Anti-Corruption Commission (ACC), granting it independent powers to investigate and prosecute matters on its own, rather than through the president-appointed attorney general. During the year President Koroma warned government officials to desist from corrupt practices, ordered a temporary ban on logging and exploitation of timber, took steps to address the lack of competitive bidding for contracts, and in September became the first Sierra Leonean head of state to declare his assets to the ACC. During 2008 the ACC indicted a former ombudsman and several low-and mid-level officials from ministries and parastatals. Several other investigations, including those involving a serving minister and two magistrates, were ongoing.

Efforts to Establish the Rule of Law

Deficiencies in the judicial system persist, including extortion and bribe-taking by officials; insufficient numbers of judges, magistrates, and prosecuting attorneys; absenteeism by court personnel; inadequate remuneration for judiciary personnel; and extended periods of pretrial detention. In 2008 some 90 percent of prisoners lacked any legal representation. Hundreds of people—over 40 percent of the country's detainees—were held in prolonged pretrial detention.

The only legal system accessible to some 70 percent of the population is one based on customary courts controlled by traditional leaders and applying customary law, which is often discriminatory, particularly against women. Local court officials frequently abuse their powers by illegally detaining persons, charging high fines for minor offenses, and adjudicating criminal cases beyond their jurisdiction.

Prisons were severely overcrowded, in violation of international standards. Some 20 people reportedly died in detention, a consequence of overcrowding and the lack of adequate food, clothing, medicine, hygiene, and sanitation in Sierra Leone's prisons. The population of the country's largest detention facility—designed for 350 detainees—stands at over 1,100.

A concerted effort by the government, UN, and UK-funded Justice Sector Development Programme (JSDP) to improve the rule of law led to some improvements in the sector, including a decrease in the number of prisoners held in pretrial detention, slight improvements in healthcare and access to water for detainees, and the opening of a separate detention facility for juvenile offenders.

In November, 11 death row prisoners were released after an appellate court overturned a December 2004 conviction for treason in connection with a 2003 coup attempt. At this writing, 12 individuals remain on death row.

Police and Army Conduct

On several occasions police were accused of using excessive force against the media and alleged criminals, or while executing a court order. There were also persistent reports of bribe-taking, extortion at checkpoints, and requiring victims of crimes to pay the police to file reports or conduct investigations. However, the police were notably professional and non-partisan during episodes of ethnic and politically-motivated violence and in their response to serious crimes, including Sierra Leone's largest drug bust. Police leadership is also increasingly more willing to investigate, discipline, and dismiss officers engaging in unprofessional or corrupt practices. In June, 94 police officers were fired after having been found guilty of professional misconduct.

Since 1999 the UK-led International Military Advisory and Training Team (IMATT) has been working to reform and advise the Republic of Sierra Leone Armed Forces (RSLAF). In 2008 there were a few reports of abuses and indiscipline by members of the army, but the RSLAF leadership demonstrated its commitment to penalize and sanction soldiers for offenses committed.

Truth and Reconciliation Commission

The 2005 report of Sierra Leone's Truth and Reconciliation Commission (TRC) attributed the civil war largely to decades of corrupt rule by the political elite and recommended abolishing the death penalty, repealing laws that criminalize seditious libel, increasing the transparency of the mining industry, improving good governance, and establishing a reparations fund for war victims. The government has been slow to implement the recommendations and openly rejected some of them, including the abolition of the death penalty. However, after a long delay, one of the commission's recommendations—the establishment of a reparations fund for war victims—was established and funded by the UN Peacebuilding Fund.

National Human Rights Commission

Increased financial support in 2008 allowed the National Human Rights Commission to more fully carry out its mandate to investigate and report on human rights abuses and push for the implementation of the TRC recommendations. During the year the commission became fully operational, establishing offices in Bo, Kenema, and Makeni, and launching a five-year strategic plan. By year's end, it had received and investigated over 100 complaints. The commission generally operated without government interference.

Accountability for Past Abuses

The trial of former Liberian president Charles Taylor—charged with 11 counts of war crimes and crimes against humanity for supporting Sierra Leonean rebel groups—resumed before the Special Court for Sierra Leone in January 2008. This followed a six-month delay due to an overhaul in Taylor's legal team after he sought to fire his lawyers over concerns that he was receiving inadequate resources to prepare his defense. The prosecution, which as of this writing has presented more than 80 witnesses, is due to complete their case in January 2009. Taylor is the first former African head of state to stand trial in front of any international or hybrid international-national war crimes tribunal. For security reasons his trial is taking place in The Hague instead of Freetown, Sierra Leone's capital.

After issuing verdicts in the cases of its first five defendants in 2007, the court in February 2008 upheld convictions on appeal by three members of the rebel Armed Forces Revolutionary Council (AFRC)—Alex Tamba Brima, Brima Bazzy Kamara, and Santigie Borbor Kanu—whom the judges noted were "responsible for some of the most heinous, brutal, and atrocious crimes ever recorded in human history." Convictions on appeal for members of the government-sponsored Civil Defense Forces (CDF)— Moinina Fofana and Allieu Kondewa—were largely upheld, although the appeals chamber rejected the trial chamber's finding that the CDF's purposes in fighting could be a basis for reducing sentences, and instead lengthened the prison terms imposed. The cases of three members of the rebel Revolutionary United Front (RUF) were concluded in June 2008, and judgment is expected in late 2008.

While states, including the UK, the US, the Netherlands, Canada, France, and Germany, continue to make important contributions to the Special Court for Sierra Leone, which relies primarily on voluntary funding, the court continued to suffer from financial shortfalls.

Key International Actors

The UN and UK government continued to take the lead in supporting Sierra Leone's transition to democracy and the rule of law.

To address the ongoing political, economic, security, and rule of law challenges, the UN Security Council in October 2008 established its fourth UN mission in Sierra Leone in 10 years—the 70-strong UN Integrated Peacebuilding Office in Sierra Leone (UNIPSIL). The mission will have a largely advisory role aimed at promoting human rights and strengthening democratic institutions and the rule of law, including efforts to address organized crime and drug trafficking. UNIPSIL will coordinate closely with the UN Peacebuilding Commission and Fund, which support projects dedicated to improving reform in the justice and security sectors. UNIPSIL follows the 300-strong UN Integrated Office for Sierra Leone (UNIOSL), whose mandate expired in September 2008.

More than one-third of Sierra Leone's national income of US$365 million is provided by donors. The United Kingdom, Sierra Leone's largest donor, gave £50 million in the last fiscal year, primarily through its international aid agency.

SOMALIA

An increasingly brutal conflict pits a deeply fragmented insurgency against Somalia's weak Transitional Federal Government (TFG) and Ethiopian military forces that are in Somalia to support it. All sides to this conflict have regularly committed serious violations of international humanitarian law amounting to war crimes with complete impunity and with devastating impact on Somalia's civilian population. The human rights and humanitarian situation in Somalia deteriorated to levels perhaps unseen since the collapse of the country's last unified central government in 1991.

Since the beginning of 2007 more than 870,000 civilians have fled war-torn Mogadishu alone and more than 6,000 civilians have been killed in the fighting. Untold numbers of Somalis bear the scars of seeing family members killed or raped. Several key international players—most notably Ethiopia, Eritrea, and the United States—have exacerbated the crisis through their policies and actions.

In 2008 violence escalated in scale and brutality while internationally supported peace talks struggled to get traction. Even traditional systems of clan protection have broken down in many areas. Key civil society activists whose talents are essential to hopes of rebuilding were killed or driven out of the country. The number of Somalis in need of humanitarian assistance surpassed 3 million, even as criminal violence, rampant piracy off the northern coasts, and targeted attacks on humanitarian workers impeded the flow of aid. Somalis attempting to flee this chaos faced brutal attacks by freelance militias along the roads.

Abuses by TFG Security Forces and Militias

TFG police, military personnel, and militias linked to leading TFG figures such as former Mogadishu mayor Mohammed Dheere are implicated in widespread abuses against Somali civilians. Throughout 2008 these forces carried out killings, murder, rape, and looting during operations across many Mogadishu neighborhoods. Following an insurgent mortar attack launched from near the Al-Mathal school in Mogadishu in June, TFG police sacked the school, smashing and burning educational materials, and shooting one child in the leg.

TFG forces repeatedly killed and wounded civilians during fighting against insurgent forces. In March, following an insurgent ambush, TFG police forces indiscriminately fired their weapons, killing four passengers in a passing minibus and injuring its driver.

TFG police and intelligence officials carried out widespread arbitrary arrests, often for the purpose of extracting ransom payments from detainees and their families. Intelligence operatives under the command of TFG National Security Agency head Mohammed Warsame 'Darwish' maintain a dungeon-like detention facility in southern Mogadishu. Conditions in this facility are appalling and intelligence personnel subject many detainees to torture during interrogation.

Abuses by Ethiopian Military Forces (see also Ethiopia chapter)

Ethiopian National Defense Force (ENDF) personnel in Mogadishu have continued to use mortars, artillery, and "Katyusha" rockets indiscriminately in response to insurgent attacks, devastating entire neighborhoods of the city. Ethiopian bombardments regularly fall on civilian homes and public spaces, sometimes killing entire families. In July ENDF forces bombarded part of the strategic town of Beletweyne after coming under attack by insurgent forces based there, displacing 75,000 people.

In 2008 ENDF personnel were implicated in numerous acts of murder, rape, and looting of Somali civilians, often alongside TFG forces. In an April raid on a Mogadishu mosque, ENDF soldiers reportedly killed 21 people; seven of the dead had their throats cut.

Since late 2007 ENDF discipline has eroded. Ethiopian soldiers frequently react to insurgent attacks by firing indiscriminately into crowds of civilians. In August a group of ENDF soldiers hit by a roadside bomb near the town of Afgooye responded by firing wildly and killing up to 60 civilians, including the passengers of two minibuses.

Abuses by Insurgent Forces

Insurgent forces have kept TFG and Ethiopian forces pinned down in heavy fighting in Mogadishu for nearly two years, gaining ground in 2008. The insurgents are deeply fragmented, but many of the worst abuses have been committed by groups linked to Al-Shabaab ("Youth" in Arabic), a militant Islamist group.

Insurgents in Mogadishu routinely fire mortar shells from populated areas towards TFG and Ethiopian installations without adequate spotting, indiscriminately killing and wounding civilians, and placing civilians under their control at risk from Ethiopian and TFG counter-battery fire. Insurgent groups, some of which are illegally recruiting—sometimes by force—under 18-year-olds, also use landmines and remote-detonated explosive devices along roads in populated areas. In August a roadside bomb in southern Mogadishu killed 21 women working as street-cleaners and wounded more than 40 other civilians.

Insurgent forces have also carried out targeted killings of civilian TFG officials, perceived TFG collaborators, and individuals the insurgents view as un-Islamic. In January a man working as a messenger among different TFG offices was shot outside of his home in Mogadishu after receiving several death threats ordering him to stop his work. In April Al-Shabaab fighters killed four foreign national teachers in the town of Beletweyne.

In October a simultaneous wave of bomb attacks struck a government office in Puntland as well as government, UN, and Ethiopian consular offices in Hargeisa. At least 28 people died in the attacks.

Attacks against Humanitarian Workers, Civil Society Activists, and Journalists

Humanitarian workers and civil society activists became the targets of an unprecedented wave of attacks in 2008. Between January and November, 25 humanitarian workers were killed in Somalia and at least 24 NGO staff were kidnapped. In January a roadside bomb in Kismayo killed three Médecins Sans Frontières staff and a journalist. In June armed men assassinated civil society activist Mohamed Hassan Kulmiye in his office in Beletweyne. In July unknown men shot dead Osman Ali Mohamed, the head of the United Nations Development Program (UNDP) office in Somalia, as he left a mosque. The head of the Somalia office of the United Nations High Commissioner for Refugees was kidnapped in June and held for more than two months.

Al-Shabaab and its more militant splinter groups are believed to have carried out many of these attacks. But many Somali activists believe that elements within the TFG are also profiting from the current environment of confusion and impunity to threaten and murder critics in civil society. Prominent activists who fled into exile in 2008 cite their inability to identify the origin of threats as the primary reason they had no choice but to leave.

At least two Somali journalists were killed in 2008, bringing the total number of journalists killed since early 2007 to 10. In June gunmen shot and killed BBC stringer Nasteh Dahir Farah outside of his home in Kismayo. TFG police and intelligence personnel have imprisoned several other journalists. In 2008 TFG security services detained the directors of two independent radio stations, Radio Somaliweyn and Radio Shabelle. A reporter from Radio Somaliweyn was also jailed, for covering an opposition meeting in Asmara. In general, however, TFG Prime Minister Nur Hassan Hussein has made efforts to reduce the level of harassment TFG security forces mete out to Somali journalists.

Key International Actors

The US, the United Kingdom, the European Commission and other key donors have failed to condemn ENDF or TFG abuses or address the scale of the Somali crisis. Instead, they have sought to support the TFG even where this risks empowering abusive TFG actors and institutions. In 2008 several donors, including the European Commission, pressured UNDP to pay the salaries of 4,000 Ethiopian-trained TFG security personnel without adequate monitoring.

US policy on Somalia is dominated by counterterrorism concerns and tends towards unwavering support for the TFG and for Ethiopian policy in Somalia. The US military has continued its practice of targeted air strikes on alleged terrorist suspects, launching two attacks on Somali soil in 2008. One attack in March injured six civilians but did not hit any suspected terrorist targets, while another in April killed Al-Shabaab's commander, Aden Hashi Ayrow, as well as several civilians.

Somalia's neighbors have played mixed roles in the ongoing crisis. Eritrea uses Somalia as a convenient theater in its proxy war against Ethiopia. Eritrea hosts a breakaway faction of the opposition Alliance for the Re-Liberation of Somalia (ARS) and actively stokes the violence. Kenya closed its border with Somalia in January 2007, but continues to accommodate nearly 7,000 new Somali refugees each month in the sprawling refugee camps around the northern town of Dadaab.

The African Union has authorized a force of 8,000 peacekeepers for Somalia, but thus far only 2,450 Ugandan and Burundian troops have been deployed. Those troops are largely limited to protecting a few key installations in Mogadishu.

The United Nations' Special Representative of the Secretary-General for Somalia, Ahmedou Ould-Abdallah, has successfully brought together the Djibouti-based ARS with TFG representatives for peace talks. The talks, hosted by the government of Djibouti, currently represent the best hope for a negotiated end to the armed conflict in Somalia. However, thus far there has been a lack of concrete progress and they have been hobbled by the fact that some factions within the TFG, along with Al-Shabaab and other powerful opposition groups, have rejected the process altogether.

SOUTH AFRICA

Poverty, unemployment, gender-based and xenophobic violence, and crime remain significant barriers to the enjoyment of human rights; the government's commitment to address them is inadequate. Vulnerable groups and NGOs are increasingly using the courts to establish the principle of progressive realization of socioeconomic rights as stipulated in the constitution.

In September 2008 leadership battles within the ruling African National Congress (ANC) resulted in the early resignation of President Thabo Mbeki after a court finding of judicial interference. ANC Deputy President Kgalema Motlanthe took over until the 2009 elections. Judicial independence has been re-emphasized by the courts, the government, and civil society in the face of public attacks, disparaging judges, and scandals involving the conduct of individual judges. Incidents of police violence are reported to be increasing.

South Africa failed to utilize its non-permanent membership of the United Nations Security Council to support resolutions or initiatives that would help protect the rights of people in various countries, most notably Sudan and Zimbabwe.

Xenophobic Attacks on Foreign Nationals

In May 2008 xenophobic violence broke out in Alexandra, Johannesburg, and rapidly spread to seven of South Africa's nine provinces, resulting in 62 deaths, including 21 South Africans, 11 Mozambicans, five Zimbabweans and three Somalis; thousands were injured. Some 40,000 foreign nationals left the country and a further 50,000 remain internally displaced.

The attacks are indicative of growing xenophobia in South Africa, where isolated incidents of violence against foreign nationals have been documented since the mid-1990s. Intolerance of migrants partly provoked by competition for resources and by increasing numbers of migrants, particularly from Zimbabwe, has created a volatile situation in poor communities, with foreign nationals becoming easy targets. Although over 1,000 people were arrested after the violence, there were fewer convictions. The climate of impunity for those responsible allowed the situation to escalate. Humanitarian measures were also inadequate. Temporary shelters constructed in June 2008 did not meet international standards, and there was insufficient clean water, food, and sanitation, and inadequate healthcare. Lack of protection for women and children resulted in incidents of sexual violence. Despite a pending Constitutional Court judgment, the Gauteng provincial government dismantled temporary shelters, leaving hundreds of people without shelter, water, food, and sanitation.

The government has yet to address longer-term issues of reintegration, resettlement, or xenophobic intolerance in local communities. While many victims of the May attacks have returned to communities from which they fled, some have experienced new attacks, with over 30 deaths being reported between June and November 2008. As a result, many are seeking greater assurances for their own safety before leaving government shelters.

Refugees and Migrants

The government opened a reception centre in Musina, near the Zimbabwean border, in response to increased migration from Zimbabwe and growing criticism from civil society organizations. However, deportation and status determination processes conducted by immigration officials and police who are insufficiently trained in basic refugee law and related procedures continue to thwart refugees' efforts to seek asylum. Tens of thousands of Zimbabwean nationals with valid refugee claims on the basis of fleeing Operation Murambatsvina or other well-founded fears of political persecution were refouled.

South Africa's reform of the Department of Home Affairs has yet to have impact on the procedural obstacles and administrative delays that plague refugee status determination. Asylum seekers remain subject to long queues in filthy conditions, face status determination officers ill-equipped to make fair decisions, and struggle to access assistance for appeals because of limited resources within the Legal Aid Board.

Excessive Use of Force by the Police

In 2008 South Africa saw a 13 percent increase in the number of deaths as a result of police action and an eight percent increase in complaints against police.

Neighbors In Need

Zimbabweans seeking refuge in South Africa

**HUMAN
RIGHTS
WATCH**

A January police raid on the Johannesburg Central Methodist Church saw the use of pepper spray and batons against 1,200 sleeping foreign nationals, including women and children seeking shelter. Some were refugees and asylum seekers. The police said they were looking for drugs, firearms, and "illegal immigrants."

The indiscriminate use of rubber bullets and other non-lethal weapons during public protests—from student protests to service delivery protests—and the number of resulting injuries call into question policing methods used during public demonstrations. During an authorized service delivery protest in Sydenham, Durban, in September 2007, police used water cannon, stun grenades and fired rubber bullets without adequate warning; six protesters required hospitalization. Rubber bullets and assaults using batons during protests injured eight people in Orange Farm in May 2008, 16 refugees in the Western Cape in July and another 18 people in Orange Farm in September. South African law clearly limits the use of weapons likely to cause bodily injury or death to situations where other methods have failed, and requires the use of proportionate force. In many reported incidents, the police failed to give adequate warning and did not try other methods to disperse demonstrations.

Socioeconomic Rights

Delivery on health rights remains inadequate, with progress being won through civil society litigation. In May 2008 the High Court ruled that the health classification policy of the South African Defence Forces was unconstitutional, ordering it to halt discrimination on the grounds of HIV status and to change policy that precluded members from external deployment because of HIV status. The increasing incidence of drug-resistant and multi-drug-resistant tuberculosis has raised concerns about the delivery of effective TB therapy and infection-control practices in South African hospitals, the confinement of patients, the conditions of confinement, and patient access to treatment.

Despite the South African government's "Breaking New Ground" housing policy, which includes development of socially inclusive housing projects, an informal settlement upgrading program, and provision of infrastructure and services for low-income communities, more than 14 percent of South Africans continue to live in inadequate housing; while over 20 percent do not have access to basic services. During his visit to South Africa in February 2008, the UN special rapporteur on adequate housing commented that living conditions in South Africa's informal settlements fall short of safe and sustainable conditions.

In April the Phiri community affirmed the right to adequate water for poor communities when it won its High Court case against the City of Johannesburg. The landmark ruling ordered the City to provide residents of Phiri with 50 liters of free water per person per day, noting that the current daily allocation of 25 liters of free water per person was insufficient, particularly for people suffering from HIV/AIDS. The City of Johannesburg halted installations of pre-paid water meters while it appealed the High Court decision.

Women's Rights

Violence against women, including rape and domestic violence, remained unacceptably high. The so-called Sexual Offences Act—officially titled the Criminal Law (Sexual Offences and Related Matters) Amendment Act, No. 32 of 2007—finally came into effect on December 16, 2007. It amends the common law definition of rape to include men and boys and no longer focuses only on penetrative offenses. It provides additional protective measures for child victims of sexual offenses and adults with mental disabilities.

Children's Rights

The Children's Act became law in April 2008 and offers increased protection for children and the promotion of children's rights. The Child Justice Act passed in June established a separate criminal justice procedural system for child offenders. It also increased the minimum age of criminal capacity from seven to 10 years, but allows for mandatory minimum sentences—including life sentences for offenses such as murder and the rape of a minor—to be applicable to children ages 16 and 17 years. This is despite constitutional provisions that children should be detained only as a last resort and for the shortest appropriate period of time, and despite the call by the UN Committee on the Rights of the Child for life imprisonment of child offenders to be abolished.

Around 122,000 children live in child-headed households, making them particularly vulnerable to discrimination, ostracism, social exclusion, and sexual exploitation. Unaccompanied refugee and asylum-seeking children face obstacles and delays in accessing the courts to formalize their status, resulting in informal foster placements and delays in accessing social welfare.

International Role

South Africa ended its two-year period as a non-permanent member of the UN Security Council in December 2008. South Africa opposed or declined to support resolutions for victims of human rights violations in Sudan, Belarus, Uzbekistan, Burma, Iran, Zimbabwe, and North Korea. Together with Libya, South Africa played a leading role in seeking to make renewal of the United Nations-African Union Mission in Darfur, conditional on a Security Council intervention to rein in the International Criminal Court, by ordering it not to proceed with the requested arrest warrant for Sudan's President Omar al-Bashir. The South African move, which would have been damaging to the court, was ultimately defeated. South Africa was a strong supporter of the court when it was founded. South Africa was reviewed under the Universal Periodic Review mechanism of the UN Human Rights Council in April, but did not make clear its commitments during the process.

South Africa's former president Mbeki continued as the Southern African Development Community mediator in Zimbabwe throughout the year but failed to confront the major election-related human rights violations committed by the Zimbabwean government.

SUDAN

With war continuing in the west and a fragile peace in the south, the dynamics of respect for human rights remain complex and the challenges severe. In Darfur hundreds of thousands remain internally displaced as the Sudanese government uses indiscriminate bombings and attacks on civilians by ground forces and allied Janjaweed militias in counterinsurgency. Throughout Sudan delay in implementing the Comprehensive Peace Agreement (CPA), signed in 2005 by the National Congress Party (NCP) government and the Sudan Peoples' Liberation Movement (SPLM), is straining relations between the parties, threatening the CPA itself.

On January 1, 2008, the hybrid United Nations-African Union Mission in Darfur, (UNAMID), formally took over peacekeeping in Darfur. However, in large part due to obstruction by the government, by late 2008 barely 10,000 of the authorized 26,000 peacekeepers were on the ground, and UNAMID was unable to provide effective protection for civilians or humanitarian operations.

In May 2008 rebels from the Justice and Equality Movement (JEM) attacked Khartoum. Government security forces arbitrarily detained hundreds of suspected rebels, severely mistreating many.

In July the International Criminal Court (ICC) prosecutor requested an arrest warrant for President Omar al-Bashir on 10 counts of war crimes, crimes against humanity, and genocide relating to Darfur. Khartoum threatened that this would lead to violence in Darfur; and, according to many observers, aiming to secure diplomatic support for suspension of the ICC investigation, Khartoum made minor concessions to UNAMID and ostensible overtures towards peace. Meanwhile, Sudan continued to refuse to hand over Ahmed Haroun, minister of state for humanitarian affairs, and Ali Kosheib, who have been subject to ICC warrants since 2007.

A national census, an important milestone in the CPA, was conducted in April, but not in much of Darfur, and it was marred by violence in parts of the south where in the weeks beforehand armed militias affiliated with the central government attacked civilians near the north-south boundary.

Also in the border area, the inability of northern and southern leaders to resolve differences over the status of oil-rich Abyei led to violent clashes between northern and southern forces in May. National elections are scheduled for 2009, but the Government of National Unity (GNU)—created under the terms of the CPA— has yet to establish an elections commission or enact critical reforms, including revised national security and press acts that would facilitate free and fair elections.

Sudan continues to sentence children to death. Sudan's 2005 Interim Constitution allows for persons under age 18 at the time of the crime to be executed for *hadd* and *qisas* (categories of crimes under Sharia law). One child was sentenced to death in 2008 and at least two other child cases are under appeal.

Darfur

Government and government-backed militias continue to attack civilian populations ethnically associated with rebel movements, both deliberately and in the course of indiscriminate bombings. Rebel factions have proliferated and criminal banditry has increased. The 2006 Darfur Peace Agreement is now widely acknowledged to be defunct.

In February, following an offensive by JEM in West Darfur, the government conducted some of the worst attacks on civilians since 2003-2005. Government forces and Janjaweed carried out a series of attacks on villages, killing and injuring hundreds of civilians, and carrying out widespread looting in violation of international humanitarian law. An estimated 40,000 people fled, 13,000 of them to Chad.

The ICC prosecutor's request for an arrest warrant for President Bashir did not, despite Khartoum's threats, appear to increase violence on the ground, but neither did it decrease. Continuing its pattern of attacks on rebel-held areas, in July government forces bombed 21 civilian locations, killing at least two civilians. In August and September government forces and militia attacked rebel positions and villages in North and West Darfur, killing an unknown number of civilians, looting property, and displacing thousands. In October militia supported by gov-

ernment forces attacked villages in South Darfur, killing scores of civilians, destroying homes, and looting animals.

In other incidents it was not clear who was responsible. Armed elements targeted both peacekeepers and humanitarian operations, usually to steal vehicles, supplies, and weapons. On July 8, armed men attacked a UNAMID convoy in North Darfur, killing five peacekeepers and two police. In September gunmen shot at UNAMID helicopters on three occasions, killing four passengers in one incident in South Darfur. A Nigerian peacekeeper was killed in an ambush in October. From January to August 2008, armed assailants hijacked 224 vehicles, attacked 139 humanitarian facilities, and killed 11 humanitarian workers. The continued insecurity has limited humanitarian operations in many areas and prompted UNAMID to tighten security restrictions.

Internally displaced populations were vulnerable to violence and attacks by a host of actors, including rebels, former rebels, and government forces. In South Darfur, government security forces conducted a raid on Kalma camp, reportedly to disarm civilians, killing 33 civilians including women and children. In September government forces entered Zamzam camp and shot indiscriminately at civilians, and looted buildings and structures, causing civilians to flee. Internally displaced women and girls were victims of sexual violence by government forces, allied militia, rebels, and criminals. The majority of victims did not seek redress or were prevented from doing so by legal and practical obstacles in the justice system.

The Darfur conflict reached the capital for the first time on May 10-12 when JEM forces attacked Omdurman, a western suburb of Khartoum. Following the attack, Sudanese National Intelligence and Security Services (NISS) arrested at least 300 individuals, including children, in public places and house-to-house searches targeting those who appeared Darfuri. Released detainees reported torture, mistreatment, and inhumane conditions in prisons and secret detention centers. Many of those arrested remain unaccounted for.

In June the government established special courts under Sudan's 2001 Anti-Terrorism Law to try those accused of participating in the attack. In trials that fell below international standards, the courts tried and sentenced to death 50 people in July and August. Their appeal is pending.

SUDAN

Five Years On

No Justice for Sexual Violence in Darfur

**H U M A N
R I G H T S
W A T C H**

Following the ICC prosecutor's request for an arrest warrant for President Bashir in July, Khartoum responded with a dual strategy of threats of further violence and promises of progress on the ground. The government made a series of minor concessions to UNAMID and ostensible overtures towards peace, aimed at securing diplomatic support for suspension of the investigation. In August President Bashir announced a "Sudan People's Initiative" to draw up a proposal for resolving the conflict, and in October expressed willingness to attend talks slated to take place in Qatar at the end of the year. On November 12, Khartoum also announced a unilateral ceasefire in advance of those talks. However, rebels refused to engage in either the People's Initiative or the Qatar talks, arguing that the government is not serious about either the peace process or the ceasefire, but only interested in securing a deferral of the ICC investigation.

Also in response to the threat of a warrant, Khartoum appointed another special prosecutor to try crimes committed in Darfur. However, at the time of writing, Sudan has made no significant progress toward domestic accountability for serious crimes.

Press Freedom

The government resumed pre-print censorship on newspapers in 2008, in the wake of a Chadian rebel coup attempt at N'Djamena on February 2-3—which the Chad government said was supported by Khartoum—and again after the JEM attack on Omdurman. Between May and September, NISS media censors removed or partly removed more than 150 articles, 50 of which covered the Darfur conflict.

Southern Sudan

Delays in implementation of the Comprehensive Peace Agreement continued to strain relations between the NCP and the SPLM. In October 2007, the SPLM temporarily suspended participation in the Government of National Unity, accusing the NCP of failing to share oil revenues, not withdrawing its troops from the south, failing to take steps to demarcate the North-South border, and, crucially, failing to implement the Abyei Protocol, an accord to resolve the status of oil-rich Abyei.

SUDAN

Crackdown in Khartoum

Mass Arrests, Torture, and Disappearances
since the May 10 Attack

**H U M A N
R I G H T S
W A T C H**

The SPLM rejoined the GNU in late 2007, but the parties did not resolve the dispute over Abyei, which led to fighting in May 2008, in which scores of civilians were killed and at least 60,000 fled their homes. The parties reached agreement to restore security to Abyei, enabling displaced residents to return. However, the underlying dispute over Abyei and other issues, including withdrawal of troops and border demarcation, continued to threaten the CPA.

In southern Sudan, the proliferation of small arms among the civilians contributed to violent communal disputes over land, cattle and resources. The semi-autonomous Government of Southern Sudan (GOSS) conducted civilian disarmament, involving human rights violations by poorly trained and sometimes undisciplined soldiers. Weak rule of law institutions were not able to provide civilian security and contributed to an environment of impunity. Human rights violations in the administration of justice—the responsibility of GOSS in the south—included arbitrary arrests and detentions, prolonged pretrial detention, and poor conditions in detention facilities.

Key International Actors

In 2008 international attention mainly focused on two issues: the deployment of UNAMID and the ICC arrest warrant request for President Bashir.

Diplomatic support for UNAMID, including at the UN Security Council, did not translate into effective pressure on Khartoum to facilitate deployment, nor the provision of critical equipment, including helicopters that the force still seeks. In early 2008 a group of governments, including the United States and Canada, formed "Friends of UNAMID," which provided additional resources to troop-contributing countries, but by late 2008 the force remained severely understaffed and ill-equipped.

In July international focus shifted when the ICC prosecutor applied for a warrant for the arrest of President Bashir, and Khartoum and its allies launched their diplomatic campaign to secure the suspension of the investigation, (which the UN Security Council can order under article 16 of the Rome Statute.)

Although both the African Union and the League of Arab States supported calls for suspending the warrant, the Security Council remains divided. Several countries, including the US, United Kingdom and France, have rejected suspension. The ICC pretrial chamber is expected to consider the prosecutor's request in early 2009.

UGANDA

In 2008 the government of President Yoweri Museveni and the Lord's Resistance Army (LRA) concluded peace talks to end the long-running war in northern Uganda, but LRA leader Joseph Kony did not sign the final peace accord. Sought by the International Criminal Court (ICC) on war crimes charges, the LRA leadership continued to commit serious abuses, preying on civilians in the Democratic Republic of Congo (DRC), to which the LRA relocated in 2006, as well as in Sudan and the Central African Republic (CAR).

In Karamoja, where the availability of firearms has aggravated cattle-raiding, the Ugandan army continued a campaign to disarm residents, but in the process committed human rights violations.

Military and security agencies illegally detained scores of persons seen as government opponents, held many of them incommunicado, and tortured some of those suspected of terrorism and treason. Police harassed opposition politicians and journalists critical of the government, charging some with sedition and defamation.

War in Northern Uganda

At the start of 2008, the government and the LRA appeared to be moving significantly closer to peace, concluding agreement in February on accountability, reconciliation, demobilization, disarmament, and reintegration. However, by the end of the year hopes of a final settlement were fading in the face of the repeated failure of Joseph Kony to show up to sign the final peace agreement. Meanwhile, LRA forces continued to commit abuses against civilians outside Uganda.

In an annex to the June 29, 2007 agreement, in February the parties agreed to the creation of a special division of the Ugandan High Court to try serious crimes committed during the conflict and broader accountability measures such as a truth commission, reparations, and traditional justice practices. Judges were appointed to the special division in May, but little else has been done since then. As the International Criminal Court's statute permits national trials of its cases where certain requirements are satisfied, LRA leaders for whom ICC arrest war-

SUDAN

Abandoning Abyei

Destruction and Displacement, May 2008

HUMAN
RIGHTS
WATCH

rants have been issued could potentially be prosecuted by the Ugandan special division, although only if the ICC judges determine that the national trials provide an adequate alternative.

Meanwhile the LRA attacked civilians in the DRC, the CAR, and Sudan. In February they reportedly abducted at least 100 persons in these three countries. After LRA combatants killed 26 civilians and abducted 95 in March in Equatoria, Sudan, the UN High Commissioner for Refugees (UNHCR) ended repatriation of Sudanese refugees from Uganda. From bases in Garamba National Park, DRC, the LRA in September, October, and November reportedly abducted at least another 100 children, killed several civilians, and looted and burned Congolese villages. Shortly after, three LRA defectors trying to turn themselves in were killed by the local community.

Disarmament in Karamoja

As part of a law enforcement campaign initiated in 2006, the army continued efforts to disarm the population in the impoverished region of Karamoja. Soldiers reportedly used excessive force, firing on civilians, killing at least six, and on several occasions torturing and arbitrarily detaining men to compel them to reveal the location of weapons, though there were fewer incidents than in previous years. In October the courts martial sentenced four soldiers to 12 years in prison for the torture and killing of a local village chief in Kotido.

In April the government launched the Karamoja Integrated Disarmament and Development Programme (KIDDP); its success will depend on more effective access to justice and protection of civilians during disarmament operations.

Extrajudicial Killings, Illegal Detention, and Torture

In 2008 Human Rights Watch documented more than two dozen cases in which treason and terrorism suspects were allegedly tortured by agents of the Joint Anti-Terrorism Taskforce (JATT) and the Chieftaincy of Military Intelligence. Victims described being arrested by agents in civilian dress and unmarked cars, especially at the time of the Commonwealth Heads of Government meeting in Kampala in November 2007. They said they were beaten and tortured with electricity, and had pepper rubbed in their eyes. Some were illegally detained for many months in the basement of JATT offices or in other irregular places of detention. Most were never brought before judicial authorities, as required by law.

Judicial Independence and Freedom of Expression

Some officials failed to implement judicial decisions, especially those involving politically sensitive issues, and used harassment and excessive force to silent opponents. On May 27, 2008, the Constitutional Court nullified a section in the Police Act that required police permission to hold a public rally, saying that it unduly limited the rights to freedom of assembly and association. When the Democratic Party organized a celebratory public rally in the capital, police officers, deployed in large numbers, used tear gas and water cannons on the assembled crowd. After party activists addressed the crowd through loud speakers from their offices, police officers stormed the building, arresting four people who they charged with environmental pollution for having used the speakers. Police prevented the party from using its offices for almost a month. The police asserted that they retain the right to determine where public rallies take place.

In February, Betty Kamya, a parliamentarian from the Forum for Democratic Change, (FDC) was questioned by the police and charged with sedition, promoting sectarianism, inciting violence, and promoting war on the person of the president for saying that Ugandans should "fight to extricate [themselves] from Museveni's paw." In June, while Conservative Party Parliamentarian Suzan Nampijja was addressing a rally in her constituency, police used tear gas to disperse the crowd, giving no reason for their action. A few days later FDC Parliamentarian Nabillah Naggayi Sempala was accosted while addressing a crowd at a Kampala market. According to her account, police officers humiliated her, stripped her of her clothing, and detained her temporarily.

Government officials also harassed opponents of a controversial land bill amendment presented to parliament in 2008. In July, Medadi Lubega, Peter Mayiga, and Betty Nambooze Bakireke, officials of the Buganda cultural institution and outspoken critics of the bill, were arrested and detained for one week, well beyond the constitutional limit of 48 hours. The three were subsequently re-arrested and eventually charged with sedition and released on bail. The case was suspended in August because a 2005 challenge to the Sedition Law, brought by journalists, was still pending in the Constitutional Court.

Government officials continue to threaten media freedom and use charges such as sedition, defamation, and inciting violence against critics. In January the Political and Media Offences Department of the Police charged Andrew Mwenda and two others with sedition. A group of journalists from *The Monitor* newspaper were charged with defaming the inspector general of government, Uganda's anti-corruption watchdog, for articles written about corruption in her office. Over 20 journalists have pending cases with the police or in the judicial system.

Lesbian, Gay, Bisexual and Transgender Activists

Police and government officials continue to harass or restrict free expression by activists supporting lesbian, gay, bisexual or transgender rights. Police arrested three LGBT activists on June 4 at the 2008 HIV/AIDS Implementers meeting in Kampala after they peacefully protested the lack of official response to HIV/AIDS among LGBT communities. They were charged with criminal trespass. Later, one was mistreated by police officers during 24 hours of detention. In August the three were acquitted of all charges.

In September two other members of the LGBT community were arrested by police and held without charge for six days. In October Ethics and Integrity Minister James Nsaba Buturo reaffirmed continued police operations to arrest LGBT individuals. He said, "the state of moral health in our nation is challenging and we are concerned about the mushrooming of lesbianism and homosexuality."

HIV/AIDS

The proposed HIV/AIDS Prevention and Control Bill 2008 criminalizes the "intentional transmission of HIV & AIDS." It also establishes compulsory HIV testing for pregnant women and their partners. In its overall HIV/AIDS strategy, the government has not made enough effort or provided sufficient resources for prevention and care services to prevent HIV transmission.

Key International Actors

International donors focused on corruption, but generally shied away from pressing the government to halt and punish human rights violations perpetrated by security forces, even those generally known among diplomats such as illegal detention and torture.

Warrants issued by the ICC for LRA leaders in 2005 remain outstanding. No major players—including the United States, United Kingdom, the European Union, and the United Nations—took steps to ensure the apprehension of the suspects, although the European Parliament adopted a resolution calling on EU and African Union member states and regional countries to help implement the warrants.

The mandate of the special envoy of the UN secretary-general for the LRA-affected areas, Joaquim Chissano, was renewed for 2008. Throughout his tenure, he has generally failed to stress the importance of justice for past crimes as a basis for any durable peace. After his June briefing, UN Security Council members could not agree on language concerning the ICC and so said nothing, providing one more example of indecision in promoting justice for the victims of abuses.

ZAMBIA

Zambia is at a political crossroads after President Levy Mwanawasa died in August 2008. Largely credited with Zambia's economic recovery, including growth of more than five percent per year since 2002, Mwanawasa had also undertaken several positive steps to address the AIDS crisis in the country.

Presidential elections in October 2008 to choose Mwanawasa's successor result-ed in a narrow victory for his former vice president, Rupiah Banda of the Movement for Multi-Party Democracy (MMD). In his inaugural speech, Banda announced that Zambia would continue its pro-market economic policies and anti-corruption programs, work to attract foreign investment, and strive to become a middle-income country by 2030.

Presidential Elections

Voter turnout was markedly low, with only 45 percent of registered voters going to the polls. The Electoral Commission of Zambia (ECZ) announced that Banda won 40 percent of the contested vote against 38 percent for his closest rival, opposi-tion Patriotic Front (PF) leader Michael Sata. The bulk of support for Banda and the MMD came from rural areas, where the MMD subsidized fertilizer supplies to enhance food security prior to the elections. Support for Sata, who ran on an anti-poverty ticket and led the polls during the first two days of counting, came from urban voters, particularly in the capital Lusaka and the Copperbelt.

The Southern African Development Community (SADC) electoral observer mission declared the elections free and fair, and the Foundation for Democratic Process (FODEP), a local electoral watchdog—described the results as consistent with the findings of their observers at polling stations. However, Sata accused the MMD of rigging the vote, citing irregularities such as late voting in two constituencies in Western Province. The Electoral Commission said this was the result of the late arrival of electoral staff and ballot papers due to transportation problems. Sata also alleged that the MMD had inflated the figures in its favor in the party's stronghold areas, citing inconsistencies between vote tallies and the number of registered voters. Refusing to accept the result, the Patriotic Front launched a legal challenge and demanded a recount in 78 of the 180 constituencies.

There was heavy police presence, especially in Lusaka, to pre-empt violence, given that the 2006 general elections saw violent clashes involving police and PF supporters in Lusaka and the Copperbelt after results from rural constituencies indicated that Mwanawasa would win those elections.

Minor riots erupted in the Copperbelt and in a couple of townships in Lusaka, after an ECZ update on the evening of November 1 indicated that Banda was likely to win the presidential race. In Lusaka, opposition protestors reportedly looted and burned makeshift shops and stoned motor vehicles. The police used teargas to disperse the protestors and arrested 14 opposition party members who have since been charged with riotous behavior and conduct likely to breach peace.

Constitutional Reform

Zambia is undergoing a constitutional review process, initiated in 2002, to address serious gaps in its 1996 constitution, such as the absence of protections for economic, social, children's and women's rights in its associated Bill of Rights. The new draft constitution rectifies these shortcomings but there has been much controversy on the review process.

The MMD government has opposed holding a constitutional conference, arguing that it would be too costly, given that a national referendum would be expected to follow. The government has insisted that Parliament is the most appropriate body to adopt the new constitution. While, the opposition—mainly PF and the Oasis Forum, an alliance of NGOs and churches—has demanded that the new constitution be adopted by a conference to avoid any possible manipulation by the party in power, and to ensure the widest possible popular support.

In response, the MMD government pushed through the controversial Constitutional Conference Act in August 2007, which set up a standing National Constitutional Conference, (NCC) but which also expanded presidential powers and bypasses a constitutional requirement for a national referendum at the end of the consultative process. However, the Oasis Forum has dismissed the NCC as unconstitutional. Opposition leader Michael Sata instructed PF members of parliament not to participate in the NCC and subsequently dismissed 26 Patriotic Front MPs who joined it.

Civil and Political Rights

Zambia's Human Rights Commission reported in 2007 that unlawful deprivation of life; unlawful detentions, poor and life-threatening prison conditions, police brutality, and torture continue to be everyday occurrences in Zambia's police cells and prisons. The chair of the Commission, Pixie Yangailo, also said people are generally subjected to unacceptable delays in receiving justice due to lack of resources and capacity.

The Zambian government has restricted the right to freedom of expression, especially in relation to the NCC. This has included threats against journalists critical of the NCC, such as in 2007 when Mwanawasa warned critics that challenging the National Constitutional Conference Act amounted to treason.

Sexual and Gender-Based Violence

Sexual and gender-based violence (SGBV) against women and children is a major endemic problem in Zambia, especially in Lusaka and the Copperbelt, fueling the country's HIV pandemic and impeding women's access to HIV treatment.

According to both a June report by Zambia's chapter of Women in Law and Development in Africa (WILDAF) and the Victim Support Unit (VSU)—the police unit that addresses abuses against women and children—the true national extent of sexual and gender-based violence in Zambia is unclear due to lack of reporting by victims and survivors. Despite this, the VSU received reports between January and August 2008 of 65 rape and 626 child rape cases in Lusaka alone.

While a 2005 amendment to Zambia's penal code made child rape punishable by a maximum penalty of life imprisonment, the country currently has no specific SGBV legislation, and provisions in the penal code do not criminalize marital rape and psychological abuse, among other shortcomings. In a positive development, the Ministry of Justice, in collaboration with a number of NGOs, is working on a draft SGBV bill, which is expected to be presented to Parliament during its January 2009 session.

In 2008 Zambia established six new one-stop centers to provide comprehensive legal, medical, and counselling services to victims and survivors of SGBV, with

ZAMBIA

Hidden in the Mealie Meal

Gender-Based Abuses and Women's HIV Treatment in Zambia

H U M A N
R I G H T S
W A T C H

"I fear to tell my husband [about my HIV status] because I fear that he can shout [at me] and divorce me. He uses bad language with me... I hide the medicine, I put it on a plate, add mealie meal, so when he takes the lid off he [does not find ART]. [When] I take the medicine... I have to make sure that he is outside. That is why I forgot to take medicine four times since I started treatment. Last year he hit me around the back with his fist."

MARIA T., 45, LUSAKA, FEBRUARY 3, 2007

funding from the United States Agency for International Development. The centers were expected to be fully operational in November. The Young Women's Christian Association, in collaboration with other NGOs and the government, has also scaled-up the operations of the existing one-stop SGBV center in Lusaka.

While chair of the Southern African Development Community in 2007, Zambia, along with several other countries, opted to defer for further national consultation adoption of the SADC Gender and Development Protocol due to apparent controversy over criminalizing marital rape, among other matters. In August 2008 SADC finally adopted the Protocol.

HIV/AIDS

The AIDS pandemic continues to devastate Zambia's population. According to United Nations estimates, HIV prevalence in Zambia was 13.1 percent in 2007. Although this represents a reduction in prevalence from one year to the next, in real terms an estimated extra 182,228 people were living with HIV in 2007 because of population growth. Prevalence of HIV among pregnant women in 2007 was estimated to be 19.3 percent. Meanwhile, access to antiretroviral treatment in Zambia has improved, according to the UN, from 82,030 in 2006 to 151,000 in December 2007.

Key International Actors

Under Zambia's SADC chair tenure between August 2007 and August 2008, the situation in Zimbabwe was the most prominent regional issue. Mwanawasa was one of a small number of regional leaders prepared to criticize the conduct of Robert Mugabe's government, unlike several other SADC leaders who remained silent.

In May the UN Human Rights Council examined the human rights situation in Zambia under its Universal Periodic Review mechanism. While commending Zambia's high-level representation and the quality of its presentation and national report, the Council noted a series of violations, particularly concerning the rights of women and children.

ZIMBABWE

The brutal response of President Robert Mugabe and the ruling Zimbabwe African National Union-Patriotic Front (ZANU-PF) to their loss in general elections in March 2008 plunged Zimbabwe deep into political turmoil. After a month's delay in releasing the results of the presidential poll, the Zimbabwe Electoral Commission declared that opposition Movement for Democratic Change (MDC) leader Morgan Tsvangirai had failed to win by a 50-percent-plus-one vote majority, necessitating a run-off on June 27.

ZANU-PF launched a campaign of violence against MDC activists and supporters, mobilizing a system of repression and violent intimidation that remained in place, if less overtly active, at the end of the year. The months leading up to the run-off were marked by widespread abuses, including killings, torture, beatings, looting, and burning of property. Perpetrators, including the police, military, and local ZANU-PF officials, as well as government-backed militia and war veterans, committed abuses with almost absolute impunity. At least 163 people were killed and some 5,000 were tortured or beaten. Tens of thousands more were displaced by the violence, which eventually forced Tsvangirai to withdraw from the poll, leaving Mugabe to declare himself the winner.

In September, in the face of international pressure and a severely weakened economy, Mugabe signed a power-sharing agreement with Tsvangirai under the mediation of then-president Thabo Mbeki of South Africa. However, the frailty of the deal was soon apparent as the parties rapidly reached a deadlock on the distribution of ministries, with violence and intimidation against the MDC still taking place. Zimbabwe's political situation remains precarious, and the future looks bleak if the political leadership does not end abuses and address accountability for both past and present abuses.

Post-Election Violence and Repression

The build up to the March elections was generally peaceful, despite some flaws in the electoral process. However, the months afterwards were marked by a well planned and systematic campaign of violence by ZANU-PF and its allies. In an attempt to overturn the vote in the presidential run-off, government-backed militia and war veterans, ZANU-PF officials and supporters, and senior military officers waged a vicious campaign of intimidation against MDC activists and suspected supporters. Entire villages were cordoned off and those suspected of having voted for the MDC were brutally beaten and tortured. The militia and war veterans beat, tortured, and mutilated suspected MDC activists, supporters, and their family members in hundreds of base camps—many of them army bases—established across the provinces as local operation centers. Thousands of people were forced to attend abusive "re-education" meetings. Suspected ZANU-PF supporters and militia targeted and killed up to 163 MDC activists.

In an effort to subvert the run-off electoral process and instill fear in election officials and observers, police arrested more than 100 presiding officers and election officials on politically motivated charges of electoral fraud. Police also arrested hundreds of MDC supporters and officials on spurious charges of inciting violence, while ZANU-PF supporters, who were responsible for the majority of the violence, were allowed to carry out abuses with almost absolute impunity.

Impunity and the Rule of Law

Zimbabwe's long history of impunity for politically motivated crimes has worsened the political crisis. Those who committed past abuses have remained free to carry out further violence and other crimes. Since 2000 the government has led an onslaught on the judiciary that has included physical and verbal attacks against judges and bribes intended to compromise the impartiality and undermine the work of the judiciary.

Law enforcement agencies have subverted the rule of law. The police are responsible for widespread violations, including harassment, threats, and violence against opposition supporters and human rights activists, as well as torture and other mistreatment. Police have routinely refused to take action against ZANU-PF supporters and militia implicated in political violence.

Public confidence in the judiciary and police—especially regarding independence and impartiality—is eroded. There have been no investigations into the role of senior government, military, and ruling party officials implicated in mobilizing and inciting militia forces responsible for election-related violence.

ZIMBABWE

"Bullets for Each of You"

State-Sponsored Violence since Zimbabwe's March 29 Elections

HUMAN
RIGHTS
WATCH

Human Rights Defenders

The violence in the aftermath of the general elections created an even more challenging environment for human rights defenders. Many NGOs are perceived by the government of Zimbabwe as being aligned to the MDC. In the capital Harare, the government clampdown forced several NGOs to shut down. In the months after March elections, police raided the offices of NGOs such as the Crisis in Zimbabwe Coalition and the Zimbabwe Election Support Network (ZESN). ZANU-PF supporters attacked hundreds of ZESN election observers, forcing many to flee their homes. Human rights defenders were intimidated and threatened by police and security agents, who in May and June arrested a number of activists, including a prominent human rights lawyer and 13 members of the NGO Women of Zimbabwe Arise.

Humanitarian Crisis

Zimabwe's humanitarian crisis shows no signs of ending, with more than 1.3 million Zimbabweans living with HIV, and millions of people facing ever more severe food shortages. According to the United Nations, nearly half the population will need food aid in 2009 and the contamination of water sources has resulted in cholera outbreaks. In June 2008 the government exacerbated the humanitarian situation by banning the operations of all local and international humanitarian agencies throughout the country. Despite lifting the ban in September, the government has tightened control over agency operations. To operate in a specific area, NGOs must obtain permission and a memorandum of understanding from the relevant government ministry. Restrictive government controls have left the delivery of humanitarian assistance open to manipulation by government agents and ZANU-PF officials. In the past, the government has used food aid as a political weapon against opposition supporters. The new government will face the challenge of addressing the humanitarian crisis in the context of an extraordinarily weakened economy, in which inflation has soared to over 200 million percent.

Key International Actors

Previous inaction to address Zimbabwe's political crisis by regional bodies such as the Southern African Development Community (SADC) and the African Union

ZIMBABWE

"Our Hands Are Tied"

Erosion of the Rule of Law in Zimbabwe

H U M A N
R I G H T S
W A T C H

(AU) emboldened the government of Zimbabwe to turn the institutions of state even more aggressively against Zimbabweans seeking democratic change. Instead, African leaders put their faith in the mediation of Thabo Mbeki, initiated on behalf of SADC in 2007 following a widely reported incident of police brutality against Morgan Tsvangirai and other MDC officials. While this led to some improvements in the electoral process leading up to the March elections, it failed to address the root causes of Zimbabwe's political crisis—the government's systematic violation of international human rights standards.

The serious violence after the March elections finally compelled several African leaders to publicly condemn abuses, although other countries, including South Africa, initially refused to acknowledge the serious nature of the situation. Differing positions within SADC prevented it from taking concerted and decisive action. At an emergency SADC summit on April 12, leaders expressed concern about the delay in the release of the presidential results, but did little to address spiraling violence and other abuses.

As the violence intensified before the June presidential run-off, SADC and AU election observers declared that it would not be free and fair. Once again African leaders failed to take a robust approach. In June at the AU heads of state summit in Sharm-el-Sheikh, Egypt, leaders not only ignored ZANU-PF's responsibility for the widespread violence, but failed to recognize the illegitimacy of Mugabe's presidency. The summit participants issued a weak resolution calling for negotiations between the two political parties, but not mentioning the violence. To their credit, several African leaders spoke publicly in condemnation of the run-off and Mugabe's brutal actions. The leaders of Botswana and Nigeria made it clear that they did not recognize Mugabe as Zimbabwe's president.

In September Mbeki's mediation led to the MDC and ZANU-PF signing a power-sharing agreement meant to bring an end to the political crisis. However, both parties remain deadlocked over the division of ministerial positions, and there have been few efforts to address abuses or accountability. The role of SADC and the AU remains crucial in ensuring a peaceful return to the rule of law and respect for human rights, but the ongoing situation is a blot on the credibility of their commitment to an effective regional solution.

The European Union, United States, and United Kingdom have each consistently condemned the government's abusive record, and maintained travel sanctions and asset freezes against senior government and ZANU-PF officials. Despite the power-sharing agreement, EU officials have indicated that sanctions and asset freezes will remain until there is a return to democracy and marked improvement in human rights conditions. International aid to reconstruct the country is also likely to remain on hold until human rights conditions improve and democracy is restored.

The ability of the UN Security Council to address the crisis was largely nullified by China, Russia, and South Africa refusing to determine that the situation was a threat to international peace and security. Nonetheless, UN Secretary-General Ban Ki-moon on numerous occasions expressed concern and appointed UN Assistant Secretary-General for Political Affairs Haile Menkerios as a special envoy for Zimbabwe.

Mexico's National Human Rights Commission

A critical assessment

HUMAN
RIGHTS
WATCH

WORLD REPORT

2009

AMERICAS

ARGENTINA

Argentina has taken important steps to bring to justice former military and police personnel accused of having committed grave human rights violations during the country's "dirty war." Since the Supreme Court struck down the "Full Stop" and "Due Obedience" laws in 2005, several police and military officials have been convicted.

Continuing human rights problems in Argentina include a juvenile justice system that provides judges broad discretion to detain children, deplorable prison conditions, and arbitrary restrictions on women's reproductive rights.

Confronting Past Abuses

Since 2003 Argentina has made significant progress in prosecuting military and police personnel responsible for "disappearances," killings, and torture during its last military dictatorship (1976-1983). The executive branch actively encouraged these prosecutions, reinforcing what began as a legal challenge to impunity in the courts. At this writing, there are more than 400 people facing charges for these crimes, the vast majority of whom are in pretrial detention.

Several important cases were reopened in 2003 after Congress annulled the 1986 "Full Stop" law, which forced a halt to the prosecution of all such cases, and the 1987 "Due Obedience" law, which granted automatic immunity in such cases to all members of the military, except those in positions of command. In June 2005 the Supreme Court declared the laws unconstitutional.

According to the Center for Legal and Social Studies, 28 people have been convicted for abuses committed during the dictatorship. For example, in June 2008 two retired federal police officers were sentenced to life imprisonment without parole for kidnapping and killing 30 detainees in the 1976 "Fatima massacre." In July 2008 a civilian intelligence agent and seven military officials, including retired General Luciano Benjamin Menendez, were convicted for kidnapping, torturing, and executing four members of the Workers' Revolutionary Party in 1977: Menendez and three others were sentenced to life imprisonment, while the rest were sentenced to 18 or 22 years in prison. In September 2008 Menendez was also sentenced, together with Antonio Domingo Bussi, to life without parole for kidnapping, torturing, and "disappearing" a legislator in 1976.

Since 2005 several federal judges have struck down pardons decreed by then-president Carlos Menem in 1989 and 1990 of former officials convicted or facing trial for human rights violations. In April 2008, for instance, a federal appeals court upheld the unconstitutionality of pardons in favor of Jorge Rafael Videla, former de facto president, Albano Eduardo Harguindeguy, former de facto interior minister, and José Alfredo Martinez de Hoz, former de facto economy minister, in a case regarding the "disappearance" of two businessmen.

The security of witnesses in human rights trials has become a serious concern since the "disappearance" in September 2006 of a torture victim who had testified in one of the cases that concluded that year. Jorge Julio López, age 77, who vanished from his home in La Plata the day before he was due to attend one of the final days of the trial, remains missing.

Criminal Justice System

Children in conflict with the law who are under age 16 are subject to a procedure that provides judges broad discretion to authorize their detention. In cases in which they are accused of having committed a crime, as well as when they are subjected to a custodial or protective measure because of their "personal or social situation," judges routinely order children to be institutionalized. The process through which "custodial sentences" are handed down lacks basic due process safeguards. At this writing, a case challenging the constitutionality of the juvenile justice system is pending before the Supreme Court.

In August 2008 Congress annulled the Code of Military Justice and created a new disciplinary process for military officials. The Congress established that crimes committed by military officials would be tried by federal civilian courts.

In detention facilities, overcrowding, abuses by guards, and inmate violence continue to be serious problems. In a landmark ruling in May 2005, the Supreme Court declared that all prisons in the country must abide by the United Nations Standard Minimum Rules for the Treatment of Prisoners. Although there have been slight improvements in the province of Buenos Aires, the situation remains critical. For instance, during 2006-07 there was a small reduction in the number of detainees held in police lockups, which for years have absorbed the overflow from the prison system. Yet, according to research by the Center for Legal and Social Studies, the number of detainees held in police installations in July 2008 exceeded the number in 2007. The high proportion of criminal suspects sent to prison to await trial, one of the causes of overcrowding, also increased in 2008, reaching nearly 77 percent of the prison population.

Freedom of Expression and Information

Defamation of public officials remains punishable by criminal penalties. At this writing, several bills to decriminalize defamation remain pending before Congress.

In June 2008 the Supreme Court ruled that public officials should be held to a high level of scrutiny, and overturned a civil judgment against a newspaper that had criticized the Judiciary's Forensic Medical Corps, an agency that carries out medical forensic testing. The court held that an opinion regarding issues of general interest, in particular related to the government, may not in and of itself lead to civil or criminal responsibility. According to the court, public officials' reputation can only be adversely affected by knowingly disseminating false information.

Some provincial governments discriminate in the distribution of official advertising by rewarding local media that provide favorable coverage and punishing those with a critical editorial line. In September 2007 the Supreme Court ruled against the provincial government of Neuquen, stating it had failed to justify why it had abruptly limited official advertising in a local newspaper that had covered a bribery scandal indirectly implicating the governor. According to the court, although there is no right to receive official advertising, a government that grants it may not apply discriminatory criteria in granting or withdrawing it. Several bills to regulate the matter have been presented since then but remain pending. In February 2008 the governor of Tierra del Fuego issued a decree establishing objective criteria to grant official advertising.

An executive decree allows Argentine citizens to obtain information held by the federal executive branch. However, bills giving Argentine citizens the right to information held by all federal offices have been pending before Congress for years. (Some provinces have access to information laws that allow individuals to obtain information from provincial governments.)

Reproductive Rights

Women and girls in Argentina face arbitrary and discriminatory restrictions on their reproductive decisions and access to contraceptives, especially emergency contraceptive pills. Therapeutic abortions and abortions for mentally disabled rape victims are legal, but women continue to face obstacles even when their right to an abortion is protected by law. For example, in October 2008 a judge ordered doctors in Bahia Blanca to delay the abortion requested by the legal representative of an 18-year-old mentally disabled woman who was raped by a family member, allegedly after a couple expressed interest in adopting her child after birth. The woman ended up having an abortion after a second judicial decision reversed the judge's initial one.

Key International Actors

In proceedings before the Inter-American Commission on Human Rights in 2005, the Argentine government formally accepted partial responsibility for failing to prevent the 1994 bombing of the Jewish Argentine Mutual Association, and for subsequently failing to properly investigate the crime, in which 85 people died. In October 2006 an Argentine special prosecutor accused Iran of planning the attack, and Hezbollah of carrying it out. The following month, a federal judge issued an international warrant for the arrest of former Iranian president Ali Akbar Hashemi-Rafsanjani and eight other Iranian former officials. In November 2007 the Interpol General Assembly voted to issue six arrest notices, and in September 2008 President Cristina Fernández de Kirchner reiterated before the UN General Assembly the Argentine government's request that Iran collaborate with the Argentine justice system.

In May 2008 the Inter-American Court of Human Rights ordered the Argentine government to modify its criminal defamation laws. The court ruled Argentina had violated Eduardo Kimel's right to free expression when a court sentenced him in 1995 to one year in prison (the sentence was suspended) and ordered him to pay

20,000 pesos (US$20,000 at that time) in damages for defamation. (Kimel had criticized the work of a judge investigating a massacre committed during the last military government.)

In September 2008 the Argentine government recognized that denying a woman's right to legal abortion violates women's human rights after a notorious 2006 case—in which a mentally disabled woman who had been raped and impregnated by her uncle had to request a private doctor to perform an abortion despite having obtained a judicial authorization to carry it out—reached the United Nations Human Rights Committee.

BOLIVIA

Bolivia's deep political, ethnic, and regional divisions and the fragility of its democratic institutions contribute to a precarious human rights situation. Almost two-thirds of the population lives below the national poverty line, and over a third—mostly indigenous peoples—lives in extreme poverty.

Since his landslide electoral victory in December 2005, President Evo Morales has sought to introduce a new constitution and other far-reaching reforms. The reform process has contributed to dramatic political polarization within the country, which has led to numerous episodes of political violence. The government's supporters and its opponents, as well as the police and military, have been accused of killings during violent clashes between rival demonstrators. Investigations into these unlawful killings are often politicized and generally fail to establish criminal responsibility. Despite judicial rulings that civilian courts should have jurisdiction, military courts usually investigate alleged abuses by army troops, further contributing to impunity.

Although Bolivia enjoys diverse media and a vibrant public debate, political polarization has brought violent attacks on journalists and media outlets by both pro-government and opposition demonstrators.

Political Violence, Accountability, and Impunity

Since 2006 there have been deep disagreements over procedures to approve a new draft constitution, and over demands for autonomy by five lowland departments. In August 2008, 67 percent of Bolivians voted in a recall referendum that Morales should remain as president, while prefects were ratified in four of the five opposition-dominated departments (there was no vote in the fifth as the prefect had assumed office recently). The tense standoff between Morales's largely indigenous supporters and the departmental prefects and their supporters in the breakaway departments led to violent clashes in 2007 and 2008 in the cities of Santa Cruz, Sucre, Tarija, and Cobija, with deaths and injuries on both sides.

Responsible officials, such as departmental prefects, failed to take firm action to curb the violence committed by their supporters in 2008. In an incident in Sucre

155

in May, students and townspeople who had surrounded the city stadium to prevent Morales from addressing his supporters threw stones, firecrackers, and dynamite to force back police and troops who were trying to secure the area. The soldiers fled in disarray, many on foot, after using up their supplies of tear gas. The protesters captured about 18 of Morales's peasant supporters, reportedly punching, kicking, and racially insulting them, and then marched them to the city square where, according to accounts, they made them strip to the waist, kneel, and burn their red (pro-Morales) ponchos.

The most serious outbreak of political violence involved a massacre of pro-Morales protesters by regional government supporters in September 2008 at the town of Porvenir, Pando department. Hundreds of indigenous peasants travelling in trucks for a demonstration in Cobija, Pando's capital, met roadblocks near Porvenir, and in violent clashes a departmental government employee and a supporter were killed. Continuing into Porvenir, the demonstrators took hostages, some of whom they beat, but they released them to police. Armed supporters of the departmental government then reportedly opened fire indiscriminately on the demonstrators, most of whom fled the town. Sixteen demonstrators were killed in Porvenir and during the ensuing chase. Some of the dozens of wounded were allegedly beaten while being taken in ambulances to hospital.

Due to the police and armed forces' failure to stop the violence, the government declared a state of siege to restore order in the department. Later, the prefect of Pando, Leopoldo Fernández, was arrested on government orders under emergency powers. As of October 2008 he was in detention facing charges of terrorism, murder, and criminal association for his alleged responsibility for the Pando killings. A multiparty congressional committee was investigating the incidents in parallel with prosecutors from the Attorney General's Office.

As of October 2008, nine shooting deaths had been attributed to the army or police in the context of crowd control since 2004. To our knowledge, no member of the armed forces has yet been convicted of an unlawful killing during law enforcement operations. Prosecutorial investigations into shootings by the army are obstructed by military courts, which insist on investigating these cases despite rulings of the Constitutional Court in favor of civilian jurisdiction. The military typically refuse to cooperate with investigations conducted by civilian prosecutors. By contrast, on more than one occasion government ministers, prefects, or top police officials have been charged with serious crimes like genocide or terrorism without prosecutors having previously identified and charged those materially responsible for shootings. In November 2007, for example, two civilians died from gunshot wounds, and a third civilian died after being hit by a tear gas shell, after students and townspeople armed with stones and firebombs confronted police and army troops in Sucre. Ballistic findings suggested that the shots were fired from guns similar to those in police use. As of October 2008 prosecutors had not identified or charged any police for the shootings, even though the attorney general had initiated impeachment proceedings for genocide against the minister of the interior and three senior police officials.

Bolivian courts still seek to establish criminal responsibility for the killing of more than 60 people in anti-government protests in September and October 2003, when the army used lethal force to quell violent protests in the highland city of El Alto. Former President Gonzalo Sánchez de Lozada resigned and left the country following the events, known in Bolivia as "Black October." In October 2007 the attorney general accused Sánchez de Lozada, 11 of his ministers, and five former military chiefs of genocide and torture in connection with the army's actions. The former president, his defense minister Carlos Sánchez Berzaín, and the former energy minister Jorge Berinduague currently reside in the United States, where Sánchez Berzaín has obtained political asylum. In November 2008 Bolivia formally requested that the US extradite the three men to face trial in Bolivia. Sánchez de Lozada and Sánchez Berzaín also face a civil lawsuit in the US for damages under the Alien Tort Claims Act and the Torture Victim Protection Act, alleging their responsibility for 10 of the Black October deaths.

Freedom of Expression

Bolivia enjoys a vibrant public debate with a variety of critical and pro-government media outlets. As political polarization has deepened, many among the media have openly taken sides. Morales often lambasts the private media for backing the opposition agenda. Government supporters sometimes physically attack journalists working for critical outlets. There have also been attacks by opposition demonstrators against state and community radio outlets and reporters working for them.

The inclusion of a norm in the draft constitution requiring that information and opinions disseminated by the media "respect the principles of truthfulness and responsibility" could lead to arbitrary restrictions of press freedom if enacted in law.

Human Rights Defenders

Supporters of regional autonomy in Santa Cruz have firebombed and ransacked offices of nongovernmental organizations defending land rights of indigenous and peasant communities. In September 2008 pro-autonomy demonstrators allegedly belonging to the Santa Cruz Youth Union broke into the office of the Center for Legal Studies and Social Research (CEJIS). The attackers smashed and set fire to furniture and documents.

Key International Actors

A United States Agency for International Development (USAID)-funded justice center in the Chapare region played a key role in investigating rights abuses during protests against US-backed eradication of coca plantations. The justice center carried out autopsies and collected valuable testimony about the circumstances of deaths in clashes between coca growers and antinarcotics police. The number of police abuses has declined significantly since the Morales government adopted a voluntary eradication policy in 2006. While there were 35 deaths from 1997 to 2003, since 2006 there have been only two, according to the Andean Information Network, an NGO which monitors US antinarcotics policy in Bolivia. In June 2008, amid mounting Bolivian criticism of USAID's activities in Bolivia, municipal authorities and coca growers' unions announced that USAID's programs in the Chapare would not be renewed. However, the justice center was still operating in October 2008, providing legal services to communities with very limited access to justice.

The Union of South American Nations (UNASUR), which was established in May 2008, helped to promote accountability following the violence in Pando. At a meeting convened by Chilean President Bachelet to discuss the Bolivian crisis, UNASUR heads of state decided to form a multinational commission to investigate the killings and" disappearances." The commission began its investigation in Pando department in late September. In a newspaper interview published in November 2008, prior to the release of the commission's findings, its president, Rodolfo Mattarollo, described the killings as a "planned massacre."

In 2008 the United Nations High Commissioner for Human Rights established an office in Bolivia to strengthen human rights protection. Its mandate includes assisting the Attorney General's Office to improve the criminal prosecution system.

Brazil

Faced with a public security crisis involving high levels of violent crime, some Brazilian police forces engage in abusive practices instead of pursuing sound policing policies. Detention conditions in the country are inhumane. Torture remains a serious problem. Forced labor persists in some states despite federal efforts to eradicate it. Indigenous peoples and landless peasants face threats and violence in rural conflicts over land distribution.

Police Violence

Brazil's metropolitan areas are plagued by widespread violence perpetrated by criminal gangs and abusive police. Violence especially impacts low-income communities. Nearly 50,000 homicides occur each year in Brazil.

In Rio de Janeiro, hundreds of low-income communities are occupied and controlled by gangs, which routinely engage in illegal drug trafficking, acts of extortion, and violent crime.

Police violence, including extrajudicial executions, is a chronic problem. For example, in the state of Rio de Janeiro, police were responsible for approximately one out of every five intentional killings in the first six months of 2008, according to official statistics. Police allege that such killings occur in confrontations with criminals, and register them as "acts of resistance"—757 police killings were registered as such in Rio de Janeiro state (an average of four per day) in the period January-June 2008. There are also reports of indiscriminate shootings by the Rio de Janeiro police, particularly during so-called mega-operations in low-income neighborhoods. In August 2008, United Nations Special Rapporteur on Extrajudicial, Summary, or Arbitrary Executions Philip Alston called the mega-operations in Rio de Janeiro "murderous and self-defeating."

Abuses by off-duty police also occur. For example, of all homicides in the state of Pernambuco, prosecutors estimated 70 percent are committed by death squads, which are believed to include police officers among their members. Militias controlling several dozen of metropolitan Rio de Janeiro's low-income communities include off-duty police officers among their members. In one such community,

Favela Batan, a resident and three employees of the newspaper *O Dia* conducting an undercover investigation into militia activities were reportedly kidnapped and tortured by militia members in May 2008. The captives endured beatings, suffocation, electric shocks, Russian roulette, threats of sexual assault, and death threats. Following a media outcry, at least two militia members have been arrested—including their alleged leader Odnei Fernando da Silva, a Civil Police inspector—and are awaiting trial.

Detention Conditions, Torture, and Ill-Treatment

Torture remains a serious problem in Brazil. The official report of the 10-month multiparty National Parliamentary Commission of Inquiry on the Penitentiary System, finalized in July 2008 and based on evidence collected from all 26 states plus Brasília, concluded that the national detention system is plagued by "physical and psychological torture." In one case from Goiás, the commission received evidence that the National Security Force subjected female detainees to kicks and electric shocks, stepped on the abdomen of a pregnant woman, and forced another woman to strip naked. The commission further noted that it received reports of torture at every single center it inspected. In six states—Rondônia, Piauí, Mato Grosso, Ceará, Maranhão, and Goiás—"as well as in many others," the commission documented the presence of "torture scars" on prisoners. The report also found beatings to be "routine in Brazilian jails." There are also abuses in juvenile centers. In Rio de Janeiro in January 2008, 17-year-old Andreu Luís da Silva de Carvalho was reportedly tortured to death by guards of the juvenile detention system, the General Department of Socio-Educational Actions.

The inhumane conditions, violence, and overcrowding that have historically characterized Brazilian detention centers remain one of the country's main human rights problems. Delays in the justice system contribute to overcrowding. According to official statistics, the inmate population has grown to 440,000 (a growth of over 40 percent in five years), approximately 43 percent of whom are pretrial detainees. There is credible evidence that some judges and prosecutors are deficient in fulfilling their inspection mandates.

In January 2008, 119 female prisoners were reportedly being held in a partially roofless jail cell built for 12 in Monte Mor jail in Sao Paulo, with less than one square meter per person. Reportedly, four of the women were pregnant, and one remained in the jail post-partum with her newborn for two days. Dozens of the women were transferred after the media broke the story. There have been reports of women and girls being incarcerated with men in violation of international standards. For example, in November 2007 in the state of Pará, an adolescent girl was repeatedly raped at a police station in Abaetetuba while locked in a cell with roughly 20 men for at least 15 days.

In the state of Rondônia, despite six provisional measures issued by the Inter-American Court of Human Rights mandating that Brazil protect inmates at Urso Branco prison, more than 100 inmates have been murdered there since the first such measures were issued by the Court in 2002. In October 2008 the attorney general moved to have Urso Branco subjected to a federal takeover due to the chronic problems there.

Forced Labor

Since 1995 the federal government has taken steps to eradicate forced labor, including creating mobile investigation units to monitor labor conditions in rural areas. However, the Pastoral Land Commission collected reports of 8,653 persons in conditions of forced labor in 2007. Of these, 5,974 were reported as having been freed. The federal government has made positive strides in its efforts to combat forced labor, but criminal accountability for offending employers remains relatively rare.

Rural Violence and Land Conflicts

Indigenous peoples and landless peasants face threats and violence as a result of land disputes in rural areas. According to the Pastoral Land Commission, 28 people were killed and 428 arrested in rural conflicts throughout the country in 2007. In March 2008, Welinton da Silva, a leader of the Landless Rural Workers' Movement, was reportedly shot at and wounded in the leg while protesting at a quarry in the state of Maranhão.

Impunity

Ensuring accountability for human rights violations remains a major challenge. In a widely followed case, Vitalmiro Bastos de Moura (Bida), the farmer alleged to have ordered the 2005 killing of Dorothy Stang, a missionary who advocated for agrarian reform, was acquitted in May 2008. The decision was questioned by two Supreme Federal Court justices and others in the federal government, including President Luiz Inácio Lula da Silva. In another case, in January 2008, the criminal investigation into the 1998 killing of Paraná land reform activist Sétimo Garibaldi was formally shelved, without anyone having been found responsible.

Brazil has never prosecuted those responsible for atrocities committed during its period of military dictatorship (1964-1985). The 1979 amnesty law has thus far been interpreted to bar prosecutions of state agents. However, at this writing, the Supreme Federal Court is considering a challenge to this interpretation of the amnesty law presented by the Brazilian Bar Association, which maintains that the amnesty does not cover crimes such as torture committed by government agents. In addition, federal prosecutors have made formal requests that criminal investigations against some individuals suspected of dictatorship-era abuses be commenced in Rio Grande do Sul, Rio de Janeiro, and Sao Paulo. In a landmark ruling in October 2008, a civil court in Sao Paulo found Col. Carlos Alberto Brilhante Ustra civilly responsible for acts of kidnapping and torture during his time as director of a dictatorship intelligence agency in Sao Paulo in the 1970s.

Human Rights Defenders

Some human rights defenders, particularly those working on issues of police violence and land conflicts, suffer intimidation and violence. Human rights lawyer João Tancredo survived an attempt on his life by two unidentified gunmen in Rio de Janeiro in January 2008. State legislator Marcelo Freixo has received death threats for his work as president of the Rio de Janeiro Legislative Assembly's Parliamentary Commission of Inquiry into militias. Joinville Frota, a trade unionist in Amapá, reported receiving death threats in May 2008 in connection with strike activities.

Reproductive Rights

In Brazil, abortion is legal only when performed by a medical doctor in order to save the life of the pregnant woman or when the pregnancy is the result of rape. Criminal investigations into women's health clinics in Mato Grosso do Sul, Sao Paulo, and Rio Grande do Sul have raised serious privacy concerns. In an ongoing 2007 criminal case from Mato Grosso do Sul, for months private medical records of thousands of women were reportedly made accessible to members of the public upon request to judicial authorities.

Key International Actors

The Inter-American Court of Human Rights ruled in May 2008 that Brazil had not fully complied with the 2006 judgment in the Damião Ximenes Lopes case. Though reparations were paid to the Ximenes family, no one has been convicted for the 1998 torture and killing of Damião, a psychiatric patient in Ceará. The court further ordered the government to undertake reform measures aimed at preventing future cases like this one.

In December 2007 an Italian court requested the extradition of 11 Brazilians in connection with the enforced disappearance of Italians carried out as part of the dictatorship-era Operation Condor. In response, the Lula government has stated that the constitution bars the extradition of native-born Brazilians.

In a positive development, in August 2008 Brazil ratified the United Nations Convention on the Rights of Persons with Disabilities. During its Universal Periodic Review before the UN Human Rights Council in April 2008, Brazil pledged to implement recommendations made by the UN Committee Against Torture and the UN Human Rights Committee.

CHILE

Since the death of former dictator Gen. Augusto Pinochet in December 2006, Chilean judges have continued to prosecute and convict former military personnel accused of committing grave human rights violations under the military government. However, the Supreme Court's criminal chamber has reduced sentences in several recent cases, with the result that convicted perpetrators eventually do not serve time in prison.

Overcrowding and ill-treatment in Chile's prisons remain serious problems. Police abuses continue to be reported in the Araucanía region, where indigenous Mapuche communities engage in sometimes violent protests in defense of land claims.

Prosecutions for Past Human Rights Violations

In the pursuit of accountability for human rights abuses under military rule, as of July 2008, 482 former military personnel and civilian collaborators were facing charges for enforced disappearances, extrajudicial executions, and torture; 256 had been convicted (of whom 83 had had their conviction confirmed on appeal), and 38 were serving prison sentences.

At the time of his death from a heart attack in December 2006, Pinochet was under house arrest, facing prosecution for torture, enforced disappearances, tax evasion, and forgery. The Supreme Court had closed three previous cases against him on medical grounds, but judges came to doubt that his mild dementia disqualified him from trial. In June 2008 Pinochet's former secret police chief, Manuel Contreras, was sentenced to life imprisonment for the car bomb murder of Gen. Carlos Prats and his wife Sofía Cuthbert in Buenos Aires in 1974. Pinochet, who had succeeded Prats as army commander just before the 1973 coup, escaped prosecution for the crime.

A majority of the five judges in the Supreme Court's criminal chamber now rule that an amnesty decreed by the military government in 1978 is inapplicable to war crimes or crimes against humanity, and that these crimes are not subject to a statute of limitations. However, not all of the judges agree that the amnesty is inapplicable. Given that court rulings in Chile are not binding in cases other than the one under review, and that the composition of the Supreme Court panel may change from case to case, the legal obstacles to convictions have not been entirely overcome. A bill promoted by the government to amend the criminal code so that crimes against humanity are not subject to amnesties or statutes of limitation remained deadlocked in Congress in 2008.

During 2007 and increasingly in 2008, the court has applied a law allowing those convicted for human rights violations to benefit from a sentence reduction in recognition of the time elapsed since the criminal act (more than 30 years in some cases). This has meant that several former military personnel sentenced to prison by lower courts have been exempted from serving time.

Prison Conditions

Chile has more prisoners per capita than any other country in South America. The prison population has grown by 28 percent since 2003. Despite the opening of six new privately contracted prisons, overcrowding remains a serious problem. For example, in 2008 the Southern Santiago Center for Preventive Detention, with a planned capacity of 3,170 places, had 6,256 inmates. In many of these older prisons sanitation and hygiene are abysmal. Inmates are sometimes crowded into dark and unventilated punishment cells without sanitary provision for up to 10 days. In August 2008 a Supreme Court official told a Senate committee that she considered this practice to be cruel and degrading.

Military Justice

Even though Chile has completely overhauled its criminal justice procedure in recent years and reinforced due process guarantees, military courts still have wide jurisdiction over civilians and also over human rights abuses committed by the *Carabineros* (uniformed police), which is part of the armed forces. At this writing, a civil-military commission is in the process of developing a new code of military justice, and has identified as a guiding principle that no civilians should be tried by military courts.

Police Abuses

Carabineros often use excessive force during operations in indigenous Mapuche communities in southern Chile. The abuses typically occur when police intervene to control Mapuche protests and prevent land occupations, or when they enter communities in pursuit of Mapuches suspected of crimes (such as theft, damage to property, and arson) allegedly committed during ongoing land disputes with farmers and logging companies.

Mapuche agronomy student Matías Catrileo, age 22, was killed on January 3, 2008, when a police officer opened fire with a submachine gun on protesters during a land occupation near the city of Temuco. The officer was reported to have said on his radio just before the shooting that the protesters were throwing stones. According to a report by the criminal investigations police, the bullet fired by the officer struck Catrileo in the back. A military prosecutor charged the police officer with "unnecessary violence resulting in death." The case remained open at this writing.

In June 2008, Citizen's Watch, a Temuco-based human rights NGO, reported the case of two Mapuche teenagers, Jorge Mariman (18) and Luis Marileo (16), who were mistreated by police when they raided the home of José Cariqueo, leader of a Mapuche community near Ercilla, while searching for a missing horse. According to Citizen's Watch, which interviewed Cariqueo, Jorge Marimán's leg was broken by a police bullet, and Luis Marileo's jaw was fractured by a blow from a riot control shotgun butt. The police, who did not show a search warrant, reportedly left the two injured without providing assistance. Citizen's Watch, which reported the case to the minister of the interior, received no substantive reply to its concern.

Reproductive Rights

Chile is one of a handful of countries in the world that prohibits abortion for any reason, even in cases of rape or incest or to save the life of the mother. Despite the comprehensive ban, an estimated 60,000 to 200,000 clandestine abortions are practiced each year. In April 2008 the Constitutional Court ruled against a legal provision that allows free distribution of emergency contraception, including the "morning after pill." The World Health Organization recognizes that emergency contraceptive pills can prevent pregnancy and does not consider them to induce abortion. However, Chile's court ruled that such methods violate the constitutional protection of the right to life of the unborn. It thus ignored the rights of living women—particularly the poor and adolescents—to health, information, autonomy, non-discrimination, freedom of conscience, and freedom to enjoy the benefits of scientific progress.

Freedom of Expression and Information

Chile has removed many of the legal norms inherited from the military dictatorship that constricted the press. In August 2008 President Michelle Bachelet enacted a law that creates an independent Council for Transparency. The four-person council will be empowered to order officials to make information available to the public, as well as to impose sanctions if they fail to do so. The law is due to enter into force in April 2009.

Key International Actors

Several rulings against Chile by the Inter-American Court of Human Rights since the return to democracy in 1990 have given impetus to reforms to strengthen the right to justice, free expression, and fair trial. However, many of the reforms demanded by the court are still outstanding.

In July 2008 the Inter-American Commission on Human Rights declared admissible a complaint against Chile filed by Karen Atala, a judge whose appeal for custody of her three children was denied by the Supreme Court on the grounds that her lesbian relationship would harm their upbringing. The commission held that the decision could violate Atala's right to equal treatment, to privacy, and to due process, as well as the rights of her children. As of October 2008 the commission had yet to rule on the merits of the case.

In August 2008 the Organization of American States rapporteur on the rights of persons deprived of their liberty, Florentín Meléndez, visited prisons in Chile. While the rapporteur praised conditions in privately contracted prisons, he expressed concern about "excessive and unnecessary force in punishment," and a "systematic practice of physical mistreatment" by guards in all the prisons he visited. He also described as "especially alarming" the deficiency of education and healthcare provision, as well as of recreational and sports programs, in the two juvenile prisons he visited.

Colombia

Colombia's internal armed conflict continues to result in widespread abuses by irregular armed groups and government forces. The Colombian government dealt serious blows to the Revolutionary Armed Forces of Colombia (FARC) guerrillas in 2008. But guerrillas continued to engage in kidnappings, use of antipersonnel landmines, recruitment of child combatants, and other abuses. Successor groups to paramilitaries, which never fully demobilized, appeared increasingly active, threatening and killing civilians, including trade unionists and human rights defenders. Reports of extrajudicial executions of civilians by the military remain frequent. Internal displacement of civilians has been steadily rising in recent years— in 2008 the number of people affected may have reached its highest level in decades.

Colombia's justice institutions have in recent years begun to make some progress in uncovering the truth about paramilitary abuses and accomplices. But in 2008 the administration of President Álvaro Uribe repeatedly took steps that could hamper the investigations.

Progress and Threats to Accountability for Paramilitaries' Accomplices

Colombia's paramilitaries are responsible for crimes against humanity and thousands of other atrocities. They have also amassed enormous wealth and influence, in part through mafia-style alliances with members of the military, politicians, and businesspeople.

Colombia's institutions of justice have recently started to uncover some of the truth about paramilitaries' abuses and accomplices. The Supreme Court has made unprecedented progress in investigating accusations against members of the Colombian Congress for collaborating with the paramilitaries. More than 60 members—nearly all from President Uribe's coalition—have come under investigation. And, in confessions to prosecutors from the Attorney General's Office pursuant to the "Justice and Peace Law," which offers them reduced sentences subject to full and truthful confessions and other conditions, paramilitary commanders have started to disclose details of some of their atrocities and to name accomplices.

However, the Uribe administration has repeatedly taken actions that could sabotage the investigations. Administration officials have issued public personal attacks on the Supreme Court and its members, in some cases making accusations that have turned out to be baseless, in what increasingly looks like a campaign to discredit the court. In mid-2008 the administration proposed a series of constitutional amendments that would have removed what are known as the "parapolitics" investigations from the Supreme Court's jurisdiction, but it withdrew the proposal in November. The administration also blocked what is known as the "empty chair" bill, which would have reformed the Congress to sanction parties that had backed politicians linked to paramilitaries.

Extraditions of Paramilitary Leaders

In May 2008 Colombia extradited most of the paramilitary leadership to the United States. The extraditions are positive in that they may help to break the groups' chains of command, and increase the likelihood that these commanders will serve lengthy prison terms for their drug crimes.

Yet the extraditions may prove fatal to obtaining justice for paramilitaries' human rights crimes. The extraditions happened at a time when several of the commanders were coming under pressure from Colombian prosecutors and courts to answer difficult questions about their abuses and accomplices. The sudden extraditions have interrupted the process of confessions and interrogation in Colombia and eliminated commanders' incentives to cooperate with the Colombian investigations.

In October two of the extradited individuals, known as "Cuco Vanoy" and "Gordolindo," received prison sentences of over 20 years each for their drug trafficking crimes, pursuant to plea bargains. They have ceased providing information to Colombian authorities about their human rights crimes, and it is unclear whether their plea bargains require that they cooperate in that regard.

New Armed Groups

The Uribe administration claims that paramilitaries no longer exist. While more than 30,000 individuals supposedly demobilized, Colombian prosecutors have turned up evidence that many of them were not paramilitaries at all, but rather, civilians recruited to pose as paramilitaries. Law enforcement authorities never investigated most of them.

Meanwhile, new armed groups often led by mid-level paramilitary commanders have cropped up all over the country. The Organization of American States (OAS) Mission verifying the demobilizations has identified 22 such groups, totaling thousands of members. The groups are actively recruiting new troops, and are committing widespread abuses, including extortion, threats, killings, and forced displacement. In Medellín, for example, after a steady decline in official indicators of violence, there has been a surge in homicides, apparently committed by these groups.

Guerrilla Abuses

Both the FARC and the National Liberation Army (ELN) continue to engage in abuses against civilians.

Government forces dealt serious blows to the FARC, including through the arrest or killing of several commanders. In June security forces rescued 15 hostages held by the FARC, including three US citizens and former Colombian presidential candidate Ingrid Betancourt. No lives were lost in the operation, but it was later revealed that members of the military who participated in the operation displayed the emblem of the International Committee of the Red Cross, in violation of the Geneva Conventions, jeopardizing the ability of humanitarian workers to fulfill their role of protecting civilians. The FARC continue to regularly engage in kidnappings, and still hold hundreds of hostages.

In August government authorities accused the FARC of planting a bomb on a crowded street in the town of Ituango that resulted in the deaths of seven people and injured more than 50 others.

The FARC and ELN continue to frequently use antipersonnel landmines. The Vice-President's Observatory for Human Rights reported 153 civilian victims of antipersonnel mines from January through September 2008.

Internal Displacement

Colombia is estimated to have more than 3 million internally displaced persons, according to the Office of the UN High Commissioner for Refugees. Displacement has steadily increased in Colombia in recent years. According to the Committee on Human Rights and Displacement (CODHES), a nongovernmental organization monitoring displacement, the first half of 2008 marked the highest rate of displacement in Colombia in 23 years, with more than 270,000 people displaced in six months (a 41 percent increase compared to the first six months of 2007). Official numbers for this period are lower, but are increasing as the period the victims have to report their displacement to the government is still open.

A 2004 Constitutional Court decision found that women are particularly vulnerable in situations of internal displacement and ruled that the government's failure to protect women's vulnerability constituted a violation of their rights. In 2008 the government began to comply with the Court's ruling by establishing programs to protect internally displaced women.

Military Abuses and Impunity

In recent years there has been a substantial rise in the number of extrajudicial killings of civilians attributed to the Colombian Army. Under pressure to demonstrate results, army members apparently take civilians from their homes or workplaces, kill them, and then dress them up to claim they were combatants killed in action.

The Attorney General's Office is currently investigating cases involving more than a thousand victims dating back to mid-2003. The Defense Ministry has issued directives indicating that such killings are impermissible. But such directives have been regularly undermined by statements from high government officials, including President Uribe, who for years publicly denied the problem existed, and accused human rights defenders reporting these killings of colluding with the guerrillas in an orchestrated campaign to discredit the military.

In September 2008 a scandal broke over the disappearance of 11 young men from Soacha, a low-income neighborhood of Bogota. Their bodies were found in the distant northeastern state of Norte de Santander, and the military—initially backed by President Uribe—claimed they were combat deaths. Attorney General Mario Iguaran disputed that claim. In October the Uribe government announced it was dismissing 27 soldiers, including three generals, in connection with the killings.

Army commander Mario Montoya, who had been the subject of allegations linking him to abuses and paramilitaries, resigned in November 2008.

Violence against Trade Unionists

For years, Colombia has led the world in killings of trade unionists, with more than 2,600 reported killings since 1986, according to the National Labor School, Colombia's leading NGO monitoring labor rights. The bulk of the killings are attributed to paramilitary groups, which have deliberately targeted unionists.

Though the number of killings annually has dropped from its peak in the 1990s, when the paramilitaries were in the midst of their violent expansion, more than 400 trade unionists have been killed during the Uribe government. In 2008 the number of killings went up again, to 41 as of October, according to the National Labor School. Unionists working in the education sector comprise a high proportion of the victims.

Impunity in the killing of trade unionists is widespread: in about 97 percent of cases there has been no conviction and the killers remain free. The rate of convictions for unionist killings under the Uribe administration was consistently low until 2007, when the number of convictions jumped to 43. As of October the Attorney General's Office reported there had been 53 convictions in 2008. This sudden increase is primarily due to pressure from the US Congress.

Threats against Human Rights Defenders, Journalists, and Victims of Paramilitaries

Human rights defenders, journalists, local community leaders, and victims of paramilitary groups, as well as trade unionists, are frequently the targets of threats.

A March 6 demonstration against paramilitary violence drew public accusations against the organizers from presidential advisor José Obdulio Gaviria, and shortly before and after the march, scores of human rights defenders and trade unionists reported being threatened and attacked. Some demonstration organizers and participants were killed. In addition to national human rights groups, the threats targeted the international organization, Peace Brigades International's Colombia Project, the news magazine *Semana*, the Workers' Central Union, indigenous organizations, and opposition politicians. In most cases, the threats were issued in the name of a group calling itself the Black Eagles.

The Ministry of Interior has a protection program for journalists and trade unionists, and during 2008 it established a separate program for victims presenting claims in the context of the paramilitary demobilization process. In May the Constitutional Court demanded a thorough review of this program, which many victims' groups consider ineffective.

High-ranking government officials continued to make public statements accusing human rights groups and defenders of collaborating with guerrillas. Such statements create an environment of intimidation that makes it difficult for human rights defenders to carry out their legitimate work.

Key International Actors

The United States remains the most influential foreign actor in Colombia. In 2008 it provided approximately US$650 million to the Colombian government, somewhat less than in past years. The bulk of the assistance continues to consist of military and police aid, though in 2008 a larger share of aid was directed toward social and economic assistance. Thirty percent of US military assistance is formally subject to human rights conditions, though the US Department of State has not consistently enforced these conditions. The United States also provides financial support for the paramilitary demobilization process, subject to Colombia's compliance with related conditions in US law.

The Democratic leadership in the US Congress has pledged to delay consideration of the US-Colombia Free Trade Agreement until there is "concrete evidence of sustained results on the ground" with regard to impunity for violence against trade unionists and the role of paramilitaries.

The United Kingdom provides military assistance to Colombia, though the full amount is publicly unknown. The European Union provides social and economic assistance, and has provided some aid to the government's paramilitary demobilization programs.

The OAS Mission to Support the Peace Process in Colombia, which is charged with verifying the paramilitary demobilizations, issued reports in 2008 that continued to express concern over the activities of new, rearmed, or never demobilized groups.

The Office of the UN High Commissioner for Human Rights is active in Colombia, with a presence in Bogotá, Medellín, and Cali. Colombia was reviewed under the Universal Periodic Review mechanism of the UN Human Rights Council in December 2008.

CUBA

Cuba remains the one country in Latin American that represses nearly all forms of political dissent. The government continues to enforce political conformity using criminal prosecutions, long- and short-term detentions, mob harassment, surveillance, police warnings, and travel restrictions.

Since Fidel Castro relinquished direct control of the government to his brother, Raul Castro, in August 2006—and finally stepped down in February 2008—Cuba has at times signaled a willingness to reconsider its long-standing disregard for human rights norms. In 2008 the country signed the two fundamental international human rights treaties and commuted the death sentences of several prisoners. Yet these measures have led to no significant policy changes in Cuba. The repressive machinery built over almost five decades of Fidel Castro's rule remains intact and continues to systematically deny people their basic rights.

Legal and Institutional Failings

Cuba's legal and institutional structures are at the root of rights violations. Although in theory the different branches of government have separate areas of authority, in practice the executive retains clear control over all levers of power. The courts, which lack independence, undermine the right to fair trial by severely restricting the right to a defense.

Cuba's Criminal Code provides the legal basis for repression of dissent. Laws criminalizing enemy propaganda, the spreading of "unauthorized news," and insult to patriotic symbols are used to restrict freedom of speech under the guise of protecting state security. The government also imprisons or orders the surveillance of individuals who have committed no illegal act, relying upon provisions that penalize "dangerousness" (*estado peligroso*) and allow for "official warning" (*advertencia oficial*).

Political Imprisonment

The Cuban Commission for Human Rights and National Reconciliation (CCDHRN), a respected local human rights group, in July 2008 issued a list of 219 prisoners whom it said were incarcerated for political reasons. The list included 11 peaceful dissidents arrested so far in 2008. Of 75 political dissidents, independent journalists, and human rights advocates who were summarily tried and sentenced in 2003, 55 remained imprisoned as of September 2008. Four others were released in February 2008 on health grounds, having been forced to choose between staying in prison, where they were denied medical treatment, and being exiled to Spain.

Family members of political prisoners are frequently harassed and blacklisted from jobs.

Travel Restrictions and Family Separations

The Cuban government forbids the country's citizens from leaving or returning to Cuba without first obtaining official permission, which is often denied. Unauthorized travel can result in criminal prosecution. In May 2008 Cuban blogger Yoani Sanchez was awarded a Spanish journalism prize. The government initially issued an exit visa to Sanchez, but the day before she was scheduled to leave the visa was put on hold without explanation, and she was unable to accept the award in person. On August 15, after repeatedly being denied exit visas, eight dissidents tried to escape Cuba aboard a primitive boat. They have not been heard from since and are presumed dead at sea.

The government frequently bars citizens engaged in authorized travel from taking their children with them overseas, essentially holding the children hostage to guarantee the parents' return. Given the widespread fear of forced family separation, these travel restrictions provide the Cuban government with a powerful tool for punishing defectors and silencing critics.

The government is also clamping down on the movement of citizens within Cuba by more aggressively enforcing a 1997 law known as Decree 217. Designed to limit migration to Havana, the decree requires Cubans to obtain government permission before moving to the country's capital. According to one Cuban official, the police have forcibly removed people from Havana in approximately 20,000 instances since 2006. In a representative case, a migrant from Granma province who had been living in Havana for seven years was stopped in the street by a police officer and told to present her papers. When she could not produce them, the police immediately sent her back to Granma.

Freedom of Expression and Assembly

The government maintains a media monopoly on the island, ensuring that freedom of expression is virtually nonexistent. Although a small number of independent journalists manage to write articles for foreign websites or publish underground newsletters, the risks associated with these activities are considerable. Access to information via the internet is also highly restricted. The only internet café in Havana charges US$5 per hour—one-third of the average Cuban monthly salary; two other cafes may be used only to send emails on a closed Cuban network.

According to the Committee to Protect Journalists, 22 journalists were serving prison terms in Cuba as of October 2008, making the country second only to China for the number of journalists in prison. Independent journalist, Oscar Sánchez Madan, was arrested in April 2007 after reporting on local corruption in Matanzas. He is now serving a four-year prison sentence for "social dangerousness."

In 2008 the Cuban government significantly increased the use of arbitrary detention to harass and intimidate dissidents, and restrict freedom of assembly. In all of 2007, the CCDHRN documented 325 arbitrary detentions by security forces; in the first half of 2008 it reported 640 arbitrary detentions. The detentions are often used to prevent dissidents from participating in a scheduled meeting or event. Security officers often offer no charge to justify the detentions—a clear violation of due process rights—but warn detainees of longer arrests if they continue to participate in activities considered critical of the government. In September 2007, for example, police detained more than 40 dissidents in several cities who were traveling to a protest in Havana at the Ministry of Justice. All were released after the protest. In April 2008, wives of political prisoners, known as the Ladies in White, were arrested when they tried to stage a peaceful sit-in in Havana's Revolution Plaza.

Prison Conditions

Prisoners are generally kept in poor and abusive conditions, often in overcrowded cells. Political prisoners who denounce poor conditions or who otherwise fail to observe prison rules are frequently punished with long periods in punitive isolation cells, restrictions on visits, or denial of medical treatment.

Death Penalty

In February 2008 the government commuted the death sentences of all prisoners except three individuals charged with terrorism. The Cuban government does not make public information about how many people are on death row, but it is estimated that between 20 and 30 sentences were commuted. Nevertheless, Cuban law continues to prescribe the death penalty for a broad range of crimes.

Human Rights Defenders

Refusing to recognize human rights monitoring as a legitimate activity, the government denies legal status to local human rights groups. Individuals who belong to these groups face systematic harassment, with the government impeding their efforts to document human rights conditions. In one 2008 case, four members of the Cuban Human Rights Foundation were arrested and sentenced to four years in prison in a summary judgment that was hidden from public view, according to the Council of Human Rights Reporters. Cuba remains one of the few countries in the world to deny the International Committee of the Red Cross access to its prisons.

Key International Actors

In February 2008 the Cuban government recognized core international human rights principles by signing the International Covenant on Civil and Political Rights (ICCPR) and the International Covenant on Economic, Social and Cultural Rights (ICESCR), although as of November it had not ratified them. At the time of signing, the government indicated it was considering making several reservations to the treaties.

In response to this and economic reforms under Raul Castro, in June the European Union lifted sanctions on Cuba, which it had originally imposed after the 2003 crackdown on dissidents. The EU publicly called on Cuba to release all political prisoners and honor the rights protected in the signed treaties. In mid-2009 the EU is due to investigate what progress Cuba has made toward fulfilling ICCPR and ICESCR commitments, and will weigh whether to maintain diplomatic relations.

The US economic embargo on Cuba, in effect for more than four decades, continues to impose indiscriminate hardship on the Cuban people and to block travel to the island. In an effort to deprive the Cuban government of funding, the US government enacted new restrictions on family-related travel to Cuba in June 2004. Under these rules, individuals are allowed to visit relatives in Cuba only once every three years, and only if the relatives fit the US government's narrow definition of family—a definition that excludes aunts, uncles, cousins, and other kin who are often integral members of Cuban families. Justified as a means of promoting freedom in Cuba, these travel policies undermine the freedom of movement of hundreds of thousands of Cubans and Cuban-Americans, and inflict profound harm on Cuban families.

GUATEMALA

A dozen years after the end of Guatemala's brutal civil war, impunity remains the norm when it comes to human rights violations. Ongoing violence and intimidation threaten to reverse the little progress that has been made toward promoting accountability. Guatemala's weak and corrupt law enforcement institutions have proved incapable of containing the powerful organized crime groups that, among other things, are believed to be responsible for attacks on human rights defenders, judges, prosecutors, and others.

Impunity for Civil War Crimes

Guatemala continues to suffer the effects of an internal armed conflict that ended in 1996. A United Nations-sponsored truth commission estimated that as many as 200,000 people were killed during the 36-year war, and attributed the vast majority of the killings to government forces.

Guatemalans seeking accountability for these abuses face daunting obstacles. Prosecutors and investigators receive grossly inadequate training and resources. The courts routinely fail to resolve judicial appeals and motions in a timely manner, allowing defense attorneys to engage in dilatory legal maneuvering. The army and other state institutions resist cooperating fully with investigations into abuses committed by current or former members. And the police regularly fail to provide adequate protection to judges, prosecutors, and witnesses involved in politically sensitive cases.

Of the 626 massacres documented by the truth commission, only three cases have been successfully prosecuted in the Guatemalan courts. The third conviction came in May 2008, when five former members of a paramilitary "civil patrol" were convicted for the murders of 26 of the 177 civilians massacred in Rio Negro in 1982.

The July 2005 discovery of approximately 80 million documents of the disbanded National Police, including files on Guatemalans who were murdered and "disappeared" during the armed conflict, could play a key role in the prosecution of those who committed human rights abuses during the conflict. By October 2008 the country's Human Rights Ombudsman's Office had processed seven million of those documents, primarily related to cases presently under active investigation. The office plans to open the first part of the archive in 2009.

In February 2008 President Álvaro Colom announced that he would open the military archives spanning Guatemala's civil war. However, the minister of defense has since delayed handing over the files, arguing that the constitution protects the confidentiality of documents related to national security. A new law passed in September 2008 challenges this argument: article 24 of the Law of Access to Public Information orders that "in no circumstances can information related to investigations of violations of fundamental human rights or crimes against humanity" be classified as confidential or reserved. The military archives remain closed, however.

Impunity for Present-Day Crimes Including Attacks on Civil Society

Impunity is not only the norm for crimes committed during the war, but also a problem that persists for present-day crimes. In 2007 an average of 16 people were killed each day in Guatemala, yet less than 3 percent of murder cases were resolved, according to a study of police data by a respected think tank. No recent case better illustrates the corrosive spread of violence and impunity in Guatemala than the murder of three Salvadorean representatives from the Central American Parliament and their driver in February 2007. Days after the crime, four Guatemalan policemen were arrested as suspects and moved to prison, but all four suspects were murdered while awaiting legal proceedings. In July 2008 the chief prosecutor in the case, Juan Carlos Martinez, was assassinated. A former mayor was arrested in August in connection with the killings, but at this writing, no one has been found guilty of any of the murders.

Attacks and threats against human rights defenders are commonplace, and pose a significant obstacle to their work. Others involved in human rights prosecutions are also routinely threatened or attacked, including forensic experts, plaintiffs, and witnesses. The Human Rights Ombudsman's Office documented nearly 200 attacks and threats against human rights defenders in 2007.

The case of Amilcar de Jesus Pop Ac, a lawyer who has been assisting an indigenous community in a dispute with a cement company, is representative. In August
2008 two armed men threatened to kill Pop, asking him why he continued to help
the community. Prior to this, Pop had received multiple death threats, which he
reported to the police and the public prosecutor, but neither had taken steps to
protect him.

The Protection Unit of Human Rights Defenders, an NGO, reported 37 attacks on
workers' advocates in the first half of 2008, an alarming increase from the previous year's total of 13 such attacks. In March, Miguel Ángel Ramírez Enríquez—co-
founder of a trade union that represents banana pickers—was murdered in his
home. A month earlier, Ramírez's daughter had been abducted and gang-raped
by four men who asked questions about her father's organizing work. No one has
been prosecuted for either crime.

Journalists, especially those covering corruption, drug trafficking, and accountability for abuses committed during the civil war, face threats and attacks for their
work. Five journalists have been killed in Guatemala since 2006. In May 2008 a
reporter who had been investigating government ties to drug traffickers died after
being shot four times in the head, a crime for which no one has been prosecuted.

From January to June 2008 four public prosecutors, a judge, and a magistrate
were assassinated, and dozens more were threatened. Most of the victims were
involved in trying cases of corruption or organized crime.

There is widespread consensus among local and international observers that the
people responsible for many of these acts of violence and intimidation are affiliated with private, secretive, and illegally armed networks or organizations, commonly referred to in Guatemala as "clandestine groups." These groups appear to
have links to both government officials and organized crime, which give them
access to considerable political and economic resources. The Guatemalan justice
system has so far proved no match for this powerful threat to the rule of law.

Excessive Use of Force

Members of the national police sometimes employ excessive force against suspected criminals and others. In September 2007 police officers arrested five men

suspected of being members of a violent drug gang in Guatemala City. The bodies of the men showed up on a ranch several days later, and two police officers are currently standing trail for their murders.

Death Penalty

Guatemalan law allows for the death penalty, but it has not been applied since 2000. In February 2008 Congress passed a decree that would have restored the practice, but the following month President Colom vetoed the decree. At this writing, Guatemala's moratorium on the death penalty continues.

Key International Actors

In September 2007 the UN secretary-general appointed a Spanish former prosecutor and judge to lead the newly-created Commission Against Impunity in Guatemala (CICIG). The commission's mandate is to work with the Guatemalan Attorney General's Office to investigate, prosecute, and dismantle the "clandestine groups" responsible for ongoing violence against human rights defenders. In its first year, the commission has taken on 15 cases, which are seen as representative of the most entrenched problems of impunity. Yet as the CICIG acknowledged in its 2008 annual report, it has also been "systematically obstructed" at times by the very corruption it seeks to root out.

In a landmark ruling, Spain's Constitutional Court held in September 2005 that, in accordance with the principal of "universal jurisdiction," cases of alleged genocide committed during Guatemala's civil war could be prosecuted in the Spanish courts. In July 2006 a Spanish judge issued international arrest warrants for eight Guatemalans and the Spanish government requested their extradition in late 2006. However, in December 2007 the Guatemalan Constitutional Court ruled that two of the accused could not be extradited to Spain. Nevertheless, the Spanish court has pushed ahead with the case: in February, May, and October 2008 it collected testimony from witnesses, victims, and experts on the conflict. Meanwhile, in Guatemala, the case continues to be held up by defense motions, while witnesses and experts are subjected to harassment and threats.

Guatemala was reviewed under the Universal Periodic Review mechanism of the UN Human Rights Council in May 2008. At that time, Guatemala pledged to ratify the Rome Statute of the International Criminal Court and the International Convention on the Protection of All Persons from Enforced Disappearance, and to accept article 14 of the International Convention on the Elimination of All Forms of Racial Discrimination (which allows individual petition to the ICERD committee). In June Guatemala ratified the Optional Protocol to the Convention against Torture and Other Cruel, Inhuman or Degrading Treatment or Punishment, and in September it ratified the Convention on the Rights of Persons with Disabilities.

The UN High Commissioner for Human Rights has maintained an office in Guatemala since 2005 that provides observation and technical assistance on human rights practices in the country. The Inter-American human rights system provides an important venue for human rights advocates seeking to press Guatemala to address past and ongoing abuses.

Guatemala is a member of the Dominican Republic-Central America Free Trade Agreement (DR-CAFTA) between the United States and several countries in Central America. In April 2008 six Guatemalan unions and the US trade union federation AFL-CIO filed a complaint with the US Department of Labor's Office of Trade and Labor Affairs alleging violations of national and international labor laws. The complaint—the first of its kind under DR-CAFTA—was accepted by the US in June and is currently being investigated.

HAITI

Despite some initial progress toward stabilization after the presidential election of 2006 and the local elections that followed, Haiti continues to suffer from high crime rates and chronic human rights problems, including inhumane prison conditions and threats to human rights defenders.

The challenges facing Haiti were compounded by food riots in spring 2008 and an exceptionally destructive hurricane season. At least five people were reportedly killed in food riots in Port-au-Prince and Les Cayes in April. The unrest led to Prime Minister Jacques Edouard Alexis's dismissal that month, leaving the post of prime minister vacant until Michèle Pierre-Louis took office in September. Haiti was hit by four hurricanes in August and September, which left hundreds dead and an estimated one million homeless or displaced and in dire need of humanitarian assistance.

Violence and Weak State Institutions

Despite some improvements in the security situation, high levels of violent crime persisted in 2008. In June United Nations police reported that 157 people had been abducted in Haiti in the first six months of the year (a rate of about one person per day). In the context of the overall high rate of kidnappings, the number of child abductions has continued to rise at an alarming rate in urban areas. Most girls who were abducted reported having been raped or sexually abused by their captors. In one highly publicized kidnapping case, despite a ransom being paid, a 16-year-old kidnapping victim was killed and his body was found on the streets of Port-au-Prince bearing signs of torture.

Police lawlessness contributes to overall insecurity. The Haitian National Police is largely ineffective in preventing and investigating crime. Reports of arbitrary arrests as well as excessive and indiscriminate use of force by police continue. There are also allegations of involvement of some police officers in criminal activity. Although some police units have received training on human rights and arrest procedures, the police continue to experience severe shortages of personnel, equipment, and training.

Haiti also continues to suffer from an ineffective justice system plagued by politicization, corruption, and a lack of personnel, training, and resources. In 2008 Haiti was ranked 177 out of 180 on Transparency International's Corruption Perceptions Index, which serves as a recognized standard for international corruption comparisons. Perpetrators of abuses are rarely held accountable. Sexual abuse of women and girls remains a serious problem, and those responsible are typically not held to account.

Accountability for Past Abuses

Accountability for past abuses remains out of reach. For example, in February 2004 in La Scierie, Saint Marc, armed anti-government gangs took over a police station, and government-linked forces responded with excessive force. There were also reports of abuses by the anti-government gangs. Several killings, including of civilians, resulted from clashes between the groups, but no one has been held responsible for the deaths. Accountability also remains lacking in regard to the 1994 case involving the killing of civilians in Raboteau by soldiers and paramilitaries during the time of the military government. In 2005 the Haitian Supreme Court overturned the convictions of 15 former soldiers and paramilitaries in the Raboteau case, basing its decision on extremely weak grounds.

Detention Conditions

The dysfunctional and politicized judicial system contributes to the severe overcrowding that plagues Haiti's prison system. Arbitrary long-term pretrial detention of suspects is commonplace. Conditions in detention facilities are dire, with prisoners held in dirty, crammed cells often lacking sanitary facilities. In September 2008 nearly 300 pretrial detainees were behind bars at a police station in Gonaives, held in small cells with a total capacity of 75 people. Detainees in some facilities take turns sleeping and standing due to a lack of space and beds, and some complain that they do not receive daily meals. Reports of untreated tuberculosis, malaria, scabies, and malnutrition are common in Haitian detention centers.

Child Labor and Access to Education

Only about half of primary-school-age children attend school and less than 2 percent of children finish secondary school, according to the United Nations Children's Fund. Although enrollment in public schools is supposed to be free, the costs of uniforms, books and other school supplies are often too high for many parents to meet.

The UN estimates there are at least 170,000 child domestic workers in Haiti. Known in Haitian Creole as *restavèks*—from the French "rester avec" (to stay with)—they form part of a long standing system by which parents from mostly low-income rural areas send their children to live with other families, typically in urban areas, in the hope that the receiving families will care for their children and provide them with food, clothing, shelter, and schooling in exchange for the children performing light chores. These children are often unpaid for their work, denied an education, and physically and sexually abused.

Human Rights Defenders

Human rights defenders remain the targets of threats and attacks. Lovinsky Pierre-Antoine, a well-known human rights advocate and former coordinator of Fondasyon Trant Septanm—an organization that worked on behalf of victims of the 1991 and 2004 coup d'états—was abducted on August 12, 2007, while serving as an adviser to a delegation of human rights advocates from Canada and the United States who were traveling in Haiti. His whereabouts remain unknown at this writing. Wilson Mesilien, a Fondasyon Trant Septanm co-founder who was serving as interim coordinator following Pierre-Antoine's disappearance, reportedly received threats and has gone into hiding with his wife and four children.

Frantzo Joseph, coordinator of the Grand Ravine Community Human Rights Council (CCDH-GR), a community group working in the Grand Ravine neighborhood of Port-au-Prince, reportedly received repeated threats and has also gone into hiding with his family. The previous CCDH-GR coordinator, Bruner Esterne, was shot dead by three unknown individuals in September 2006.

Investigations into these three human rights defender cases have not progressed.

On March 7, 2008, the Inter-American Court of Human Rights heard the case of *Fleury v. Haiti*. Lysias Fleury is a human rights activist who was arbitrarily arrested, beaten, and tortured by members of the Haitian National Police in 2002.

Key International Actors

In the wake of the 2008 hurricanes, Haiti received promises of humanitarian aid, particularly from countries throughout the region and in Europe. The delivery of humanitarian aid to areas most affected by the storms has been delayed, in part due to the damage caused to the country's infrastructure by the storms.

The UN Security Council voted in October 2008 to extend the mandate of the UN stabilization mission in Haiti (known by its French acronym, MINUSTAH) to October 15, 2009. The UN force, present in Haiti since 2004 and currently under Brazilian command, contains 6,854 troops and 1,858 police officers. There have been reports of serious abuses over the course of MINUSTAH's mandate, including by personnel from Brazil, Jordan, and Sri Lanka. In February 2008 the UN Office of Internal Oversight Services issued conclusions from its investigation into allegations of violations against children by the personnel of the 950-member Sri Lankan troop contingent, finding that acts of sexual exploitation and abuse were "frequent" and occurred "at virtually every location where the contingent personnel were deployed." Though reports of MINUSTAH abuses appear to have decreased over the past year, problems remain. For example, in August 2008 witnesses reported seeing MINUSTAH forces beating two plainclothes Haitian police officers during a security operation in Cité Soleil.

In 2008, in its first ever judgment in a case against Haiti, the Inter-American Court of Human Rights sharply criticized Haiti's current and former governments for their detention and mistreatment of former Prime Minister Yvon Neptune. It found Haiti responsible for violating 11 different provisions of the American Convention on Human Rights, including the right to physical integrity, the right to personal liberty, and the right to a fair trial and judicial protection. Haiti was ordered to adopt judicial reforms, improve prison conditions, quickly resolve Neptune's criminal case, and pay Neptune US$95,000 in damages and costs.

MEXICO

Mexico's criminal justice system continues to be plagued by human rights problems. Persons under arrest or imprisonment face torture and ill-treatment. Law enforcement officials often neglect to investigate and prosecute those responsible for human rights violations, including abuses perpetrated during law enforcement operations, those committed during Mexico's "dirty war," and sexual and domestic violence against women and girls.

The human rights requirements included in the Merida Initiative, an aid package that the United States government signed into law in June 2008 to help Mexico address the increasing violence and corruption of heavily armed drug cartels, provide a unique opportunity to increase international scrutiny of Mexican security forces' poor human rights records. Other developments in 2008 include a constitutional reform to overhaul the criminal justice system and a Supreme Court ruling upholding a Mexico City law that legalized abortion in the first 12 weeks of pregnancy.

Criminal Justice System

The criminal justice system routinely fails to provide justice to victims of violent crime and human rights violations. The causes of this failure are varied and include corruption, inadequate training and resources, and abusive policing practices without accountability.

Torture remains a widespread problem within the Mexican criminal justice system. One perpetuating factor is the acceptance by some judges of evidence obtained through torture and other mistreatment. Another is the failure to investigate and prosecute most cases of torture.

Over 40 percent of prisoners in Mexico have never been convicted of a crime. Rather, they are held in pretrial detention, often waiting years for trial. The excessive use of pretrial detention contributes to prison overcrowding. Prison inmates are also subject to abuses including extortion by guards and the imposition of solitary confinement for indefinite periods. Children are often detained in poor conditions in police stations and other institutions, and many juvenile detainees do not have access to educational programs.

In June 2008 Mexico passed a constitutional reform that is, in some respects, an historic step forward. It creates the basis for an adversarial criminal justice system with oral trials and contains measures that are critical for promoting greater respect for fundamental rights, such as including presumption of innocence in the constitution. However, two new provisions violate Mexico's obligations under international law. The first allows prosecutors, with judicial authorization, to detain individuals suspected of participating in organized crime for up to 80 days before they are charged with a crime. The second denies judges the power to decide, in cases involving offenses on a prescribed list, whether a defendant should be provisionally released pending and during trial.

Impunity for Military Abuses

Mexican soldiers continue to commit egregious abuses while engaged in law enforcement activities. For instance, in February 2008 soldiers in Tamaulipas used excessive force when they opened fire at a car, killing one man and injuring another. In April soldiers in Chihuahua allegedly arbitrarily detained four police-women, two of whom were blindfolded and held naked in front of soldiers.

With army abuses routinely charged to military authorities to investigate and prosecute, impunity ensues. The military justice system lacks the independence necessary to carry out reliable investigations and its operations suffer from a general absence of transparency. The ability of military prosecutors to investigate army abuses is further undermined by a fear of the army, which is widespread in rural communities and inhibits civilian victims and witnesses from providing information to military authorities.

Impunity for "Dirty War" Crimes

During its five-year existence, the Special Prosecutor's Office that former President Vicente Fox established in 2001 to address abuses committed during the country's "dirty war" in the 1960s, 1970s, and 1980s made very limited progress in investigating and prosecuting these crimes. It did not obtain a single criminal conviction. Of the more than 600 "disappearance" cases, it filed charges in 16 cases and obtained indictments in nine. The office determined the whereabouts of only six "disappeared" individuals, finding that four were sent to psychiatric institutions and two were killed while in detention.

After President Felipe Calderon officially closed the Special Prosecutor's Office, the cases were transferred to another, non-specialized office within the federal Attorney General's Office, which has not made significant advances in the investigations.

Reproductive Rights, Domestic Violence, and Sexual Abuse

Mexican laws do not adequately protect women and girls against domestic violence and sexual abuse. Some laws on violence against women run directly counter to international standards, including provisions of Mexican law that define sanctions for some sexual offenses with reference to the "chastity" of the victim, and penalize domestic violence only when the victim has been battered repeatedly. Legal protections that do exist are often not enforced vigorously. Girls and women who report rape or violence to the authorities are generally met with suspicion, apathy, and disrespect. As a result, victims are often reluctant to report crimes and such underreporting in turn undercuts pressure for necessary legal reforms. The net effect is that sexual and domestic violence against women and girls continues to be rampant and shrouded in impunity.

In a landmark decision, the Mexican Supreme Court affirmed in August 2008 the constitutionality of a Mexico City law of April 2007, which legalized abortion in the first 12 weeks of pregnancy and established the responsibility of public healthcare providers to offer first trimester abortions without restriction and with no residency requirements. However, abortion continues to be criminalized in the rest of Mexico, though every federal state in the country allows abortion in certain specific circumstances, including after rape. Yet pregnant rape victims who seek to terminate their imposed pregnancy are often thwarted from doing so by the dismissive and even hostile treatment they receive from authorities.

Freedom of Expression and Information

Journalists, particularly those who have investigated drug trafficking or have been critical of state governments, have faced harassment and attacks. In June 2008, for example, two days after the severed head of a man was found in front of a newspaper in Tabasco, a note saying "you're next, director" was left nearby. Seven Mexican journalists have gone missing since 2005, including five who had investigated links between local officials and organized crime. Such cases have generated a climate of self-censorship in parts of the country.

Since 2007, defamation, libel, and slander are no longer federal criminal offenses. However, at the state level, criminal defamation laws continue to be excessively restrictive and tend to undermine freedom of expression.

A 2002 federal law on transparency and access to information and a 2007 constitutional reform increased avenues for public scrutiny of the Mexican government. However, progress made in promoting transparency within the federal executive branch has not yet been entirely matched in other branches of government, in autonomous institutions, or at the state level.

Labor Rights

Legitimate labor-organizing activity continues to be obstructed by collective bargaining agreements negotiated between management and pro-management unions. These agreements often fail to provide worker benefits beyond the minimums mandated by Mexican legislation. Workers who seek to form independent unions risk losing their jobs, as inadequate laws and poor enforcement generally fail to protect them from retaliatory dismissals.

The National Human Rights Commission

The National Human Rights Commission, Mexico's official human rights organ, has had limited impact. The Commission has provided detailed and authoritative information on specific human rights cases and usefully documented some systemic obstacles to human rights progress. But, by falling short of making full use of its broad mandate and immense resources, it has routinely failed to press gov-

ernment institutions to remedy the abuses it has documented and to promote
reforms needed to prevent them.

Key International Actors

The Merida Initiative, an aid package that US President George Bush signed into
law in June 2008, includes US$400 million for Mexico as part of a multi-year
regional partnership to address the increasing violence and corruption of heavily
armed drug cartels. The package also provides that most of the aid for Mexican
police and military forces can be made available immediately. However, 15 percent will only be available after the US secretary of state reports to Congress that
the Mexican government has met four human rights requirements. These include
ensuring that civilian prosecutors and judicial authorities investigate and prosecute federal police and military officials who violate basic rights; consulting regularly with Mexican civil society organizations regarding the implementation of the
Merida Initiative; enforcing the prohibition on the use of testimony obtained
through torture or other ill-treatment; and improving the transparency and
accountability of police forces.

The United Nations High Commissioner for Human Rights (OHCHR) maintains an
in-country office that provides valuable documentation of human rights problems
and recommendations for addressing them. In May 2008 the OHCHR removed the
head of its Mexico office amidst credible reports that the Calderon administration
had requested this due to the UN representative's "high profile."

In August the Inter-American Court of Human Rights ruled that Mexico had violated former Foreign Relations Minister Jorge Castañeda's right to judicial review in a
case challenging electoral laws in Mexico. Castañeda had questioned the laws
that establish that presidential candidates must be nominated by political parties, arguing that he should be allowed to run as an independent candidate. The
Court also ruled, however, that Mexico had not violated the articles of the
American Convention that guarantee political rights and the right to equality
before the law.

PERU

Justice for past abuses continues to be a leading human rights concern in Peru. For the first time in its history, the country is currently trying a former president for grave human rights violations. While authorities have made some progress in holding accountable others responsible for abuses committed during Peru's 20-year internal armed conflict (1980–2000), most perpetrators continue to evade justice. Investigations of massacres and enforced disappearances by government forces have been delayed by lack of cooperation from the military.

Cases of torture and ill-treatment continue to occur. Journalists reporting on corruption in Peru's provincial cities face harassment and physical attacks. Government officials have aggressively sought to discredit nongovernmental organizations that advocate for human rights accountability.

Accountability and Impunity

According to Peru's Truth and Reconciliation Commission, almost 70,000 people died or were "disappeared" during the country's internal armed conflict. Many were victims of atrocities committed by the Shining Path and the Tupac Amaru Revolutionary Movement (MRTA), and others of human rights violations by state agents.

On December 10, 2007, the trial began in Lima of former President Alberto Fujimori, who was extradited from Chile to face charges of human rights violations and corruption. Fujimori is accused of the extrajudicial execution of 15 people in the Barrios Altos district of Lima in November 1991, the enforced disappearance and murder of nine students and a teacher from La Cantuta University in July 1992, and two abductions. He faces a sentence of up to 35 years' imprisonment. During 2008 the three judges of the Special Criminal Court heard evidence from Fujimori and scores of witnesses, including victims' relatives, members of the Colina group (an army death squad responsible for the killings), high-ranking military officers, journalists, and human rights experts.

In a separate trial, Gen Julio Salazar Monroe, former head of the National Intelligence Service (SIN) during the Fujimori government, was sentenced in April 2008 to 35 years in prison for ordering the Cantuta killings.

Efforts to investigate and prosecute former officials and military officers implicated in scores of other killings and disappearances dating from the beginning of the armed conflict have had meager results. Lack of cooperation by the military has hampered investigation of human rights cases. The excessive workload of prosecutors, inefficiency, and inexperience in dealing with human rights cases also contribute to the delays.

According to information published by the human rights Ombudsman in December 2007, of 192 cases monitored by the institution—which include abuses committed by insurgent groups— only six had led to convictions, while 110 were still under investigation by prosecutors several years since the investigations were opened. In all, only 19 individuals had received prison sentences. In August 2008 the Ombudsman noted with concern that court proceedings were stagnating.

A decree law enacted in July 2007 to address the problem of organized crime contains a provision that could undermine accountability for police abuses. The law exempts from criminal responsibility members of the police or military who cause death or injury using firearms in the line of duty. The Ombudsman has expressed concern that this law could be invoked to halt ongoing human rights prosecutions and has called for legislation to regulate the use of lethal force in accordance with international standards.

Torture and Ill-Treatment

Torture and ill-treatment of criminal suspects continue to be problems in Peru. A poor record of prosecuting state agents for abuses hinders eradication of these practices. The human rights Ombudsman investigated 139 complaints of torture or ill-treatment between August 2006 and September 2007. The nongovernmental Human Rights Commission (COMISEDH) documented 19 cases from January to September 2008.

The crime of torture was incorporated into the criminal code in 1998, but by the end of 2007 courts had obtained only 11 convictions. Verdicts on torture have been erratic. Although in 2008 the Supreme Court increased prison sentences in one case, another Supreme Court panel annulled a conviction for torture on the erroneous grounds that torture exists only at times of political conflict.

Media Freedom

Journalists who publicize abuses by local government officials are vulnerable to intimidation, assault, and even murder by individuals acting in support of, or working for, municipal authorities. Between January and August 2008 the Press and Society Institute (IPYS), a nongovernmental press freedom monitoring group, issued 20 alerts on behalf of provincial journalists who alleged they had been physically attacked, threatened, or intimidated by mayors and regional authorities or their employees.

Reproductive Rights

In Peru, interrupting a pregnancy is legal only in order to save the life of the woman or to avoid serious and permanent damage to her health, but there are significant barriers to accessing lawful abortions. Human Rights Watch has documented statements by women and adolescent girls who were clearly eligible for legal abortions but who were refused or were unable to access the service, with serious consequences for their mental and physical health.

Major obstacles to accessing therapeutic abortion in Peru include; vague and restrictive laws and policies on therapeutic abortion, the absence of a national protocol on eligibility and administrative procedures, ad hoc approval and referral procedures for legal abortions, and lack of accountability for non-service. These problems are compounded by healthcare providers' fear of prosecution or malpractice lawsuits, and low levels of awareness among women and healthcare providers about exceptions to the criminalization of abortion.

Human Rights Defenders

Former president Fujimori's supporters in Congress, as well as some top govern-ment officials, have aggressively sought to discredit NGOs who advocate for human rights accountability. Such NGOs have been falsely accused of sympathy with terrorist groups.

In April 2008, for example, President Alan García accused the Association for Human Rights (APRODEH), of "treason," after two of its leading members sent a letter to the European Parliament pointing out that the MRTA, one of the armed groups responsible for widespread abuses during the armed conflict, was no longer active, and arguing that to include it in a list of current terrorist groups would be to exaggerate its importance. Vice-President and congressman Luis Giampetri accused APRODEH's director, Francisco Soberón, of justifying terrorism (*apologia del terrorismo*), and called him a "conspicuous agitator of the masses whom the state will have to hold to account."

Soon after, the Peruvian Agency for International Cooperation (APCI), a state body that monitors development aid, announced that it was investigating APRODEH's accounts. In September 2008 APCI announced that the Legal Defense Institute (IDL), a human rights NGO that has campaigned vigorously in Peru for accounta-bility for past human rights violations and on corruption issues, was also to be subject to a full inspection. APCI audits a random sample of NGOs every year, but it was the third time IDL had been selected in less than two years.

Key International Actors

Rulings against Peru in the Inter-American Court of Human Rights on cases involv-ing human rights violations during the armed conflict have provoked negative reactions from the government. In November 2006 the Court ruled on a case involving the indiscriminate killing in 1992 of 41 Shining Path prisoners at the Miguel Castro Castro prison in Lima. It ordered the government to pay compensa-tion of about US$20 million to the families of the dead and to individuals tor-tured during the operation. President García protested that he could not accept paying compensation to "terrorists," and, in a request for clarification filed with the Court, Peru asked if the state or private creditors could demand that the vic-

tims pay damages mandated by Peruvian courts from their compensation payments. In August 2008 the Court ruled that it was up to the Peruvian state to
resolve this issue in accordance with its domestic laws.

Peru was reviewed under the Universal Periodic Review mechanism of the UN
Human Rights Council in May 2008. During the review Peru pledged to report
back to the Human Rights Council on its efforts to implement the recommendations of the Truth and Reconciliation Commission, in particular with regard to victims' compensation and institutional reform, including bringing to justice those
responsible for human rights violations during the 20-year armed conflict.

Venezuela

Venezuela currently lacks a credible, independent judiciary that can serve as a check on arbitrary state action and a guarantor of fundamental rights. In the absence of judicial oversight, the government of President Hugo Chavéz has undermined journalists' freedom of expression, workers' freedom of association, and the ability of civil society groups to promote human rights.

Police abuses remain a widespread problem. Prison conditions are among the worst on the continent, with a high rate of fatalities from inmate violence.

Independence of the Judiciary

The Chávez government has effectively neutralized the judiciary as an independent branch of government. In 2004 the president and his supporters in the National Assembly launched a political takeover of the Supreme Court, filling the court with government supporters and creating new measures that make it possible to purge justices from the Court. Since then, the Court has largely abdicated its role as a check on executive power. It has failed to uphold fundamental rights enshrined in the Venezuelan constitution in key cases involving government efforts to limit freedom of expression and association.

Freedom of Expression and the Media

Venezuela enjoys vibrant public debate in which anti-government and pro-government media are equally vocal in their criticism and defense of Chávez. However, in its efforts to influence the control and content of the media, the government has engaged in discriminatory actions against media that air opposition viewpoints, strengthened the state's capacity to limit free speech, and created powerful incentives for government critics to engage in self-censorship.

In March 2005, amendments to the Criminal Code came into force that extended the scope of Venezuela's *desacato* (disrespect) laws, which criminalize expression deemed to insult public officials or state institutions, and increased penalties for criminal defamation and libel. A broadcasting law introduced in December 2004 has encouraged self-censorship by allowing the arbitrary suspension of

201

channels for the vaguely defined offense of "incitement." Should the government choose to utilize the expanded speech offenses and incitement provisions more aggressively to sanction public expression, the existing political debate could be severely curtailed.

The government has abused its control of broadcasting frequencies to punish stations with overtly critical programming. President Chávez has repeatedly responded to critical coverage by threatening television stations that they would lose their broadcasting rights as soon as their concessions expired. Radio Caracas Television (RCTV) lost its concession in 2007, after Chávez announced at a nationally broadcast military ceremony that RCTV would not have its concession renewed because of its support for an April 2002 coup attempt. Neither this accusation nor an alleged breach of broadcasting standards was ever proved in a proceeding in which RCTV had an opportunity to present a defense. At the same time, the government renewed the concession of Venevisión, a rival channel that Chávez had also repeatedly accused of involvement in the coup but which had since cut its overtly anti-Chávez programming.

Globovisión, the only remaining channel on public airwaves that continues to overtly criticize Chávez, has been denied permission for additional broadcasting frequencies and frequently warned about possible sanctions for critical programs. By contrast, the government has quickly granted frequencies to pro-government channels that it controls or finances.

On the positive side, the government has actively supported the creation of community radio and TV stations, whose broadcasting contributes to media pluralism and diversity in Venezuela. In May 2008 more than 450 such outlets were operating across the country, according to a government official.

Labor Rights

The Chávez government has engaged in systematic violations of workers' rights aimed at undercutting established labor unions while favoring new, parallel unions that support its political agenda.

The government requires that all union elections be organized and certified by the National Electoral Council (CNE), a public authority. This mandatory oversight of

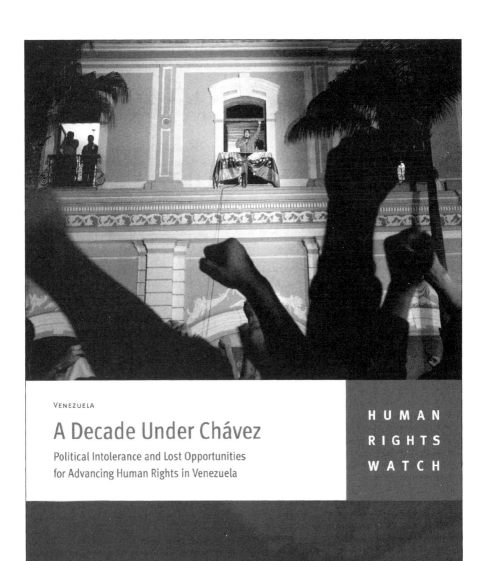

VENEZUELA

A Decade Under Chávez

Political Intolerance and Lost Opportunities
for Advancing Human Rights in Venezuela

HUMAN
RIGHTS
WATCH

union elections violates international standards, which guarantee workers the right to elect their representatives in full freedom and according to the conditions they determine. The government has been promising for several years to reform the relevant labor and electoral laws to restrict state interference in union elections. Yet at this writing these proposals remained under discussion by the National Assembly and the CNE.

Established unions whose elections have not been certified by the CNE are barred from participating in collective bargaining. In the public sector alone, more than 250 collective bargaining agreements are reported to have expired while unions were waiting for the CNE to approve their requests to hold elections and certify their election results.

In bypassing established unions on the grounds that they lack state certification for their elections, the government has promoted and negotiated with new, pro-government unions that are exempt from electoral restrictions when first formed. This practice has created strong incentives for workers to switch labor organizations and join the new organizations preferred by the government.

The government has also undermined the right to strike by banning some legitimate strike activity and engaging in mass reprisals against striking oil workers. Former state oil workers dismissed for participating in a strike in December 2002 are still barred from being rehired in either the public or private sector of the oil industry.

Police Abuses

Violent crime is rampant in Venezuela and extrajudicial killings by security agents remain a recurring problem. Thousands of extrajudicial executions have been recorded in the past decade. Impunity for these crimes remains the norm. Between January 2000 and February 2007 the attorney general's office registered 6,068 alleged killings by the police and the National Guard. Of 1,142 officials charged, only 204 were convicted.

In April 2008 the Chávez government issued by decree an Organic Law of Police Service and National Police, which includes measures aimed at improving police accountability. It created a new office within the Ministry of Interior and Justice, called the Police Rector, to evaluate the performance of all police departments, including their compliance with human rights standards. The law also requires all police forces to establish internal affairs units and independent disciplinary units. At this writing none of these reforms had been implemented.

Prison Conditions

Venezuelan prisons are among the most violent in Latin America. Weak security, insufficient guards, and corruption allow armed gangs to effectively control prisons. Overcrowding, deteriorating infrastructure, and the poor training of guards contribute to the brutal conditions. Despite much fanfare, government plans to "humanize" the penitentiary system have not resulted in any notable improvements. Venezuelan Prison Watch, a Caracas-based group that monitors prison conditions, reported 249 prison deaths as a result of violence and 381 injuries in the first six months of 2008.

Human Rights Defenders

The Chávez government has aggressively sought to discredit local and international human rights organizations. Officials, including the president, have repeatedly made unsubstantiated allegations that human rights advocates were engaged in efforts to destabilize the country. The government has sought to block local rights advocates from participating in international human rights forums, typically on grounds that their work is political or that they receive US or other foreign funding. Rights advocates have also faced prosecutorial harassment and unsubstantiated allegations aimed at discrediting their work. The Supreme Court has ruled that nongovernmental organizations that receive funds from foreign governments are not to be considered part of civil society.

Key International Actors

The Venezuelan government has increasingly rejected international monitoring of its human rights record.

In September 2008 the Chávez government expelled two Human Rights Watch representatives from the country hours after they had presented a critical report on human rights at a news conference in Caracas. The foreign minister falsely accused Human Rights Watch of receiving funding from the US government and of "insulting the institutions of Venezuelan democracy." He also announced, "Any foreigner who comes to criticize our country will be immediately expelled."

In its report covering events in 2007, the Inter-American Commission on Human Rights (IACHR) stated that the Venezuelan government's failure to invite the commission to carry out a fact-finding mission since its last visit in 2002 hindered it from carrying out its mandate in the country. The commission condemned Human Rights Watch's expulsion from Venezuela in September 2008. The government of Chile sent a diplomatic note to Venezuela in protest of the expulsion.

"One Year of My Blood"

Exploitation of Migrant Construction Workers in Beijing

HUMAN
RIGHTS
WATCH

WORLD REPORT

2009

ASIA

AFGHANISTAN

Afghanistan is experiencing its worst violence since the fall of the Taliban government. Widespread human rights abuses, warlordism, and impunity persist, with a government that lacks the strength or will to institute necessary reforms. Corruption and an escalating cost of living are affecting millions.

The Taliban and other militants have extended their control into parts of the country previously considered relatively stable, such as Logar and Wardak which border Kabul province, and parts of Herat province in the west. Kabul was a target of several audacious militant attacks in 2008, with several major roads out of the capital becoming dangerous to travel. Civilians continue to bear the brunt of militants' bomb attacks. Civilian deaths resulting from international military actions also remain high, with hundreds of preventable deaths occurring in 2007 and 2008.

Violence and Insecurity

As the violence spirals, each year that passes is declared bloodier than the last. 2008 was no exception. Insurgent groups have been responsible for approximately two-thirds of civilian deaths. In the first seven months of 2008, the UN estimates that improvised explosive devices and suicide attacks killed almost 500 civilians. Antigovernment forces routinely violate the laws of war by launching attacks from civilian areas or retreating to such areas, knowingly drawing return fire.

The targeting of individuals associated with the government is also on the rise, from school teachers to human rights defenders, with the United Nations recording over a hundred assassinations in 2008. The Taliban claimed responsibility for the September killing of Afghanistan's highest-ranking female police officer, Lieutenant-Colonel Malalai Kakar.

Despite operational improvements, significant numbers of civilians also continue to be killed by US and NATO-led International Security Assistance Force (ISAF) airstrikes, inflaming public opinion and undermining the government. In July 2008, a mistaken US bombing of a wedding party in Deh Bala, Nangahar

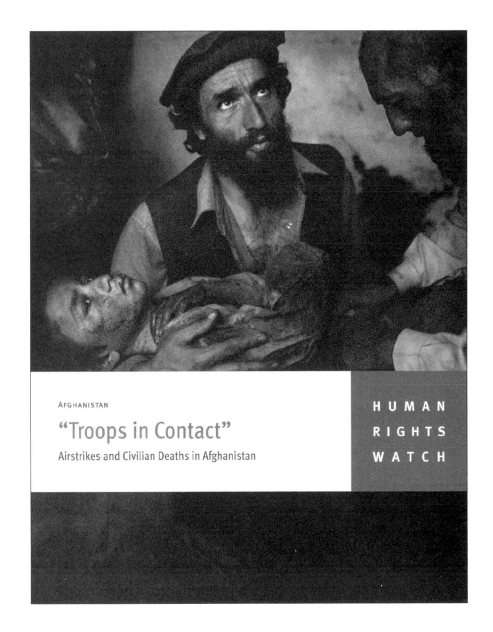

AFGHANISTAN

"Troops in Contact"

Airstrikes and Civilian Deaths in Afghanistan

HUMAN
RIGHTS
WATCH

province, killed 47 civilians. Denials and lack of transparency have made the situation worse. In August, US forces bombed the village of Azizabad; the UN, the government, and the Afghan Independent Human Rights Commission said more than 90 civilians were killed. The US initially denied that any more than seven civilians had been killed, but weeks later raised the figure to 33.

Increasingly under joint command, the US and ISAF have now agreed to hold joint investigations with the Afghanistan government. Too often a faulty condolence-payment system has not provided timely and adequate compensation to assist civilians harmed by US and ISAF actions.

Outside the conflict areas, organized crime and warlords terrorize Afghans with impunity. Kidnapping of Afghans for ransom is common, but the police seem largely incapable or unwilling to tackle it.

Governance and Impunity

The Afghan government continues to lose public legitimacy because of widespread corruption, failure to improve living standards, and lack of progress in establishing the rule of law even in areas under its control. Afghans frequently cite police corruption as a problem, with internationally funded police reform efforts showing limited impact. The UN special rapporteur on extrajudicial killings, Philip Alston, visited Afghanistan in May 2008 and drew attention to the impunity police generally enjoy after they have been accused of killing civilians.

President Hamid Karzai's government has done little to implement the Action Plan for Peace, Reconciliation and Justice, a five-year plan for implementing transitional justice in Afghanistan, part of the Afghanistan Compact which the government officially initiated on December 12, 2006. The legal status of an amnesty for war criminals, passed by parliament in 2007, is still unclear. But the tone of the debate on transitional justice is still being dominated by the influential group of parliamentarians that pushed the resolution through, including Abdul Rabb al Rasul Sayyaf, Burhanuddin Rabbani, and Taj Mohammad, all of whom have been implicated in war crimes and other serious human rights abuses. The Karzai administration appears powerless to challenge them.

Women and Girls

Afghan women and girls rank among the world's worst-off by most indicators, including maternal mortality, life expectancy, and literacy.

Insecurity prevents the vast majority of girls from attending school in the south and southeast. In Kandahar in November 2008, several schoolgirls had acid thrown at their faces on their way to school. Even in conflict-free areas, Afghan girls continue to face immense obstacles to education such as lack of girls' schools, sexual harassment en route to school, and early marriage which tends to prematurely end schooling. According to Ministry of Education data, 46 percent of primary school-aged girls were enrolled in primary school, compared with 74 percent of boys. At the secondary level only 8 percent of girls and 18 percent of boys were enrolled.

Women still confront widespread discrimination, significant barriers to working outside the home, and restrictions on their mobility; many still cannot travel without an accompanying male relative and a burqa.

Children

As part of their campaign of terrorizing the civilian population, the Taliban and other insurgent groups continue to target schools, and in particular girls' schools. According to the Ministry of Education, over one hundred schools were attacked between March and October 2008, with the Afghanistan NGO Security Office recording more than 30 teachers and students killed in the first 10 months of 2008.

According to the Afghan Independent Human Rights Commission, child labor is prevalent throughout the country and is another reason children do not attend school.

The UN special representative for children and armed conflict drew attention in 2008 to the largely taboo practice of *bacha bazi* (the keeping of boys as sex slaves by wealthy or powerful patrons). The government of Afghanistan has done little to tackle this abusive cultural tradition.

Human Rights Defenders

Freedom of expression for those who criticize government officials, insurgents, or powerful local figures remains limited. Threats, violence, and intimidation are regularly used to silence opposition politicians, critical journalists, and civil society activists.

In January 2008, 23-year-old student Sayed Parviz Kambakhsh was sentenced to death on blasphemy charges, accused of downloading, doctoring, and distributing among friends an article about the role of women in Islam. In October, the death sentence was commuted to 20 years in prison—still an excessive punishment. Kambakhsh's detention and trial were marred by denials of justice including confessions extracted under duress, excessive periods in detention, limited access to lawyers, a closed and abbreviated trial, the use of inappropriate evidence, and severe delays during the appeal process.

Media Freedom

The blossoming of an independent media sector was once seen as a rare success of the post-Taliban government. But the increasingly authoritarian government has repressed critical journalism, leading to self-censorship. Dozens of journalists have been detained, some held without charge for days, weeks, or months.

In July 2008 a private TV program airing accusations of government corruption was pulled off the air on the orders of the president's office. The intelligence services detained the presenter, Mohammad Nasir Fayaz, for two days.

Journalists are also attacked by warlords, insurgents, parliamentarians, and the security forces. The body of 25-year-old journalist Abdul Samad Rohani, a BBC correspondent, was found with multiple knife and bullet wounds in June 2008. The government's response to such crimes remains weak.

The most dangerous areas for journalists are in the south and east of the country where the armed conflict and the resulting propaganda war are most fierce. Insurgent groups have used murder, arson, and intimidation to try to stop reporting they see as unsympathetic. The government also exerts undue pressure on reporters in conflict areas who have legitimate journalistic contacts with insurgent groups.

Key International Actors

In the immediate aftermath of the overthrow of the Taliban in 2002-2003, the international community's stated aim was to extend the reach of central government, in order to avoid the vacuum of weak or absent government being exploited by the insurgency. Foreign military powers, donors, and the UN have since failed to prioritize governance and the rule of law, contributing to the growth of insurgency in Afghanistan and the diminution of central government control.

The Paris donor conference in June 2008 offered donors a chance to address fundamental problems of impunity, women's rights, freedom of expression, transitional justice, and judicial reform. Instead, donors largely offered more of the same, with few conditions attached to aid.

The UN operation in Afghanistan remains understaffed, with the human rights and rule of law office well below capacity. The UN special representative for Afghanistan, Kai Eide, who took charge in April 2008, has not prioritized human rights.

International security forces, in particular US forces, have focused much of their efforts on killing or capturing al Qaeda and Taliban leaders, rather than providing a safer environment for Afghans to enjoy their basic rights.

The US military operates in Afghanistan without an adequate legal framework, such as a status-of-forces agreement, and continues to detain hundreds of Afghans without adequate legal process. The expanding US-run Bagram detention facility holds over 600 prisoners, including children, who are given negligible legal rights. Unlike at Guantanamo, prisoners at Bagram are not allowed to see lawyers. Administrative review of detainees' cases is cursory. The detainees have no right to a personal advocate, no opportunity to review the evidence against them, and very little means of contesting the grounds for their detention.

BANGLADESH

A military-backed interim government ruled Bangladesh for the second year in a row in 2008 under a state of emergency. This was despite the absence of any visible internal or external threats justifying emergency rule. Fundamental rights were suspended during most of the year, but were partially restored in the run-up to parliamentary elections in December and the expected return to democratic rule.

In the second half of 2008, the government released dozens of senior politicians and businesspersons arrested in an anti-corruption drive initiated in 2007. Extrajudicial executions, custodial torture, arbitrary arrests, and impunity for members of the security forces continue to characterize the human rights situation in Bangladesh.

Political Developments

The military-backed government headed by "Chief Advisor" Fakhruddin Ahmed claimed to be a non-party "caretaker government" constitutionally mandated to undertake routine government functions and ensure that the Election Commission can hold free and fair parliamentary elections. However, it interpreted its mandate broadly, and throughout 2008 adopted dozens of ordinances with little or no direct link to preparations for national elections. In December 2007 the President issued an ordinance for the establishment of a National Human Rights Commission. At this writing, the commission had not yet been made operational.

Many of the country's political and business leaders were detained and charged in an unprecedented and initially welcomed anti-corruption drive that began in 2007. The drive has been plagued by perceived political favoritism and has so far had limited impact in reducing overall corruption.

In the course of negotiations between the government and political parties over planned December 2008 elections, authorities released former prime ministers Khaleda Zia, leader of the Bangladesh Nationalist Party, and Sheikh Hasina, leader of the Awami League, together with dozens of other high profile prisoners who had been held on corruption-related charges.

BANGLADESH

The Torture of Tasneem Khalil

How the Bangladesh Military Abuses Its Power
Under the State of Emergency

HUMAN
RIGHTS
WATCH

Extrajudicial Killings

The police force and the Rapid Action Battalion(RAB)—an elite anti-crime and anti-terrorism force—continue to kill people in what the authorities refer to as "crossfire" killings, "encounters," and "shootouts," but which in fact are thinly disguised extrajudicial executions. After strong national and international criticism the number of killings decreased in 2007 and early 2008.

According to the human rights organization Odhikar, law enforcement officials killed 116 people between January 1 and September 30, 2008. Alleged members of outlawed left wing political parties are often targeted. On July 26, the mother of Dr. Mizanur Rahman Tutul, the head of the outlawed Purbo Banglar Communist Party (Red Flag faction), informed the media that RAB officers had arrested her son in Dhaka. She urged the government to save him from "crossfire." According to the police, Tutul was killed in a shootout between his group and the police on July 27, the day after his mother talked to the press.

Torture

Torture remains widespread in Bangladesh and is frequently used by law enforcement officials to coerce confessions in criminal investigations and to extort money. It is also used for politically motivated purposes against perceived government critics and alleged national security suspects. The bodies of those who are killed by RAB and the police regularly have physical marks and injuries indicating that they have been tortured.

After their release in 2008, businesspersons and politicians targeted in the government's anti-corruption campaign alleged that the Directorate General of Forces Intelligence (DGFI)—Bangladesh's most important military intelligence agency—illegally detained them at its offices inside the military cantonment in Dhaka for days or weeks and subjected them to physical torture, harsh interrogations methods, and sleep deprivation. Former detainees also allege that the DGFI used threats and extortion to force suspects to transfer arbitrary sums of money to state coffers and individual accounts.

Freedom of Expression and Assembly

Emergency provisions limiting the rights of expression and assembly remained in force during most of 2008, but the interim government lifted some restrictions in advance of elections.

Military and civilian government agencies have regularly interfered in the day-to-day work of the media. While direct intimidation and harassment of journalists was less frequent during the second part of 2008, members of DGFI provided "friendly advice" to journalists on editorial content and the media continued to exercise a high degree of self censorship, especially when reporting on allegations of corruption and other illegal acts by members of the armed forces. Military figures and their associates continue to increase their ownership of both electronic and print media.

2008 saw a sharp decrease in the number of criminal defamation cases filed against journalists. At this writing, no journalist had been murdered and none were known to be arbitrarily detained.

Law enforcement agencies continue to use excessive force to break up demonstrations. On May 19, the Bangladesh Rifles, a paramilitary law enforcement agency, reportedly injured at least 50 people demonstrating against an assault on a sub-district commissioner by members of the Rifles.

In June 2008 security forces detained thousands of grassroots political activists following the refusal of the major political parties to participate in a government-initiated dialogue about the country's political future until party leaders were released from detention. Most of those arrested were released shortly afterwards.

Freedom of Association

Union activities remain banned under the state of emergency. But factory workers continue to hold frequent, large-scale demonstrations protesting non-payment of salaries, below-minimum wages, and the failure of employers to respect basic labor standards. Several union and labor rights activists were arrested during 2008, while others went into hiding for fear of being subjected to harassment. In January 2008, National Security Intelligence agents arrested Mehedi Hasan of the

Dhaka branch of the Worker Rights Consortium, an organization that monitors labor practices on behalf of US colleges and universities. Hasan was detained for ten days.

Women's Rights

Discrimination against women is common in both public and private spheres. There are few women in decision-making positions and women generally are paid lower wages than men. Maternal mortality rates remain extremely high, despite significant improvements over the past 20 years. Domestic violence is a daily reality for many women and dowry-related crimes are reported to be increasing.

Following adoption of a new National Women's Development Policy in March 2008, a number of Islamist groups organized violent protests, arguing that provisions calling for equality in acquisition and control of property violate Sharia inheritance rules. In response to the protests, the government established a committee of Islamic scholars which among other things recommended that references to equal rights be taken out of the policy. At this writing, it remained unclear whether the policy would be amended or its implementation shaped by the recommendations.

Privacy

Section 377 of Bangladesh's criminal code, an inheritance of British colonialism, punishes consensual homosexual conduct with up to life imprisonment.

Impunity

The interim government's efforts to hold people accountable for corruption stand in sharp contrast to its complete inaction with regard to abuses committed by members of the security forces. No progress has been made in recent years to address the longstanding problem of impunity and at this writing not a single member of the security forces had been sentenced to prison for extrajudicial killings or torture.

Impunity for security forces and officials has been further entrenched by a constitutional provision permitting authorities to suspend court enforcement of fundamental rights during the state of emergency.

Despite considerable civil society pressure, there has been no move by the interim government to prosecute individuals believed responsible for atrocities in the 1971 Bangladesh liberation war.

Human Rights Defenders

Bangladesh's NGO Affairs bureau, which approves projects and funding of NGOs, has created obstacles for some human rights organizations seeking permission to receive foreign donor funding. Organizations critical of the regime and outspoken against human rights abuses appear to be particularly affected. There were some reports of staff members of nongovernmental human rights organizations being harassed by members of the security forces.

Key International Actors

Foreign governments and intergovernmental organizations, including the US, UK, and EU, stressed the importance of parliamentary elections being held before the end of 2008 and publicly urged the interim government to relax or lift the state of emergency before the elections.

Several international donor agencies such as the Asia Development Bank, United Nations Development Programme, and World Bank are providing support to the government's anti-corruption efforts. They have rarely raised publicly any concerns about abuses resulting from the campaign.

The United Kingdom conducted human rights training for selected RAB members in 2008, apparently in hopes of future cooperation with RAB, on organized crime, Islamic militancy, and terrorism. The US also has explored possibilities for future cooperation. The EU and some foreign missions continue to raise concerns about extrajudicial executions and other abuses.

Multinational companies buying garments from Bangladesh were slow in reacting to the state of emergency ban on trade union activities even though their own codes of conduct stress the importance of freedom of association. In September 2008 some major brands asked the interim government to lift restrictions on such activities

Bangladesh is due to be reviewed under the Universal Periodic Review mechanism of the UN Human Rights Council in February 2009.

Burma

Burma's already dismal human rights record worsened following the devastation of cyclone Nargis in early May 2008. The ruling State Peace and Development Council (SPDC) blocked international assistance while pushing through a constitutional referendum in which basic freedoms were denied.

The ruling junta systematically denies citizens basic freedoms, including freedom of expression, association, and assembly. It regularly imprisons political activists and human rights defenders; in 2008 the number of political prisoners nearly doubled to more than 2,150. The Burmese military continues to violate the rights of civilians in ethnic conflict areas and extrajudicial killings, forced labor, land confiscation without due process and other violations continued in 2008.

Cyclone Nargis

Cyclone Nargis struck the Irrawaddy Delta and Burma's largest city Rangoon on the night of May 2-3, 2008. The storm rendered 2.4 million people across 37 townships homeless or in need of food or medical assistance with an estimated 84,000 dead and 53,000 missing.

The SPDC tightly controlled emergency international assistance and in some cases blocked aid in the crucial early stages following the cyclone. The government denied visas to disaster relief experts and aid workers and prevented them from travel inside Burma. More than 2 million people waited for weeks for relief operations to reach them.

United Nations Secretary-General Ban Ki-moon visited Burma in late May, and the UN, the Association of Southeast Asian Nations (ASEAN), and the SPDC created a Tripartite Core Group (TCG) as a multilateral mechanism to coordinate delivery and distribution of emergency relief aid. The SPDC subsequently relaxed restrictions on some agencies and enabled helicopters and boats to operate more freely. But two months after the cyclone an estimated 700,000 people had received no aid whatsoever because of SPDC obstruction.

While some UN agencies and international NGOs have reported continuing travel restrictions and obstructions, others say they have been permitted free travel and unfettered operational space. Pro-government organizations such as the Myanmar Red Cross and the Union Solidarity and Development Association operate extensively in the Irrawaddy Delta, but some private civil society efforts have been either discouraged or co-opted by the authorities.

In cyclone-affected areas, there have been reports of land confiscations, forced labor, and forced evictions of displaced people by Burmese authorities.

Constitutional Referendum

The SPDC announced in February 2008 that its long awaited constitutional referendum would take place on May 10. The constitution itself was publicly released only in April, and then under limited distribution. A new law made any "disruption" of the referendum process potentially punishable by three years' imprisonment.

The new constitution entrenches military rule and limits the role of independent political parties. It empowers the commander-in-chief to appoint military officers to a quarter of all seats in both houses of parliament, and gives the military even broader representation in the selection of the president and two vice-presidents.

Despite the devastation of the cyclone, the referendum took place throughout Burma on May 10, with a delayed vote on May 24, for 47 townships affected by the storm. The referendum was carried out in an environment of severe restrictions on access to information, repressive media laws, an almost total ban on freedom of expression, assembly, and association, and the continuing widespread detention of political activists. There were no independent international observers and Burmese and foreign media could only clandestinely cover it. The referendum was marred by voter registration irregularities, coercion and intimidation in communities and at polling stations, and widespread government corruption including ballot stuffing.

In late May the SPDC announced a national voter turnout of 98.12 percent, of which 92.48 voted in favor of the constitution. Widespread international condemnation denounced the referendum as a sham. The referendum completed the

BURMA

Vote to Nowhere
The May 2008 Constitutional Referendum in Burma

HUMAN RIGHTS WATCH

fourth step of the SPDC's Seven Step Road Map to Democracy, with the SPDC announcing multi-party elections for 2010.

Human Rights Defenders

Intimidation of political activists and human rights defenders increased in 2008. The number of political prisoners rose from 1,100 in mid 2007 to over 2,150 in late 2008. On September 23, the SPDC announced the release of 9,002 prisoners, of which only seven were political activists, including 78 year old U Win Tin who had been incarcerated since 1989. Days later, the SPDC arrested five members of the National League for Democracy (NLD). On May 27, NLD leader Aung San Suu Kyi had her house arrest order extended for another year, her sixth straight year of confinement. Reports indicate her health is deteriorating, and the SPDC denies her visitors or contact with the outside world.

In October and November, more than 70 political activists, monks, nuns, labor activists, and journalists were tried in secret proceedings in prison or closed sessions in court. Many received harsh sentences for offenses related to the 2007 demonstrations; 14 of them were sentenced to 65 years each. Members of the 88 Generation Students faced 22 charges, including contact with exiled political groups and unlawfully publishing documents, and faced sentences of 150 years. Four lawyers representing activists were also jailed for contempt of court after they attempted to withdraw from legal representation to protest the unfair proceedings.

Journalists continued to be harassed and arrested in 2008, including Thet Zin and Sein Wun Aung in February for their investigation into the SPDC's brutal crackdown against peaceful protestors. Prominent blogger Nay Phone Latt received a 20-year prison sentence in November.

Authorities arrested several prominent former political prisoners for their role in cyclone relief activities including, on June 4, 2008, prominent comedian and dissident Zargana, who distributed aid through his activist networks to Nargis victims. Zargana had criticized the SPDC's relief efforts in interviews with the foreign media.

Child Soldiers

Burma continues widespread and systematic forced recruitment of child soldiers. Non-state armed groups also recruit and deploy children in conflict areas.

The UN Security Council working group on children and armed conflict reviewed Burma's record for the first time in 2008. Despite the SPDC's ongoing failure to curtail use of child soldiers, it did not recommend concrete measures to spur the SPDC to act. The Security Council's failure—in large part due to efforts by China to block a more principled response—was particularly glaring given its previous pledges to seriously consider arms embargoes and other targeted measures against parties that repeatedly recruit and use child soldiers.

Continuing Violence against Ethnic Groups

The Burmese military continues to attack civilians in ethnic conflict areas, particularly in Karen State and Shan State. Abuses such as forced labor, sexual violence against women and girls, extrajudicial killings, torture and beatings, and confiscation of land and property are widespread. In 2008 army counterinsurgency tactics and security operations for infrastructure developments displaced more than 40,000 civilians in these two areas.

There are an estimated 450,000 to half a million internally displaced people in eastern Burma. The Burmese army and non-state armed groups extensively use landmines, including near civilian settlements and food production sites— a clear violation of international humanitarian law.

In Arakan State in western Burma, the Rohingya Muslim minority faces widespread rights violations including religious persecution, forced relocation, land seizures, and denial of citizenship and identity papers. Ethnic Chin people in Chin State and Sagaing Division continue to face forced labor, beatings, sexual violence, and land confiscation by the Burmese military; a famine in the region affected over 100,000 civilians, with reports that relief efforts were hampered by the Burmese army.

Refugees and Migrant Workers

Thousands of Burmese refugees and migrant workers continue to travel to Bangladesh, India, Thailand, Malaysia, and Singapore where they face abuses and harassment. Some 140,000 refugees remain in nine camps along the Thai-Burma border. Over 50,000 refugees have been resettled in third countries such as the United States, Canada, Australia, and Norway since 2004.

In July 2008, Thai military officials forcibly returned 52 ethnic Karen people, including children, back to Burma, clearly violating the principle of non-*refoulement*, and threatened further returns from other camps. In December 2007, Thai security forces shot dead a man in Karenni Site 1 camp, and have since obstructed the official Thai investigation into the killing. Sexual violence by Thai camp guards against female refugees remains prevalent.

Key International Actors

The UN secretary-general's special advisor on Burma, Ibrahim Gambari, visited Burma twice in 2008 but made no progress in engaging the SPDC on political reform. In his March visit, Burmese officials lectured Gambari and criticized his attempts at impartial mediation. The UN Security Council expressed its frustration with the slow pace of dialogue with Burma and called on Gambari to show "tangible progress." In August, Aung San Suu Kyi and senior generals refused to meet with Gambari.

The UN special rapporteur on human rights in Burma, Tomas Ojeá Quintana conducted a five-day official visit to Burma in August 2008. Quintana's visit was tightly managed by the SPDC; including a tour of the cyclone-affected Irrawaddy delta, and meetings with government-screened political prisoners, Burmese officials, pro-SPDC political parties, and civil society organizations. Quintana expressed cautious optimism about engaging the SPDC on improving the human rights situation.

ASEAN was a key diplomatic focal point after Cyclone Nargis, with ASEAN Secretary General Surin Pitsuwan making frequent visits to Burma to organize relief efforts. ASEAN's early criticism of Burma following the 2007 crackdown was muted as it focused on aid efforts. Indonesia lifted its ban on granting credentials to Burmese ambassadors, and Singapore continued to voice support for Burma in international forums.

After Cyclone Nargis, the international community reacted with shock and anger at the SPDC's reluctance to allow international aid and aid workers into affected areas, with the French government raising the "Responsibility to Protect" principle and arguing for international intervention to assist victims. A European Parliament resolution "strongly condemned" the disruption of cyclone aid, referred to the referendum as "implausible," and directly warned that further blockades by the SPDC should result in a charge of crimes against humanity and Burma's referral to the International Criminal Court.

China, Russia, India, and Thailand continue to provide diplomatic support for the SPDC and are major trade and investment partners. Foreign investment in Burma's oil and natural gas sector increased in 2008, particularly in connection with a major offshore gas project led by a Korean consortium and a planned over-land pipeline to the Burma-China border. Sales of natural gas account for the largest share of the SPDC's revenue.

Countries including Australia, Canada, the European Union, Switzerland, and the US continue to impose targeted sanctions on Burma. In July 2008 the US updated its sanctions on Burmese leaders and close business allies by adding Burmese military conglomerates and related companies. It also tightened its gem embargo, making imports of Burmese rubies and jade illegal even if processed in other countries. In August, President George Bush met with exiled Burmese dissidents in Thailand.

Cambodia

Cambodia continued its drift toward authoritarianism in 2008 as Prime Minister Hun Sen and his Cambodian People's Party (CPP) consolidated power through flawed national elections in July. The elections were criticised by the European Union and the United Nations special representative for human rights in Cambodia for failing to meet international standards.

Authorities continue to use the criminal justice system to silence critics. Human rights defenders, journalists, trade unionists, and opposition party members face intimidation, violence, spurious legal action, imprisonment, and even death. Endemic impunity, rampant corruption, and illegal plundering of natural resources remain pressing issues.

National Elections

The CPP won National Assembly Elections on July 27 by a wide majority, taking 91 of 123 seats. While there was less political violence than in past elections, the vote was marred by the CPP's near monopoly over the media, bias within the electoral apparatus, and coerced defections of opposition Sam Rainsy Party (SRP) members to the CPP. Lucrative offers of high-paying government positions and threats of reprisals, including arrest or violence against those who refused, led hundreds of opposition party members to join the CPP.

In March 2008 police arrested and detained SRP leader Tuot Saron in Kampong Thom. He was charged with illegal confinement after assisting a distressed former party colleague following her alleged defection to the CPP under controversial circumstances. He remains in prison at this writing.

Freedoms of Expression, Association, and Assembly

The Cambodian government controls all television and most radio stations and regularly suspends, threatens, or takes legal action against journalists or news outlets that criticize the government. Freedom of speech is hampered by provisions in Cambodian laws that allow individuals to be criminally prosecuted for peaceful expression of their views. Reporters risk dismissal, physical attack, or even death for covering controversial issues.

In July gunmen shot and killed Khim Sambo, a journalist for *Moneaksekar Khmer* (Khmer Conscience), an SRP-affiliated newspaper. In June, the newspaper's editor, Dam Sith, an SRP electoral candidate, was arrested after the paper reported allegations that the foreign minister had served the Khmer Rouge regime. Sith was released after one week, but still faces criminal defamation and disinformation charges. In May, Radio Free Asia journalist Lem Piseth, who was covering alleged involvement of government officials in a drug trafficking and murder case, fled the country after receiving death threats.

The government confiscates, bans, or suspends controversial publications. In May 2008 the government shut down an independent radio station in Kratie after it sold air time to opposition parties. Cambodian authorities also threatened Buddhist monks for circulating bulletins advocating for the rights of Khmer Krom people (ethnic Khmer from southern Vietnam).

A 2007 law on demonstrations requires organizers to give local authorities five days' notice and holds organizers responsible for any misconduct that occurs. Authorities reject requests or forcibly disperse many demonstrations. For example, in May 2008 authorities in Ratanakiri province prohibited indigenous ethnic minority villagers from conducting a peaceful march to protest land confiscation.

The government continues to fail to resolve cases involving violence against trade union activists. Four years after the murder of labor leader Chea Vichea, the perpetrators remain at large while two men unfairly convicted for the crime are serving 20-year prison sentences. In September 2008, judicial authorities closed the investigation into the murder of labor leader Hy Vuthy in 2007, despite previous police statements that warrants had been issued for two suspects.

Workers who organize or strike for better wages and working conditions are subject to harassment, physical attacks, and unfair dismissal. In February 2008 police and military police forcefully dispersed a strike by garment factory workers at the Kingsland factory in Phnom Penh who were demanding reinstatement of fired union representatives. In March union activist Keo Sokun was attacked and beaten by four men.

Land Confiscation

The rural and urban poor continue to lose their land to illegal concessions awarded to foreign firms, government officials, and those with connections to government officials. This has become one of the most critical economic and social problems in Cambodia. In Phnom Penh, 85,000 people have been forcibly evicted during the last 10 years, with another 70,000 currently facing eviction proceedings. Authorities often provide insufficient notice of impending evictions and inadequate housing and compensation to displaced people afterwards. For example, more than two years after 1,000 families were forcibly evicted from Sambok Chap village in Phnom Penh, the government had not yet provided adequate health care, water, sanitation, schools, and other basic services to the evictees, relocated to a remote site far from the city.

On numerous occasions police and soldiers have used excessive force in evictions. In February 2008, 100 police and military police officers fired AK-47 rifles into the air and used tear gas to forcibly evict 23 families from Russey Keo district in Phnom Penh. In July villagers in Kampot were beaten and arrested when soldiers dismantled their houses and evicted them for a land concession.

Khmer Rouge Tribunal

The Extraordinary Chambers in the Courts of Cambodia, a hybrid tribunal presided over by both Cambodian and international judges to address Khmer Rouge era crimes, continued in 2008 to make slow progress toward holding its first trials. At this writing, five senior Khmer Rouge officials remain in detention, including Kaing Khek Iev (Duch), the former chief of Tuol Sleng prison; Pol Pot's deputy, Nuon Chea; former Khmer Rouge Foreign Minister Ieng Sary, former Khmer Rouge Social Affairs Minister Ieng Thirith, and former Khmer Rouge head of state Khieu Samphan. All are charged with crimes against humanity and war crimes, except for Ieng Thirith, who was charged only with crimes against humanity.

Serious concerns remain about political interference in the court from the Cambodian government, corruption among Cambodian personnel, lack of sufficient victim and witness protection, and the limited number of cases brought to address the deaths of as many as 2 million people from 1975-1979. Criticism of the tribunal has mounted, with many in Cambodia saying they are losing interest as the process drags on without tangible results.

Prisons and Arbitrary Detention

Prisons remain overcrowded, with inadequate food, water, health care, and sanitation. Police routinely use torture to force confessions from detainees. In February 2008 a police officer in Kep municipality involved in a land dispute with Princess Marie Ranariddh was arrested, beaten, and detained for a month—part of the time in shackles—without a court order. In June, Cambodian human rights organization Licadho uncovered abusive conditions—including lack of food, medical care, and physical mistreatment—at government-run "social rehabilitation centers" where sex workers, homeless children and families, beggars, and drug addicts are detained after arbitrary police round-ups.

Refugees and Asylum Seekers

Cambodia continues to violate its obligations under the UN Refugee Convention by forcibly returning Vietnamese Montagnards before they are able to apply for asylum with the UN High Commissioner for Refugees (UNHCR). During 2008 UNHCR provided shelter in Phnom Penh to approximately 500 Montagnard asylum seekers, including about 200 new arrivals.

Cambodians who help Montagnard asylum seekers exercise their right to seek asylum are subject to arrest. In June, the Phnom Penh Court sentenced two men to four months' imprisonment for sheltering Montagnards after they had entered Cambodia to seek asylum.

In October UNHCR announced that Cambodian immigration police, and not UNHCR, would begin screening all asylum seekers in Cambodia other than ethnic minority Montagnards from Vietnam.

Rule of Law

No progress was made in 2008 on legal and judicial reform. The Supreme Council of Magistracy, established to ensure judicial independence, remains politicized and ineffectual, while the Constitutional Council fails to safeguard the constitutionality of legislation. Despite 15 years of commitments, the government and parliament have still not passed a new criminal law, anti-corruption law, or other legislation critical to the protection of human rights.

Key International Actors

Cambodia's donors still have not seriously pressed Hun Sen and the Cambodian government to keep their annual promises to promote and protect human rights and establish the rule of law and judicial independence.

Instead of demanding that the Cambodian government allow the US Federal Bureau of Investigation to complete its investigation into the March 30, 1997 grenade attack on a rally led by opposition party leader Sam Rainsy—in which at least 16 were killed and which the US branded a terrorist act—the US in 2008 worked with individuals implicated in that attack and other incidents of political violence in counterterrorism programs with the Cambodian government. In June the US raised Cambodia's anti-trafficking ranking to Tier 2 to reflect its assessment that the country's practices had improved. The US continues to provide funding and training to the Cambodian military.

In September the UN Human Rights Commission decided to create the post of a special rapporteur on Cambodia to replace the former functions of the secretary-general's special representative. The last special representative, Yash Ghai, resigned in September 2008, noting that Cambodia still faces serious human rights challenges and "deep-seated systematic deficiencies in the judiciary and other key institutions charged with upholding the rule of law and protecting the rights of individuals."

Cambodia is due to be reviewed under the Universal Periodic Review mechanism of the HRC in December 2009.

CHINA

The Chinese government broke its promise to improve human rights in conjunction with its hosting of the 2008 Summer Olympic Games. The months prior to the Olympics were marked by a significant tightening of restrictions on freedom of association, expression, and religion.

Fundamental rights and freedoms are not guaranteed in China, particularly as the government continues to control and direct judicial institutions and decisions. Such control raises serious concerns about the integrity of legal proceedings in controversial cases and has made courts a less attractive venue for citizens seeking redress for official corruption, illegal land seizures, labor rights violations, and other abuses. With nowhere else to turn, people increasingly are taking to the streets, with tens of thousands of public protests, at times violent, now taking place across China each year.

2008 Beijing Olympics

In the run-up to the Olympics, authorities tightened restrictions on human rights defenders, obstructed the activities of civil society organizations, including groups devoted to assisting China's population living with HIV/AIDS, and heightened security controls on Tibetans and Uighurs. More stringent visa rules curtailed business and tourist travel into China for the duration of the games.

Olympics-related temporary regulations for foreign media freedom in effect from January 1, 2007, to October 17, 2008, gave foreign correspondents some increased freedom but failed to prevent dozens of incidents of harassment, detention, and physical assault by government officials and security forces. The government obstructed foreign journalists from reporting on "sensitive" issues, including instances of civil unrest, corruption, and detention facilities.

Despite pledges to allow foreign journalists unfettered access to the internet during the games, the Chinese government only did so after coming under intense international pressure in the days just prior to the games. It allowed access to previously blocked websites, including those of international human rights organizations. However, websites of pro-Tibetan independence groups and the Falun Gong remained blocked throughout the duration of the games.

The government targeted high-profile critics who linked human rights abuses to preparations for the games. For example, land rights activist Yang Chunlin was sentenced to five years in prison on March 24, 2008, on charges of "inciting subversion of state power," for initiating a petition titled "We Want Human Rights, Not the Olympics" that protested officials' illegal land seizures.

The government also backtracked on its promise to allow citizens to demonstrate at designated protest zones in three Beijing parks. Instead, officials announced on August 20 that that they had denied all 77 protest applications that had been filed, claiming that they had successfully resolved the applicants' concerns through "dialogue and communication." They also detained several people who made such applications, including two elderly women, Wu Dianyuan, 79, and Wang Xiuying, 77, who received a one-year sentence of "Re-education through Labor" on August 17 for seeking more compensation for the demolition of their homes. International condemnation prompted the government to rescind the sentence two weeks later.

Freedom of Expression

The Chinese government continues to strictly control journalists, and sanctions individuals and print and online media which fail to comply with extremely restrictive but unpredictably enforced laws and regulations. Potential punishments for journalists, webmasters, writers, bloggers, and editors who write or post articles critical of the political system or send news outside China range from instant dismissal to prosecution and lengthy imprisonment.

At this writing, at least 26 Chinese journalists remain in prison due to their work, many on ambiguous charges including "revealing state secrets" and "inciting subversion." They include freelance reporter Lü Gengsong, who was sentenced to four years in prison in February 2008 on charges of "inciting subversion" for stories he had written for overseas websites on corruption and the trial of a Chinese human rights activist.

CHINA

China's Forbidden Zones

Shutting the Media Out of Tibet and Other "Sensitive" Stories

HUMAN
RIGHTS
WATCH

Foreign media have been effectively barred from freely reporting in Tibetan areas with the exception of five government-organized and controlled tours since protest by monks and violence in the Tibetan capital Lhasa in March 2008. On June 26, the Foreign Ministry announced that Tibet was officially reopened to foreign media "in line with previous procedure," a process which rarely resulted in permission to freely visit Tibet.

China's censors temporarily loosened tight controls on freedom of expression in the aftermath of the May 12, 2008, Sichuan earthquake. Within days, however, domestic media were instructed to avoid reporting on topics including protests by parents of some of the thousands of children who died in the collapse of public schools during the quake. In mid-June, the Chinese government imposed tighter restrictions on foreign correspondents in the area.

The global consequences of stifled expression in China dominated post-Olympics coverage of the country. On September 10, the state media finally began to report that milk powder tainted by melamine continued to be sold domestically and internationally. Five weeks earlier, after being forced to admit the problem by an international partner, the Sanlu dairy group appealed to the government to "control and coordinate" media coverage of the issue rather than publicize it. 53,000 infants became sick and four died.

On October 17, 2008, the Chinese government permanently lifted certain restrictions on foreign journalists. However, the new freedoms do not extend to Chinese journalists and foreign journalists still have limited access to certain parts of the country, including Tibet.

Legal Reform

Despite significant achievements over the past decade in strengthening legal institutions, the Chinese Communist Party's domination of judicial institutions and inconsistent enforcement of judicial decisions has meant that the legal system remains vulnerable to arbitrary and often politically-motivated interference. In 2008 the pace of legal reforms appeared to slow.

Police torture and coerced confessions remain important criminal justice concerns. Such concerns are particularly acute in death penalty cases, though judi-

CHINA

"Walking on Thin Ice"

Control, intimidation and harassment of lawyers in China

HUMAN
RIGHTS
WATCH

cial authorities have announced a substantial decrease in the number of sentences imposed since the People's Supreme Court regained the authority to vet death penalty cases in 2007. The police also continue to make frequent use of the "Re-education through Labor" system, including for political and religious dissidents, which allows detention of "minor offenders" for up to four years without trial.

In March 2008 revisions to the Law on Lawyers were promulgated. These included some limited advances, such as affirmation of defense attorneys' procedural rights to meet their clients in detention, but failed to offer meaningful remedies for when these rights are violated. A top official from the Supreme People's Procuratorate (the public prosecution) announced in late April that defense attorneys' right to meet with criminal suspects in detention did not extend to cases involving "state secrets." The revisions also introduced a provision prohibiting lawyers from making statements in court that "harm national security."

Party and government authorities often associate lawyers with their clients' causes, rendering the lawyers vulnerable to official reprisals and undercutting efforts to establish the rule of law. In late May the Ministry of Justice threatened not to renew the professional licenses of a dozen Beijing lawyers who had publicly offered to represent Tibetan protesters. The ministry also prohibited lawyers from representing victims in two major national scandals that shook public opinion: the shoddy construction of schools that collapsed in the Sichuan earthquake, and dairy companies' poisoning of baby formula.

On May 1, new regulations regarding the disclosure of government-held information went into effect, allowing ordinary citizens to force government departments to disclose information. But an important exception is made for information classified as "state secrets," a broad category not limited to matters of national security but also to "social, economic, and cultural" information.

That tens of thousands of public protests—a fraction of them violent that erupt each year highlight the inherent dangers of not providing meaningful avenues for expression and redress for official misconduct. In one of several similar incidents in 2008, up to 30,000 people rioted in Weng'An county (Guizhou province), following suspicions that the police had tried to cover up the murder of a 15-year-old girl. The crowds torched a police station, ransacked government buildings, and overturned police cars. Chinese media disclosed shortly after the unrest that the number of such "mass incidents" had reached 90,000 in 2006—the highest number ever reported.

Human Rights Defenders

Human rights defenders faced greater than usual difficulties in 2008 as the government strove to present a picture of "harmony" to the world ahead of the Olympics. Police warned defenders and dissidents not to talk to foreign media, monitored their phone and internet communications, tracked their movements, and subjected them to varying degrees of house arrest. Other independent observers—NGO leaders, intellectuals, civil rights lawyers—were also subjected to unprecedented surveillance and monitoring.

In the months before the Olympics, petitioners trying to come to the capital to seek redress for local abuses were systematically rounded up and sent back to their home province by police and agents paid by provincial authorities, often after having been fined or detained without legal process. As a result, many activists chose to postpone or suspend their work until the games were over. Several of those who did not were jailed.

China's leading human rights activist, Hu Jia, was sentenced on April 3, 2008, to three-and-a-half years in prison after having been found guilty of "inciting subversion of state power." In August 2007, Hu was one of 42 Chinese intellectuals and activists who co-signed an open letter calling for greater attention to human rights in China. In September 2007, Hu and lawyer Teng Biao published another open letter, "The Real China and the Olympics," assessing specific human rights concerns in China in the context of the Beijing Games. On December 27, 2007, Hu was detained prior to being formally arrested on January 30, 2008. His wife, fellow activist Zeng Jinyan, remains under police surveillance in Beijing. Zeng Jinyan was detained in a hotel in Dalian in Liaoning province during the Olympics to prevent her from speaking with journalists.

Huang Qi, a Chinese internet pioneer and founder of a website through which he investigates and publicizes human rights abuses of the "nameless and powerless" was also arrested in 2008. After the May 12, 2008, earthquake in Sichuan province, Huang published reports about the efforts of parents of schoolchildren who had been killed to hold local authorities accountable for constructing sub-standard schools. Huang was detained by authorities on June 10 and formally arrested on July 18 for "illegal possession of state secrets."

Labor Rights

On January 1, 2008, the Chinese government unveiled a new Labor Contract Law, which aims to eliminate the widespread problem of employers denying workers labor contracts or failing to provide workers with copies of contracts after they have been signed. The success of the law will hinge on whether authorities enforce relevant worker protection regulations and punish employers who flout them.

A ban on independent trade unions leaves the Party-controlled All-China Federation of Trade Unions (ACFTU) as the sole legal entity dedicated to workers' rights protection. Although the ACFTU plans to extend membership rights to the estimated 150 million internal migrants who labor in Chinese towns and cities, that status is unlikely to protect them all from rampant wage exploitation, danger-ous work environments, and lack of medical and accident insurance.

China's official household registration system, or hukou, continues to deny inter-nal migrants public benefits including medical care and children's education. The Chinese government has introduced temporary household registration certificates specifically for such workers, but only a small percentage of migrants obtain the documents.

Women's Rights

Chinese women, particularly in rural areas, continue to be victims of violence, gender-based discrimination, and unequal access to services and employment. In March, the official Xinhua News Agency called domestic violence the most serious problem facing women in China. In July 2008 a Sichuan provincial court delivered China's first-ever sexual harassment conviction, sentencing a man to five months' imprisonment for harassing a female colleague.

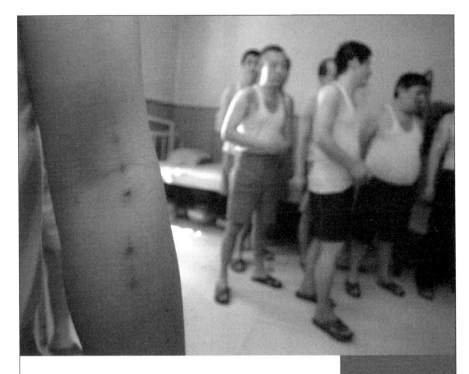

CHINA

An Unbreakable Cycle

Drug Dependency, Mandatory Confinement, and HIV/AIDS
in China's Guangxi Province

**HUMAN
RIGHTS
WATCH**

HIV/AIDS

China's HIV/AIDS policies continue to be both pragmatic and punitive. On January 1, 2008, the government took an important step in controlling the spread of HIV/AIDS and other blood-borne disease by implementing compulsory screening of all blood products. Yet overall prevention efforts were undercut by intensified repression of HIV/AIDS activists and grassroots organizations as part of a wider crackdown on "embarrassing" issues ahead of the Beijing Olympics and by abusive policies towards injecting drug users.

While the government has increased some services to injecting drug users, anti-narcotics policies continue to emphasize detention without due process in detoxification and "Re-education through Labor" centers. Drug users in such centers often have minimal access to health care or drug dependency treatment, are subject to forced labor, and are exposed to TB and HIV. In June 2008 a new anti-narcotics law went into effect which gives police broader authority to conduct searches.

Freedom of Religion

China's constitution guarantees freedom of religion, but the government restricts spiritual expression to government-registered temples, monasteries, mosques, and churches. The government vets religious personnel, seminary applications, and religious publications, and periodically audits religious institutions' activities, financial records, membership, and employees. The Chinese government considers all unregistered religious organizations, including Protestant "house churches," illegal; members risk fines and criminal prosecution. It also continues to designate certain groups as "evil cults," including the Falun Gong, and regularly cracks down on followers.

Official repression of religious activists continued during the Beijing Olympics. On August 10, police detained veteran house church leader Hua Huiqi as he was en route to a church in Beijing where US President George W. Bush was scheduled to attend religious services. Hua was confined to a makeshift detention center for several hours until he managed to escape.

Tibet

The situation in Tibetan areas sharply deteriorated in 2008. Against a backdrop of ever-more intrusive controls over religious and cultural activities, accelerated state-led economic development, and large-scale compulsory resettlement of farmers and nomads, major protests against Chinese rule erupted on March 10 in Lhasa and spread across the Tibetan plateau.

That date marked the anniversary of the failed 1959 uprising against Chinese rule. Over the next four days, hundreds of monks from Drepung, Sera, and Ganden temples peacefully protested in different locations and encountered varying degrees of police obstruction, including arrest. On March 14 near Romoche temple, members of the public started protesting police preventing monks from leaving the compound; some protesters turned violent and burned several police cars. The police retreated and then inexplicably disappeared from Lhasa for much of the rest of the day. Rioters burned Chinese shops and government buildings and attacked Chinese-looking passersby.

Chinese authorities claim that troops never opened fire but numerous witnesses say there was widespread shooting by security forces over a 36-hour period. Authorities say that 11 Chinese civilians and a Tibetan were burned to death after hiding in shops set on fire by the rioters, and that a policeman and six other civilians died from beatings of unknown causes. The Tibetan government-in-exile claims that over 80 Tibetans were killed in the police crackdown.

As protests spread throughout Tibetan areas, the government blanketed the entire plateau with military, armed police, and public security forces, and progressively expelled all foreign media. It also launched an aggressive propaganda offensive that covered only the March 14 violence and blamed the Dalai Lama for conspiring to "sabotage the Olympics Games." Several thousand alleged protesters were arrested, and although the government has announced that it subsequently released most of them, the whereabouts of several hundred remain unknown. Police and Party authorities arbitrarily arrested, detained, or fined Tibetans suspected of passing information abroad through relatives, friends, or foreigners. Two groups of foreign journalists later permitted to visit Lhasa were told by monks of a massive "patriotic education campaign" launched by the government in monasteries and places of worship.

In response to international condemnation, the government permitted 15 foreign diplomats to visit Lhasa in late March, but severely restricted their ability to speak freely to Tibetans, visit those in detention, or otherwise investigate aspects of the protests. In early April, a request from Louise Arbour, the then-UN High Commissioner for Human Rights, to visit Tibet was declined on grounds that it was "inconvenient." A separate appeal issued jointly by six UN Special Rapporteurs was similarly declined. The Olympic Torch, however, passed through Lhasa on June 21.

Xinjiang

Tensions worsened in 2008 in the Xinjiang Uighur Autonomous Region. Beijing identified Uighur separatism as one of "the top three security threats for the games," and launched a year-long security campaign focusing on "the three evil forces"—"terrorism, religious extremism, and separatism"—which resulted in even more drastic restrictions on religious, cultural, and political rights. Many Uighurs feel increasingly marginalized by rapid economic development but the government continues to prohibit domestic discussion of or reporting on human rights issues concerning Xinjiang.

The government prohibited employees and students from fasting during Ramadan, tightened control over religious personnel and mosques, reinforced civil militias, and deployed army and police patrols to prevent protests. Police also continued to confiscate Muslims' passports in an apparent bid to prevent them from making non-state-approved pilgrimages to Mecca. In February new regulations were published prohibiting "23 types of illegal religious activities," including praying in public or at wedding ceremonies. In March the authorities put down a large, peaceful demonstration in the town of Khotan.

At several points in 2008 police authorities in Xinjiang and Beijing announced that they had foiled "terrorist plots" and arrested "terrorist gangs" seeking to carry attacks during the games, but without releasing information sufficient to dispel concerns that Beijing was using counterterrorism concerns, which were legitimate—as cover for a crackdown on peaceful political opposition.

The government alleged terrorist involvement in two serious incidents. On August 4 in Kashgar two men rammed a truck in a patrol of soldiers, killing 16, and on August 10, attackers detonated a series of small home-made bombs against government buildings and Chinese shops before dawn, killing one or two people.

These incidents, which the government says demonstrate that it is facing a serious armed separatist threat in Xinjiang, have deepened the polarization between Han Chinese and Uighurs.

Hong Kong

Following a December 2007 decision by China's National People's Congress Standing Committee, Hong Kong authorities repeatedly stated that the government had a "clear timetable" to move toward election by universal suffrage of the chief executive in 2017 and of all members of the Legislative Council in 2020.

Immigration authorities' refusal to allow several visitors critical of China's human rights record into Hong Kong ahead of the Olympics raised concerns that the territory's autonomy was being eroded.

Key International Actors

International criticism of China's rights record remained muted in 2008. Many of the abuses taking place in conjunction with the Olympics were enabled by near-total silence from other governments, the International Olympic Committee, and the corporate sponsors of the games, many of which had justified their support for the games by claiming the event would improve human rights.

Formal human rights dialogues with the Chinese government—conducted by the United States and others—failed to produce any measurable improvements. In October 2008 the European Parliament awarded the Sakharov Prize to Chinese activist Hu Jia.

China is due to be reviewed under the Universal Periodic Review mechanism of the UN Human Rights Council in February 2009.

INDIA

Despite an overarching commitment to respecting citizens' freedom to express their views, peacefully protest, and form their own organizations, the Indian government lacks the will and capacity to implement many laws and policies designed to ensure the protection of rights. There is a pattern of denial of justice and impunity, whether it is in cases of human rights violations by security forces, or the failure to protect women, children, and marginalized groups such Dalits, tribal groups, and religious minorities. The failure to properly investigate and prosecute those responsible leads to continuing abuses.

While India claims that its national and state human rights commissions ensure protection of human rights, these commissions are not fully independent—their members and chair are appointed by the government—they lack sufficient resources to conduct their own investigations, and they are not empowered to investigate violations by the army.

Violence continues in secessionist conflicts in northern Jammu and Kashmir and in Manipur, low intensity insurgencies in other parts of the northeast, and the Maoist conflict in several states of central India. In efforts to contain the armed groups, Indian security forces are responsible for extrajudicial killings, arbitrary detention, due process violations, and ill-treatment in custody. Laws such as the Armed Forces (Special Powers) Act sanction impunity.

Armed groups are responsible for human rights abuses against civilians including the use of explosive devices and landmines, forced recruitment including of children, threats, extortion, and killings. Bomb blasts in Guwahati, Ahmedabad, Jaipur, Delhi, and other Indian cities in 2008 claimed hundreds of lives. Police attributed most of these attacks to Muslim extremists.

Protests in Jammu and Kashmir

While the level of violence has decreased, failure to investigate human rights violations transparently and prosecute those responsible remains a strong reason for public anger. Kashmiris believe that many of the thousands "disappeared" over the last two decades were dumped into unmarked graves. The government has ignored calls for an independent investigation by human rights groups to determine the fate of the victims.

Widespread protests erupted in Jammu and Kashmir after a state government decision in May 2008 to transfer forest land to a Hindu trust to build temporary shelters during an annual Hindu pilgrimage called "Amarnath Yatra." Several people were killed and many injured in the protests, and the issue fueled religious tension. Security forces used tear gas and opened fire using live ammunition as well as rubber bullets to control protesters who set fires, damaged government property, hurled stones, and in some cases attacked policemen.

Separatist groups announced a boycott of state assembly elections in late 2008 and called for demonstrations.

Violence in Manipur and Other Northeastern States

Violence has continued in the northeast, particularly in Manipur, where over 300 people, including nearly a hundred civilians, were killed in the armed conflict in 2008. Caught between the armed groups and security forces, civilians also remain victims of human rights abuses.

A series of bomb attacks in Guwahati and other cities in Assam on October 30, 2008, killed 84 people and injured hundreds. Police believe the bombings may have been acts of revenge for earlier attacks on Bangladeshi Muslim settlers by local tribes in which nearly 50 people were killed.

In Manipur, security forces have been responsible for extrajudicial killings and torture. The impunity and free rein given to government forces has led to a culture where many soldiers and police officers appear to believe it is easier to kill suspects than gather evidence to secure convictions.

Despite the large deployment of government forces, armed groups claiming to protect the rights of the various ethnic communities in Manipur have succeeded in imposing their will on many communities. Manipuris are forced to build alliances with one group to ensure protection from the rest. Armed groups are responsible for extortion, killings, forced recruitment—including of children—and imposition of moral diktats, often by force.

INDIA

"These Fellows
Must Be Eliminated"

Relentless Violence and Impunity in Manipur

**HUMAN
RIGHTS
WATCH**

Naxalite Conflict

Maoist armed groups, also called Naxalites, continue to carry out bombings, abductions, beatings, and killings in several Indian states including Chhattisgarh. Security forces have responded with arbitrary detention, torture, and extrajudicial killings of suspected Naxalites or their alleged supporters.

The Naxalites claim to be fighting for the rights of the marginalized tribal groups, Dalits, and the poor, but have been responsible for forced recruitment and severe punishment of those who refuse to submit to demands for cash, shelter, and protection.

In Chhattisgarh, government security forces and state-government-backed vigilantes called the Salwa Judum are responsible for attacking, killing, and forcibly displacing tens of thousands of people in armed operations against Maoist rebels. The Naxalite rebels retaliate in a brutal manner, abducting, assaulting, and killing civilians perceived to be Salwa Judum supporters. The government has chosen to view those who do not join the Salwa Judum as Naxalite supporters.

All parties to the Chhattisgarh conflict have used children in armed operations. The Naxalites admit that it is standard practice to recruit children age 16 and above in their forces; they have used children as young as 12 in some armed operations. The Salwa Judum have included children in their violent attacks against villages as part of their anti-Naxalite campaign. The Chhattisgarh state police admit that in the past they recruited children under age 18 as special police officers, but claim they did so due to the absence of age documentation and that all children have now been removed from the ranks. Human Rights Watch investigators in Chhattisgarh found that underage special police officers continue to serve with the police and are used in counter-Naxalite combing operations.

Impunity

While law enforcement is needed to end the violence perpetrated by militants, India continues to provide extraordinary powers to its troops and grants them immunity from prosecution when they abuse those powers and commit human rights violations.

INDIA

"Being Neutral
is Our Biggest Crime"

Government, Vigilante, and Naxalite Abuses in India's Chhattisgarh State

HUMAN
RIGHTS
WATCH

The Armed Forces (Special Powers) Act was enacted on August 18, 1958, as a short-term measure to allow deployment of the army in the northeast. The law has remained in force in various parts of the country for five decades. It provides the armed forces with sweeping powers to shoot to kill, arrest, and search in violation of international human rights law. The law has led to widespread human rights abuses and protects troops from prosecution for such crimes.

Protection of Vulnerable Communities

The government has failed to protect vulnerable communities including Dalits, tribal groups, and religious minorities.

Since August 2008, supporters of the Hindu militant groups Vishwa Hinud Parishad and Bajrang Dal in Orissa have attacked Christians, many of them tribal minorities or Dalits. The militants have burned churches, beat priests and nuns, and destroyed property. Several policemen were suspended for dereliction of duty after a nun alleged that she was raped. At this writing, at least 40 persons had died in the violence, with scores injured and thousands internally displaced.

Failure to secure justice for the 2002 Gujarat riots—in which more than 2,000 Muslims were killed following an attack on a train carrying Hindu pilgrims—has fueled anger amongst Muslims. Police continue to arbitrarily round up and detain Muslims nationwide after bomb blasts; many have alleged they were tortured during interrogation and forced into signing false confessions. Muslims also face discrimination in access to housing and jobs and the Indian government does little to protect them.

Despite a scheme launched four years ago to provide universal education, millions of children in India still have no access to education and work long hours, many as bonded laborers. Many children continue to be trafficked for marriage, sex work, or employment. Others languish in substandard orphanages or detention centers.

A case is still pending before the Supreme Court seeks to strike down Section 377 of the Indian Penal Code—a British colonial provision—so as to decriminalize consensual homosexual conduct between adults. While some officials, including the health minister, support repealing the law, others have vigorously defended it. In

INDIA

Getting Away With Murder

50 Years of the Armed Forces Special Powers Act

HUMAN
RIGHTS
WATCH

October 2008, police in Bangalore arrested five *hijras*—transgender women—and then detained 37 human rights defenders and activists who came to assist them, beating and sexually abusing some of them.

According to the National AIDS Control Organization, more than 2.5 million people are living with HIV. Four southern states (Andhra Pradesh, Maharashtra, Tamil Nadu, and Karnataka) account for nearly two-thirds of those infected. Although antiretroviral therapy is supposed to be freely available at public health facilities, there are significant regional disparities in implementation of the policy.

Children and adults living with HIV/AIDS, as well as those whose marginalized status puts them at highest risk—internal migrants, sex workers, injection drug users, men who have sex with men, and transgender populations—face widespread stigmatization and discrimination, including denial of employment, access to education, orphan care, and healthcare.

Human Rights Defenders

The trial of Dr. Binayak Sen, a physician and human rights activist with the People's Union for Civil Liberties (PUCL), began in May 2008 in Chhattisgarh. Sen was detained in May 2007 under the Chhattisgarh Special Public Security Act and accused of having links to the Naxalites. In May 2008 police arrested filmmaker and PUCL member Ajay TG under the same act for alleged links to unlawful Maoist organizations. He was granted bail in August after the government failed to file charges within the mandatory 90 days stipulated in the act.

Key International Actors

As a strong emerging economy, India has built crucial trade links with the European Union and United States. After signing a deal with the US to secure nuclear supplies for civilian use, in 2008 India won a waiver from the 45-nation Nuclear Suppliers Group to lift restrictions on nuclear commerce. The restrictions were imposed after India carried out its first nuclear test in 1974.

In 2008 several key international partners were disappointed by India's refusal to take a strong public position against ongoing human rights violations in Burma

and Sri Lanka. In response to the renewed crackdown on dissent in Burma, New Delhi stopped the supply of lethal weapons to the Burmese military but otherwise offered only a tepid response, saying it believed in private engagement with the Burmese regime.

India initially refused to join the international community in demanding better human rights protections during the ongoing war in Sri Lanka. In September 2008 India finally expressed concern amid unconfirmed reports that civilians were increasingly being caught in the middle of the fighting, at risk from both government forces and the Liberation Tigers of Tamil Eelam. In November India agreed to ship relief materials for distribution by the International Committee for the Red Cross.

India has routinely ignored recommendations from UN human rights bodies including, UN committees on the elimination of racial discrimination and discrimination against women. India is a member of the UN Human Rights Council (HRC) and in 2008 came up for Universal Periodic Review by the HRC, agreeing to several recommendations including that it sign and ratify UN treaties banning torture and enforced disappearances.

INDONESIA

Indonesia saw little human rights progress in 2008. Basic freedoms in the country expanded dramatically following the resignation of President Suharto in 1998, transforming Indonesia from an authoritarian state to a vibrant if chaotic democracy. Today, there is a loss of momentum, with reforms in key areas bogged down and backtracking in some areas.

Apart from halting progress in prosecutions for the murder of prominent activist Munir Said Thalib, efforts to pursue accountability for past human rights crimes remain at a complete standstill. Current abuses, including endemic police torture, also routinely go unpunished.

In a major setback for religious freedom, the government in 2008 bowed to pressure from hard-line Islamic groups and banned the Ahmadiyah sect from publicly practicing their faith.

Indonesia has a diverse and lively media sector, but freedom of expression has been undermined by powerful officials and businessmen using criminal and civil defamation laws to silence criticism.

In Indonesian Papua, deeply rooted distrust of Jakarta is still a time bomb; failure to address human rights—including security force abuses—is one important reason the distrust has not been dispelled.

Impunity

Former president Suharto died in January 2008 having escaped prosecution for abuses committed during his 32-year rule. The list of abuses is extensive, and includes anticommunist pogroms that killed half a million or more people in 1965-1966, security force atrocities in East Timor, Aceh, southern Sumatra, and Papua, and the Trisakti and Semanggi killings in Jakarta in 1998-1999. Many collaborators in Suharto-era abuses still hold positions of power. Several are candidates for the forthcoming 2009 elections, including General Wiranto and Suharto's son-in-law Prabowo Subianto, implicated in abuses in East Timor and other crimes.

In March 2008 the Indonesian Supreme Court overturned the conviction of former militia leader Eurico Guterres for instigating violence following the 1999 UN-sponsored referendum on independence for East Timor. Indonesian-army-backed militias killed hundreds of Timorese and destroyed much of East Timor's physical infrastructure. With the reversal of the conviction, all 18 people indicted by the Indonesian Ad Hoc Human Rights Court on East Timor have been acquitted.

The Indonesian and Timorese joint Commission on Truth and Friendship released its final report in July 2008 assigning institutional responsibility for the 1999 atrocities to the Indonesian military, police, and government. UN Secretary-General Ban Ki-moon urged accountability, but President Susilo Bambang Yudhoyono insisted that no such action would be taken.

In August a military court convicted 13 marines for killing four civilians and wounding eight in a 2007 incident involving a land dispute in Pasuruan, East Java. The marines received light sentences of 18 months to three-and-a-half years.

Also in August, a US court ruled that a lawsuit against Exxon Mobil for alleged complicity in military abuses in Aceh could proceed to trial.

Military Business

Efforts to end Indonesian military business activity, a barrier to full civilian control of the armed forces, showed few results in 2008. An April presidential decree created a new advisory team on military business reform but it remained unclear whether the government would fully dismantle the military's economic interests before October 2009 as mandated by law.

While the government has focused on legal businesses, military involvement in illegal businesses, including in the logging and oil palm sector, also continues to feed corruption and generate conflicts of interest.

Freedom of Religion

In June 2008 the government ordered members of the Ahmadiyah sect to cease public religious activities or face up to five years' imprisonment. In the weeks following the decree, Muslim hardliners attacked Ahmadiyah mosques in Cianjur,

West Java, and Islamic Defenders Front members closed the local Ahmadiyah headquarters in Makassar, South Sulawesi. In September the South Sumatra provincial government issued a total ban on Ahmadiyah, claiming the ministerial decree did not go far enough.

In January 2008 a mob burnt down the Sangkareang Hindu temple in West Lombok and in July, Muslim hardliners attacked students at a Christian theology school in East Jakarta, injuring 18 and forcing the school to shut its 20-year-old campus.

In April, Abdul Salam, the self-proclaimed prophet and founder of the Islamic sect Al-Qiyadah Al-Islamiyah, was sentenced to four years' imprisonment for "blasphemy." Indonesian laws prohibiting blasphemy are primarily applied to practices perceived to deviate from mainstream Islam.

Migrant Domestic Workers

Approximately two million Indonesians, mostly women, work abroad. Many migrate as domestic workers and are subject to a range of human rights violations (see Saudi Arabia and Malaysia chapters). Prior to departure, poorly monitored labor recruiters often deceive workers about their jobs abroad and impose excessive fees, placing the migrants at risk of trafficking and forced labor.

Many Indonesian foreign missions in the Persian Gulf and Asia operate temporary shelters for the thousands of domestic workers facing abuses each year. Despite recent improvements, foreign missions often fall short of meeting minimum requirements including in the areas of shelter, case management, and legal representation.

Child Domestic Workers

More than 700,000 children, mainly girls, work as domestic workers in Indonesia. Typically recruited between the ages of 12 and 15, often on false promises of decent wages and working conditions, they may work 14 to 18 hours a day, seven days a week, earning far less than the prevailing minimum wage. In the worst cases, child domestic workers are paid no salary at all and are physically, sexually, and psychologically abused.

Domestic workers are excluded from existing national labor laws, which afford protections such as minimum wage, an eight-hour work day, weekly day of rest, and vacation time. At this writing, draft national legislation that would mandate an eight-hour work day, a weekly day of rest, and an annual holiday for domestic workers remained stalled in the Ministry of Manpower.

Aceh

Six political parties in Aceh will take part in general elections in 2009. All party candidates must take a Quran reading test administered by Aceh's election commission, which discriminates against qualified secular or non-Muslim Acehnese.

There remains no accountability for past human rights violations committed during or after the Aceh conflict and there has been no movement toward establishing a truth and reconciliation commission.

Papua and West Papua

Despite dozens of Indonesian government statements pledging a new approach in Papua and positive developments on some fronts, justice has noticeably lagged.Security forces, including special Mobile Brigade (Brimob) police units, continue to engage in abuses in remote highland regions with virtual impunity.

Freedom of expression also continues to be corralled. In March police jailed nine Papuan activists for displaying the Papuan "Morning Star" flag. They remain in detention charged with rebellion (*makar*), a crime punishable by life imprisonment. In July police assaulted 46 protesters and charged six with rebellion for raising the Morning Star flag in Fakfak, West Papua. In August police fired live ammunition into a crowd, killing a peaceful demonstrator after protesters raised the Morning Star flag in Wamena.

Death Penalty

After a 14-month hiatus, Indonesia resumed executions in June 2008, killing two Nigerians convicted of drug trafficking. In July and August four Indonesians convicted of multiple murders were executed. In November, authorities executed Amrozi, Mukhlas, and Imam Samudra, convicted for the 2002 Bali bombings that killed 202 people.Over 100 people remain on death row in Indonesia.

Freedom of Expression and Press

In April 2008, the House of Representatives passed a freedom of information law after seven years of debate. Critics are concerned with a vaguely worded provision criminalizing "deliberate misuse" of public information.

Criminal and civil defamation laws continue to be used to silence press criticism. In February 2008, *Time Magazine* submitted a petition to reverse the $US110 million libel ruling against it in favor of the Suharto family. In September a Jakarta court found Indonesia's *Tempo* magazine guilty of defaming agribusiness giant Asian Agri for an investigative report on alleged tax evasion. In June 2008 a court convicted and jailed Risang Bima Wijaya, a Yogyakarta-based reporter, for an article on sexual harassment ruled to have insulted the manager of a local newspaper.

Human Rights Defenders

In January 2008 the Supreme Court reconvicted Garuda Airways pilot Pollycarpus Budihari Priyanto, and sentenced him to 20 years in prison for the 2004 murder of human rights defender Munir Said Thalib. An Indonesian court sentenced Indra Setiawan, a former airline official, to one year in prison for being an accessory.reinvigorated police investigations uncovered key evidence linking Muchdi Purwopranjono—a former general, special forces commander, and deputy national intelligence chief—with Pollycarpus and the murder of Munir.

In a January 2008 report on Indonesia, Hina Jilani, UN expert on human rights defenders, concluded that defenders in Papua are particularly vulnerable to threats, harassment, arbitrary detention, and torture. She also noted that while conditions for defenders in Aceh have improved since the 2005 peace agreement, no perpetrators have been brought to justice for abuses committed against defenders there between 2001 and 2005.

Key International Actors

United States Defense Secretary Robert Gates visited Indonesia in February 2008 offering increased military assistance to the Indonesian military. The US military has not resumed cooperation with Kopassus (special forces) and Brimob (antiriot police), units notorious for rights abuses.

Forty members of the US House of Representatives sent a letter to Yudhoyono in July 2008, requesting the release of Papuan political prisoners Filep Karma and Yusak Pakage.

Relations between Indonesia and Australia were strengthened through the June 2008 visit of Australian Prime Minister Kevin Rudd. Rudd and Indonesian President Yudhoyono discussed security cooperation and signed a joint Forest Carbon Partnership agreement, but Indonesia's commitment to curbing deforestation remained in doubt with corruption rampant in the forestry section and inadequate timber and financial tracking systems.

In April 2008 the UN Human Rights Council examined Indonesia's human rights record as part of the new Universal Periodic Review (UPR) process. Concerns put to Indonesia during the UPR dialogue included continuing impunity, torture, arrests, detention of peaceful political activists, and human rights violations in Papua.Indonesia made no clear commitments to address ongoing violations in Papua, but it agreed to criminalize torture and ratify the Optional Protocol of the Convention against Torture.

In May 2008 the UN Committee against Torture issued findings that both police and military routinely use torture; it expressed concern that no Indonesian official has been convicted of the offense.

As a key ASEAN member, Indonesia continues to press Burma to release Aung San Suu Kyi. Indonesia played a pivotal role in ASEAN efforts to convince Burma to lift a ban on foreign assistance following the devastating Cyclone Nargis in May.

In October Indonesia's Parliament ratified the ASEAN Charter, but lawmakers and officials said they would press for future changes to strengthen its compliance with international standards and establish penalties for non-compliant members.

In September 2008 the Norwegian government abandoned its US$1 billion investment in Rio Tinto over concerns with unethical conduct and environmental devastation at the Grasberg gold and copper mine in Papua.

MALAYSIA

Hopes that Malaysia's human rights climate would improve following elections in March 2008 proved unfounded. The ruling National Front coalition lost the two-thirds parliamentary majority it had enjoyed since Malaysia became independent in 1957 but was still in power at this writing. National Front leaders continue to insist that Malaysia's multiethnic society is too fragile to sustain genuine freedom of assembly and expression or full due process rights for all suspects.

The government continues to use outdated repressive laws and regulations to silence its critics and extend its rule. One such critic is former Deputy Prime Minister Anwar Ibrahim, now leading the opposition coalition People's Alliance. In what was widely viewed as a politically motivated attempt to discredit him, police charged him with consensual sexual relations with a male aide in August 2008.

The People's Volunteer Corps, a largely volunteer paramilitary force, continues to commit abuses against undocumented migrants, refugees, and asylum seekers.

Detention without Charge or Trial

Malaysia uses the Internal Security Act (ISA) to indefinitely detain, without charge or trial, individuals deemed by officials to threaten Malaysia's national security. This includes not only individuals suspected of planning terrorist attacks, such as members of the militant Islamist groups Jemaah Islamiah and Darul Islam, but also individuals allegedly promoting ethnic or religious discord.

On December 13, 2007, after the Hindu Rights Action Force (Hindraf) organized a massive rally to draw attention to discrimination faced by Malaysia's Indian population, the government detained five of its leaders. In October 2008, the government declared Hindraf an illegal organization on the grounds that it constituted a "threat to public order and morality." As of late November 2008, the leaders remained in ISA custody.

On September 12, 2008, police detained three government critics under the ISA. Raja Petra Kumaruddin, founder and editor of Malaysia's most popular website *MalaysiaToday*, was originally detained for two years for insulting Islam but was

freed on procedural grounds on October 7. The government is appealing the ruling. Authorities also detained opposition Democratic Action Party parliamentarian
Teresa Kok for a week for involvement in "activities that may spark a religious dispute," and Tan Hoon Cheng, a *Sin Chew Daily* reporter, for 18 hours.

According to the Abolish ISA Movement (Gerakan Mansuhkan ISA), 64 individuals
were in ISA detention as of October 2008.

Migrant Workers, Refugees, and Asylum Seekers

According to Malaysia's Immigration Department, there were 2.1 million documented migrants in Malaysia in November 2007. Undocumented migrants are
estimated at over 400,000, some 150,000 of whom are refugees or asylum seekers.

As the Malaysian Immigration Act of 1959/1963 does not distinguish between
undocumented migrant workers and refugees, all those without valid residency
status are subject to arrest, detention, and deportation. The People's Volunteer
Corps (RELA), numbering half a million members, is empowered by law to enter
any premises and arrest "undesirable persons" and suspected undocumented
migrants. No search or arrest warrants are necessary. During 2007, close to
60,000 migrants—including children—were arrested, imprisoned, or deported.
Most migrant children are denied access to schools and some end up in exploitative forms of child labor.

In May and June 2008, migrants told Human Rights Watch researchers how RELA
members abused them with impunity during detention and in the immigration
detention centers where RELA is responsible for security. Abuses include physical
assault, intimidation, forced entry into living quarters, extortion, theft, destruction of residency papers, and sexual abuse.

Testimonies from migrants, refugees, and asylum seekers deported from Malaysia
to the Thai border indicate collusion between Malaysian immigration officials and
human smuggling gangs who charge steep fees to facilitate deportees' return to
Malaysia or back to Burma.

Cases of severe physical abuse of migrant domestic workers continue to be reported. In September 2008 a Malaysian employer forced an Indonesian domestic worker to drink boiling water. The criminal justice system has been slow to respond. A verdict in the case of Nirmala Bonat, burned and brutally beaten by her employer in 2004, was expected in late November 2008.

Many of the approximately 400,000 primarily Indonesian domestic workers in Malaysia experience withheld wages, forced confinement, and excessively long work hours without days off; some face physical and sexual abuse. Domestic workers are excluded from key provisions of Malaysia's 1955 Employment Act and their work permits tie them to a particular employer, making it difficult to report abuse for fear of deportation.

Freedom of Assembly and Police Abuse

Article 10 of Malaysia's constitution guarantees freedom of assembly, but the Police Act of 1967 severely restricts its exercise in practice. No more than four persons may assemble in public without a police license. Police are empowered to break up unlicensed demonstrations, arrest participants, and use force if orders to disperse are ignored. In January 2008 a peaceful protest organized by NGOs and opposition political parties targeting inflationary pressure resulted in 56 short detentions.

Excessive use of force at public demonstrations is one of the reasons that a May 2005 Royal Commission recommended the establishment of an Independent Police Complaints and Misconduct Commission. No such commission has been created.

Freedom of Expression

An increasingly vibrant blogosphere and use of electronic media and communications are challenging longstanding restrictions on free expression, but authorities continue periodic crackdowns on dissent.

On August 25, the Malaysian Communications and Multimedia Commission ordered all 19 internet service providers to block *MalaysiaToday*, suggesting it published "libelous, defamatory and slanderous" material threatening public order. Postings had probed government activities the leadership apparently did not want exposed. The Malaysian cabinet overturned the closure order on September 11.

The broadly worded 1948 Sedition Act has been used to silence bloggers who express grievances against the government or who "promote feelings of ill will and hostility between" ethnic groups in Malaysia. In October 2008, Kamaruddin was put on trial for sedition for an article he wrote about a 2006 murder case.

The 1984 Printing Presses and Publications Act censors newspapers by requiring annual renewal of publishing licenses and by controlling production and distribution of foreign publications. The Home Affairs Ministry can restrict or ban a publication outright on several different vaguely defined grounds and no legal remedy or judicial review is available.

In September 2008 the ministry instructed three newspapers to "show cause" why their publication licenses should not be suspended or rescinded. *Sin Chew Daily*, a Chinese-language paper, had reported on allegedly sensitive issues affecting ethnic relations; *The Sun*, an English Daily, was cited for "manipulating and playing up numerous sensitive issues," and *Suara Keadilan*, the People's Justice Party internal publication, had claimed that an official became paralyzed after heart surgery.

Freedom of Religion

Islam is Malaysia's official state religion, but the constitution protects freedom of religion for all. Tensions periodically arise over whether Malaysia is a secular or religious state and over attempts to widen or restrict the jurisdiction of Sharia courts.

On August 9, 2008, some 300 protestors disrupted an open forum entitled "Conversion to Islam," sponsored by the Malaysian Bar Council. The protestors contended that non-Muslims had no right to discuss Islam. The forum addressed issues faced by families caught in jurisdictional disputes on matters such as civil marriage, divorce and custody battles, and burial rites.

Privacy

Section 377 of Malaysia's criminal code criminalizes "carnal intercourse against the order of nature," both consensual and non-consensual. Activists have urged Malaysian authorities to repeal provisions on consensual relations and replace the section on non-consensual sexual acts with a modern, gender-neutral law on rape.

Human Rights Defenders

The NGO community, the Malaysian bar, lawyers, journalists, and some opposition politicians actively defend human rights despite serious personal and professional risks. Police arrested and detained overnight eight activists including members of the bar and local non-governmental organizations during a December 2007 peaceful march to commemorate International Human Rights Day. Six of the eight went on trial in October 2008.

On January 6, 2008, police used water cannons to break up a vigil organized by the Abolish ISA movement. On September 26 and October 9, after more ISA arrests, police broke up additional candlelight vigils opposing the ISA. In the latter incident, police confiscated the camera of a newspaper reporter, one of 23 people temporarily detained after the vigil.

Key International Actors

Tension in the US-Malaysia relationship surfaced in 2008. While the US praised Malaysia as a regional counterterrorism leader, officials in August expressed concern over the filing of sodomy charges against Anwar Ibrahim, and in September summoned Ilango Karuppannan, the charge d'affaires at the Malaysian embassy, to protest Malaysia's crackdown on critics.

Lord Malloch-Brown, the UK's minister of state in the Foreign and Commonwealth Office, said the UK had also spoken with Malaysian officials about the crackdown and had raised the issue with its EU partners and the Commonwealth Secretariat.

In a September address to the UN, Malaysian Foreign Minister Dr. Rais Yatim objected to interference in Malaysia's internal affairs.

Although the US Department of State's June 2008 "Trafficking in Persons Report" upgraded Malaysia's status from Tier 3 to Tier 2, US Senator Lugar expressed concern about continuing reports of trafficking of Burmese at the Thai-Malay border.

Malaysia has supported the creation of an ASEAN regional human rights mechanism, but in July 2008 Foreign Minister Yatim said that its standards should reflect the "ASEAN value system," hearkening back to the "Asian values" debate and the discredited notion that Asians value human rights less than others.

NEPAL

National elections in April 2008 with the participation of former Maoist rebels and the subsequent seating of a Constituent Assembly marked a new era in Nepal after a decade of conflict that claimed over 13,000 lives. On May 28, the assembly abolished the monarchy and declared the country a republic. The deposed king moved out of the Kathmandu royal palace in June.

The Communist Party of Nepal (Maoist) (CPN-M) won more than a third of the assembly's 601 seats, making it the largest party. After months of political deadlock, the CPN-M in August formed a coalition government and Maoist leader Pushpa Kamal Dahal, also known as Prachanda, became prime minister. Women make up a third of the new assembly, a historic jump in women's representation in government.

Marginalized communities, particularly Dalits, ethnic minorities, and women, continue to face widespread discrimination. There is hope that proposed constitutional protections and new resolve from the Maoist-led government—the rebellion was fueled in part by a desire to remove discrimination against such groups—will lead to new legal protections and a significant reduction in abuses.

The new government has shown little interest in ending impunity for the widespread human rights violations committed before, during, and after the armed conflict.

Impunity

During the 1996-2006 armed conflict both security forces and the Maoist rebels were responsible for human rights abuses. Security forces committed hundreds of extrajudicial killings, widespread torture, and, in some years, the largest number of "disappearances" in the world. Maoist forces abducted, tortured, and killed civilians suspected of being "informers" or "enemies of the revolution," extorted "donations" from villagers, recruited children as soldiers, and abducted students for political indoctrination. Maoists often executed their victims in public, forcing the victim's relatives and other villagers to observe the killing.

NEPAL

Waiting for Justice

Unpunished Crimes from Nepal's Armed Conflict

HUMAN
RIGHTS
WATCH

Even after they signed a peace agreement in November 2006, both the army and Maoists failed to cooperate with police investigations. At this writing, not a single perpetrator had been brought to justice before a civilian court. The Nepal Army continues to resist accountability. The police, subservient to the army, resist filing cases of human rights violations.

In one success, Kavre District police on August 11, 2008, following a Supreme Court order, finally registered a complaint for the murder of royalist party member Arjun Bahadur Lama in December 2005. But despite court orders and interventions from local and international organizations, no arrest followed.

Morang District police still have not filed a criminal complaint in the case of civilian Madhuram Gautam, allegedly killed by army personnel in December 2004, despite court orders and repeated appeals by local and international organizations.

The lack of political will to address such crimes is also reflected in proposals to grant an amnesty for serious human rights abuses committed during the conflict. Draft laws on both a truth and reconciliation commission and a disappearances commission contain such an amnesty.

In September 2008 the ruling parties affirmed their commitment to establish commissions on national peace and rehabilitation, truth and reconciliation, "disappearances," and land reform, but had not made significant progress on establishing any of them at this writing.

Impunity for killings continues. Paramilitary police deployed for the security of Khum Bahadur Khadka, a former minister and Nepali Congress candidate, killed seven Maoists on April 7, 2008. Accounts conflict as to who initiated fire, but reports suggest that police used excessive force. The families of the victims have filed complaints, but police had taken no action at this writing.

There were widespread protests after the May 8, 2008, torture and killing of businessman Ram Hari Shrestha. Members of the People's Liberation Army, the armed wing of the CPN-M, are believed responsible.

Armed Combatants in UN Cantonments

Under the November 2006 Comprehensive Peace Agreement, Maoist cadres were registered in cantonment sites under the protection of the United Nations Mission in Nepal (UNMIN), which also took custody of their weapons. According to UNMIN, after the verification of registered Maoist combatants was completed in December 2007, 15,756 men and 3,846 women remain in the cantonments. CPN-M wants to ensure that the former fighters are integrated into government security forces or provided alternate livelihoods.

In October 2008 the government said it would set up a special committee to ensure proper rehabilitation of combatants, but at this writing, there were still disagreements on the extent to which Maoist combatants should be integrated into the Nepal army.

Child Soldiers

During the conflict, an estimated 6,000 to 9,000 Maoist cadres were believed to have been children. Not all were cantoned after the conflict, however, making a precise count impossible. UNMIN has reported that over 3000 child recruits remain in the cantonment sites.

The government of Nepal now including the Maoists has said it will not use or enlist children age 18 or below in any military force and that all child soldiers will be properly rehabilitated. To date, these policies are not being properly implemented. Without proper rehabilitation and reintegration, many child combatants have found their way into violent groups such as the Young Communist League (YCL), the youth wing of the CPN-M.

Youth Communist League

The YCL has been implicated in abductions, beatings, and killings since it was re-established in December 2006. Violent attacks attributed to the YCL against perceived political opponents intensified before and after the April 10, 2008, elections. The YCL is comprised mainly of former People's Liberation Army commanders; its members are age 16-40.

The YCL has assumed broad powers to patrol communities across the country and "arrest" and punish offenders, saying police are failing to perform this function. Anointing itself the moral guardian and arbiter of disputes, the YCL has attacked political opponents, journalists, alleged drug users, and individuals suspected of extramarital relations. On August 6, ahead of his election as prime minister, Maoist chairman Prachandra ordered all party members including the YCL to halt violent activities.

Torture

Despite Nepal having ratified the Convention against Torture and other Cruel, Inhumane or Degrading Punishment, torture is still not a criminal offense in Nepal. Between January 1 and June 30, 2008, Advocacy Forum, a Nepal-based NGO, interviewed 1,423 detainees in their regular visits to 35 detention centers across 16 districts. Of this number, 396—124 of them children—claimed they had been tortured or ill-treated by police. The cases show a pattern of police abuse of juvenile suspects, with long periods of illegal detention, lack of access to adequate medical and legal assistance, and inhumane treatment including frequent and multiple beatings.

Situation in the Terai Region

Ethnic tensions continued in Nepal in 2008 over the rights of Madheshi communities in the southern Terai region. In February a strike by Madheshi groups turned violent. While the protesters threw stones and petrol bombs, targeting police posts and destroying government property, the police used lethal force to control the protest. At least six persons were killed and hundreds, including some police officers, were injured.

Arbitrary Arrest and Torture of Tibetans

After March 10, 2008, Tibetans living in Katmandu conducted a series of protests against the Chinese government's harsh crackdown in Tibet. Nepali authorities, in their efforts to appease China, opposed such demonstrations and engaged in unnecessary and excessive use of force, arbitrary arrest, sexual assault of women

during arrest, arbitrary and preventive detention, beatings in detention, unlawful threats to deport Tibetans to China, and unnecessary restrictions on freedom of movement in the Katmandu Valley.

The government has in effect sealed the border to prevent the arrival of Tibetan refugees and has allowed Chinese security personnel to operate on the Nepali side of the border.

Lesbian, Gay, Bisexual, and Transgender Rights

In December 2007 Nepal's Supreme Court directed the government to repeal laws criminalizing homosexual conduct and laws otherwise discriminating against sexual minorities. The court also directed the government to official recognize a "third gender" in addition to "male" and "female," and established a committee to explore same-sex marriage for Nepal. No other country in South Asia has taken these steps.

Human Rights Defenders

Human rights defenders, especially women defenders, continue to face attacks. The Youth Communist League has been involved in several violent attacks against defenders, journalists, and political opponents but such cases are usually not investigated by police.

Key International Actors

Nepal relies on the aid and support of foreign governments including India, China, the United States, the United Kingdom, the European Union, and Japan. These actors have at times played an important role in strengthening human rights protection and demanding an end to impunity and security sector reform.

The US has still not removed the CPN-M from its terrorist exclusion list.

Nepali Prime Minister Dahal visited India in September and November 2008, and India assured him of economic assistance and help drafting a new constitution. Dahal also visited China to build economic and strategic ties.

On July 23, the Security Council extended the UNMIN monitoring mission until January 23, 2009. Despite budget reductions, the Office of the High Commissioner for Human Rights continues to play a significant role in Nepal investigating human rights violations, including "disappearances," and seeking accountability for abuses committed during the conflict.

North Korea

Human rights conditions in the Democratic People's Republic of Korea (North Korea) remain dire. There is no organized political opposition, independent labor unions, free media, or civil society. Arbitrary arrest, detention, and lack of due process remain serious concerns.

North Korea runs large prison camps where hundreds of thousands of its citizens—including children—are enslaved in deplorable conditions. Periodically, the government publicly executes individuals for stealing state property, hoarding food, and other "anti-socialist" crimes. There is no freedom of religion.

Individuals who leave the country without state permission are often considered traitors and can face lengthy prison terms and possible execution upon return. Ahead of and during the Beijing Olympic Games, China stepped up the arrest and repatriation of North Korean refugees and migrants.

Officials in Washington and Seoul said leader Kim Jong Il was believed to have suffered a stroke in September 2008. Because Kim Jong Il wields such extensive power, his failing health, if true, could have far-reaching consequences for human rights and governance in North Korea.

Right to Food

While the nationwide famine of the 1990s has not returned, food shortages persist and the country's vulnerable population suffered another hungry year in 2008. Non-elite members of society now purchase their food and necessities at markets that have replaced the largely defunct ration system. Only a small minority of the population, mostly high-ranking members of the Workers' Party and the security and intelligence forces, still receive regular rations.

Food prices in North Korea continued to rise in 2008, although not as steeply as in 2007, while experts on North Korea's agriculture industry offered widely different assessments of the extent of food shortages.

North Koreans in China

Hundreds of thousands of North Koreans fled to China in the 1990s. Many settled in the Yanbian Korean Autonomous Prefecture in eastern Jilin Province, near China's border with North Korea. As a state party to the 1951 Refugee Convention, China has an obligation to offer protection to refugees, but Beijing categorically labels North Koreans in China "illegal" economic migrants and routinely repatriates them. As noted above, the consequences for returnees can be severe.

North Korean women who live with Chinese men in de facto marriages—even if they have lived in China for years—are not entitled to legal residence and remain vulnerable to arrest and repatriation. Some North Korean women and girls are abducted or duped into marriage or prostitution in China.

Ahead of and during the August 2008 Olympic Games in Beijing, Chinese police arrested and repatriated many North Koreans from Yanbian. While no official statistics are available, local residents say that in some villages only a small minority of North Koreans who had lived there a year ago remain. Some fled to third countries with the ultimate goal of reaching South Korea, while others were arrested and repatriated.

Thousands of children in Yanbian who were born to North Korean mothers live without a legal identity or access to elementary education. North Korean children who migrate to China have no legal right to obtain the household registration papers that many schools demand. Children with Chinese fathers sometimes are not registered in the household registration to avoid exposing their mothers.

By law, neither North Korean nor half-North Korean children should be required to submit legal identity papers for admittance to schools since Chinese law provides that all children regardless of nationality are entitled to nine years of free education, but in reality, most schools require such documentation. Some parents and guardians of North Korean children resort to bribery or trickery in order to ensure children can go to school.

Refugees and Asylum Seekers outside China

A relatively small number of North Koreans in China have managed to reach South Korea, Japan, or the United States via other countries in the region, including Mongolia and Thailand. South Korea accepts all North Koreans as citizens under its constitution. South Korea has admitted more than 13,000 North Koreans, Japan has accepted more than 100, and the US has accepted a few dozen so far. Canada, Japan, Germany, the United Kingdom, and a few other European countries have granted refugee status to several hundred North Koreans in recent years.

North Korean Workers

In North Korea's Kaesong Industrial Complex, more than 35,000 North Korean workers produce mostly consumer goods for South Korean businesses. The law governing working conditions in the complex falls far short of international standards on freedom of association, the right to collective bargaining, gender discrimination and sexual harassment, and hazardous child labor.

North Koreans are also reportedly employed in Bulgaria, China, Iraq, Kuwait, Mongolia, and Russia. In some countries, activists have expressed concern for workers' basic rights, including efforts by the North Korean government to restrict freedom of movement, expression, and association, the constant presence of "minders" accompanying workers, and indirect salary payments under which large portions of salaries allegedly are recouped by agencies or the North Korean government.

Abductees

The issue of foreigners allegedly abducted by North Korea mostly in the 1970s and 1980s remains unresolved. South Korea says 496 of its citizens, abducted by North Korean agents, remain in North Korea against their will. Pyongyang insists that the South Koreans defected to North Korea, and remain of their own free will, but refuses to allow South Korean relatives to communicate with them.

CHINA/NORTH KOREA

Denied Status, Denied Education

Children of North Korean Women in China

HUMAN RIGHTS WATCH

North Korea, meanwhile, has admitted that it abducted 13 Japanese—returning five to Japan in 2002, but claiming the other eight died, and that no other Japanese citizens were abducted. Japan insists that several more of its citizens have been abducted.

Key International Actors

South Korea's President Lee Myung-bak took office in February 2008 with a pledge to change South Korea's policies on North Korea, saying he would speak out on the latter's human rights record and demand the return of South Korean prisoners of war and abductees. Under former presidents Kim Dae-jung and Roh Mu-hyun, both of whom had summit meetings with North Korea's leader Kim Jong Il, South Korea offered large amounts of aid and started major economic projects in North Korea, but largely remained silent on human rights violations.

After Lee took office, relations between the Koreas deteriorated rapidly. In March, North Korea fired missiles off its west coast, close to South Korea, and in July, a North Korean soldier shot and killed a South Korean tourist near the Diamond Mountain resort. In August, South Korea's National Prosecutors' Office announced the arrest of a man and a woman (a North Korean refugee who had settled in South Korea) for allegedly spying for North Korea.

The deteriorating relationship appeared responsible for an interruption in food aid, with North Korea initially rejecting offers of aid, and South Korea then failing to respond promptly to an August plea from the World Food Program to provide new food aid. Together with China, South Korea has been the largest donor of unconditional food aid to North Korea in recent years.

Pyongyang's relationship with Washington, however, appeared to improve. On February 26, the New York Philharmonic performed in Pyongyang, with many observers cautiously calling it a prelude to a thaw between the two countries. In May, the United States announced that it would offer 500,000 tons of food aid by mid-2008; at this writing in November it had delivered about 120,000 tons. On October 12, 2008, Washington removed North Korea from its list of state sponsors of terrorism.

In a March 2008 report for the UN Human Rights Council, Vitit Muntarbhorn, UN special rapporteur on human rights in North Korea, criticized North Korea for "appalling" prison conditions and "extensive use of torture and public executions."

PAKISTAN

2008 was a tumultuous year for Pakistan. Elections in February that ushered in a return to civilian rule were followed by the formation and rapid collapse of a coalition government, the forced resignation of former army chief Pervez Musharraf as president after nearly nine years in power, and the ascension to the presidency in September of Asif Zardari, the controversial widower of assassinated Pakistan People's Party (PPP) leader Benazir Bhutto. The new civilian government inherited a dramatically worsening security situation and skyrocketing food and fuel prices.

The new government initially agreed to an uneasy cohabitation with Musharraf and accepted demands from the army for transfer of power on the basis of "legal continuity," whereby the new government would not challenge the legal basis of Musharraf's rule nor attempt to hold him or the army legally accountable for Musharraf's coups and abuses during his time in power. Many arbitrary measures enacted under emergency rule can only be rolled back through constitutional amendments that require a two-thirds majority in both chambers of parliament. Musharraf was forced out in August 2008, but Zardari inherited all the powers Musharraf had accrued.

Since the civilian government came to power, civil and political rights protections have improved. Media restrictions have been revoked, opposition rallies and demonstrations have been allowed to proceed without government hindrance or violence, and military personnel have been withdrawn from civilian administrative and political positions. The government has emphasized dialogue to resolve the political dispute between the federal government and Balochistan province and to extend meaningful political rights to the troubled tribal areas bordering Afghanistan.

While the new government has been keen to promote civil liberties and human rights, its rhetoric has not always been matched by action. Ongoing structural concerns include lack of an independent judiciary and fair trials; mistreatment, torture, and unresolved enforced disappearance of terrorism suspects and opponents of the previous military government; military abuses in operations in the tribal areas; the failure to commute death sentences; and legal discrimination against and mistreatment of religious minorities and women.

PAKISTAN

Destroying Legality

Pakistan's Crackdown on Lawyers and Judges

**HUMAN
RIGHTS
WATCH**

Elections

On February 18, 2008, Pakistanis went to the polls to vote in elections for the National Assembly (the lower house of parliament). The elections took place in a period of tumult, after President Musharraf's imposition in November 2007 of a state of emergency, his controversial and illegal November 2007 reelection, his sacking and arrest of many Supreme Court and other senior judges, and the December 27 assassination of former prime minister Benazir Bhutto. In a rebuke to Musharraf, major opposition parties made serious gains and formed a short-lived coalition government.

The pre-election period was marred by widespread electoral manipulation and a concerted attempt by the government to prevent or reduce the scale of an opposition victory. Human Rights Watch documented the abuses and released an audio tape of Musharraf's attorney general speaking of his awareness of a plan to "massively rig" the elections. The European Union Election Observer Mission concluded that the elections "fell short of a number of international standards for genuine democratic elections."

Judicial Independence

Upon assuming power, the government released all judges detained by Musharraf and restored their salaries. Most of the 42 judges fired by Musharraf returned to work under a deal with the PPP-led government that required them to take a fresh oath of office under the constitution.

However, despite repeated public assertions to the contrary, President Zardari reneged on commitments and his signed agreement with opposition leader Nawaz Sharif to restore to office deposed Supreme Court Chief Justice Iftikhar Muhammad Chaudhry, who had been arbitrarily fired and detained by Musharraf during emergency rule.

The lawyers' movement, which rose to prominence in 2007, has weakened as a political force since the advent of an elected government but retains significant support in the legal fraternity and in civil society.

Balochistan

The Pakistani government apologized in 2008 to the people of Balochistan for excesses and abuses under Musharraf, released high-profile political prisoners in the province, and affirmed its intention to reach a rights-respecting political compact between the Pakistani federation and the province. These overtures calmed the situation in Balochistan considerably and attacks by both Baloch militants and the Pakistani military stopped.

The dispute in Balochistan is essentially political, centered on issues of provincial autonomy and exploitation of mineral resources. The Zardari government has accepted that hundreds of political opponents were "disappeared" from Balochistan during Musharraf's rule, but progress in locating them or informing their next-of-kin has remained slow.

Terrorism, Counterterrorism, and "Disappearances"

Pakistan was rocked by a spate of suicide bombings in 2008 that targeted the political and military elite of the country and the symbols of its power. The most high-profile attack took place on September 20 in Islamabad, destroying the Marriot Hotel, killing 54, and injuring hundreds. The attack came just hours after President Zardari had delivered his first address to a joint session of parliament.

Terrorism suspects are frequently detained without charge or, if charged, are often convicted without proper judicial process. Human Rights Watch has documented scores of illegal detentions, instances of torture, and "disappearances" in Pakistan's major cities. Counterterrorism laws also continue to be misused. It is impossible to ascertain the number of people "disappeared" in counterterrorism operations because of the secrecy surrounding such operations. Pakistan's Interior Ministry, now controlled by the elected government, has estimated the total at 1,100. However, the government has not provided details of how many were suspected of links to al Qaeda and the Taliban and has made negligible progress in resolving cases and recovering victims.

Until the imposition of the state of emergency in November 2007, the Supreme Court was investigating 400 cases of enforced disappearance. In response to pressure from the Supreme Court, scores were freed or produced in court and

charged. The Supreme Court under Musharraf-appointed Chief Justice Abdul
Hameed Dogar has notably failed to pursue such cases.

Pakistan has yet to become a signatory to the international treaty banning
enforced disappearances.

Security Operations and Displaced Persons

At the urging of the United States, the Pakistani armed forces have engaged in
increasingly aggressive counterterrorism operations in Pakistan's Federally
Administered Tribal Areas along the Afghan border. The operations at times have
been accompanied by massive civilian displacement, extrajudicial executions,
house demolitions, and arbitrary detentions.

Since September 2008, US drones are believed to have carried out more than a
dozen missile attacks on alleged militant targets in the tribal areas, killing dozens
of people amid persistent claims of civilian casualties. The air raids have been a
political liability for Zardari, who has called on the US to stop them. In the Bajaur
agency area, where the fighting has been most intense, more than 200,000 people have been displaced by the Pakistani army offensive.

Armed groups in Pakistan's tribal areas continue to engage in vigilantism and violent attacks on civilians, including suicide bombings, murder, and public behead-
ings. Despite selective military operations and periodic peace deals, the government has not succeeded in preventing the Taliban and members of other militant
groups from committing serious human rights abuses.

Throughout 2008 Taliban suicide bomb attacks and operations continued in the
settled areas of the North West Frontier Province. Battles between pro-Taliban militants and government security forces in the NWFP's Swat valley displaced civilians and led to severe insecurity.

Discrimination

Legal discrimination against religious minorities and women continues to be a
serious concern.

The Ahmadi religious community continues to be targeted. Blasphemy cases were registered against Ahmadis in 2008 and two members were murdered in the province of Sindh after Dr. Aamir Liaquat Hussain, a popular religious talk-show host on Geo TV, declared Ahmadis appropriate targets for murder under Islamic law.

Violence against women and girls, including rape and domestic violence, and forced marriage remain serious problems. "Honor killings" were perpetrated across the country in 2008, with particularly gruesome cases reported from Sindh and Balochistan provinces. In one case, five women were reported to have been shot and buried alive for marrying against their families' wishes.

Despite condemnation from human rights groups, Israrullah Zehri, a senator from Balochistan province who publicly defended honor killings as "tribal custom," and legislator Hazar Khan Bijrani, accused of presiding over a tribal *jirga* (council) that in 2006 ordered the handing-over of five girls, aged six and younger, as "compensation" in a dispute, were elevated to Pakistan's cabinet by President Zardari in November 2008.

Growing extremism poses new threats to women's rights, particularly in the tribal regions bordering Afghanistan. In 2008, the Taliban and other insurgent groups destroyed more than 100 girls schools and imposed other barriers to prevent girls from attending schools.

Freedom of Expression

Journalists continue to face pressure and threats from non-state actors and elements of Pakistan's intelligence apparatus, but there has been a marked decrease in government-sponsored attacks since Musharraf was forced to step down. The elected government revoked sweeping curbs on the media put in place by Musharraf.

Death Penalty

Pakistan's prime minister announced in June 2008 that more than 7,000 inmates on death row in Pakistan would have their sentences commuted. In a July meeting with Human Rights Watch the prime minister again emphasized his intention to commute the death sentences. Between the June announcement and this writing in late 2008, however, 15 more people were executed, according to the Human Rights Commission of Pakistan.

Despite commitments to reduce the number of offenses for which the death penalty is applicable, Zardari actually increased their number in November by adding "cyber-terrorism" to the list of crimes punishable by death. Pakistan's Law Ministry appears to be stalling the commutation of death sentences and blocking proposals to limit the applicability of the death penalty.

Key International Actors

The United States and United Kingdom, the key external actors in Pakistan, remain focused on counterterrorism in their dealings with Pakistan, subordinating all other issues. The US, working closely with Pakistan's notoriously abusive Inter-Services Intelligence agency, has had a direct role in "disappearances" of counterterrorism suspects.

While the US and UK supported a return to electoral democracy in 2008, they backed Musharraf even after the February elections, despite his personal unpopularity and the illegality of his hold on office. When it became clear that his continuation in office was untenable, they successfully urged the elected government not to prosecute or hold Musharraf legally accountable for abuses under his rule in return for facilitating his resignation. In contrast, they notably failed to urge full restoration of the judiciary.

On April 17, 2008, the Pakistani government ratified the International Covenant on Economic, Social and Cultural Rights and signed both the International Covenant on Civil and Political Rights and the UN Convention against Torture.

Under Musharraf, Pakistan played an extremely negative role at the UN Human Rights Council (HRC); the change in government has been accompanied by some improvements in approach. Still, Pakistan's positions at the HRC often do not fully reflect the administration's stated commitments to human rights and it continues to play an actively obstructive role on some issues. Pakistan was reviewed under the Universal Periodic Review mechanism of the HRC in May 2008.

Papua New Guinea

Papua New Guinea's government acceded to the International Covenant on Civil and Political Rights and the International Covenant on Economic, Social and Cultural Rights in July 2008. Police rape and torture and gender-based violence and discrimination nevertheless remain widespread. Many people, especially girls and women, lack access to basic education and healthcare.

Police Violence, Juvenile Justice, and Detention of Children

Despite statements by the police commissioner in 2008 promising respect for human rights, police routinely use excessive force, torture, and sexual violence against individuals in custody. Because girls and women are rarely formally charged, their contact with the police, including rape in police stations, is often not reflected in official data. In the face of widespread violent crime, such tactics have deeply eroded the public trust and cooperation crucial to effective policing. Impunity and corruption fuel abuse as police are rarely held accountable for violence or other crimes, either through internal disciplinary mechanisms or by the criminal justice system.

Progress in developing a juvenile justice system continues, but so does police violence against children. More police were trained on new standards for dealing with children. Thirteen of 20 provinces now have some form of juvenile court, but children rarely receive legal representation.

Police frequently detain children with adults in police lockups where they are denied medical care and are at risk of rape and other violence. In prisons and other juvenile institutions, children awaiting trial are mixed with those already convicted. Conditions in many facilities are poor; even the prison in the capital Port Moresby lacks formal education for children. Children may spend months or even years awaiting trial. Notably, the number of children in correctional facilities has decreased since 2000, corresponding to the establishment of juvenile courts and an increased use of community-based sentences and pre-sentence diversion.

As of October 2008 at least one child—a 16-year-old boy—was imprisoned under a death sentence for murder. No one has been executed in Papua New Guinea since the death penalty was reintroduced in 1991.

Violence and Discrimination against Women and Girls

Violence against women and girls—including domestic violence, gang rape, and torture and murder for alleged sorcery—is pervasive and rarely punished. Police often ignore complaints, or demand money or sex from victims. Girls' and women's low status is also reflected in disparities in education, healthcare, and employment; heavy household workloads; early marriage; and polygamy. Although the prime minister and other officials condemned violence against women in late 2007 following several well-publicized cases, these statements have yet to result in improved protection for women, services for victims, or an expectation of accountability for perpetrators.

There is only one female member of parliament.

Human Rights Monitoring Mechanisms

Several NGOs document human rights abuses connected with logging and mining operations; some have faced threats and physical violence. In August 2008 three men attacked Jethro Tulin, director of an NGO documenting abuses at Barrick Porgera Joint Venture gold mine, breaking his arm and telling him he would not be allowed to return to Canada. Tulin had delivered a statement in Canada in May at Barrick's annual shareholders meeting. Human Rights Watch has no evidence as to whether his attackers were linked in any way to Barrick.

The Ombudsman Commission, which has taken useful steps to monitor government corruption, has a human rights unit, but its capacity to pursue cases is weak and it has not taken up police violence against children. A 2007 agreement gave the commission limited oversight over selected complaints against police. In October 2008 the commission reported that it had jointly investigated two cases with police, one involving allegations that a provincial police commander had raped a woman who came to the station for assistance. The officer was suspended but was free on bail at this writing, awaiting trial.

In 2008 juvenile magistrates conducted monitoring visits to some prisons and police stations. Magistrates documented children being whipped, kicked, slashed, and beaten by police; children being held without a court order; and appalling detention conditions.

In September the National Court found that five men had a cause of action for breach of their human rights. The men alleged that police had detained them for three weeks without charge and tortured them, including forcing two of them to have sexual intercourse with each other.

The government held public consultations during 2008 on the creation of a National Human Rights Commission.

Right to Health

The closure of rural aid posts and health centers, declining transportation infrastructure, failure of allocated funds to reach local governments, and a shortage of drugs, medical equipment, and trained health professionals limit access to quality healthcare. Rates of maternal and child mortality are among the highest in the Pacific. Around 40 percent of women receive no antenatal care, according to government reports.

Papua New Guinea has the highest prevalence of HIV/AIDS in the Pacific: around 60,000 people are living with the disease (1.61 percent of adults in 2007). Antiretroviral therapy is inaccessible to most. Gender-based violence and discrimination, and poor access to healthcare also fuel the virus's spread. People living with HIV/AIDS often face violence and discrimination. Despite police training on HIV/AIDS, police undermine prevention efforts by targeting female sex workers and men and boys suspected of homosexual conduct for beatings and rape. Police are able to do so in part because they can threaten arrest using laws criminalizing homosexual conduct and certain forms of sex work, and because social stigma against homosexuality and sex work shields police from public outrage. Sections 210 and 212 of Papua New Guinea's penal code, an inheritance of British colonialism, punish consensual homosexual conduct between men with up to 14 years' imprisonment.

Education

Primary education is neither free nor compulsory. According to the education department, net primary enrollment rates are low, ranging from around 22 percent in one province to 65 percent in the capital in 2007. Only 56 percent of primary school entrants reach the final grade of primary education; secondary school enrollment rates are around 25 percent.

Barriers include long distances to schools, a shortage of upper secondary placements, and school closures due to insecurity. Girls in particular suffer from sexual abuse by other students and teachers, lack of water and sanitation facilities, and dangerous journeys to and from school. School fees—ranging from 90 kina (US$35) for lower primary school to 1,300 kina (US$508) for grade 12 boarding students—are prohibitively high for many families. Average annual income was around US$770 in 2006. Despite partial government subsidies in some provinces and the secretary of education's urging that schools should turn away students only as a last resort, high fees have been linked to non-attendance, dropout, and entry into child labor.

Key International Actors

The UN special rapporteurs on torture and education, and the UN Working Group on Arbitrary Detention have all requested permission to visit the country, but, at this writing, the government had not responded. Nor had the government responded to a January 2008 letter from the special rapporteur on extrajudicial, summary or arbitrary executions seeking information on the killing of at least eight people by private security forces at the Barrick Porgera Joint Venture gold mine and the government's failure to investigate and prosecute those responsible.

The United Nations Children's Fund assists juvenile justice reform efforts, and the Office of the High Commissioner for Human Rights stationed a human rights advisor in the country at the beginning of 2008.

Australia remains the most important external actor and largest foreign donor, playing a significant role in, among other areas, the law and justice sector and HIV/AIDS response. Relations between the two countries improved following the election of Australian Prime Minister Kevin Rudd, and Australia sent a few additional federal police to serve as advisors in 2008. It remains to be seen whether Australia will adopt more specific commitments to human rights in its development policy.

THE PHILIPPINES

The Philippines is a multiparty democracy with an elected president and legislature, a thriving civil society sector, and a vibrant media. Several key institutions, including the judiciary and law enforcement agencies, however, remain weak.

Under intense domestic and international pressure, the number of extrajudicial killings and enforced disappearances implicating security forces dropped significantly in 2008. The government of President Gloria Macapagal Arroyo continues to deny complicity of security forces in most such acts despite considerable evidence to the contrary. Hundreds of activists, journalists, and outspoken clergy have been killed or abducted since 2001. While a few people have been successfully prosecuted, not a single solider has been brought to justice for crimes committed during this period.

Armed encounters between the Armed Forces of the Philippines (AFP) and groups such as the communist New People's Army (NPA), the Moro Islamic Liberation Front (MILF), and the Abu Sayaff Group (ASG) continue. Starting in August 2008, the conflict in Mindanao rapidly escalated, with clashes between the AFP and the MILF displacing hundreds of thousands of civilians.

Extrajudicial Killings and Enforced Disappearances

The government maintains that most extrajudicial killings and "disappearances" are the result of internal purges within the communist movement, but UN expert Philip Alston and human rights organizations have found evidence of military involvement in many cases. Alston presented his report on the Philippines to the UN Human Rights Council in April 2008. A new government taskforce said in November 2008 that out of 260 compiled "disappearances" cases, 19 cases involved members of the military.

Abductions of activists continue, with the military or police sometimes resurfacing abductees and charging them with killings or other offences.

On May 15, 2008, unidentified gunmen shot and killed Celso Pojas, secretary-general of a leftist farmers' organization in Davao City, in southern Mindanao.

Pojas had campaigned against military operations that allegedly displaced indigenous people and farmers in Compostela Valley. At this writing, the police have not arrested any suspects.

On the same day, in Cagayan Valley, unidentified men abducted Randy Malayao, former vice president of the College Editors Guild of the Philippines and a consultant to the National Democratic Front (NDF), a coalition of underground left-leaning organizations. A few days later, the military produced him, saying he was a rebel leader involved in the killing of former congressman Rodolfo Aguinaldo. At this writing, he remains in jail in Tuguegarao City, Cagayan Valley, facing murder and attempted murder charges.

In August 2008 a regional court in Tagaytay City found the arrest and detention of the "Tagaytay Five" unlawful and ordered their release. Security forces had abducted and detained Riel Custodio, Axel Pinpin, Aristides Sarmiento, Enrico Ybanez, and Michael Masayes in a joint military-police operation in April 2006 and forced them to admit they were members of the NPA. Rebellion charges were later filed against the five, all of whom are farmers' advocates and organizers in the provinces of Cavite and Batangas in southern Luzon.

On September 13, the Court of Appeals in Manila dismissed charges against Berlin Guerrero, a church pastor, and ordered his immediate release. Armed men abducted Guerrero on May 27, 2007, in Laguna province and several days later he appeared in police custody. He subsequently was accused of being a rebel and charged with sedition and murder.

Meanwhile, initial optimism over new Supreme Court writs to compel military and other government agents to release information on people in their custody—the writs of *amparo* and *habeas data*—was dampened by a series of lower court decisions dismissing cases seeking the release of or information on persons in government custody. Among the cases dismissed was that brought on behalf of Jonas Burgos, a farmers' rights advocate, abducted in April 2007 in Quezon City. Local activists have expressed concern that courts are putting unreasonable obstacles in the way of petitioners in such cases.

From January to September 2008, five journalists, mostly radio commentators tackling corruption and other issues, were killed. On August 4, 2008, gunmen killed radio commentator Dennis Cuesta in General Santos City. Although witness-es identified one of the gunmen as a known police officer, no arrest had been made at this writing.

Summary Executions of Petty Criminals and Street Youth

Reports of execution-style killings continue in several cities, particularly in Mindanao. Local activists say more than 100 people were killed from January to September 2008 in Davao City alone. Execution-style killings have been reported in the cities of Davao, Digos (Davao del Sur), Tagum (Davao del Norte), General Santos, Cagayan de Oro, and Cebu.

The majority of the victims are street children or petty criminals, including gang members. An increasing number of victims are bystanders and victims of mistak-en identity. Killings are often perpetrated in broad daylight, some near police sta-tions and detention centers. The perpetrators often do not hide their faces and ride in twos or threes aboard motorcycles with missing license plates. Gunmen sometimes threaten witnesses, warning them that they could be targeted as well.

Police and local authorities deny the existence of vigilante groups and attribute the killings to gang wars, but many of the killings followed tough anti-crime pro-nouncements by top local officials including Mayor Rodrigo Duterte of Davao City, Mayor Arsenio Latasa of Digos City, and Mayor Tomas Osmena of Cebu City. Local residents and activists told Human Rights Watch in 2008 that death squads have been operating in the cities for years with virtual impunity. In most of the cases documented by human rights groups, no formal criminal investigation has been opened and the perpetrators remain unpunished.

Conflict in Mindanao

On August 5, 2008, after almost eight years of negotiations, the Philippine gov-ernment and MILF were to sign a comprehensive agreement in Kuala Lumpur to address the Moro secessionist issue in the southern Philippines. On the eve of the signing, however, the Supreme Court, acting on a petition filed by local execu-tives and politicians in Mindanao who were opposed to the agreement, issued a temporary restraining order stopping the process.

The aborted peace agreement was followed by sporadic armed clashes between government forces and MILF rebels in several provinces of Central Mindanao resulting in at least 62 civilian deaths. Fighting displaced more than 100,000 families, comprising more than 500,000 individuals, mostly women, children, and the elderly. Some soldiers and politicians reportedly began arming non-Moro civilians to fight the MILF. Human rights groups have warned that if the government and MILF do not return to the negotiating table, a full-blown civil war may again erupt.

Clashes with Other Armed Groups

Under a military operation entitled *Oplan Bantay Laya 2* (Operational Plan Freedom Watch), the stated aim of which is to crush the NPA by the end of Arroyo's term in 2010, the government accelerated counterinsurgency operations in central Luzon, southern Tagalog, Bicol, eastern Visayas, southern Mindanao, and northern Mindanao. In 2008, armed confrontations between the AFP and the NPA displaced thousands of people. Indigenous communities in Surigao del Sur, Davao del Norte, and Compostela Valley were most affected.

Local human rights groups have expressed concern that the military's regular use of aerial and heavy artillery bombardment is putting civilian lives at risk. In February 2008 security forces in Sulu killed seven civilians including two children and a pregnant woman during an attack on a village suspected of hosting ASG members. In September a pregnant woman and five children were killed in Maguindanao during an air force attack on a village where MILF rebels were allegedly hiding.

Filipino Workers Abroad

Approximately 1.7 million Filipinos work abroad, including hundreds of thousands of women who work in other parts of Asia and the Middle East as domestic workers. While the Philippine government has made some efforts to support and protect domestic workers, many women continue to experience abuses including unpaid wages, food deprivation, forced confinement in the workplace, and physical and sexual abuse (see Saudi Arabia, UAE, and Malaysia chapters.)

Key International Actors

The United States is the most influential ally and the largest donor to the Philippines. The US military has access to Filipino lands and seas under a Visiting Forces Agreement, and the two militaries hold joint annual exercises. In fiscal year 2008 (October 2007–September 2008), the US government provided the Philippines almost US$30 million under Foreign Military Financing for procurement of military equipment and almost US$1.5 million in the International Military Exchange Training program under which AFP officers are trained in the United States. The US Foreign Operations Bill approved in December 2007 requires the Philippine government to show progress in addressing human rights abuses, including extrajudicial killings, in order for some additional US military funding to be approved.

In April 2008 the UN Human Rights Council examined the human rights record of the Philippines under its Universal Periodic Review mechanism. Several member states raised the issue of impunity for extrajudicial killings and enforced disappearances but the Philippine government rejected recommendations for a follow-up report.

SINGAPORE

Singapore remains an authoritarian state with strict curbs on freedom of expression, assembly, and association; denial of due process rights; draconian defamation laws; and tight controls on independent political activity. Since 1959 the ruling People's Action Party (PAP) has won all elections.

Internal security and criminal laws permit prolonged detention of suspects without trial. Caning is obligatory for certain categories of crimes, as is the death penalty for others. Although reforms have improved employment conditions for some of the country's 180,000 migrant domestic workers, the government still fails to guarantee them basic rights.

Freedom of Expression and Assembly

Singapore's constitution guarantees freedom of assembly and expression, though parliament can and does limit both on security, public order, and morality grounds. Opposition politicians and their supporters are at constant risk of prison and substantial fines for simply expressing their views.

On October 13, 2008, Singapore's High Court ruled that opposition Singapore Democratic Party (SDP) Secretary General Dr. Chee Soon Juan and his sister, Chee Siok Chin, must pay Minister Mentor Lee Kuan Yew and his son, Prime Minister Lee Hsien Loong, US$416,000 in damages for an article in the SDP's newsletter. The article had compared how the government is run to a scandal at a well-known charity. The ruling may bankrupt the SDP and permanently shut it down. Dr. Chee and Ms. Chee are already bankrupt because of previous defamation rulings against them.

In September 2008 the Lees also won a defamation suit against the *Far Eastern Economic Review* and its editor Hugo Restall for commentary on the same case. Damages had yet to be assessed at this writing. The government is also seeking contempt proceedings against the publisher and two editors of the *Asian Wall Street Journal* for editorial comments related to the case.

In May Dr. Chee and a colleague were fined for speaking in public without a permit during the 2006 election campaign. They were charged with trying to sell copies of the SDP newsletter on a Singapore street.

Movies, music, and video games are routinely censored in Singapore. The Media Development Authority controls website licensing. In May 2008 the authority interrupted a private screening, sponsored by the SDP, of the video *One Nation Under Lee.*

The Newspaper and Printing Presses Act requires that locally published newspapers renew their licenses each year, and empowers authorities to limit the circulation of foreign publications deemed to "be engaging in the domestic politics of Singapore."

How far Singapore's leadership will loosen curbs on assembly and expression, as Prime Minister Loong suggested in August 2008, remains to be seen. The only step taken in 2008 was the government's decision in September to rescind the need for police permission for gatherings and rallies of more than four people at a popular park site officially labeled the Speaker's Corner. Race and religion still may not be publicly discussed, police may still intervene on public order grounds, and a permit is still required elsewhere in the city.

In March, on World Consumer Rights Day, police stopped a protest against rising prices outside Parliament House. The organizers, among them Dr. Chee, had been refused a permit; 18 protesters have since been charged with illegal assembly and procession. A day after the attempted rally, the non-political Consumer Association of Singapore was able to hold a public event without incident.

Due Process

Singapore's Internal Security Act (ISA), Criminal Law (Temporary Provisions) Act (CLA), Misuse of Drugs Act (MDA), and Undesirable Publications Act permit arrest and detention of suspects without a warrant or judicial review. Both the ISA and the CLA also authorize preventive detention. The MDA permits the Central Narcotics Bureau chief to send suspected drug users for rehabilitation without recourse to trial.

The ISA is used against suspected Islamist militants, many of whom have been detained for long periods without trial. There is no right to challenge detention on substantive grounds. As of April 2008 some 30 suspected Muslim militants were being held, almost all members of Jemaah Islamiah. Another 25-30 former detainees live under restriction orders.

Caning

Singapore's penal code mandates caning combined with imprisonment for some 30 offenses, including drug and immigration felonies. It is discretionary for other offenses. Courts reportedly sentenced 6,404 men and boys to caning in 2007, some 95 percent of whose sentences were carried out.

Death Penalty

Although death penalty statistics are secret in Singapore, available information indicates that it has one of the world's highest per capita execution rates. In December 2007 Singapore joined with 53 other states in voting against a non-binding UN General Assembly resolution calling for "a moratorium on executions with a view to abolishing the death penalty." Earlier, Singapore's home affairs minister, referring to the law's deterrent effects, commented that "there is no room to go soft."

Migrant Domestic Workers

Singapore's labor laws exclude some 180,000 migrant domestic workers from key protections guaranteed to other workers, such as a weekly day off, limits on working hours, annual leave, paid holidays, and caps on salary deductions. In May 2008 acting Minister for Manpower Gan Kim Yong said it was unnecessary to mandate a weekly rest day. He instead supported the current standard contract provision that provides for at least one day off a month or compensatory pay. However, many employers forbid domestic workers to take a rest day; their isolation and employers' power to have them deported at will make it difficult if not impossible for them to bargain effectively for their due.

The government has prosecuted some employers who physically abuse domestic workers and imposed penalties on labor recruitment agencies for unethical practices. However it has failed to regulate exploitative recruitment charges that can consume a third or more of workers' two-year wage total.

Privacy

In October 2007 Singapore's parliament rejected a proposal to repeal law 377A, which bans private and consensual sexual relations between men. Although prosecutions are rare, those found in violation can be jailed for up to two years on charges of "gross indecency."

In April 2008 the Media Development Authority fined a local television station for featuring a gay couple and their baby under regulations that prohibit promotion of gay lifestyles. It also fined a cable network for airing a commercial that showed two women kissing.

Human Rights Defenders

State laws and political repression effectively prevent the establishment of human rights organizations and deter individuals from speaking out publicly against government policies.

Unless they are registered as political parties, associations may not engage in any activities the government deems political. Trade unions are under the same restrictions and are banned from contributing to political parties or using their funds for political purposes. Most unions are affiliated with the umbrella National Trade Union Congress, which does not allow members supportive of opposition parties to hold office.

Key International Actors

Singapore is a key member of the Southeast Asia Regional Centre for Counter-Terrorism, along with the US, Malaysia, and others, and is an active participant in regional and sub-regional security issues. It is also an important financial and banking center for Southeast Asia.

In February 2008 Singapore Foreign Minister George Yong-Boon Yeo, then chair of the Association of Southeast Asian Nations (ASEAN), expressed ASEAN's concern about the conditions under which Burma's constitutional referendum took place. Since July 2008, after Singapore's term as chair of ASEAN ended, the government has shown more support for Burma's government, even refusing to renew residency permits for Burmese citizens who appear to have taken part in peaceful activities critical of Burmese government policies.

SRI LANKA

On January 2, 2008, the Sri Lankan government formally pulled out of its cease-fire agreement with the secessionist Liberation Tigers of Tamil Eelam (LTTE). The agreement had effectively been a dead letter since mid-2006, when major military operations by both sides resumed. Since then, the human rights situation in the north and east of the country has deteriorated markedly, with numerous reports of killings, abductions, and enforced disappearances by government forces, the LTTE, and paramilitary groups.

All parties are responsible for harmful and unnecessary restrictions on humanitarian access to populations at risk. The LTTE has continued bomb attacks on civilians in several cities, including the capital Colombo.

The government's state of emergency continued in 2008, with increasing numbers of arrests and detentions taking place under emergency regulations and the Prevention of Terrorism Act (PTA). The culture of impunity deepened, with investigations and inquiries into human rights violations failing to bring significant results, and a group of prominent international figures pulling out of an inquiry into grave human rights abuses because of "an absence of political and institutional will" on the part of the government.

Humanitarian Crisis

Since mid-2006 fighting in the north and east has created a series of humanitarian crises. On September 8, 2008, the government ordered the United Nations and other international agencies to withdraw foreign and non-resident local staff and suspend their aid operations in the LTTE-controlled Vanni region. At this writing, reports indicated there were over 240,000 displaced persons in Kilinochchi and Mullativu Districts. The withdrawal raised fears of shortages of food and essential items in the area and inadequate shelter.

Restrictions imposed by the LTTE make it extremely difficult for civilians to leave the Vanni for government areas, including the LTTE requirement that civilians have a "guarantor"—in effect, a hostage—who remains behind. Such restrictions have resulted in entire communities being trapped in areas threatened by fighting and with minimal humanitarian assistance.

Those who manage to escape the Vanni have faced an uncertain future, as the government suspects Tamils from the area of being LTTE supporters. Many families have been moved by the government to "welfare centers," as in Kallimoddai and Sirukondal in Mannar District, where their movements are severely restricted. Concerns remain about security, sustainability, and freedom of choice for displaced persons returning to or resettling in areas in the east, particularly in the High Security Zone in Sampur, Trincomalee District.

Threats and Attacks against Civilians

Threats and attacks against civilians continue. In 2008 bomb blasts in urban areas resulted in over 70 civilian deaths and some 250 casualties; the LTTE was the prime suspect. According to local media, as many as 47 civilians were killed in Kilinochchi District after hostilities escalated in May. T. Maheswaran, a Tamil member of parliament and vocal critic of the government, was killed on January 1, 2008, while attending religious services at a Hindu temple in an area with high security.

Fear of killings and abductions in the northern Jaffna peninsula is so great that at this writing over 300 people were in protective custody in the Jaffna prison. Many serious abuses in Jaffna have been reported during curfew hours and in high-security areas, suggesting the complicity of government security forces.

As many as 22 people were killed and 26 abducted in May 2008 before and after council elections in Eastern Province. The elections resulted in the appointment of Pillayan, a former LTTE member and current Tamil Makkal Viduthalai Pulikal (TMVP) leader, as chief minister. The TMVP, originally a breakaway faction of the LTTE called the Karuna Group, continues to be responsible for abductions and child recruitment with the complicity of the security forces.

Tamil civilians, including many who relocated to Colombo from Jaffna and other locations in the north and east, continue to face arbitrary arrests and detentions, round-ups, orders of eviction, and new forms of registration.

Abductions and Enforced Disappearances

Abductions and enforced disappearances continued in 2008, with approximately 43 reported cases in Vavuniya in August alone. Many cases are not reported due to fear of reprisals. Besides a few arrests of persons alleged to be involved in abductions for ransom, Human Rights Watch is unaware of any serious action by the government to address the hundreds of new "disappearances" of the past few years, the great majority of which remain unresolved. Most cases of enforced disappearances implicate government security forces.

Emergency Regulations and the Prevention of Terrorism Act

Emergency regulations provide broad powers to the security forces to investigate, arrest, and detain people in the name of "national security." The government uses the regulations to arrest and detain political opponents, journalists, human rights defenders, and members of the Tamil minority community.

On March 7, 2008, the Terrorist Investigative Department arrested prominent journalist J.S. Tissainayagam and detained him without charge for more than 150 days for alleged links to the LTTE. He was later charged both under the emergency regulations and the Prevention of Terrorism Act for printing and distributing *North Eastern Monthly* magazine in 2006. A new emergency regulation introduced in August 2008 gives the secretary of defense power to detain persons for 18 months without producing them before the courts.

Impunity

Despite government commitments to address impunity, rights violators continue to face no serious threat of prosecution. There were no convictions of perpetrators of serious human rights violations in 2008. The Presidential Commission of Inquiry, formed under international pressure to investigate 16 incidents of grave human rights abuses, failed to make any significant progress. The process was so flawed that the International Independent Group of Eminent Persons, after regularly raising serious concerns, eventually withdrew from its observer role. Four Sri Lankan commissioners also resigned.

In a shocking display of impunity, Karuna Amman, former LTTE deputy commander implicated in numerous serious abuses both with the LTTE and his breakaway armed group, was reinstated as a leader of the TMVP upon his return to Sri Lanka in July 2008. He had just been released after serving time for immigration fraud in the United Kingdom. On October 7 he was inducted as a member of parliament with the full support of the president and government.

Child Soldiers

In October the United Nations Children's Fund reported 1,424 outstanding cases of recruitment of child soldiers by the LTTE, including 108 still under age 18, and 133 by the TMVP, including 62 still under age 18. New child recruitment continues: reports from Ampara District indicated an increase in TMVP abductions in late 2008 and unconfirmed reports suggest that the LTTE has sharply increased child recruitment in response to government military operations in Kilinochchi District. Many cases are not reported due to fear of reprisals.

Human Rights Defenders, Journalists, and Humanitarian Workers

Threats and attacks against human rights defenders and journalists worsened in 2008. On September 27, grenades were thrown at the house of human rights lawyer and executive director of Transparency International Sri Lanka, J.C. Weliamuna. According to the Free Media Movement, since 2005, 14 journalists have been killed, 7 abducted, and 13 arrested.

Humanitarian space shrunk considerably in 2008, with the government ordering withdrawal of agencies from the Vanni region. Aggressive public statements from senior government officials continued against international agencies, including the UN, with many accused of being LTTE supporters or sympathizers. Humanitarian aid agencies' operations were significantly affected with restrictions on movement and difficulties obtaining visas and work permits for expatriate staff. No progress was made in the August 2006 execution-style slayings of 17 Action against Hunger (ACF) aid workers despite strong new evidence that state security forces were responsible.

Sri Lankan Migrant Workers

More than 710,000 Sri Lankan women work abroad as domestic workers, nearly 90 percent of them in Saudi Arabia, Kuwait, Lebanon, and the United Arab Emirates. Once abroad, many domestic workers face abuses, including long hours, no rest days, forced confinement, low and unpaid wages, physical and sexual abuse, and conditions that amount to forced labor (see Saudi Arabia and Lebanon chapters).

Some Sri Lankan foreign missions have created shelters to assist the thousands of domestic workers complaining of unpaid wages and abuse each year. These foreign missions have inadequate staffing and resources, the shelters are grossly overcrowded and unhygienic, and the services they provide often fail to meet minimum standards. The government and the Sri Lankan association of recruitment agencies have attempted to negotiate higher salaries for Sri Lankan domestic workers working abroad, but enforcement in labor-receiving countries is uneven.

Key International Actors

On May 21, Sri Lanka lost its bid for reelection to the UN Human Rights Council. A broad coalition of national and international NGOs raised strong objections to Sri Lanka's candidacy, pointing to its poor human rights record and failure to meet past commitments to the HRC. In May during the HRC's triennial review of Sri Lanka's record, the government agreed to implement a national action plan on human rights.

In 2008 several influential actors, including co-chairs of the peace process in Sri Lanka—the European Union, Japan, Norway, and the United States—denounced abuses by government and LTTE forces and called on all sides to respect civilian life and humanitarian space.

Many eminent international figures who commented on the deteriorating human rights situation in Sri Lanka were sharply criticized by senior government officials, some even accused of being LTTE dupes or sympathizers, including UN Secretary-

General Ban Ki-moon and Nobel Laureates Bishop Desmond Tutu, Adolfo Pérez Esquivel, and Jimmy Carter.

THAILAND

The end of a military-installed administration has not led to the restoration of rights and democracy in Thailand. Within months of general elections in December 2007 and formation of a new civilian government in January 2008, political polarization between pro- and anti-government groups led to protracted protests and occasional deadly clashes; media freedom and freedom of expression were undermined by harassment and interference from both the government and anti-government groups.

In the southern border provinces, Thai security forces continue to engage in extrajudicial killings and torture. Insurgent groups continue their brutal and deadly attacks on civilians.

New "War on Drugs"

During the inaugural presentation of government policy to the parliament on February 20, 2008, then interior minister Chalerm Yubamrung announced that a new "war on drugs"—similar to that carried out in 2003 by the government of Thaksin Shinawatra—would be launched. Chalerm vowed that, "if this will lead to 3,000-4,000 deaths of those who break the law, then so be it." Although the campaign was scrapped due to strong domestic and international opposition, the government showed no interest in reopening investigations into the 2,819 extrajudicial killings that allegedly accompanied the 2003 campaign. On November 7, 2008, Prime Minister Somchai Wongsawat announced a new anti-drug campaign.

The government failed to end systematic police brutality and abuse of power in drug suppression operations. For example, Police Captain Nat Chonnithiwanit and seven other members of the 41st Border Patrol Police (BPP) unit allegedly abducted and tortured more than 60 people over a three-year period in order to extort money and force them to confess to drug offenses. Despite the much publicized arrest of a BPP member on January 25, 2008, little progress has been made to bring perpetrators to justice.

People's Alliance for Democracy

Starting on May 25, 2008, the People's Alliance for Democracy (PAD) staged protracted protests in Bangkok and other cities to express opposition to the government. Labeling Prime Minister Samak and his successor, Somchai Wongsawat (former prime minister Thaksin's brother-in-law), as surrogates for Thaksin, the PAD accused the government of corruption, abuse of power, and being unpatriotic. Protesters blocked roads and traffic in the capital, in some cases for months at a time. Pro-government groups often violently attacked PAD rallies while police stood by.

On August 26, PAD protesters besieged many government buildings in Bangkok, including the National Broadcasting of Thailand (NBT) building and Government House, where the prime minister and cabinet members have their offices. The government obtained injunctions and arrest warrants from the courts against PAD leaders, but could not end the siege of Government House. After clashes between police and PAD protesters on August 29, the PAD closed international airports in Thailand's southern provinces and imposed worker strikes on train services across the country.

Violence escalated when the pro-government Democratic Alliance against Dictatorship (DAAD) engaged in street fighting with the PAD on September 2, resulting in one death and more than 40 injuries. Prime Minister Samak declared a state of emergency in Bangkok, but army chief General Anupong Paochinda refused to use the emergency powers to crack down on the PAD and suppress basic freedoms. After Samak was removed from office by the Constitutional Court—the court ruled he had violated the constitution by accepting payment for appearances on a cooking show—the new prime minister, Somchai Wongsawat, approved General Anupong's proposal to lift the state of emergency on September 9.

On October 7, thousands of PAD protesters surrounded the parliament in an attempt to block Prime Minister Somchai from delivering a policy statement. To clear the area, police riot units and BPP units used tear gas and rubber bullets, in some cases firing tear gas from close range directly at the protesters. PAD protesters responded by firing guns, shooting slingshots, throwing bricks and metal pipes, trying to run over police officers with pickup trucks, and stabbing police with flagpoles. According to the Public Health Ministry, two PAD supporters died and 443 were injured, including four cases of amputation. About 20 police were injured.

On October 13, Thailand's National Human Rights Commission concluded that Chinese-made tear gas canisters and grenades used by police on October 7 may have caused many of the deaths and severe injuries.

To date, there has been no independent and impartial investigation into politically motivated violence and human rights abuses committed by the PAD.

At this writing, the PAD was still occupying Government House. PAD leaders were demanding that the military have the right to intervene in politics to check corruption and to protect the monarchy and national sovereignty. They also were proposing that the number of elected MPs be reduced to 50 percent of the total—with the remainder filled through appointment.

Freedom of Expression and Media Freedom

The government has continued to interfere in the media. A news talk radio program hosted by former senator Jermsak Pinthong was taken off the air on February 13, 2008, after he claimed that Prime Minister Samak distorted the truth about a massacre of students at Thammasat University on October 6, 1976. On April 19, Jakrapob Penkair—who was then in charge of the government's Public Relations Department—ordered some 500 community radio operators to allocate three hours a day to promote the government or risk closure.

Prime Minister Samak attempted to use the NBT broadcast to counter daily attacks by PAD-controlled media outlets, ASTV, and Manager Radio. On July 21, the time slot for the political talk show "Page Four News" on NBT TV Channel 11 was reassigned to commentators affiliated with the ruling People's Power Party (PPP) to host a pro-government program called "Truth Today."

The PAD's protests included criminal violence against the media. On August 26, armed PAD protesters stormed into NBT headquarters and attempted to stop the broadcast of NBT television and radio stations. On that day, PAD protesters harassed NBT reporters and staff at Government House and chased them out of their mobile broadcast trucks.

Pro-government groups also have harassed the media. On November 3, about 200 red-clad members of the Love Chiang Mai 51 Group stormed into the regional office of the Thai Public Broadcasting Service in Chiang Mai province. They cut open the fence and blocked the building's entrance with tents, threatening to cut electricity and water supplies after TPBS reported that members of the Love Chiang Mai 51 Group were paid 2,000 baht (about US$57) each to join the pro-government rally in Bangkok organized by the pro-government DADD on November 1.

The PAD, the opposition Democrat Party, and senior military officers have actively advocated the arbitrary use of *lese majeste* (insulting the monarchy) charges against supporters of the government. Jakrapob had to resign from office on May 30 after he was charged with *lese majeste* for a speech at the Foreign Correspondent's Club about the patronage system. On July 22, government supporter Daranee Charnchoengsilpakul was arrested for allegedly insulting the monarchy in her speech at a DAAD rally. In 2008 authorities also closed down more than 400 websites after accusing them of promoting anti-monarchy sentiments.

Thai authorities have warned the vibrant international media in Thailand not to comment on the role of the monarchy. Jonathan Head—a Bangkok-based reporter for the BBC—faced a criminal investigation for allegedly making anti-monarchy comments in his stories.

Violence and Abuses in the Southern Border Provinces

Attacks on civilians by both Thai security forces and armed separatist groups in Thailand's southern border provinces continued in 2008. Soldiers from the Army's 39th Taskforce in Rue Soh district of Narathiwat province were implicated in the highly publicized torture and murder of imam Yapa Kaseng on March 21. On June 21, armed insurgents stormed a passenger train in Ra Ngae district and executed a Buddhist Thai train police officer and three Buddhist train workers. Car bombs were used in a March 15 attack on CS Pattani Hotel in Pattani province and an August 21 attack in Su Ngai Kolok district of Narathiwat province. Some insurgents aimed to spread terror among the Buddhist Thai population, most notably by beheading victims or setting their bodies on fire. Insurgents burned down government schools and continued to engage in roadside ambushes and targeted assassinations of teachers and students.

Although the government and General Anupong vowed to deliver justice to the ethnic Malay Muslim population, Thai security forces still faced little or no consequences for extrajudicial killings, torture, and arbitrary arrests of suspected insurgents. After a sharp decline in 2007, new cases of enforced disappearances emerged again in 2008.

Refugees and Migrant Workers

The international law prohibition against *refoulement*—returning refugees to any country where they are likely to be persecuted or their lives put at risk—continued to be breached in 2008, as ethnic Karen refugees and asylum seekers were deported to Burma. Similarly, Lao Hmong seeking asylum in Petchabun province were rounded up from camps and sent back to Laos.

Thailand hosted the Association of Southeast Asian Nations (ASEAN) Labor Ministerial Meeting in May 2008, but migrant workers remain largely unprotected by Thai labor laws. They continue to be vulnerable to arrest and extortion by corrupt officials, and risk exploitation, abuse, and death. On April 10, 54 Burmese migrants died of suffocation in an unventilated truck while being smuggled to work in Ranong province. Decrees in Ranong, Rayong, and Phang Nga provinces have made it unlawful for migrants to go out at night, carry mobile phones, and ride motorcycles.

Human Rights Defenders

There has been little progress in official investigations into the cases of 20 human rights defenders killed during the Thaksin administration. This includes the "disappearance" and presumed murder of well-known Muslim lawyer Somchai Neelapaijit.

Thai authorities have threatened to revoke the registration of international NGOs in order to deter them from speaking up about government abuses in southern border provinces.

Key International Actors

Thailand assumed the rotating chairmanship of the ASEAN in 2008, but has yet to ratify the ASEAN charter. Thailand's efforts to set the terms of reference for the ASEAN human rights mechanism have been discredited by its poor human rights record and close alliance with military rulers in Burma. Prime Minister Somchai used the October ASEAN-Europe Meeting in Beijing to launch a diplomatic campaign to support the Burmese military government, asserting that lifting economic sanctions and supporting government-led development is the best path to democratization in Burma.

The United States and other western governments resumed normal relations with Thailand after an elected government came to power in 2008. The US used its strong bilateral relationship with Thailand to raise human rights concerns regarding the political confrontation in Bangkok and violence in Thailand's southern border provinces.

Together with the United Kingdom, Australia, and the European Union, the US sought to promote the restoration of democracy in Thailand and expressed strong opposition to attempts by conflicting political factions to incite a military coup and suppress civil liberties.

TIMOR-LESTE

Timor-Leste faced one of its gravest challenges since independence with the near fatal shooting of President Jose Ramos-Horta in February 2008. The police and military united in efforts to maintain order and search for rebels following the attack, a positive development given recent clashes between the services, but the response was marred by continuing reports of security force abuses.

Failures of justice remain a central human rights concern. The most prominent examples are continuing impunity for crimes committed during the 2006 crisis, when fighting between soldiers and police triggered wider violence in which at least 37 people were killed and crimes committed before, during, and after the 1999 UN-sponsored referendum on independence, in which Indonesian-army-backed militias killed hundreds of Timorese and destroyed much of Timor-Leste's physical infrastructure. Impunity for human rights crimes was boosted in 2008 by a series of presidential pardons.

Attacks on Leaders

On February 11, 2008, Alfredo Reinado, former commander of Timor-Leste's military police unit, led an armed group to attack the prime minister and president of Timor-Leste. Reinado and his militia had been in hiding since 2006, when he played a pivotal role in initiating violence in Dili. During the 2008 attack, Reinado was shot and killed and Horta suffered a near fatal injury, requiring treatment for two months in Australia before he was able to resume his presidential duties. Prime Minister Xanana Gusmão escaped unharmed. After the attacks, Reinado associate Gastoa Salsinha assumed command of the armed group and fled with the rebels to the Ermera district. Salsinha and his 11 armed rebels surrendered peacefully on April 29, 2008.

Impunity

On July 15, 2008, the Indonesian and Timorese joint Commission on Truth and Friendship released its report to the leaders of both countries. The report concludes that crimes against humanity occurred in Timor-Leste in 1999 and attributes institutional responsibility to the Indonesian military, police, and government.

UN Secretary-General Ban Ki-moon urged the leaders of Indonesia and Timor-Leste to follow the release of the report with initiatives to "ensure full accountability" and "end impunity." The leaders, however, rejected calls to bring individuals to account and formally accepted the findings of the report, emphasizing their determination to "bring closure to a chapter of our recent past."

In May President Horta issued a decree granting full and partial pardons to 94 prisoners. As a result at least 20 prisoners have been released, including former Interior Minister Rogerio Lobato, who played an instrumental role in the 2006 crisis and had been jailed for manslaughter and illegal distribution of weapons. Nine prisoners serving sentences for committing crimes against humanity in 1999 also received commuted sentences with four released in June 2008. A petition against the president's decision to pardon the criminals was rejected by the court of appeal in September 2008. Timorese politicians and human rights activists backing the petition felt that the decision "strengthens impunity, weakens the people's faith in the justice system and undermines the rule of law."

In July 2008 Horta unveiled new draft legislation addressing the 2006 crisis. If passed by parliament, the law would provide a wide-ranging amnesty for perpetrators: even individuals responsible for murder and other serious crimes would be able to immunize themselves from prosecution by issuing an apology. Several individuals responsible for crimes against humanity in the 1999 carnage already enjoy impunity under a May 2008 clemency decree. Continuing failure to hold those behind the 2006 violence to account will further erode confidence in the Timorese justice system and send a message to disaffected former fighters and other armed groups that politics trumps justice.

Security Sector

The United Nations Integrated Mission in Timor-Leste (UNMIT) police continue to act as the primary law enforcement agency while taking steps to train and strengthen the National Police Force of Timor-Leste (PNTL). In December 2007 UNMIT established a PNTL Task Force of 100 police officers in Dili. UNMIT recorded a significant decrease in Dili-based crime in the months following the creation of the Task Force. But UNMIT reported that this was accompanied by an increase in allegations of "excessive use of force and ill-treatment during arrest, unlawful searches of houses and abusive behaviour."

Following the February 11 attacks on Timor-Leste's leaders, the government declared a state of emergency and members from the army and police of Timor-Leste temporarily formed a Joint Command. The Joint Command was tasked with coordinating the response, assisting in apprehending the rebels, and preventing violence from spreading.

Under the state of emergency citizens were subject to a night curfew limiting their freedom of movement. Freedom of assembly was suspended and security forces had authority to conduct searches at night without warrants.

During the state of emergency, 58 incidents of ill-treatment by the Joint Command were reported to UNMIT. Allegations included death threats and beatings resulting in hospitalization. The state of emergency had ended by the end of April everywhere except Ermera district, which remained under a state of emergency until May 22.

Human Rights Defenders

Despite a rise in allegations of human rights violations, no attacks on human rights defenders were reported in Timor-Leste in 2008.

The Office of the Provedor for Human Rights and Justice encouraged the public to report human rights violations during the state of emergency and opened investigations into 44 allegations of human rights abuses. Following investigations of these alleged abuses, cases deemed to warrant further action will be sent to the Prosecutor General's Office, though there is a current backlog of 4,700 criminal cases before the courts.

Key International Actors

Relations strengthened between the leaders of Timor-Leste and Indonesia after both countries accepted the findings of the Commission on Truth and Friendship report and agreed not to pursue individual accountability for gross human rights violations committed in Timor-Leste in 1999.

On February 25, 2008, the United Nations Security Council extended UNMIT's mandate for 12 months. In September Secretary-General Ban Ki-moon announced the appointment of Takahisa Kawakami of Japan as Deputy Special Representative for Security Sector Support and Rule of Law in Timor-Leste.

In August Prime Minister Gusmão visited Australia hoping to secure the inclusion of Timor-Leste in the Pacific Islander guest worker scheme. Australian Prime Minister Kevin Rudd did not commit to including Timor-Leste in the scheme. Rudd did pledge an increase in grants for Timorese students and funding of approximately US$5 million to build a military training centre in Timor-Leste. During his visit Gusmão announced that security was improving in Timor-Leste and suggested that Australia's troop commitment could be reduced in 2009.

From May to September 2008 the International Organization for Migration assisted Timor-Leste in returning and reintegrating 5,930 families (displaced by the 2006 unrest) from camps in and around Dili. As of November 2008, the government had closed 24 such camps but some 30 camps remained in operation.

Vietnam

The Vietnamese government continues to crackdown on democracy activists, journalists, human rights defenders, cyber-dissidents, and members of unsanctioned religious organizations.

Social unrest increased in 2008 as thousands of workers joined strikes for better pay and working conditions. An informal nationwide land rights movement swelled, as thousands of farmers traveled to Ho Chi Minh City and Hanoi to publicly express their grievances about land seizures and local corruption.

Ethnic Khmer Buddhists in the Mekong Delta and Montagnard Christians in the Central Highlands protested against land confiscation and religious persecution. 2008 saw the harshest crackdown on Catholics in Vietnam in decades as Vietnamese authorities sought to curtail mass prayer vigils in Hanoi calling for the return of government-confiscated church properties.

Political and Religious Prisoners

More than 400 political and religious prisoners remain behind bars in harsh prison conditions. Prisoners are placed in solitary confinement in dark, unsanitary cells, and there is compelling evidence of torture and ill-treatment of political prisoners, including beatings and electric shock. Credible sources report the use of forced prison labor in a cashew processing facility at Xuan Loc prison, where many political prisoners are imprisoned.

Arbitrary Detention and Unfair Trials

National security laws are used to imprison members of opposition political parties, independent trade unions, and unsanctioned media outlets and religious organizations. Political dissidents are often tried without access to legal counsel in proceedings that take less than a day.

Laws such as Ordinance 44 authorize the detention without trial of dissidents at "social protection centers" and psychiatric facilities if they are deemed to have violated national security laws. In March 2008 police arrested Bui Kim Thanh, an activist who defended victims of land confiscation and involuntarily committed her to a mental hospital for the second time in two years.

In May a Ho Chi Minh City Court sentenced three members of the opposition Viet Tan party to up to nine months' imprisonment on charges of terrorism and threatening national security for planning to distribute leaflets about their party.

Several land rights activists and landless farmers petitioning for redress were imprisoned during 2008, including seven in July on charges of causing public disorder. In September an appeals court upheld the two-year prison sentence of activist Luong Van Sinh, who had circulated reports and photographs of farmers' protests on the internet.

Media and Internet Restrictions

The Vietnamese government strictly controls the media. Criminal penalties apply to authors, publications, websites, and internet users who disseminate information or writings that oppose the government, threaten national security, reveal state secrets, or promote "reactionary" ideas. The government controls internet use by monitoring online activity, harassing and arresting cyber-dissidents, and blocking websites of democracy and human rights groups and independent media based in Vietnam and abroad.

In July 2008 the Kien Giang People's Court upheld a five-year prison sentence for internet reporter, land rights activist, and Vietnam Populist Party member Truong Minh Duc for "abusing democratic freedoms."

In September, prominent internet writer Nguyen Hoang Hai (or Dieu Cay), was sentenced to 30 months in prison. Following his trial, police detained at least a dozen other democracy activists and bloggers, many of whom, like Dieu Cay, had protested China's claims to the disputed Spratly and Paracel islands.

In October a Hanoi court sentenced reporters Nguyen Viet Chien of *Young People* (*Thanh Nien*) newspaper to two years in prison and Nguyen Van Hai from *Youth* (*Tuoi Tre*) to two years' "re-education" for having exposed a major corruption scandal in 2005.

Freedom of Religion

Vietnamese law requires that religious groups register with the government. Those that do not join one of the officially authorized religious organizations—the governing boards of which are under the control of the government—are considered illegal.

Authorities harass and arrest church leaders campaigning for rights or choosing not to affiliate with state-controlled religious oversight committees. For decades, Buddhist monk Thich Quang Do, now Supreme Patriarch of the banned Unified Buddhist Church of Vietnam, has either been in prison or under house arrest for publicly protesting government policies.

Five ethnic Khmer Buddhist monks remain in prison in Soc Trang province after participating in a peaceful protest in 2007 calling for greater religious freedom. On June 28, ethnic Khmer monk Tim Sakhorn was released from a year's imprisonment in An Giang province. Although a recognized citizen of Cambodia, Vietnamese authorities have prohibited him from returning to Cambodia since his release.

Authorities beat and arrest members of ethnic minorities in remote areas, such as Montagnards in the Central Highlands, for refusing to join state-sanctioned church organizations, protesting land confiscation, making contact with relatives or groups abroad, or trying to seek political asylum in Cambodia. In April police arrested Y Ben Hdok in Dak Lak province after other Montagnards in his district tried to flee to Cambodia to seek political asylum. After three days in detention, police told Y Ben's family to pick up his battered body. According to his family, his head was bashed in, his ribs and limbs broken, and his teeth had been knocked out. Police labeled the death a suicide.

Freedom of Association and Labor Rights

The government bans all independent political parties, unions, and human rights organizations. Decree 88 provides for strict government control of associations, which effectively serve as agencies of government ministries or the Vietnamese Communist Party.

Vietnamese workers are forbidden from organizing unions independent of the government-controlled labor confederation. Activists announced the formation of independent trade unions in 2006, but were arrested, imprisoned, harassed, intimidated, and "disappeared" for doing so; at least 10 independent trade union members have been arrested since 2006. The whereabouts of Le Tri Tue, one of the founders of the Independent Workers' Union, has remained unknown since his "disappearance" in May 2007.

Government regulations impose fines on workers who participate in strikes not approved by the government, enable local officials to force striking workers back to work, and ban strikes in strategic sectors, including power stations, railways, airports, and oil, gas, and forestry enterprises.

Despite these restrictions, thousands of workers participated in strikes calling for better wages and working conditions during 2008, including 10,000 workers at Keyking toy factory in Danang in February.

Freedom of Assembly

Decree 38 bans public gatherings in front of places where government, party, and international conferences are held, and requires organizers of public gatherings to apply for and obtain advance government permission.

Despite the restrictions, public protests and social unrest grew during 2008 as citizens throughout Vietnam publicly aired their grievances over land confiscation, corruption, religious persecution, confiscation of church property, and China's claims to offshore islands.

During 2008 unprecedented numbers of Catholics—one of the largest officially recognized religions in Vietnam—gathered in Hanoi for prayer vigils calling for return of government-confiscated church property. In September police used tear gas and electric batons to disband the vigils, detained protesters, and bulldozed properties considered sacred to Vietnamese Catholics. Hundreds of thugs, some in the blue shirts of the Communist Youth League, harassed, cursed, and spat at parishioners and destroyed church statues. The state-controlled press conducted a smear campaign against the Archbishop of Hanoi after he publicly defended the vigils. On September 19, police detained and beat an American reporter covering the events.

Police continue to forcefully disperse land rights demonstrations. In February 2008, police used dogs and electric batons to break up a land rights protest by ethnic Khmer farmers in An Giang province, injuring several protesters. In April 2008, police and soldiers forcibly dispersed Montagnard Christians demonstrating in the Central Highlands, and arrested dozens of protesters. In August four Montagnards were imprisoned on charges of organizing protests and helping people flee to Cambodia.

Women and Children

Vietnam continues to be a source of and transit point for women and girls trafficked for forced prostitution, fraudulent marriages, and forced domestic servitude to other parts of Asia. Sex workers, trafficking victims, street children, and street peddlers—officially classified by the government as "social evils"—are routinely rounded up and detained without warrants in compulsory "rehabilitation" centers, where they are subject to beatings and sexual abuse.

Key International Actors

Various governments including New Zealand, Norway, Switzerland, Canada, Sweden, Australia, the United Kingdom, France, and the European Union made representations to the Vietnamese government on behalf of activists, independent journalists, and prisoners of conscience. In October 2008 the European Parliament called on Vietnam to cease its "systematic violations of democracy and human rights" before finalization of a new EU-Vietnam cooperation agreement. Relations with the United States continued to warm with Prime Minister Dung's June 2008 visit to the US. The US raised concerns about arrests of journalists and the government's crackdown on Catholic protesters, but asserted that religious freedom continued to improve. In May the US Commission on International Religious Freedom urged the Bush administration to reinstate Vietnam's designation as a "Country of Particular Concern" (CPC) for religious freedom violations, but it did not do so. The United States, which designated

Vietnam a CPC in 2004, lifted the designation just days before President Bush's visit to Hanoi in November 2006.

Vietnam is due to be reviewed under the Universal Periodic Review mechanism of the UN Human Rights Council in May 2009.

Stuck in a Revolving Door

Iraqis and Other Asylum Seekers and Migrants
at the Greece/Turkey Entrance to the European Union

HUMAN
RIGHTS
WATCH

WORLD REPORT

2009

EUROPE
AND CENTRAL ASIA

ARMENIA

Armenia experienced one of its most serious civil and political rights crises since independence when security forces used excessive force on March 1 against opposition demonstrators protesting the results of the February 2008 presidential election. Violent clashes erupted between police and demonstrators, and authorities arrested several hundred demonstrators and prosecuted more than a hundred opposition supporters. A state of emergency temporarily restricted several basic freedoms, including freedom of assembly. International condemnation of the use of excessive force during the March 1 events and of the state of emergency was widespread.

Elections and Election-Related Violence

The February 19 presidential election was won by Prime Minister Serj Sargsyan, but was marred by election-day violence and irregularities. On election day, assailants threatened and attacked opposition activists protesting what they believed to be electoral fraud, domestic observers, and journalists at eight polling stations. Several assaults occurred in the presence of police and election officials who did not intervene; in one case a policeman appeared to assist assailants. International observers also reported violations, including campaigning near polling stations, ballot stuffing, vote buying, and counting and tabulation irregularities. Observers criticized the Central Election Commission for its apparent failure to properly investigate complaints.

On February 20, tens of thousands of supporters of Levon Ter-Petrossian, the main opposition candidate, took to the streets in downtown Yerevan. The protests continued peacefully for 10 days.

On March 1, special police forces confronted the demonstrators using excessive force, beating them with batons and attacking fleeing demonstrators. Some demonstrators also resorted to violence, including throwing stones and burning vehicles. The clashes resulted in at least 10 deaths (eight demonstrators and two police officers), and scores of people were injured. Police detained several hundred demonstrators, charging more than one hundred opposition supporters and others with organizing or participating in illegal demonstrations and mass disturbances. Police committed due process violations including incommunicado detention, denial of access to counsel, and failure to investigate allegations of ill-treatment. Subsequent trial proceedings raised fair trial concerns: several detainees were convicted solely on police testimony and in expedited trial proceedings.

The government declared a state of emergency on March 1, temporarily restricting freedom of movement, assembly, expression, and access to information. The state of emergency was lifted fully on March 21.

Under pressure from the Parliamentary Assembly of the Council of Europe (PACE), the Armenian authorities have taken steps to establish an independent inquiry into the March 1 events, but have yet to hold anyone responsible for the deaths.

Media Freedom

Police targeted journalists covering the February demonstrations. On February 29, police attacked photojournalist Gagik Shamshyan while he was attempting to photograph them. On March 1, police detained Shamshyan, took his camera, and beat him; he needed hospital treatment for his injuries and was released after the intervention of the Armenian ombudsman. Also on March 1, police hindered a Radio Liberty correspondent's work and beat the driver of her car. Police detained at least two other journalists during demonstrations in Yerevan and Gyumri.

Under the state of emergency, media could use only official information from state agencies to report on national affairs. The National Security Service (NSS) prevented at least seven opposition and independent newspapers from publishing, and blocked websites. At least two newspapers protested the restrictions and refused to print. Although media restrictions were lifted on March 13, NSS representatives interfered with the same seven newspapers' printing, allowing them to publish only on March 21. In late March tax authorities hit at least four newspapers with apparently politically-motivated audits.

In October, the Court of Cassation overturned a February 29 ruling against the founder of the Gyumri-based television station GALA for allegedly illegally using the local television tower, but left in force a March 19 fraud conviction. The cases emerged following an October 2007 tax audit that was widely seen as retaliation for GALA's airing a September 2007 Ter-Petrossian speech critical of the government. The Asparez Journalism Club of Gyumri was apparently targeted for supporting GALA. On January 19, an assailant attempted to set fire to the Asparez office, and on March 21 two unidentified men torched a car being used by Asparez director Levon Barseghyan as he returned to the car from GALA.

In June 2008 the European Court of Human Rights ruled that Armenia had violated article 10 (freedom of expression) of the European Convention on Human Rights in relation to the independent broadcast company A1+. The court held that laws regulating awarding of broadcast licenses failed to protect against arbitrary interference and that denials of a license to A1+ were unlawful. As of April, A1+ had made 12 unsuccessful attempts to regain a license since going off air in 2002. In September 2008 the National Assembly amended the law on television and radio to suspend all licensing until a digital switchover scheduled for 2010. The amendments are seen as further efforts to deny A1+ a license.

The Yerevan Press Club reported several apparently arbitrary arrests of journalists, and the beating of two journalists, Lusine Barseghyan, an *Armenian Times* reporter, and Hrach Melkumyan, Radio Liberty acting director, by unknown assailants in separate incidents in August. The journalists believe they were targeted for their professional activities.

On July 18, a presidentially-appointed commission rejected an early release request by Arman Babajanyan, editor of the independent newspaper *Zhamanak Yerevan*, who had been convicted in 2006 of forging documents in order to evade compulsory military service. Babajanyan had served two years of a three-and-a-half-year sentence and was eligible for early release on parole for good conduct.

Freedom of Assembly

Just before the government lifted the state of emergency, on March 17, 2008, the National Assembly passed restrictive amendments to the law on meetings, which were criticized by the Council of Europe and the Organization for Security and Cooperation in Europe (OSCE). Subsequent further amendments in April eased some of the restrictions. The government denied numerous opposition requests to hold public rallies in late March, and at least 90 people participating in peaceful "public walks" organized by opposition supporters in Yerevan were briefly detained.

Torture and Ill-Treatment

According to local human rights defenders, torture and ill-treatment in custody remain widespread. Several people detained in connection with the March 1 events alleged physical abuse during apprehension, transfer to police stations, and in custody. At this writing, the authorities have not investigated these claims.

In June a Yerevan court ordered additional investigation into the May 2007 death of Levon Gulyan, who was found dead after police arrested and interrogated him. The authorities allege that Gulyan jumped from a second-storey window of a police station while trying to escape, a claim denied by Gulyan's relatives who believe he was tortured.

Attacks on Human Rights Defenders and Political Activists
In November 2007 a group of unknown assailants beat Narek Galstyan, leader of the youth wing of the opposition Social-Democratic Hnchakyan Party. Two days earlier, police had briefly detained Galstyan and another activist for posting leaflets critical of Serj Sargsyan.

In May 2008 the chairman of the Armenian Helsinki Association, Mikael Danielyan, was wounded when an assailant shot him from a pneumatic gun, following an argument while both men were stopped at a traffic light. It was reported that the assailant was a former leader of the Armenian Progressive Party. Criminal investigation into the attack is ongoing.

Also in May, Arsen Kharatyan, a leading member of the pro-opposition democratic youth movements Sksela and Hima, was beaten in Yerevan by several unknown assailants, and sustained serious head injuries. Another Hima member, Narek Hovakimyan, was attacked and beaten in June.

Key International Actors

International election observers from the OSCE, Council of Europe, and the European Parliament declared that the February elections were "mostly in line" with international standards, but noted concerns about the election process. International and domestic observers also criticized uneven media coverage of candidates prior to the elections.

Citing concerns about the Armenian authorities' reaction to the March 1 events, the United States froze further payments to Armenia from the Millennium Challenge Corporation, a five-year US$235.65 million program for reducing rural poverty. In several statements, the European Union expressed concern about the authorities' use of force and arrests of demonstrators.

Following a visit to Armenia in early March, the OSCE's special envoy for the South Caucasus called on the Armenian authorities to lift the state of emergency and expressed "regret" that "maximum restraint" had not been used during the crisis.

During its urgent debate on Armenia in April, the PACE threatened to suspend Armenia's voting rights unless it took a series of urgent measures, including revoking the amendments to the law on meetings, conducting an independent inquiry into the March 1 events, and releasing those detained on seemingly politically motivated charges who had not committed any violent or serious offense. At its June session, the PACE welcomed progress in some of these areas, but regretted that Armenia had not complied with all requirements.

Council of Europe Commissioner for Human Rights Thomas Hammarberg conducted three visits to Armenia in 2008. In addition to gathering information about the March 1 events, Hammarberg provided support for establishing an independent inquiry.

AZERBAIJAN

With its October 2008 presidential election Azerbaijan largely wasted an opportunity to demonstrate improvements in human rights. Opposition parties boycotted the election, and freedom of assembly and media remained restricted. President Ilham Aliyev was re-elected with 82.6 percent of the vote.

The release of five journalists in December 2007 was a welcome step, but at least five other journalists remain in prison on questionable charges relating to their work. Torture and ill-treatment in police custody, political prisoners, and harassment and intimidation of human rights defenders remain serious problems.

On November 2, 2008, at talks convened by Russian President Dmitry Medvedev, President Aliyev and his Armenian counterpart signed an agreement to intensify efforts for a political settlement over Nagorno-Karabakh. Some commentators hailed it as the most significant step toward a breakthrough over the separatist enclave and contiguous Armenian-occupied territories since the 1994 ceasefire.

Elections

Azerbaijan has a history of seriously flawed elections. All major opposition parties boycotted the October 15 presidential election, charging that the government failed to implement the recommendations of the Organization for Security and Co-operation in Europe (OSCE) and Council of Europe from past elections. International observers from the OSCE, Council of Europe Parliamentary Assembly (PACE), and the European Parliament cited some progress in 2008's election, but noted as shortcomings the lack of competition and little media discourse, and that it "thus did not reflect all principles of a meaningful and pluralistic democratic election."

In the pre-election period, domestic election observers noted improvements in voter list verification, but documented local officials interfering in signature collection during the nominating process. Experts also noted that June election code amendments did not address Council of Europe or local NGO recommendations.

The authorities prevented the opposition from organizing demonstrations prior to the election. On July 11, police prevented the Musavat party from holding a rally near the Baku municipal building to protest violations of freedom of assembly; eight people were detained briefly. Police prevented another Musavat demonstration on June 17, briefly detaining 16 party members and two journalists.

In September the government banned foreign television and radio companies from using satellite equipment for live broadcasting during the presidential election, apparently intending to prevent or delay broadcast of election information.

Media Freedom

Journalists, particularly those critical of the government, continue to face politically-motivated charges. In December 2007 five journalists serving sentences for criminal libel or other charges were released under a presidential pardon, but five remained in prison—two of them already convicted and the other three pending trials completed in 2008. On November 14, 2008, a court sentenced the editor-in-chief of the *Ideal* newspaper, Ali Hasanov, to six months' imprisonment on criminal libel charges.

Eynulla Fatullayev, the outspoken founder and editor-in-chief of two newspapers—*Realny Azerbaijan* and *Gundelik Azerbaijan*—was convicted in October 2007 on charges of fomenting terrorism and libel and sentenced to eight-and-a-half years in prison. He continues to serve his sentence, which was upheld on appeal by the Supreme Court on June 3, 2008. Fatullayev has filed an application with the European Court of Human Rights. Mirza Sakit, a reporter and satirist for the opposition daily *Azadlyg*, is serving a three-year prison sentence for alleged narcotics possession.

Ganimed Zahid, *Azadlyg* editor-in-chief, was sentenced to four years' imprisonment in March 2008 on questionable hooliganism charges. Mushfig Husseinov, a *Bizim Yol* newspaper journalist, was sentenced to six years in January and banned from journalism for two years on questionable extortion charges; in April the appeals court reduced Husseinov's sentence to five years and left the ban unchanged. Novruzali Mammadov, editor of the *Talishi Sado* newspaper and head of the Talysh Cultural Center and of the Science Academy's Linguistics

Department, was sentenced to 10 years' imprisonment on June 24 for high treason. After more than 16 months in pretrial detention, he was convicted for "distribution of Talysh nationalist ideas and attempts to destroy the foundations of the Azerbaijani state," and for spreading "a negative image of Azerbaijan" internationally by writing about abuses against minorities.

On October 7 *Azadlyg* and *Yeni Musavat* were allowed to resume publishing temporarily, after having been closed following court decisions in libel cases.

The government failed to meaningfully investigate violence against journalists. In February two security officers beat *Azadlyg* correspondent Agil Khalil. One month later, four unknown assailants stabbed Khalil in the chest. On July 15 a Baku court sentenced Sergei Strekalin, whom they claim was Khalil's former lover, for the stabbing, to which Strekalin allegedly confessed; the conviction apparently "demonstrated" that the attack on Khalil was not political. In September 2007 Hakimeldostu Mehdiyev, a reporter for *Yeni Musavat*, was detained, threatened, and beaten severely in police custody. He was sentenced to 15 days' imprisonment for a misdemeanor.

Four years after the murder of Elmar Huseynov, the editor-in-chief of the independent journal *Monitor*, the case remains unresolved.

In November the government announced the discontinuation in 2009 of local transmission of three international radio services—BBC, Radio Free Europe/Radio Liberty, and Voice of America, making them accessible only through satellite receiver or the internet.

Torture and Ill-Treatment

Torture and ill-treatment in custody continues to be a widespread problem. Three teenage boys convicted in June 2007 of murdering another boy have stated repeatedly, including at trial, that they confessed after beatings and other ill-treatment by police and investigators. The government failed to conduct a meaningful investigation into these allegations. In October, imprisoned journalist Ganimed Zahid was beaten in custody. Azerbaijan has not allowed publication of the European Committee for the Prevention of Torture's reports on its last three visits. In November 2007 Faina Kungurova, a member of the Democratic Party of

Azerbaijan, died of starvation following a hunger strike, after six weeks in detention on drug-related charges believed to be politically motivated. From 2002-2004 she had also served a prison sentence on politically-motivated charges.

In October videos of Azeri army officers beating conscripts, apparently as part of a hazing ritual, became widely available. Two officers were subsequently arrested for their role in the beatings.

Political Prisoners

Government officials, businessmen, and opposition politicians arrested prior to the November 2005 parliamentary elections on allegations of attempting to overthrow the government remain in custody, including brothers Farhad and Rafig Aliyev, respectively former economics minister and former president of the Azpetrol oil company, and former health minister Ali Insanov. Parts of their trials were completely closed and lawyers cited procedural violations, raising concerns about the trials' fairness.

Human Rights Defenders

Human rights defenders continue to face pressure and harassment. On June 14, police detained Emin Huseynov, chairman of the Institute for Reporter Freedom and Safety (IRFS), an outspoken media monitoring organization. Police beat and threatened Huseynov in custody, and he was hospitalized for 24 days. Huseynov filed a complaint, but the court refused to open an investigation, and an appellate court upheld that refusal on September 2. IRFS staff had been the target of attacks and government surveillance in 2007.

On May 14, a Baku court found the Election Monitoring Center (EMC), an independent domestic observer organization, in violation of registration laws and ordered its liquidation. EMC staff and others believe the decision was politically motivated. After being denied registration six times, the EMC had received registration in February, but in April the Ministry of Justice suspended it, claiming the EMC had provided inaccurate information, and petitioned for its liquidation. In June the EMC lost an appeal against the May court decision.

Key International Actors

A number of international and regional institutions and bilateral partners criticized Azerbaijan's human rights record, especially regarding media freedoms. In a strongly-worded June resolution, the Council of Europe Parliamentary Assembly expressed concern about the deteriorating human rights situation and outlined urgent reforms needed prior to the presidential election. The PACE also called for decriminalization of defamation; an immediate moratorium on criminal libel charges; the release of journalists and political prisoners; and implementation of the European Court of Human Rights judgments. In a February report on his April 2007 visit to Azerbaijan, the United Nations special rapporteur on freedom of opinion and expression, Ambeyi Ligabo, encouraged the government to consider repealing criminal defamation laws and to institute a moratorium on criminal libel prosecutions. He also noted the problem of impunity for crimes targeting media professionals. Others making strong statements on the media situation in 2008 included Council of Europe Secretary-General Terry Davis; the PACE rapporteur on Azerbaijan, Andreas Herkel; OSCE Representative on the Freedom of the Media Miklos Haraszti; and United States Assistant Secretary for Democracy, Human Rights, and Labor David J. Kramer.

On January 8, 2008, the European Union welcomed the presidential pardon of the imprisoned journalists, and called for the release of the remaining journalists and for a moratorium on defamation proceedings. The EU's European Neighbourhood Policy Action Plan progress report released in April also noted that "the rapid solution" of the cases of the remaining journalists in jail, and a revision of the current norms on libel and defamation "would contribute to improving the attainment of the relevant Action Plan objectives." It highlighted the problem of torture, noting that "effective investigation of allegations of torture remained minimal." It also called for the government to ensure judicial independence.

Azerbaijan is due to be reviewed under the Universal Periodic Review mechanism of the UN Human Rights Council in February 2009.

Belarus

Belarusian authorities continue to use the criminal justice system and onerous administrative demands to control civil society, political opposition, and the media. In 2008, as in previous years, several opposition activists and journalists were arrested and jailed for participating in unsanctioned protests. Violence was used against some activists and journalists during demonstrations.

Belarus has demonstrated some progress by releasing its last remaining political prisoners in 2008, but at least 10 activists continue to serve "restricted freedom" sentences that permit them only to be at home or at work. Belarus introduced new restrictions on the media that take effect in early 2009.

Political Freedoms and Civil Society

Belarus held parliamentary elections on September 28, 2008. The elections failed to meet international standards for free and fair elections, according to the United States, the European Union, and the Office for Democratic Institutions and Human Rights of the Organization for Security and Co-operation in Europe (OSCE/ODIHR). The ODIHR noted minor improvements over previous elections, including opposition representatives' increased ability to participate in election commissions and conduct meetings without interference; but cited a major lack of transparency in the vote count, more than 35 percent of OSCE election observers having been denied permission to observe that process. Observers who were granted access observed falsification of results in several cases.

The government controls political opposition groups, NGOs, and trade unions through costly and burdensome registration requirements, and often denies registration for unfounded reasons. Some requirements, such as a legal address in a nonresidential building, are often too expensive for applicants to meet, while authorities have denied registration to NGOs for such minor technical reasons as incorrect birth date information and typos in names on applications, rather than giving them an opportunity to make corrections.

Activists are also required to apply for demonstration permits, but the onerous application process serves as a tool to restrict the right to hold peaceful assemblies. Belarusian authorities continue to fine, jail, and search the homes of opposition activists in relation to organizing and participating in "unauthorized events." In 2008 such events in Minsk included the annual Freedom Day demonstration on March 25 and the April 26 Chernobyl rally, as well as rallies on January 10 and 21 against new policies affecting small businesses. In December 2007 riot police beat political opposition leader Anatol Labiedzka and Young Front leader Dmitry Fiedaruk during a protest, leaving Fiedaruk unconscious.

The Ministry of Justice has not legally registered any new NGO since 2000. Some organizations operate despite repeated denials of registration, and the authorities have harassed and arrested dozens of activists for acting on behalf of unregistered organizations, a criminal offense. Even for registered NGOs, authorities monitor correspondence and telephone conversations and conduct frequent inspections of premises.

The Belarusian Helsinki Committee (BHC) remains under threat of closure for alleged tax violations, following a 2007 court ruling that it is liable for back taxes and fees of 160m rubles (about US$75,000). Authorities harassed several BHC senior staff members. On May 1, 2008, Belarusian border guards stopped BHC Chairperson Aleh Hulak, his wife Anastasia Hulak, and a BHC regional coordinator, Eduard Balanchuk, at the Belarus-Poland border and searched them for more than 10 hours. Belarusian customs officials confiscated their money and computer for supposed "verification"; their belongings have not been returned. Pavel Levinov, a human rights lawyer and representative of the BHC in Vitebsk, was detained on May 26 and fined 700,000 rubles (approximately US$330) in connection with legal aid he provided to journalists under investigation for televising cartoons that allegedly insulted President Alexander Lukashenka. Officers of the KGB (Belarus' state security agency) broke into BHC activist Leonid Svetik's home in May, seized office equipment and printed materials, and interrogated Svetik for nine hours about an ethnic hate case he allegedly witnessed.

Political Prisoners

In February 2008 the government unexpectedly released several political prisoners, including Young Front leaders Artur Finkevich and Zmicier Dashkevich. In 2006 Finkevich had received a sentence of two years' corrective labor for "malicious hooliganism" for allegedly writing political graffiti. In November 2006 Dashkievich had been sentenced to 18 months in prison for "organizing or partici-pating in the activities of an unregistered organization."

In August 2008 the authorities granted early release to Belarus's three remaining political prisoners. Alexander Kazulin, a candidate in the March 2006 presidential election, was released from a five-and-a-half-year prison sentence handed down in July 2006 for hooliganism and disturbing public order after his arrest during a peaceful post-election opposition march. Andrej Kim, a youth activist, was released early from an 18-month sentence handed down in April 2008 for "petty hooliganism" and "violation of rules of organizing and holding mass actions" in connection with the two January demonstrations against new policies for small businesses. Siarheji Parsiukevich, a businessman and former police officer, was released from a two-and-a-half-year sentence handed down in April for "violence or threat of violence against a policeman" during the January 10 protest, in which more than 2,000 small business owners took part.

Kim had stood trial with 10 other youth activists for the January protests. Seven of Kim's co-defendants received two years of "limitation of freedom without transfer to an open correctional institute" (a version of house arrest that restricts them to home and work) and two received fines for blocking traffic.

Media Freedom

The government continues to tightly control the media. Several privately-owned Belarusian newspapers are printed in Russia because local, state-run printing companies are not permitted to print material that "discredits Belarus" by "fraud-ulent representation" of developments in the country. There are no independent television or radio stations and authorities monitor the internet; politically-sensi-tive sites are often temporarily shut down. In August Belarusian authorities approved a new law that will further restrict the media effective from February 2009. The new restrictions include requiring online media to register with authori-ties and for registered media to reregister. The law also prohibits media outlets from receiving foreign funding.

Journalists are affected by the restrictive measures against peaceful assembly. In 2008 police on several occasions searched, detained, interrogated, and arrested journalists for covering demonstrations. The homes of roughly 30 journalists in several cities were searched for materials that allegedly defamed the president in connection with coverage of the peaceful March 25 demonstrations, and *Nasha Niva* reporters Syamyon Pechanko and Andrei Lyankevich were beaten and detained while reporting from a rally in Minsk that day. Pechanko was sentenced to 15 days in prison for participating in an unsanctioned protest.

Death Penalty

Belarus is the only country in Europe that continues to use the death penalty. As of mid-November 2008, three executions had been carried out this year, all in February; there is no public information on the number of executions in 2007. Families of those executed are not provided with information on the date of the execution or where the body is buried.

Key International Actors

The United States and the European Union welcomed the August releases of political prisoners and expressed hope that it would lead to improved relations. Both have expressed clearly that more progress needs to be made, especially in regard to free and fair elections, civil society, and the media. In October EU foreign ministers decided to suspend the travel ban imposed on President Lukashenka and also suspended the travel restrictions imposed on most of his inner circle, although six Belarusian officials are still barred entry to the EU, and the financial measures imposed against the Belarusian administration remain in place. The US maintains a visa ban against Lukashenka and his inner circle, as well as economic sanctions including against the energy company Belneftekhim, imposed in response to the flawed 2006 election and subsequent arrests and detention of independent political activists. In September 2008 the US lifted economic sanctions against two subsidiaries of Belneftekhim, however.

US-Belarusian relations deteriorated in late 2007 and early 2008 when Belarusian authorities demanded expulsion of US Embassy staff after the US imposed sanctions on Belneftekhim, but relations thawed somewhat following the prisoner releases. In May the US Congress extended and amended the Belarus Democracy Act of 2004, which authorizes assistance to organizations that promote democracy and civil society in Belarus. The United States remains concerned about imprisoned US lawyer Emanuel Zeltser, who was arrested by the KGB on March 12, 2008, and has been convicted and sentenced to three years' imprisonment for economic espionage and using false documents. US officials were refused access to his closed trial and were denied consular access to Zeltser several times.

The Council of Europe's Parliamentary Assembly (PACE) welcomed Alexander Kazulin's release, but noted that he should never have been jailed in the first place. In April PACE adopted the resolution "Abuse of the criminal justice system in Belarus," urging Belarus to "mitigate the effects of abusive legislation" and abolish the death penalty, among other recommendations. The resolution "encouraged" the EU and the US to continue targeted sanctions, and called for a mechanism to assist victims of human rights abuses, such as a working group of local and international human rights defenders with tasks such as identifying officials responsible for abuses. In a July statement PACE's rapporteur on the situation in Belarus condemned the new media law.

Bosnia and Herzegovina

The discovery in August 2008 of a mass grave near Kamenica, believed to hold the bodies of up to 100 victims of the 1995 Srebrenica massacre, was a reminder that Bosnia remains marked by the legacy of the 1992-95 war. The appearance of Radovan Karadzic in the dock of the International Criminal Tribunal for the former Yugoslavia (ICTY), 13 years after his indictment, was a major blow against impunity; but progress in prosecuting war crimes in Bosnia's courts was mixed. The number of refugees and displaced persons returning to their areas of origin continues to decline. The climate for civil society in Republika Srpska worsened.

War Crimes Accountability

On July 30, 2008, Radovan Karadzic was transferred from Serbia to The Hague (for his apprehension see Serbia chapter). His initial appearance before the ICTY took place the following day. Karadzic is charged with genocide, including at Srebrenica; crimes against humanity; and war crimes. Karadzic refused to enter a plea during his second appearance in August, saying he did not recognize the court's jurisdiction. A "not guilty" plea was entered on his behalf. In September prosecutors streamlined the indictment, narrowing the geographic scope and clarifying the allegations against Karadzic. In a disappointing move, the amended Karadzic indictment remains vague on charges of sexual violence.

Ratko Mladic, fellow indicted architect of the Srebrenica massacre, remains at large.

In November Karadzic testified as a defense witness in the ongoing ICTY appeal of Momcilo Krajisnik, a Bosnian Serb wartime leader convicted in 2006 of crimes against humanity.

In June Stojan Zupljanin, accused of war crimes and crimes against humanity against non-Serbs principally in Republika Srpska, was transferred to the ICTY. In July the appeals chamber acquitted Naser Oric, Bosniak (Bosnian Muslim) wartime commander in Srebrenica, on all counts, reversing his 2006 conviction and two-year sentence for crimes against Serb civilians. In September the ICTY sentenced Rasim Delic to three years' imprisonment for crimes against Serb prisoners; his conviction is under appeal.

In July 2008 a Dutch district court in The Hague ruled that it lacked jurisdiction to hear a civil claim against the United Nations brought by some 6,000 relatives of Srebrenica massacre victims.

Bosnia's War Crimes Chamber (WCC) continued successfully to pursue its mandate of prosecuting those responsible for war atrocities. In September 2008 the chamber launched a new national war crimes strategy to address the backlog of cases, which could involve as many as 10,000 suspects. According to the strategy, prosecutions before the WCC will focus on "those who planned the worst atrocities" during the war.

In November 2007 the WCC appeals chamber sentenced Gojko Jankovic, the former commander of Republika Srpska military units operating in Foca, to 34 years' imprisonment for sexual violence and other wartime abuses in Foca. Notable developments in the WCC during 2008 included sentences ranging from 38 to 42 years handed down in July to seven Serb defendants in the "Kravica case" convicted of genocide in and around Srebrenica.

Local (district and cantonal) criminal courts continue to face challenges in their efforts to effectively tackle war crimes trials. According to the Organization for Security and Co-operation in Europe (OSCE), Republika Srpska prosecutors have brought a total of 21 indictments against 44 accused, with district courts reaching 12 verdicts and 9 cases ongoing. In the Federation, cantonal courts have decided a total of 85 verdicts against 119 defendants, with 16 cases still in process.

The absence of witness support or protection services in most local courts discourages witnesses from testifying. Other shortcomings include an insufficient number of prosecutors and support staff; inadequate cooperation between prosecutors and police, as well as between police across entity lines; lack of legal harmonization; and insufficient outreach to affected communities.

EUROPE AND CENTRAL ASIA

Return of Refugees and Internally Displaced Persons

Returns of refugees and internally displaced persons (IDPs) to their areas of origin continued to decline. As of June 2008 more than 132,000 Bosnians remained displaced. The United Nations High Commissioner for Refugees registered 286 IDP and 246 refugee returns during the first half of 2008, the majority in both categories being Bosniaks. Not all registered returnees remain permanently, especially in areas where the returnees' ethnic group now constitutes a minority. Limited economic opportunities and lack of adequate housing constitute the two main practical obstacles to sustainable return.

Roma refugees in Bosnia, the majority from Kosovo, remain vulnerable and dependent on periodic extensions of their temporary protection status.

Citizenship and National Security

The Bosnian commission that reviews wartime decisions on the naturalization of foreign citizens, including those who came to fight alongside Bosniaks, continued its work. Attou Mimoun, a naturalized Bosnian of Algerian origin, was stripped of his citizenship and expelled in December 2007. Many others (now estimated at around 300 persons) also had their citizenship revoked. While the process is said to be motivated solely by concerns over irregularities in naturalization decisions, it appears also to be linked to concerns about the presence of alleged Islamist radicals in Bosnia with links to terrorism.

Some whose citizenship was revoked left Bosnia voluntarily. Others appealed against the loss of their citizenship and have been allowed to remain in Bosnia pending the outcome of those appeals. In a February report, the Council of Europe Human Rights Commissioner Thomas Hammarberg echoed NGO concerns about the lack of adequate safeguards against the risk of return to serious human rights abuse, including torture or ill-treatment, for those subject to forced removal. His comments followed the January 2008 intervention by the European Court of Human Rights to halt the removal to Syria of Imad Al-Husin, pending the decision of the Bosnian Constitutional Court on his appeal against revocation of citizenship and deportation. At this writing, Al-Husin remains in detention in Bosnia.

The six Algerian national security suspects illegally transferred to Guantanamo Bay in 2002 with the complicity of the Bosnian authorities remain there at this writing. Their cases were among those considered by the US Supreme Court when it ruled in June 2008 that detainees held at Guantanamo have the right to challenge their detention in civilian courts in the United States. Their petition to the European Court of Human Rights was expedited for consideration, but at this writing the court has yet to rule on the petition.

Human Rights Defenders

Branko Todorovic, the president of the Republika Srpska Helsinki Assembly, received threatening phone calls directed toward him and his family on July 23. While the police responded promptly by opening an investigation and providing protection, Republika Srpska authorities failed to condemn the threats. In May the Bijelina district court convicted two men for their role in the unrelated February 2007 murder of the organization's previous head, Dusko Kondor, and the wounding of his daughter. The defendant convicted of the murder received a 20-year prison sentence, while his accomplice received seven years. An appellate court rejected the latter's appeal against conviction in June.

Transparency International Bosnia and Herzegovina temporarily closed its office in Banja Luka in July following what the Office of the High Representative (OHR) called a "propaganda campaign" against the organization by Republika Srpska authorities. Republika Srpska Prime Minister Milorad Dodik accused the organization of racketeering and extortion, and offered "full witness protection" to citizens who came forward with information on its alleged wrongdoings. Dragomir Babic, a human rights activist from Republika Srpska, had alerted OHR about the campaign in an anonymous letter in February 2008. Babic came forward as the author following the July office closure, and received anonymous death threats during that month.

Lesbian, Gay, Bisexual, and Transgender Rights

The inauguration of Bosnia's first cultural festival for lesbian, gay, bisexual, and transgender people in September 2008 met with widespread denunciation and

anonymous death threats. Violence at the opening injured at least eight participants; organizers were forced to make the rest of the festival a private event.

Key International Actors

In June the Peace Implementation Council agreed, despite Russian opposition,
that no date should be set for closure of the Office of the High Representative, a
further move away from its 2006 assessment that Bosnia would be ready for full
self-governance by mid-2007.

In a positive move, the European Union concluded a Stabilization and
Association Agreement with Bosnia on June 16, 2008, the first step toward opening membership negotiations, although its progress report in November was
somewhat downbeat.

In May the European Court of Human Rights ruled in *Rodic v. Bosnia* that Bosnian
Serb prisoners serving sentences for war crimes in Zenica prison had been subject to prohibited ill-treatment in 2005 because Bosnian authorities failed to protect the men from abuse at the hands of Bosniak prisoners. The European Court
also received written submissions during 2008 in *Finci and Sedjic v. Bosnia,*
which contests Bosnia's constitutional requirement that its three-person presidency must consist of a Serb, a Croat, and a Bosniak; thereby barring Jews, Roma,
and other minorities from standing for election.

CROATIA

Croatia made modest improvements in human rights in 2008, motivated by its desire to join the European Union, but it has yet to fully address obstacles to the return and reintegration of Serbs. The impartiality and effectiveness of domestic war crimes prosecutions remains in doubt. The closure of the Organization for Security and Co-operation in Europe mission in December 2007 created a human rights monitoring gap.

Return and Integration of Serbs

Despite government declarations expressing commitment to the issue, Serb returns to Croatia slowed to a trickle. Most of the 231 displaced persons and 610 refugees who returned to their home areas during the first half of 2008 were ethnic Croats. According to United Nations High Commissioner for Refugees, around 125,000 ethnic Serbs who fled the 1991-1995 conflict are registered as having returned to Croatia, of whom around 55,000 remain permanently.

Serb returnees continue to suffer violence and intimidation, particularly in north Dalmatia, although at a declining rate. Most attacks were directed at property rather than people. Police generally increased their presence at the scene following such attacks and opened investigations, but did not identify the perpetrators. The most serious incident occurred in March, when a group of young men stoned a house of a Serb returnee family in the area of Benkovac, injuring a family member. Police arrested the alleged perpetrators, who are on trial for ethnically-motivated violent assault charges at this writing.

Serbs continue to face difficulty repossessing occupied homes, despite court judgments in their favor. Repossession cases sometimes linger in the courts. There is still no effective remedy for those seeking the return of occupied agricultural land. At this writing, there are 7,743 pending appeals (mostly from Serbs) against rejected applications for reconstruction assistance.

While the two existing government-sponsored housing care programs enable those who wish to return to apply for and receive housing, there was no progress toward a viable solution for Serbs stripped during the war of the right to occupy socially-owned property (an impediment to Serb return to urban areas). The government fell short by around 100 units on its pledge to provide 1,400 housing units for Serb returnees by mid-2008.

The government adopted a procedure in May to allow Serbs to register periods of work in formerly occupied areas (an impediment to Serbs qualifying for Croatian pensions). Increased government funding for legal aid for the general population has partly benefited displaced and returnee Serbs in housing and other wartime-related disputes.

War Crimes Accountability

The trial of Croatian generals Ante Gotovina, Ivan Cermak, and Mladen Markac began in March at the International Criminal Tribunal for the former Yugoslavia (ICTY). The three are accused of war crimes and crimes against humanity, including persecution and murder committed during a 1995 military operation against rebel Serbs in Krajina, during which around 200,000 ethnic Serbs were forced out of the region. While Croatia has handed over all its indictees to the ICTY, it was criticized by the tribunal in June for failing to deliver all requested documents related to the Gotovina case, a charge rejected by Croatia.

In May the Zagreb county court sentenced Gen. Mirko Norac to seven years' imprisonment for war crimes against ethnic Serb civilians in the "Medak pocket," and acquitted Gen. Rahim Ademi of the same charges. The case was the first transferred from the ICTY to Croatia. The prosecution has appealed against Norac's sentence and Ademi's acquittal.

In September delays in the prosecution of Branimir Glavas, caused by the summer recess and wrangling over a co-defendant's legal representation, led to a breach in prosecution time-limits and forced a retrial in the Osijek county court. Glavas and six others are charged with war crimes against Serb civilians. Glavas, who is at liberty, remains a sitting member of the Croatian parliament.

Serbs continued to make up the majority of defendants in war crimes trials. According to the OSCE, during the first nine months of 2008 there were 20 active war crimes trials across eight county courts, involving 72 defendants, 45 of whom are Serb. Nine of the trials (involving 17 defendants) reached final verdicts, with

14 defendants convicted (eight Serbs and six Croats) and three acquitted (two Serbs and one Albanian).

In absentia prosecutions against Serbs continued in Vukovar, Sisak, and Osijek, despite opposition from the State Attorney's Office. A similar trial in Rijeka appears to have been suspended indefinitely. Retrials began in three cases involving a total of four Serbs, after the Supreme Court overturned the previous in absentia convictions because of insufficient evidence or poorly reasoned judgments.

In September the government indicated a willingness to extradite its citizens to neighboring countries to face trial on war crimes and other charges, "if other states were prepared to do the same." Despite regional mechanisms for judicial cooperation, Croatia and Serbia currently prohibit the extradition of their citizens, widely seen as an impediment to war crimes accountability.

Media Freedom

In July the Association of Croatian Journalists threatened a general strike in protest at pressure and intimidation of journalists reporting on war crimes and other sensitive topics. The protest came after threats in February against Drago Hedl, a reporter with *Feral Tribune* newspaper, apparently related to his coverage of wartime abuses in Osijek, and a violent assault in June on Dusan Miljus, a well-known journalist covering organized crime and corruption. At this writing, the police have yet to identify Miljus' assailants. The government condemned both incidents.

On October 28, Ivo Pukanic, a well-known editor of the prominent political weekly *Nacional*, and his marketing director Niko Franjic, were killed by a car bomb in Zagreb. The killings, and the murder in Zagreb two weeks earlier of Ivana Hodic, a prominent lawyer's daughter, shocked Croatia and prompted a crackdown on organized crime, including dozens of arrests within Croatia and in neighboring states.

Migration and Asylum Policy

A new law on asylum and another on foreigners entered into force on January 1, 2008, intended to harmonize Croatian legislation with EU law. According to the Croatian Law Center, there continue to be shortcomings in Croatia's asylum practice. Although the law on asylum prescribes that asylum seekers will not be punished for illegal entry, in practice asylum seekers still risk administrative sanction for misdemeanor for doing so. Some asylum seekers lack access to legal advice or interpreters during misdemeanor proceedings, which can lead to them being given expulsion decisions and deported before there is any consideration of the asylum claim.

Asylum seekers are subject to detention if facing misdemeanor proceedings for illegal entry, rather than being transferred to appropriate conditions at the Kutina asylum center. Detention conditions for such asylum seekers are often inadequate, with overcrowding, instances of inadequate heating, and limited space for movement. This is especially the case in the Jezevo migrant facility near Zagreb, where some detainees threatened a hunger strike in September in protest at conditions.

Children's Rights

The European Court of Human Rights ruled in July 2008 that Croatia did not discriminate against Roma pupils by placing them in separate classes at school, pointing to the fact that separate classes for Roma took place within mainstream schools and were temporary in nature (until pupils' Croatian language skills improved). Roma organizations expressed their disappointment at the decision.

Human Rights Defenders

Human rights groups continue to be viewed with suspicion, but remain largely free to operate. The positive work of the Human Rights Ombudsman was undermined by the frequent failure of national and local authorities to respond to its recommendations and information requests.

The closure of the OSCE Mission in Croatia on December 24, 2007, created a significant human rights monitoring gap in the country. Although the OSCE retains a residual presence in Zagreb, primarily to monitor war crimes trials, it lacks the capacity to engage effectively with the Croatian government across the range of human rights issues affecting the country.

Key International Actors

The European Union remains the most influential international actor in Croatia, an official candidate for EU membership. In March 2008 Croatia received an entry target date of 2010. An EU Council decision in February identified among the priorities refugee return, adequate housing for tenancy-right holders, recognition of Serb wartime working time for pensions, and the reconstruction and repossession of property. In response, the Croatian authorities are developing action plans containing deadlines by which clear progress should be attained. The European Commission (through its annual progress report) and the European Parliament (through its Croatia rapporteur) reiterated the need for Croatia to address these priority issues and to ensure that legal and institutional changes on housing and pensions deliver practical benefits to affected Serbs.

In July NATO ambassadors in Brussels signed accession protocols allowing Croatia to join the alliance at a later stage, possibly as early as spring 2009.

Croatia signed the Council of Europe Convention on Action against Trafficking in Human Beings in February 2008.

EUROPEAN UNION

The process of improving human rights protections in European Union law stalled in June 2008, a consequence of the Lisbon Treaty being rejected by referendum in Ireland. The treaty would make the EU party to the European Convention on Human Rights, and the EU Charter on Fundamental Rights and Freedoms binding in EU law. At present, EU institutions are not explicitly bound by the convention, unlike individual EU member states.

The European Union and leading member states continue to pursue counterterrorism measures that violate human rights. National security removals despite the risk of ill-treatment on return, inadequate safeguards in detention, and curbs on freedom of expression and the right to privacy, are among the key concerns.

Migration and asylum policies remain focused on keeping irregular migrants, including children, out of the EU and removing those who are present rather than ensuring their rights are protected. Racist and xenophobic incidents and policies, particularly affecting the Roma and Sinti, Jewish, and Muslim populations, as well as migrants, were an issue in a number of EU states.

Counterterrorism Measures and Human Rights

The EU Council approved in April an amendment to the EU Framework Decision on Combating Terrorism, introducing new offenses of provocation (intended to give effect to provisions in the Council of Europe Convention on the Prevention of Terrorism), and terrorist recruitment and training, including when committed over the internet. The provocation offense gives rise to concern about criminalization of speech with little connection to terrorism. In September the European Parliament recommended narrowing the amendment, so that only speech intended to directly incite specific terrorism offenses is criminalized.

The lack of safeguards in the EU's implementation of United Nations financial measures against terrorism was highlighted in September, when the European Court of Justice ruled in the case of *Kadi* that the inability of non-EU nationals whose assets are frozen to effectively challenge the decision violates the right to a fair hearing. This reversed the finding of the EU's Court of First Instance that the binding nature of the measures imposed by the UN Security Council, outweighed human rights obligations.

European Union member states continued to seek the expulsion of terrorism suspects, including through the use of diplomatic assurances, to a risk of torture or other prohibited ill-treatment on return, despite opposition from the courts, human rights bodies, and NGOs. In February 2008 the European Court of Human Rights unanimously reaffirmed the absolute prohibition on return to torture or other prohibited ill-treatment in its judgment in *Saadi v. Italy*, which concerned Italy's attempted expulsion of a terrorism suspect to Tunisia, with the use of assurances. It rejected a submission by the United Kingdom government to allow risk of ill-treatment on return to be balanced against a threat to national security. It also rejected the notion that diplomatic assurances necessarily constitute a guarantee against torture.

Earlier allegations in Parliamentary Assembly of the Council of Europe (PACE) and European Parliament reports of CIA renditions programs having used secret detention centers in Poland and Romania were finally being addressed in Poland, but Romania has taken no significant steps. In August, at the request of Polish Prime Minister Donald Tusk, the public prosecutor initiated an investigation into the allegations. Critics are concerned that the scope and powers of the investigation will not be sufficient to address serious allegations of torture and other human rights abuses.

Common EU Asylum and Migration Policy

A "European Pact on Immigration," adopted by the European Council in October, was the centerpiece of the migration focus under France's EU Presidency in the latter half of 2008. The non-binding pact foresees stricter controls on family reunification for migrants and calls on EU states to pursue expulsion, paying migrants to return home, and readmission agreements with countries of origin, to remove irregular migrants. The pact raises concerns about its potential impact on the right to family life and the prohibition on return to a risk of persecution or ill-treatment.

The continued focus of EU migration policy on border enforcement rather than human rights protection was reflected in the €30 million increase to the 2008 budget for the EU border control agency, Frontex. At this writing, the Frontex operation "Hera" during 2008 has "deterred" or "diverted" back to West Africa 4,373 undocumented migrants heading to the Canary Islands.

In June the European Parliament adopted the controversial Council Directive on common standards and procedures in Member States for returning illegally staying third-country nationals, known as the Returns Directive. The measure, which will come into effect in 2010, permits the detention of undocumented migrants and failed asylum seekers, including unaccompanied children, for up to 18 months and allows for a five-year ban on reentry. In October 2008 the UN High Commissioner for Human Rights criticized the detention periods in the directive as excessive and an erosion of the right to liberty for migrants.

Human Rights Concerns in EU Member States

France

Reviews by the UN Human Rights Council in May under Universal Periodic Review and the Human Rights Committee in July identified serious human rights concerns with France's counterterrorism law and policy. The Human Rights Committee called on France to end the practice of denying terrorism suspects in police custody access to a lawyer for 72 hours after arrest and not informing them of their right to remain silent.

The lack of an automatically suspensive appeal against expulsion in cases involving national security was identified as a particular problem; since it can result in the removal of suspects at risk of torture or ill-treatment before any appeal is determined (a similar concern applies in asylum cases subject to expedited procedures). In April the European Court of Human Rights ordered France to suspend the national security deportation of Kamel Daoudi to Algeria, highlighting the need for an effective in-country procedure.

In a welcome development, France ratified the Optional Protocol to the UN Convention against Torture in July, following the appointment in June of France's first Inspector General of Places of Detention (fulfilling a protocol obligation).

A law adopted in February allows certain former violent offenders to be detained for renewable one-year periods of preventive detention after they have served their prison sentence. This undermines the presumption of innocence, the right to liberty, and the right not to be punished twice for the same crime.

In June France's top administrative court, the Conseil d'Etat, denied citizenship to a Moroccan Muslim woman married to a French man on the grounds that her "radical" religious practices (including wearing the niqab) were incompatible with French values, in particular that of gender equality.

Germany

The German Constitutional Court gave important rulings in February and March that laws relating to surveillance and the storing of internet and telephone data disproportionately restrict the right to privacy. Changes to the law governing Germany's federal criminal police operations adopted by the Bundestag (lower house) in November would allow investigators to use intrusive surveillance techniques on terrorism suspects based on generalized suspicion; the changes are pending before the Bundesrat (upper house) at this writing. Employment-based restrictions continue on teachers and other civil servants wearing the headscarf, despite concerns that the measures discriminate on the grounds of religion, with courts in three states upholding headscarf bans for teachers since December 2007.

The European Centre for Constitutional Rights, an NGO, filed a lawsuit against the German government at the Berlin Administrative Court in June for its failure to formally request the extradition of 13 CIA agents who had been charged in Germany for involvement in the kidnapping of Khaled el-Masri, a German citizen of Lebanese descent apprehended in Macedonia and flown to Afghanistan, where he was imprisoned for five months and tortured.

An attempt by Germany to extradite to Turkey Hassan Atmaca, a refugee suspected of links to the Kurdistan Workers Party, using diplomatic assurances, is subject

FRANCE

Preempting Justice

Counterterrorism Laws and Procedures in France

HUMAN
RIGHTS
WATCH

to a pending appeal to the European Court of Human Rights. Challenges in German courts to deportation proceedings against two Tunisian national security suspects using assurances are pending at this writing.

Following an August review of Germany, the United Nations Committee on the Elimination of Racial Discrimination noted an increase in reported racism-related incidents against members of the Jewish, Muslim, and Roma and Sinti communities, as well as German nationals of foreign origin and asylum seekers (in particular Africans), and called for "more resolute action" to prevent and punish the perpetrators. Germany is due to be reviewed under the Universal Periodic Review mechanism of the UN Human Rights Council in February 2009.

Greece

In April the UN High Commissioner for Refugees (UNHCR) leveled sharp criticism at Greek asylum and detention policies and recommended that other European states not return asylum seekers to Greece, a blow to EU rules that asylum claims should generally be heard in the first EU country entered, and that reception conditions and asylum procedures must meet common standards. UNHCR said that asylum seekers in Greece "often lack the most basic entitlements, such as interpreters and legal aid, to ensure that their claims receive adequate scrutiny from the asylum authorities." Greece recognized only 1.2 percent of asylum claims at first instance in 2007.

Greek police systematically arrest migrants on Greek territory, including a large proportion of Iraqis, detain them for days without providing legally required registration, and in some cases beat or otherwise ill-treat them. Migrants are regularly forcibly and secretly expelled to Turkey without consideration of their protection needs.

Around 1,000 unaccompanied children entered Greece in 2008, the majority from Afghanistan. There were numerous examples of such children being beaten and kicked by Greek coastguard, police, and port police officers upon interception at the border or during arrest and detention. Children are often detained together with adults. Most fail to seek asylum, lack status, and are at risk of deportation. Many live outside sponsored care and are exploited in dangerous working condi-

tions. Unaccompanied girls in particular are at high-risk of falling into the hands of trafficking networks.

Italy

Silvio Berlusconi was reelected prime minister in April, gaining a clear majority in both houses of parliament. His government in July declared a national state of emergency in relation to undocumented migration. As a result, undocumented status in Italy is now a crime punishable by up to four years in prison as well as being an aggravating factor for other crimes, increasing associated prison sentences.

In a memorandum in July, Council of Europe Commissioner for Human Rights Thomas Hammarberg criticized the rise of racist and xenophobic incidents in Italy as well as increased discrimination against Roma and Sinti in government policies.

Against a backdrop of vigilante incidents, including two attacks in which Roma camps were destroyed by petrol bombs in May, and public concern about several violent crimes allegedly perpetrated by Roma individuals, the government declared a state of emergency for "nomad communities" (code for Roma) in the Campania, Lazio, and Lombardy regions, giving local authorities special powers including to conduct censuses and to raid and dismantle Roma camps. In July a lawsuit was filed in Italy challenging the legality of these measures and the European Parliament adopted a resolution calling on Italy to stop fingerprinting Roma including children. The European Commission muted its criticism of the policy following assurances from the Italian government that it was not collecting ethnic data.

The trial of 26 US citizens and 7 Italian citizens for the abduction in Milan and rendition to Egypt of the Egyptian cleric Hassan Mustafa Osama Nasr, known as Abu Omar, resumed in March, amid allegations that the government had acted "disloyally" in pursuing a claim before the Constitutional Court that the Milan prosecutors' office violated state secrecy laws in the conduct of the investigation. In October the court agreed to hear arguments on the state secrets claims in a closed hearing scheduled for March 2009. Also in October the Court of Cassation confirmed the conviction of Rabei Osman for links to the March 2004 Madrid train bombings.

Despite the ruling in *Saadi v. Italy*, Italy expelled Essid Sami Ben Khemais to Tunisia in June, in breach of interim measures issued by the European Court of Human Rights requesting that Italy suspend the expulsion until the court had considered the case. This drew criticism from Commissioner Hammarberg. The Italian authorities justified the expulsion on the grounds that they had obtained diplomatic assurances from the Tunisian government guaranteeing that Ben Khemais would not be tortured and would receive a fair trial. At this writing, the case is pending before the European Court of Human Rights.

Migrants continue to die attempting to reach Italy by sea in unseaworthy boats. The trials of seven Tunisian fishermen for abetting illegal immigration after they rescued 44 migrants and brought them to safety on Lampedusa, an island off Sicily, were ongoing at this writing. There are fears that such prosecutions risk discouraging rescues at sea and exacerbate the dangers for migrants attempting the crossing.

Malta

Malta continued to be criticized for its failure to rescue migrants in distress at sea and unwillingness to allow ships carrying migrants rescued at sea to enter its ports. More than a thousand migrants reached Malta in 2008. In August, 71 migrants drowned in the Mediterranean Sea when their dinghy capsized; eight survivors were rescued by a fishing vessel. The Maltese government has been calling for "burden sharing" among EU states on irregular migration.

Migrants, including children, who come to Malta are held in closed detention centers for up to 18 months while their claims are processed. Detention facilities for migrants in Malta were criticized in a PACE report in May. An investigation ordered by the Maltese government into allegations of ill-treatment against detainees involved in a disturbance in the Safi detention center in March concluded that there had been excessive use of force by staff, but failed to identify those responsible.

The Netherlands

A bill on administrative measures for national security aimed at preventing acts of terrorism passed the House of Representatives in March 2007 and is pending before the Senate at this writing. It contains provisions severely limiting the freedom of movement and right to privacy of persons suspected of being "connected to" or supporting terrorist activities. The bill has been criticized by rights groups for its lack of clear definitions and the absence of judicial supervision over such measures.

In January 2008 the Hague Appeals Court refused to characterize the militant Hofstad network as a "terrorist group" when it cleared seven men, including Mohammed Bouyeri, the murderer of Dutch filmmaker Theo Van Gogh, of the charge of belonging to a terrorist group. In October the Amsterdam Appeals Court upheld the conviction of Samir Azzouz and four others on terrorism charges.

The European Committee for the Prevention of Torture and Inhuman or Degrading Treatment of Punishment in a February report expressed concern about the placement of terrorism suspects in special high-security "terrorist departments" in prisons, the conditions of which it considered so strict as to amount to de facto isolation.

There were successful court challenges to discriminatory law and policies restricting the ability of legal residents to bring family members into the Netherlands from non-Western countries. In July Amsterdam's district court ruled that it is unlawful to require migrants from certain countries wishing to join relatives in the Netherlands to pass an integration test demonstrating knowledge of Dutch language and society before being allowed into the country, although it did not determine whether the policy violates human rights law. The test, which disproportionately affects Moroccan and Turkish Muslim migrants, has been criticized by Dutch MPs and NGOs. Earlier the same month, a court in Roermond overturned a related law requiring residents wishing to bring a non-Dutch spouse to the Netherlands to earn at least 120 percent of the minimum wage. The Ministry of Justice is appealing both rulings, and policies are the subject of an ongoing government review.

Poland

Government expressions of homophobia remain a problem. In March, in a nationally televised speech, President Lech Kaczynski threatened to block ratification of the Lisbon Treaty, claiming that the EU Charter on Fundamental Rights and Freedoms would force Poland to legally recognize same-sex relationships.

Reproductive rights remain extremely limited, with lack of sex education and limited access to contraceptives. Access to safe and legal abortion is severely restricted by law, which criminalizes abortion in most circumstances. The law also protects a doctor's right to refuse to provide abortion services for reasons of "conscience." As a result, there is a high incidence of illegal and generally unsafe abortions, jeopardizing women's health and lives.

Spain

Following the reelection of Jose Luis Rodriguez Zapatero as prime minister in March, the Spanish cabinet contained equal numbers of men and women for the first time, including a female minister of defense.

In September the Supreme Court overturned the convictions of four of the 21 people found guilty in 2007 in relation to the Madrid train bombings of 2004. It also convicted one Spanish man who had previously been acquitted of providing the explosives for the attack. In October the same court acquitted 14 of 20 men convicted in February for plotting a bomb attack on the Audiencia Nacional, Spain's counterterrorism court.

In addition to ongoing cases involving international terrorism, there were a number of attacks by the Basque separatist group ETA and arrests of alleged ETA members throughout 2008, as well as ongoing prosecutions of individuals and groups allegedly connected to ETA.

In May the UN special rapporteur on the protection and promotion of human rights while countering terrorism, Martin Scheinin, issued a series of recommendations to the Spanish government, highlighting the need for the "complete eradication" of incommunicado detention and for a review of overly-broad terrorism offenses. These concerns were echoed by the Human Rights Committee in its Concluding Observations in October.

Scheinin also criticized the use of diplomatic assurances in an extradition case to Russia. In February the Audiencia Nacional had approved the extradition of Chechen Murat Ajmedovich Gasaev on the basis of diplomatic assurances from Russia that he would be treated humanely. At this writing Gasaev is still in detention pending a decision from the Council of Ministers on whether to go ahead with the extradition.

In May an Audiencia Nacional judge ordered the government to provide detailed information about stopovers of US military planes in Spain on their way to or from Guantanamo Bay between 2002 and 2007. The Ministry of Defense responded in September that US military flights to Guantanamo had passed through Spain but asserted that none carried passengers or cargo that could be "controversial." The judge requested further information.

An unrelated request by a different judge in the same court for the transfer of Jamil El-Banna and Omar Deghayes from the UK to stand trial in Spain for terrorism offenses following their release from Guantanamo was dropped in March.

There continued to be a marked drop in arrivals by sea of irregular migrants—down 8 percent in the first eight months of 2008 compared to the same period in 2007 and down 64 percent since 2006, according to Spain's Interior Mministry. In September-October 2008, however, Spanish authorities intercepted two boats off the Canary Islands containing a total of 329 irregular migrants, including children.

The Spanish Ombudsman confirmed reports of ill-treatment and criticized inadequate care facilities for unaccompanied migrant children in the Canary Islands. The Spanish government continued to push for the return of unaccompanied children to Senegal and Morocco without adequate safeguards. More than two dozen court decisions blocked children's repatriations because the repatriation decisions did not comply with Spanish or international law.

SPAIN

Returns at Any Cost

Spain's Push to Repatriate Unaccompanied Children
in the Absence of Safeguards

**HUMAN
RIGHTS
WATCH**

United Kingdom

Serious human rights concerns about the UK's counterterrorism law and practice were raised by international bodies during 2008, including the UN Human Rights Committee, the UN Human Rights Council under its Universal Periodic Review, and the Council of Europe.

Following a crushing defeat in the House of Lords, the government withdrew from a draft counterterrorism bill measures extending pre-charge detention for terrorism suspects from 28 to 42 days. It also removed a proposal to allow inquests in secret on national security grounds. The government has said that it may reintroduce both proposals, widely criticized as incompatible with human rights law, in future bills. At this writing, the bill includes the power to impose blanket lifelong notification requirements for individuals convicted of terrorism offenses in the UK or abroad, breach of which would be a criminal offense.

The Court of Appeal overturned a number of convictions for terrorism offenses. In February it quashed a 2007 conviction of five students under section 57 of the Terrorism Act 2000 for downloading and sharing material considered to be terrorism-related. The court ruled that the offense requires proof of intent that the material is for a terrorist purpose. In July the court reversed the November 2007 conviction of Samina Malik under section 58 of the Terrorism Act 2000 for possession of information useful to terrorists. The ruling followed a separate February 2008 Court of Appeal decision that section 58 does not apply to mere propaganda.

In May a staff member and a graduate student at Nottingham University, Hicham Yezza and Rizwaan Sabir, were arrested for possessing a document ("the Al Qaida Manual") freely available on the internet. They were detained for six days before being released without charge. The case raises concerns about the impact of terrorism legislation on academic freedom.

In September the inquest opened into the killing of Jean Charles de Menezes, an innocent man, by police officers during a counterterrorism operation in July 2005.

UK courts continued to block attempts to deport terrorism suspects on the basis of diplomatic assurances. In April 2008 the Court of Appeal ruled that Omar

UNITED KINGDOM

Not the Way Forward
The UK's Dangerous Reliance on Diplomatic Assurances

H U M A N
R I G H T S
W A T C H

Othman, (known as Abu Qatada) could not be deported to Jordan, on the grounds that torture evidence would be used against him at trial. He was subsequently released on bail from a high-security prison on strict security conditions including a 22-hour curfew. In October the Law Lords considered the appeal court's ruling in *Othman*, and a second appeal about removals to Algeria using assurances. It has yet to deliver a judgment in either case at this writing.

The Court of Appeal blocked the deportation of two Libyans to Libya in April, ruling that a memorandum of understanding with Libya was unreliable, and finding that the men would face a "complete" denial of fair trial if they were returned. The UK government is not appealing the ruling on Libya.

The use of the British Indian Ocean territory of Diego Garcia as part of the US renditions program was confirmed. In February CIA Director Michael Hayden admitted that the US had used Diego Garcia twice to refuel aircraft taking terrorism suspects to Guantanamo Bay and Morocco in 2002. The UK government maintains that it had not given consent for or been informed of this use of Diego Garcia.

In August 2008 the High Court ruled that the Foreign and Commonwealth Office should in principle disclose material in its possession that would assist the lawyers of Binyam Mohamed, a former UK resident facing trial before a military commission at Guantanamo Bay, in demonstrating that confessions used in evidence against him had been extracted through torture and were therefore inadmissible at trial. At this writing, a further hearing to consider national security arguments against disclosure has been adjourned pending the outcome of US proceedings in which the US government has been directed to hand over the materials. In October the home secretary asked the attorney general to investigate possible criminal wrongdoing by the UK Security Service and the CIA in Mohamed's treatment.

During a review by the UN Committee for the Rights of the Child in September, the UK government announced that it would withdraw its reservation to the Convention on the Rights of the Child in immigration cases. The committee welcomed the announcement but expressed regret that the best interests of the child are not given primary consideration in the areas of juvenile justice, immigration, freedom of movement, and peaceful assembly.

GEORGIA

The August conflict over the breakaway region of South Ossetia dominated events in Georgia during the second half of 2008. All sides of the conflict committed serious violations of international human rights and humanitarian law. The Georgian government used indiscriminate force, including cluster bombs.

Georgian authorities failed to comprehensively investigate past use of excessive force. The government lowered the minimum age for criminal responsibility, while failing to resolve overcrowding and poor conditions in prisons.

Conflict over South Ossetia

After months of escalating tensions and clashes between Georgian and South Ossetian forces, on the night of August 7-8 Georgia launched a military assault on Tskhinvali, the capital of South Ossetia, a breakaway region. Russia deployed significant military forces to South Ossetia, forcing a Georgian military retreat. Russian and South Ossetian forces pursued Georgian forces beyond the South Ossetian administrative border and occupied significant portions of uncontested Georgian territory until October 10. Russian forces also entered Abkhazia, a second breakaway region.

All parties committed serious violations of international human rights and humanitarian law (see also Russia chapter), resulting in many civilian deaths and injuries. The Office of the United Nations High Commissioner for Refugees estimated that 133,000 people were displaced by the conflict, but at least 80 percent have now returned to their homes. Thousands of Georgians from South Ossetia still remain displaced.

During the attack on South Ossetia, Georgian forces used indiscriminate force, firing Grad multiple rocket launchers, an indiscriminate weapon that should not be used in civilian areas. The Georgian military used tanks and machine guns to fire at buildings in Tskhinvali, including at apartment buildings where civilians sheltered; South Ossetian forces had fired on Georgian forces from at least some of these buildings.

The Georgian military also used cluster munitions against Russian military, including in Georgian territories adjacent to the administrative border with South Ossetia populated by civilians. Cluster munitions are indiscriminate weapons and cause unacceptable humanitarian harm. Some civilians were killed or injured as a result of Georgian- and Russian-fired unexploded ordnances, including cluster duds.

Some Ossetians detained during the conflict complained of ill-treatment during transfer to Georgian detention facilities.

Lack of Accountability for Excessive Use of Force

Despite repeated calls from key international actors, including the United States and the Parliamentary Assembly of the Council of Europe (PACE), the government has refused to launch a comprehensive investigation into the events of November 7, 2007, when police used excessive force against largely peaceful political demonstrations in the capital, Tbilisi, resulting in at least 500 injured. Authorities initiated investigations into only a handful of cases of possible excessive use of force. The authorities paid the independent television station Imedi US$2.5 million compensation for damage to its equipment during the November 7 police raid on the station.

The government has also failed to conduct a comprehensive investigation into the March 2006 operation to quell a riot in Tbilisi Prison No. 5, which left seven prisoners dead and dozens injured.

Criminal Justice System

The government has taken steps to reduce prison overcrowding, including issuing two presidential pardons and amnesties in 2008, and opening a new prison in Gldani. However, overuse of pretrial detention perpetuates overcrowding. As of October 1, 2008, the prison population totaled 19,929, a 50 percent increase in two years. In March the government closed the infamous Tbilisi Prison No. 5, which the European Committee for the Prevention of Torture and human rights organizations had repeatedly criticized for its overcrowding and appalling conditions. Poor conditions persist in many facilities, and allegations of ill-treatment of prisoners continue, including at the new Gldani prison.

In 2007 the government lowered the minimum age of criminal responsibility from 14 to 12 for certain crimes, further weakening protections for children in conflict with the law. The new minimum age entered into force in July 2008. However, the minister of justice issued a moratorium on implementation of the law until the creation of a separate juvenile justice system for young offenders. In its June review of Georgia, the United Nations Committee on the Rights of the Child expressed "deep regret" about the new minimum age and urged the government to reinstate it at 14.

In October parliament passed amendments on judicial restructuring, creating a new Ministry of Probation and the Penitentiary System and merging the General Prosecutor's Office with the Ministry of Justice. Independence of the judiciary in Georgia is a longstanding concern; the merger risks weakening the judiciary further.

Elections

Joint Organization for Security and Co-operation in Europe (OSCE), PACE, and European Parliament observer missions lauded the January 5, 2008 presidential election as "the first genuinely competitive presidential election" in Georgia, and noted that both it and the May parliamentary elections were essentially consistent with international standards. Observers still cited shortcomings, for instance, during the presidential election, widespread allegations of pressure—including on public employees and opposition activists— as well as irregularities in vote counting and tabulation during both elections. They noted that presidential election coverage lacked balance on most television stations, with President Mikheil Saakashvili generally receiving the most coverage.

Media Freedom

The media environment remains mixed, with a vibrant print media, but increasingly limited television news broadcasting, apparently due to government pressure. Only the state-owned Georgian Public Broadcasting station and the pro-government Rustavi 2 maintained nationwide news programming throughout the year.

Following its closure during the November 7 events, the private television station Imedi resumed broadcasting on December 12, 2007, but two weeks later Imedi suspended broadcasts, citing pressure from the authorities and its co-owner. Although Imedi resumed broadcasting in May 2008, it only resumed news programming in September. In June the independent television station Mze, widely considered pro-government, suspended news programs, allegedly for channel reorganization. However, the cable television company Maestro successfully challenged an April decision by the National Communications Commission depriving it of its license to broadcast news.

Independent television station Kavkazia experienced two suspicious transmission interruptions, including during a September 1 program criticizing Georgian government actions during the conflict over South Ossetia. Kavkazia's director questioned whether the transmitter's technical problems were coincidental. Kavkazia also alleged that financial police targeted companies buying advertising from the station.

During the conflict over South Ossetia, the Georgian government blocked access to Russian cable television stations and websites.

Journalists alleged pressure and attacks, including during the elections. A government supporter attacked Hereti radio correspondent Khatuna Gogishvili on the day of the presidential election by taking her recording device and physically assaulting and threatening to kill her. In February independent journalist Gela Mtivlishvili alleged that state security officials subjected him to surveillance and intimidation before and after the election. Journalists reported interference with their professional duties during the May parliamentary elections, including several Rustavi 2 and Mze television journalists and Eliso Chapidze, editor of the newspaper *Resonance*.

Key International Actors

During the conflict over South Ossetia, international actors unanimously called for restraint by all parties, but insufficiently highlighted the need for compliance with international human rights and humanitarian law and for transparent investigations and accountability for abuses, and the parties' obligations in this regard.

In response to the conflict, the OSCE chairman-in-office, the United Nations high commissioner for refugees, the United Nations representative of the secretary-general on the human rights of internally displaced persons, the Council of Europe commissioner for human rights, the United Nations Office for the Coordination of Humanitarian Affairs, and the PACE conducted missions to Georgia.

Holding the rotating European Union presidency, French President Nicolas Sarkozy brokered a six-point peace plan between Russia and Georgia. The EU appointed a special representative for the crisis in Georgia to prepare October talks chaired by the UN, OSCE, and the EU and aimed at resolving tensions between Georgia and Russia. The talks stalled on the first day and were set to resume in mid-November. In October the EU deployed more than 200 unarmed monitors to Georgia under the European Defense and Security Policy. On October 22, the EU and World Bank hosted a donor conference to mobilize support for a US$660 million assistance package dispersed over three years for reconstruction, economic recovery, and aid to the internally displaced in Georgia.

Both the European Court of Human Rights and the International Court of Justice issued decisions calling on all parties to comply with international human rights conventions. The International Criminal Court (ICC)—to which Georgia is a state party—announced that crimes committed by all parties to the conflict are under analysis by the ICC prosecutor.

In October the PACE issued a resolution declaring that both Georgia and Russia had violated Council of Europe principles, and called for an international investigation.

Following the conflict, the OSCE Mission to Georgia increased the number of its military monitoring officers. Russia has not allowed the monitors to enter South Ossetia.

In September the United States approved aid for Georgia that could total up to US$1 billion over two years, a sum 30 times greater than past annual US aid to

Georgia. After an October visit to Georgia, US Assistant Secretary of State for European and Eurasian Affairs Daniel Fried stated that NATO membership is still possible for Georgia, but the country should do more to strengthen its democratic institutions, particularly independent media and the judiciary.

KAZAKHSTAN

Despite hopes for meaningful reform, spurred by the country's selection as the 2010 chair of the Organization for Security and Co-operation in Europe (OSCE), human rights in Kazakhstan improved little in 2008. Draft laws on election legislation and mass media fell short of promised improvements, and parliament is considering legislation that observers fear would severely restrict the right to manifest religion or belief.

Kazakhstan's bid for the OSCE chairmanship was controversial because of its poor human rights record. Responding to OSCE members' concerns, Foreign Minister Marat Tazhin pledged in November 2007 that Kazakhstan would take several reform steps prior to assuming the chairmanship. These included amending the media law, reforming the law on elections, and liberalizing the registration requirements for political parties by the end of 2008. Tazhin further pledged that Kazakhstan would incorporate recommendations by the OSCE's Office for Democratic Institutions and Human Rights (ODIHR) into its election legislation and promised not to weaken the ODIHR during its chairmanship. Minister Tazhin's pledges were unprecedented and welcome, but so far have not resulted in meaningful reform.

Election Legislation

At the start of 2008 the government established a working group of government and civil society representatives to address election law reform. Members of the working group reported that they were prevented from considering the repeal of seriously flawed provisions: for example, there are currently no term limits for Kazakh President Nursultan Nazarbaev, he has sweeping powers to dissolve parliament, can appoint a third of the members of the upper chamber, and chooses the chair and two members of the seven-member Central Election Commission.

On November 11, the government sent to parliament a raft of amendments to election-related legislation. These leave unchanged the requirement that political parties gain at least seven percent of the vote to be represented in parliament. They stipulate that at least two political forces must be represented in parliament (no doubt a response to strong criticism of the 2007 parliamentary elections, which produced a single-party parliament). If only one party gets past the seven percent threshold, parliamentary seats may be distributed to the party garnering the next largest number of votes. Other draft amendments include lowering from 50,000 to 40,000 the minimum number of supporters for a party to be registered.

Freedom of Expression and Information

Most media outlets in Kazakhstan remain de facto under government control through a variety of direct and indirect means. Of some 2,500 functioning media outlets, the government owns a growing proportion outright. In March 2008 Samgau, a state-owned company, purchased all the remaining privately-held stock in Khabar, once the country's most important private media group. In July the government combined its media assets, including Khabar, into a special holding company, Arna Media.

In February 2008 the Ministry of Culture, Information and Public Accord declined for the second time a draft media law—including key reforms on registering media outlets—proposed by a working group of civil society representatives. After creating a new working group, the government hedged on supporting reforms, such that the media rights organization Adil Soz called the resulting draft law at best "a tiny first step" toward international standards.

One of the weaknesses of this draft law is that it focuses solely on media operations, while ignoring other relevant criminal and administrative law. For example, the government failed to enact essential reforms on criminal libel, which is often invoked to intimidate journalists and political critics. In the first six months of 2008 authorities opened seven criminal cases against journalists for alleged libel, slander, and defamation. In 2007 there were 27 such cases.

In April 2008 authorities released Kazis Toguzbaev, a journalist sentenced to two years in prison in January 2007 for insulting President Nazarbaev in articles he wrote criticizing the government, and expunged his verdict. The judges concluded that Toguzbaev had "demonstrated by his behavior that he was reformed." The release is welcome, but so long as such a broad criminal libel regime remains in place, others risk spending time and effort in defending themselves against it. In August 2008 a court in Shymkent ordered the release of Nurlan Alimbekov, a

An Atmosphere
of Quiet Repression

Freedom of Religion, Assembly and Expression in Kazakhstan

**HUMAN
RIGHTS
WATCH**

philosopher arrested in 2007 on charges flowing from an email he wrote questioning Kazakhstan's close relationship with Russia, which the government argued constituted incitement of racial hatred. Authorities had confined Alimbekov to a high-security psychiatric institution. Although the court freed him to return home, it did not dismiss the charges or conclude that Alimbekov was mentally fit under the law—only that his "treatment" does not currently require institutionalization.

In February 2008 an Astana court ordered the independent newspaper *Law and Justice* closed on grounds that it was improperly registered. Editors at the paper believed the case to be politically motivated: it had recently published allegations of corruption among the judiciary.

Beginning in April, the government-controlled internet monopoly Kaztelecom blocked access to the English- and Kazakh-language services of Radio Free Europe/Radio Liberty for seven weeks. The sites were made available again after expressions of concern from key international actors. The websites of several political opposition movements remain blocked.

Freedom of Religion

Kazakh authorities continue to restrict freedom of religion, primarily by pursuing members of "non-traditional" religions. Addressing members of Kazakhstan's ruling political party in January 2008, President Nazarbaev urged lawmakers to take steps to curb the activities of foreign missionaries. Misleading, fear-promoting statements about religious minorities in media and government statements continued during the year. In September a new draft law on religion passed the lower house of parliament. While the bill was in draft, local human rights groups characterized it as "repressive," arguing that it imposes inappropriate restrictions on religious groups and is open to arbitrary interpretation. The draft law makes a distinction between religious groups, which have no legal status and therefore no rights, and religious associations, which must have at least 50 members in a given locality. A religious association is the only legal entity religious communities can form. The draft law requires all communities to reregister within 18 months. On October 31 the upper house of parliament returned the draft to the lower house, requesting several insignificant changes.

Human Rights Defenders

Granting Kazakhstan the OSCE chairmanship has rendered the work of local human rights groups that press for reform more challenging. On the one hand, the government has established a number of human rights-related working groups, including one to draft a National Plan on Human Rights 2008-2011. But on the other hand, the government deflects or even ignores criticism and proposals for reform from rights groups, by portraying its 2010 OSCE chairmanship as evidence that its human rights record is in good order. In July 2008 five local human rights groups signed a memorandum to jointly monitor the implementation of the government's reform promises prior to its OSCE chairmanship.

Key International Actors

The OSCE remained engaged with Kazakhstan throughout 2008 on issues relating to the promised reforms and the upcoming chairmanship. After a visit to Kazakhstan in late July, OSCE Chairman-in-Office Alexander Stubb said the OSCE hoped to see "swift continuation of reforms in fields such as media, elections and political parties" and encouraged dialogue on other reforms.

Although the United States endorsed Kazakhstan's bid to chair the OSCE, US officials remained vocal about the country's slow progress on democratic and human rights reforms. In his July testimony before the US Commission on Security and Cooperation in Europe, Assistant Secretary of State for South and Central Asian Affairs Richard A. Boucher expressed the administration's support for Kazakhstan's chairmanship but admitted that reforms were uneven. Visiting Kazakhstan in October, it was reported that Secretary of State Condoleezza Rice raised with President Nazarbaev the commitments for Kazakhstan's democratic reform made in November 2007, stressing that the US looked to Kazakhstan "to show leadership by example and, working closely with OSCE and civil society, make steady progress toward meeting all of its ... commitments, including the adoption of laws governing independent media and elections," comments that suggest the US did not assess Kazakhstan as having made sufficient progress so far.

In September the European Union underlined "the importance of reforms in view of the Kazakh Chairmanship of the OSCE, including in the areas of media freedom, the electoral law and the registration of political parties, as confirmed at the OSCE ministerial in Madrid in December 2007." The first round of what is to become an annual human rights dialogue in the framework of the EU's Central Asia strategy was held in mid-October. The EU did not make public what specific issues it raised or what results the dialogue yielded.

KYRGYZSTAN

Pluralism and fundamental freedoms that facilitate public scrutiny of government are increasingly at risk in Kyrgyzstan. Legislative changes passed or pending in 2008 curbed freedom of assembly and threatened to restrict religious freedoms. The government is failing to meet its obligations to prevent and investigate torture and domestic violence. Harassment of journalists and NGO activists intensified, and arbitrary suspensions and terminations of asylum-seeker certificates exposed flaws in Kyrgyzstan's refugee protection system.

Elections

As a result of the December 2007 parliamentary elections, which the Organization for Security and Co-operation in Europe (OSCE) called "a missed opportunity," President Kurmanbek Bakiev's Ak-Zhol party now dominates parliament. Controversy surrounding impending local elections heightened in September 2008 when the head of the Central Election Commission fled the country after accusing the president's son of threatening her. Local NGOs reported pressure on election observers and voters during the October 5 poll.

Civil Society

NGOs can operate freely but face increasing government intimidation. Police conducted harassing inspections and searches of the offices of local and international human rights NGOs, including Citizens against Corruption, Kylym Shamy, Labrys, Mir-Svet-Kultura, and the Norwegian Helsinki Committee. For example, on the evening of April 8 three policemen forced their way into Labrys's shelter for women and transgender people. The police searched Labrys's files without a warrant and threatened to arrest anyone who did not produce identification, though no charges were filed.

Saidkamal Akhmedov, a defense lawyer and human rights activist, was tried in Osh on bogus embezzlement charges. Akhmedov had had refugee status in Kazakhstan but in 2007 was forcibly returned to Kyrgyzstan by the Uzbek government when he was visiting relatives in Uzbekistan. On February 1, 2008, he received a one-year suspended sentence after spending five months in detention in both Uzbekistan and Kyrgyzstan. The sentence was upheld on appeal.

Ivar Dale, the Norwegian Helsinki Committee's regional representative, was denied entry into Kyrgyzstan for unknown reasons on October 12, 2008. One month prior, a court ruled in Dale's favor on the state's charges that he had worked illegally in Kyrgyzstan and had provided "untruthful information" on his visa application.

In December 2007, 13 youth activists and human rights defenders were detained for two days in a cold, rat-infested cell for holding small, peaceful demonstrations in Bishkek.

Freedom of Assembly

In July 2008 the Constitutional Court ruled that any licensing regime for public assemblies is unconstitutional. The decision effectively voided the highly restrictive 2007 Bishkek City Council ordinance regulating assemblies in the capital. Nevertheless, on August 6 President Bakiev signed amendments to the 2002 law on freedom of assembly that essentially establish a licensing regime and limit possibilities for timely and spontaneous protests: The amended law requires assembly organizers to notify local authorities 12 days in advance of any planned event, regardless of the size, does not enumerate grounds for "reasonable disagreement" by the authorities, and allows provincial governors excessive powers to interfere with the planning of public assemblies.

Media Freedom

According to the Media Representative Institute, an NGO, at this writing at least seven criminal cases and more than 30 defamation suits were filed against Kyrgyz journalists and media outlets in 2008.

Most worrisome is the prosecution of the editors of two opposition newspapers, *De Facto* and *Alibi*, on charges that they libeled the president's nephew. They were first sentenced in June 2008 to a prohibitively high fine of 1 million Kyrgyz soms (US$28,500) each, and then criminally prosecuted for not paying the fine.

As a result, *Alibi* editor Babyrbek Jeenbekov was detained for two days in early September, while *De Facto* editor Cholpon Orozbekova fled the country. On June 14 police raided the *De Facto* offices, confiscated its financial records and computers, and sealed the newsroom as part of a separate criminal investigation into allegations that a letter the newspaper had published about official corruption amounted to a "knowingly false denunciation." At this writing, the investigation is ongoing.

The investigation into the October 2007 murder of independent journalist Alisher Saipov was suspended in February 2008, but then reopened. No information is publicly available about whether it has identified any suspects.

Amendments to the press law adopted in June empower the president to appoint the executive director of state-run television and radio, reversing previous initiatives to turn them into public broadcasters.

Violence against Women

In Kyrgyzstan the government does not adequately prevent and punish domestic violence and bride kidnapping. Thousands of women are isolated in their homes, beaten, humiliated, raped, and sometimes killed, generally with impunity. According to nationwide statistics provided by the governmental judiciary committee, in the first nine months of 2008, in three court cases involving forced marriage the defendant was found guilty, and four other cases were dismissed.

In June parliament held its first hearing on the 2003 domestic violence law. Participants highlighted the absence of national gender institutions, insufficient resources, poor statistics, and inadequate training of law enforcement bodies as factors that hinder the law's effectiveness.

Torture

On April 14, 2008, Kyrgyzstan ratified the Optional Protocol to the Convention against Torture. Despite this welcome move, torture and ill-treatment of detainees remain pervasive. In the first nine months of 2008, a network of human rights defenders, Golos Svobody, submitted approximately 40 complaints of torture and ill-treatment to prosecutors' offices throughout the country. In response, prosecutors initiated about a dozen inquiries, but for the others either determined "allegations not confirmed" or did not reply. No case was heard by Kyrgyz courts in 2008 under the criminal code article banning torture.

One of the rare criminal investigations in 2008 related to allegations of torture—involving police treatment of four minors and one adult—began in March. All five had been arrested between February 29 and March 3 in Bishkek and reported severe beatings by the police to compel confessions of theft. At this writing, only one police officer, implicated in abuse of one of the minors, remains under investigation, for abuse of office.

Refugee Protection

The government of Kyrgyzstan hosts hundreds of refugees and asylum seekers from Afghanistan, Iran, and Uzbekistan, most of whom are awaiting resettlement to third countries. However, it has also been complicit in the forced return of asylum seekers to Uzbekistan, despite the risk of torture there.

In August the State Committee for Migration and Employment arbitrarily stopped extending asylum-seeker certificates issued to Uzbek nationals who were seeking asylum. In mid-September the committee renewed extensions for some asylum seekers, but in many cases not for the full three months required by law; and in some asylum seekers' certificates the committee noted, "No right for further extension." Newly arrived asylum seekers face difficulties in registering. For example, in 2008, 20 asylum seekers from Afghanistan and Iran challenged in court the denial of registration on the grounds of illegal entry, as it contradicts international and domestic law. At this writing the court decision is pending.

In its first decision on Kyrgyzstan (*Maksudov et al. v. Kyrgyzstan*) the UN Human Rights Committee ruled in July that Kyrgyzstan breached the rights to personal liberty, freedom from torture, and right to life of four Andijan refugees (see Uzbekistan chapter) and should provide effective remedy and put in place effective monitoring of their situation. The four had been extradited to Uzbekistan in August 2006 despite interim measures of protection requested by the committee. The committee also noted that Kyrgyz extradition legislation does not comply with

KYRGYZSTAN

These Everyday Humiliations

Violence Against Lesbians, Bisexual Women,
and Transgender Men in Kyrgyzstan

H U M A N
R I G H T S
W A T C H

the state's non-refoulement obligations. The government so far has taken no action to implement the decision.

Key International Actors

The Cooperation Council between the European Union and Kyrgyzstan held its tenth meeting in July 2008. The Council welcomed progress achieved toward the implementation of the EU's Central Asia Strategy but regretted recent developments, "especially in the area of media freedom and freedom of assembly". The first round of what is to become an annual human rights dialogue was held at the end of October, concluding "that EU strives to reinforce overall, broad-based cooperation with Kyrgyzstan," and failing to indicate any specific human rights benchmarks.

In March the United States and Kyrgyzstan signed a two-year US$16 million Millennium Challenge Corporation agreement. The program aims to implement measures such as reforming the judicial system and combating corruption. Kyrgyz human rights groups had urged the US to suspend the signing of the agreement until "the government proves its commitment to the [program's] objectives."

International governmental and nongovernmental actors expressed concerns about a new draft religion law adopted by parliament on November 6, 2008. The US Department of State noted in its Annual Report on International Religious Freedom that the draft law "severely obstructs citizens' right to freedom of religion" with such changes as "an increase from 10 to 200 members required for official registration of a religious organization, the elimination of alternative military service for all but priests and religious laymen, a ban on proselytizing, and the prohibition of the conversion of Kyrgyz citizens to a different faith." At this writing, the draft is with the president for approval.

RUSSIA

Russia's armed conflict with Georgia over South Ossetia and its subsequent temporary occupation of parts of Georgia sparked international concern over the balance of power in the region and Russia's willingness to use force to protect its interests. The election of Dmitry Medvedev to the Russian presidency did not result in immediate improvements in the rule of law or the environment for civil society, with the government continuing to crack down against independent groups and activists.

International criticism of Russia's human rights record remains muted, with the European Union failing to challenge Russia on human rights issues in a consistent and sustained manner.

Elections

In February the Office for Democratic Institutions and Human Rights of the Organization for Security and Co-operation in Europe cancelled its planned observation mission to the presidential election, citing "severe restrictions on its observers."

On March 2, Dmitry Medvedev was elected president by over 70 percent of the vote in an election that was orderly but uncompetitive. The Parliamentary Assembly of the Council of Europe (PACE) characterized the election as a "plebiscite" on outgoing president Vladimir Putin's rule and his handpicked successor rather than a truly democratic election. Medvedev assumed the presidency on May 7 and immediately appointed Putin prime minister.

The Armed Conflict over South Ossetia

After months of escalating tensions and clashes between Georgian and South Ossetian forces, Georgia launched a military assault on Tskhinvali, the capital of South Ossetia, a breakaway region in Georgia, on the night of August 7-8. Russia moved significant forces into South Ossetia, ostensibly to protect Russian peacekeepers and Russian citizens there. After several days of heavy fighting, Georgian forces retreated, and Russian and South Ossetian forces pursued the Georgian army beyond the South Ossetian administrative border and occupied significant portions of uncontested Georgian territory. On August 15-16, Russia and Georgia signed a peace agreement.

On August 26, Russia recognized the independence of South Ossetia and Abkhazia, a breakaway region in western Georgia. On October 10, Russia withdrew from uncontested areas of Georgia.

All parties committed serious violations of international human rights and humanitarian law during the conflict (see also Georgia chapter). The fighting resulted in many civilian deaths and injuries. The Office of the United Nations High Commissioner for Refugees estimated 133,000 people were displaced by the conflict, but at least 80 percent have now returned to their homes. The majority of those still displaced are Georgians unable to return to their homes in South Ossetia.

Immediately following the fighting, Ossetian militias and looters systematically destroyed Georgian enclave villages in South Ossetia, with some militia members admitting that they wanted to prevent ethnic Georgians from returning.

Russian forces used cluster bombs in areas populated by civilians in the Gori and Kareli districts of Georgia, leading to civilian deaths and injuries. Russia also launched indiscriminate rocket attacks on civilian areas, causing casualties.

Russian forces in Georgia failed to protect civilians in areas under their effective control and prevented Georgian authorities from policing these areas, creating a security vacuum. Ossetian militias and armed criminal gangs looted and burned homes and killed, raped, beat, and threatened civilians in these areas.

Ossetian forces unlawfully detained at least 160 civilians, mainly elderly, in South Ossetia and the Gori district. Detainees were held in conditions that amounted to degrading treatment. Some were subjected to beatings and forced labor. Russian troops and Ossetian militias detained at least 14 Georgian servicemen, subjecting them to severe torture and ill-treatment, including beatings, burnings, and starvation, and summarily executed at least one Georgian soldier.

RUSSIA

"As If They Fell From the Sky"

Counterinsurgency, Rights Violations, and Rampant Impunity
in Ingushetia

HUMAN
RIGHTS
WATCH

Civil Society

The government continues tightening control over civil society through selective implementation of the law on NGOs, restriction and censure of protected expression and the media, and harassment of activists and human rights defenders. These actions form an unmistakable part of the Russian government's efforts to weaken—in some cases beyond recognition—the checks and balances needed for an accountable government. In May oversight of NGOs was transferred from the Federal Registration Service to the Ministry of Justice, raising hopes that the law would be implemented less selectively, but as of this writing the transfer appears to have had little practical effect.

In April Russia's Supreme Court upheld the liquidation of Sodeistvie, a refugee assistance NGO in Vladimir. Sodeistvie had submitted an activity report in 2007 but was liquidated for failure to submit past reports; a violation the government argued could not be remedied.

Two offices of the voters' rights NGO Golos suffered harassment, apparently to interfere with elections-related work. In the two weeks before the presidential election, Novosibirsk authorities made numerous onerous demands for documents from Golos's regional affiliate. In Samara the prosecutor ordered the Golos director to undergo psychiatric and drug examinations while investigating specious accusations of software piracy.

2007 amendments to the extremism law allow any politically or ideologically motivated crime to be designated extremist. Russian authorities apply these provisions to silence government critics, and in 2008 initiated cases against NGOs, activists, and independent media, including internet sites and blogs. The Nizhni Novgorod environmental NGO Dront received a warning for unspecified extremist content on its website. In August the Moscow City Court upheld the liquidation of the independent news website Ingushetiya.ru for extremism.

In July a court in Syktyvkar convicted Savva Terentyev for inciting hatred against police for a blog comment. A blogger associated with the youth political organization Oborona came under investigation for allegedly inciting hatred against the Federal Security Service (the state security police), having criticized them for corruption and attempting to close Oborona. In both cases incitement provisions

were applied on the basis of officially characterizing the respective police forces as "social groups."

The North Caucasus

In Chechnya the armed conflict has subsided and significant reconstruction is ongoing in Grozny, the capital. However, security forces loyal to Chechen President Ramzan Kadyrov continued to use torture and illegal detention, especially against those with suspected rebel ties. A growing atmosphere of intimidation fostered by the government in Chechnya inhibits human rights monitoring and accountability for human rights abuses.

Local human rights groups continued to report a decline in the number of enforced disappearances, documenting 30 abductions leading to nine disappearances by September. However, few efforts have been made to address the cases of as many as 5,000 people "disappeared" since 1999. On August 3, 2008, Mokhmadsalakh Masaev was abducted and "disappeared," less than a month after a newspaper published his account of ill-treatment during four months in a secret prison in Chechnya. A local police station refused to register the abduction report filed by Masaev's brother.

Violence continued elsewhere in the North Caucasus, with armed clashes between rebels and police in Ingushetia and Dagestan. In Ingushetia law enforcement and security forces involved in counterinsurgency committed serious human rights abuses including summary and arbitrary detentions, acts of torture and ill-treatment, enforced disappearances, and extrajudicial executions.

On January 26, police in Nazran, Ingushetia, arrested 10 journalists and two human rights defenders monitoring a violent demonstration against government repression and corruption. Two of the journalists, Said-Khussein Tsarnaev and Mustafa Kurskiev, were kept overnight in custody and denied access to counsel, food, and water. Police severely beat Kurskiev, then denied him access to medical care.

In July approximately 50 armed members of the security forces in military vehicles took Zurab Tsechoev of the human rights group Mashr from his home in Magas, Ingushetia. Tsechoev was blindfolded and driven to an unknown location. His abductors accused him of working for Ingushetiya.ru, beat him causing serious injuries to his chest and legs, and threatened his family.

On August 31 Magomed Yevloev, owner of Ingushetiya.ru, was shot in the head while in police custody after being detained at Nazran airport. The killing was ruled accidental, and no disciplinary measures were taken. Yevloev's killing and the lack of accountability for the perpetrators prompted public indignation against the Ingush authorities. Alleged insurgent attacks increased in the republic in the latter part of 2008. Against this background, on October 30 President Medvedev dismissed Murat Zyazikov as president of Ingushetia and replaced him with a military general, Yunus-Bek Yevkurov. Political and civic activists in Ingushetia expressed hopes that the new president would be capable of overcoming the republic's pressing human rights and security challenges.

In October the trial of 59 alleged participants in the 2005 Nalchik uprising, in Kabardino-Balkaria, began again after a long delay. Many of the defendants have alleged torture and other abuses while in custody.

Migrant Construction Workers

Russia has between 4 and 9 million migrant workers, over 80 percent of whom come from other countries of the former Soviet Union. Forty percent of migrant workers are employed in construction, where they face abuses that include confiscation of passports, denial of contracts, non-payment or delayed payment of wages, and unsafe working conditions. Some employers threaten or use violence to intimidate workers who protest against non-payment. Police frequently use document inspections to extort money from visible minorities, including migrant workers, and may physically abuse them or force them to perform work for free. Although Russia has liberalized migration policy in recent years, migrant workers have few effective options for redress for these abuses.

HIV and Drug Dependence

Hundreds of thousands of people in Russia are dependent on drugs and at immediate risk of HIV infection. While Russia has made considerable progress expanding access to antiretroviral treatment for people living with HIV, its efforts to ensure that injection drug users have access to effective drug dependence treatment services—a key factor in both general HIV prevention and treatment for injection drug users—have fallen far short.

Methadone maintenance therapy helps reduce HIV infections as it enables many patients to stop using illicit drugs or helps them adopt less risky injection behavior; it also helps drug users obtain and adhere to antiretroviral treatment. Yet Russia refuses to make maintenance therapy available to drug-dependent people and has banned the use of methadone for treatment purposes. Available drug treatment services are insufficiently accessible, incomplete, and often not based on scientific evidence.

Key International Actors

While many global leaders expressed concern over developments in Russia, such as the war over South Ossetia and restrictions on civil society, human rights issues remained on the margins of Russia's bilateral and multilateral relations, with many key interlocutors failing to press Russia for reform or to challenge it on entrenched problems.

The European Union held two rounds of human rights consultations with Russia, meetings ultimately undermined by the lack of high-level Russian participation or adequate follow-up mechanisms. Human rights did not figure prominently in the broader EU-Russia agenda. Due to Russia's military actions in Georgia, in September the EU froze negotiations to renew its Partnership and Cooperation Agreement with Russia, which expired in December 2007, but the EU decided in November 2008 to resume the negotiations.

The United States government issued several strong statements on human rights but lacked the leverage to challenge Russia meaningfully on its worsening human rights record.

Russia has served on the new United Nations Human Rights Council since its inception in May 2006, and is due to be reviewed under its Universal Periodic Review mechanism in February 2009. The government has not fulfilled its obligation to cooperate fully with UN human rights mechanisms, including the UN special rapporteur on torture, who canceled a visit planned for October 2006 and has remained unable to visit the country due to the government's continued refusal to provide conditions that accord with the mandate's terms of reference.

The Parliamentary Assembly of the Council of Europe resumed its monitoring mandate on Chechnya. An introductory memorandum declassified in April 2008 concluded that "abductions, secret detentions and torture" remained "commonplace" and termed the rights situation in the North Caucasus "by far the most alarming in the whole of the geographical area covered by the Council of Europe." A fact-finding visit and full report were repeatedly postponed, most recently due to the conflict over South Ossetia.

The International Criminal Court (ICC) announced that crimes committed by all parties to the conflict over South Ossetia are under analysis by the ICC prosecutor. Although not an ICC state party, Russia has provided the ICC with evidence of what it claims are Georgian crimes.

Unable to secure justice domestically, hundreds of victims of abuse in Chechnya have filed applications with the European Court of Human Rights. In more than 50 rulings to date, the court found Russia responsible for serious human rights abuses in Chechnya, including torture, extrajudicial executions, and enforced disappearances. In every ruling the court has found a failure by the Russian government to launch a meaningful investigation. Russia has not sufficiently implemented the general measures recommended by the court to remedy systemic problems and prevent abuses from recurring. Russia remains the only Council of Europe member not to have ratified Protocol 14 of the court's charter, which would streamline the court's procedures and reduce backlog.

SERBIA

Kosovo declared independence from Serbia on February 17, 2008. This is rejected by Serbia, and it has not clarified Kosovo's international legal status, although an independent Kosovo has been recognized by a number of key bilateral partners of both Serbia and Kosovo including several European Union states.

In Serbia the formation in June of a new coalition government produced dramatic results on war crimes, with the arrest of Radovan Karadzic and his transfer to the International Criminal Tribunal for the former Yugoslavia (ICTY). But the government failed to arrest Ratko Mladic. There was a wave of attacks against ethnic Albanian businesses and homes following Kosovo's independence declaration. The Roma minority remains vulnerable. Human rights defenders and journalists came under renewed pressure.

War Crimes Accountability

On July 30 Radovan Karadzic was transferred from Serbia to the ICTY, 13 years after his indictment (see also Bosnia chapter). The arrest was a significant breakthrough in Serbia's cooperation with the tribunal, reflecting the growing authority within the government of President Boris Tadic's Democratic Party. The previous month Serbia transferred to the ICTY Stojan Zupljanin, a former commander of Bosnian Serb police. Widespread public hostility to the ICTY persists.

ICTY indictees Ratko Mladic and Goran Hadzic remain at large at this writing. Serbia's special prosecutor for war crimes, Vladimir Vukcevic, reiterated in August that the arrest of both fugitives was a priority for Belgrade. In August the president of Serbia's national council on ICTY cooperation, Rasim Ljajic, said that Mladic hid in military barracks in Belgrade from June 2002 until the end of 2005. During a September visit to Serbia ICTY Prosecutor Serge Brammertz expressed "careful optimism" that Mladic would be "arrested soon," but declined publicly to assess Serbia's cooperation with the ICTY.

In October ICTY judges upheld the conviction of Milan Martic for crimes committed during the shelling of Zagreb in 1995, sentencing him to 35 years' imprisonment. The trial of Vojislav Seselj at the tribunal continued during 2008, where he is accused of helping to orchestrate the wartime mass expulsion of Muslims, Croats, and other non-Serbs from Croatia, Bosnia, and Serbia. Other continuing high-profile trials included those of Milan Milutinovic, Dragoljub Ojdanic, Nikola Sainovic, Nebojsa Pavkovic, and Vladimir Lazarevic.

The Belgrade War Crimes Chamber continues its efforts to hold alleged perpetrators accountable for wartime abuses, despite limited funding, inadequate political support, and little public awareness of its work. In August the chamber indicted Branko Grujic and Branko Popovic for war crimes against Bosniak civilians in the area of Zvornik. The "Suva Reka" trial, relating to the killing of Kosovo Albanians in 1999, was among the seven ongoing prosecutions in the chamber during 2008. The trial of four "Scorpion" paramilitary members, accused of war crimes against Kosovo Albanians, resumed in October. In September Serbia's Supreme Court ruled on appeals against the 2007 convictions of four members of another "Scorpion" paramilitary unit operating in the area of Srebrenica. It upheld the convictions of three defendants (reducing one sentence from 20 to 15 years), and ordered the retrial of the fourth, pointing to alleged irregularities in the original trial.

War crimes special prosecutor Vukcevic continued to receive death threats, especially following the arrests and transfer of Karadzic and Zupljanin. In October Vukcevic made a formal request to the Albanian government to visit Albania to investigate the alleged abduction, transfer to Albania, and murder of Kosovo Serbs in 1999. Albanian authorities responded positively, but the visit had yet to take place at this writing.

In June the Supreme Court sentenced former secret police chief Radomir Markovic to 40 years' imprisonment, and several other defendants to long prison terms, for the attempted murder of opposition leader Vuk Draskovic in October 1999. Four aides to Draskovic had been killed in the staged road accident. The verdict concluded an eight-year cycle of trials, during which three earlier decisions of lower courts had been annulled by the Supreme Court, which ultimately tried the case itself.

Treatment of Minorities

Kosovo's declaration of independence on February 17 triggered public anger in Serbia. In the days that followed, ethnic Albanians suffered acts of harassment and intimidation, many involving smashing the windows of business and homes, as well as attempted arson, the spraying of hate graffiti, and intimidating protests in front of homes and businesses. The response of the Serbian authorities was inadequate: The police were more active in safeguarding minority-owned businesses after the attacks than during a wave of similar attacks in 2003 and 2004, but they failed to take preemptive action to protect minority homes and businesses and generally failed to identify perpetrators, even when police were present during attacks. Few perpetrators were charged with attacks by misdemeanor judges or by municipal and district prosecutors.

The Roma minority continues to suffer discrimination and economic and political marginalization; it has the highest rate of unemployment and school dropouts, and over half live below the poverty line. During a September visit to Serbia the Council of Europe commissioner for human rights highlighted the "inhumane conditions" and "social exclusion" experienced by Roma.

In August Roma activists and 450 residents in Kursumlija called for a public investigation into allegations that three local police officers beat two Roma men. Following public pressure, the police suspended the three officers and launched an investigation to determine whether excessive force had been used.

Internally Displaced Persons and Refugees

There was little progress in finding durable solutions for the more than 200,000 internally displaced persons and almost 100,000 refugees in Serbia. Both groups face ongoing problems with documents, housing, and employment. More than 7,000 refugees from Bosnia and Croatia, and displaced persons from Kosovo remain in collective centers, often in substandard conditions. The forced removal from Western Europe of Roma from Kosovo and elsewhere in Serbia continues to place a burden on Roma communities.

SERBIA

Hostages of Tension

Intimidation and Harassment of Ethnic Albanians
in Serbia After Kosovo's Declaration of Independence

**HUMAN
RIGHTS
WATCH**

Media Freedom

The independent news organization B92 received threats in February, and during mass protests in Belgrade linked to Kosovo on February 21, an arson attempt was made on its offices, but was prevented by a police cordon. B92 cameraman Bosko Brankovic and Beta news agency correspondent Milos Djorelijevski were severely beaten while covering a protest in July against the arrest of Radovan Karadzic, but in August and October members of two ultranationalist groups forced their way into Beta's offices, demanding coverage of protests against Karadzic's arrest. They were removed by police.

Two journalists from the news weekly *Nedeljni Telegraf* received death threats on March 24 in a letter signed by the "Red Berets" (a disbanded special police unit). The reasons for the threats were unclear. Vukasin Obradovic, owner and editor-in-chief of the weekly *Vranjske*, received repeated threatening phone calls in early November, apparently related to the magazine's coverage of organized crime. The police promptly deployed patrols around the *Vranjske* offices and Obradovic's home.

Human Rights Defenders

In February the executive director of the Humanitarian Law Center, Natasa Kandic, was subjected to threats after attending the session of the Kosovo Assembly at which it proclaimed independence from Serbia. Activists from the Socialist Party of Serbia collected signatures to lodge a criminal complaint against Kandic, accusing her of threatening the constitution and the state; she was not charged, however. The newspapers *Kurir* and *Vecernje Novosti* respectively referred to Kandic as a "traitor" and "a woman who does not exist."

The Helsinki Committee for Human Rights in Serbia and its director Sonja Biserko received threats in September linked to their work on war crimes accountability. Ultranationalists protested outside the group's office on September 30. On October 2, Biserko's home address was published by a tabloid newspaper article calling her a "traitor." She was subsequently placed under police protection.

Key International Actors

The European Union signed a Stabilization and Association Agreement with Serbia in April, despite its failure to transfer Mladic to the ICTY. At this writing, EU member states have yet to ratify the agreement, a move dependent on full cooperation with the ICTY. In September the EU decided not to offer interim trade benefits to Serbia, after the Dutch government refused to ratify the deal, citing Serbia's failure to apprehend Ratko Mladic and Goran Hadzic. The European Commission's regular report on Serbia published in November highlighted Mladic, and the plight of Roma.

The UN Human Rights Council was due to consider Serbia under its Universal Periodic Review mechanism in December 2008.

The Council of Europe's Commission against Racism and Intolerance published a report on Serbia in April. It recommended improved legal protection for religious minorities, enhanced legal remedies for racial discrimination, bringing to justice the perpetrators of attacks against religious and ethnic minorities, and improved living conditions for Roma.

Kosovo

Not only did Kosovo's declaration of independence from Serbia in February fail to clarify its international legal status, but it also brought no visible improvements to human rights conditions. The weak criminal justice system frustrates efforts to tackle impunity for ethnic violence and other serious crimes. Minorities face continued violence and discrimination. Few displaced persons and refugees returned to their homes, even as forced returns from Western Europe increased.

Uncertainty over the status of the UN interim administration in Kosovo (UNMIK) and successor EU missions hindered their effectiveness. Kosovo's status plan, based on the so-called "Ahtisaari plan" (envisioned by the UN chief negotiator Martti Ahtisaari) proposed that an EU-led International Civilian Office (ICO) and EU police and justice mission (EULEX) would assume responsibility from UNMIK following Kosovo's declaration of independence. But the UN Security Council failed to agree the change, delaying the deployment of EULEX, and leaving a gap in oversight of the justice system. The UN secretary-general approved in June a more informal transfer of responsibility to EULEX and a scaled down role for UNMIK. At this writing EULEX has yet to deploy to the Serb-controlled north of Kosovo, a process complicated by objections from authorities in Pristina and Belgrade about the implications for Kosovo's status. The status of the ICO remains unclear.

The NATO-led Kosovo peacekeeping force, KFOR, remains deployed throughout Kosovo, including in the north. In the first six months of 2008 the number of troops decreased from 15,900 to 14,759.

Protection of Minorities

There was limited violence following Kosovo's declaration of independence, most of it concentrated in the north of Mitrovica. Forty-five ethnically motivated incidents (18 in Mitrovica) were recorded by the Kosovo Police Service (KPS) in the first six months of the year, down from the 31 it recorded in Mitrovica during the same period in 2007. UNMIK, which recorded almost 200 "inter-ethnic" incidents in 2007, did not provide figures for 2008.

In January and February 2008, buses carrying Serbs and Gorani were stopped and searched by armed masked men. No one was hurt and the perpetrators have not been identified. On two separate occasions in April shots were fired at the Serbian village of Banjski Suvi Do from a nearby Albanian village. The KPS and KFOR attended promptly on both occasions, but the perpetrators have not been identified. In May an elderly Serbian returnee to Decani was beaten up. The investigation into this incident was still ongoing at this writing.

A Ukrainian policeman was killed and more than 150 people injured during clashes in Mitrovica on March 15, after Serbs tried to storm a UN courthouse. Tension persisted in Mitrovica in subsequent months, resulting in renewed clashes on August 4 during which three Serbs and one international policeman were injured.

Roma, Ashkali, and Egyptians (RAE) face persistent discrimination, particularly in employment and access to public services, and continue to be affected by the highest unemployment, school drop-out, and mortality rates in Kosovo.

Kosovo

Kosovo Criminal Justice Scorecard

HUMAN RIGHTS WATCH

Return of Refugees and Displaced Persons

The number of voluntary returns to Kosovo, including from Serbia, continues to decline, with only 229 (including 80 Serbs) registered during the first eight months of the year. Returns are hampered by the unstable political situation and the lack of conditions for sustainable return, including employment and social services. According to the United Nations High Commissioner for Refugees, Serbs, Roma, and Albanians from areas where they are in the minority remain in need of international protection.

A survey by the Mitrovica Institute of Public Health in May concluded that lead levels among displaced RAE in camps in North Mitrovica remain dangerously high, despite efforts to administer treatment for lead contamination. The Ombudsperson launched an investigation into the issue in July 2008. Efforts to return RAE to their homes in Mitrovica continued, with 14 families returned to newly reconstructed homes in 2008.

Forced returns from Western Europe continued, with 1,727 persons returned in the first eight months of 2008, including 437 from Germany and 290 from Switzerland. While UNMIK continues to directly manage such returns, the Kosovo Ministry of Internal Affairs is now responsible for monitoring the process. But the government's reintegration strategy, which foresees 5,000 returns per annum, lacks mechanisms to ensure the access to documentation and housing necessary to facilitate reintegration.

Impunity and Access to Justice

Ramush Haradinaj, a former commander of the Kosovo Liberation Army, was acquitted by the ICTY on April 3, 2008. Haradinaj, who was Kosovo's prime minister at the time of his indictment, had been accused of murder, persecution, rape, and torture during the Kosovo conflict. ICTY judges found him not guilty on all counts. The court cited significant difficulties in obtaining testimony of many witnesses due to security concerns. One co-defendant, Idriz Balaj, was found not guilty on all counts, while another, Lahi Brahimaj, was convicted and sentenced to six years' imprisonment. Prosecution appeals against the two acquittals and

Brahimaj's sentence, and an appeal by Brahimaj against conviction, are pending at this writing.

In July the ICTY convicted well-known Kosovar journalist Baton Haxhiu for contempt of court for revealing the identity of a protected witness who testified during the Haradinaj trial. He was fined €7,000.

Kosovo's criminal justice system continued to be the weakest of its main institutions. A 2004 law requiring prosecutors, rather than judges, to take the lead in investigating cases has yet to be fully implemented. Insufficient coordination between police and prosecutors, and between national and international actors, remains a barrier to the effective administration of justice. The absence of designated judicial police, as required by the law, undermines the ability of police to meaningfully assist prosecutors. The electronic case management system is still not operational.

Witness protection is a particular problem, especially in cases involving organized crime, war crimes, and attacks on minorities. Widespread witness intimidation and harassment mean that many witnesses are unwilling to come forward. Kosovo lacks a witness protection law, and judges and prosecutors often fail to use those measures that are available. Reluctance on the part of Western governments to host witnesses and their families hampers witness relocation.

The number of active war crimes prosecutions remains low. The ongoing trials include that of ethnic Albanian Gani Gashi, accused of killing Albanian civilians in 1998. Ethnic Serb Momcilo Jovanovic was arrested in March for crimes against Albanian civilians in 1999. In May ethnic Serb Miroslav Vuckovic was sentenced to eight years' imprisonment for crimes against ethnic Albanian civilians in May 1999, including endangering lives through the use of explosives and firearms, property destruction, theft, and looting.

There was little progress in bringing to justice persons responsible for the most serious crimes arising from riots in the March 2004. According to the latest statistics from UNMIK, by the end of October 2008, 35 people had been convicted on charges of arson, looting, inciting racial, religious and ethnic hatred, and assault, the same number as at the end of January.

There was also little progress in determining the fate of missing persons. As of April 2008, 1,963 persons—the majority Kosovo Albanian—remain missing. In June the Parliamentary Assembly of the Council of Europe nominated Dick Marty as rapporteur to investigate the fate of missing Serbs allegedly transferred to northern Albania after June 1999. The Kosovo government has refused to investigate the allegations.

Human Rights Defenders

Human rights defenders are largely free to operate without hindrance from international authorities or the Kosovo government.

The Ombudsperson Institution remains compromised by the failure of the Kosovo Assembly to appoint an ombudsperson, with the process restarted in September 2008 for the third time. The institution has had an acting ombudsperson since 2006. But UNMIK's cooperation improved, with progress on addressing the backlog of correspondence and requests from the Ombudsperson. At this writing, EULEX had yet to initiate cooperation with the institution.

The Human Rights Advisory Panel has received over 30 cases, dealing with alleged property rights violations, access to court, and challenges to UNMIK executive decisions. At this writing EULEX had yet to indicate whether the panel can receive complaints against it. In December 2007 the families of two protestors killed by Romanian UN police in 2007 filed their claim with the panel. In September the UN Special Representative of the Secretary General (SRSG) argued that the claim was inadmissible because of a failure to exhaust alternative remedies. The SRSG has not provided a response to the merits of the complaint to date, despite a request from the panel. The panel decided in October to convene a public hearing in January 2009 to consider the admissibility and merits of the case. At this writing, it had yet to issue a recommendation in relation to any case before it.

Key International Actors

In October the United Nations General Assembly approved Serbia's request for a ruling by the International Court of Justice on whether Kosovo's unilateral declaration of independence accords with international law.

TAJIKISTAN

Tajikistan's human rights problems are numerous and chronic, including lack of access to justice, due process violations, and ill-treatment in custody. The government also exercises excessive control over NGOs, religious organizations, political parties, and the media.

Tajikistan is on the United Nations list of 12 countries most adversely affected by the global food crisis. At the start of 2008 severe lack of electricity, due in part to low water levels and government mismanagement, left many without heat during an unusually cold winter. As urban renewal continues in several cities, numerous people have been evicted from their homes without adequate compensation. These problems prompted an unusually high number of popular protests, all small-scale and peaceful.

In March the International Monetary Fund demanded that Tajikistan give back more than US$47 million in loans, after the Central Bank of Tajikistan intentionally gave false information about the country's financial state. The incident exposed serious flaws in Tajikistan's governance.

Institutional Human Rights Reform

In a positive move, in March 2008 the Constitutional Court's mandate was extended to include, among other things, the right to initiate a review of any law's compliance with the constitution and to consider complaints by legal persons.

On March 20, President Emomali Rahmon signed the Law on the Human Rights Ombudsman, under which the ombudsman is appointed by the president and later confirmed by parliament. At this writing, the ombudsman has not yet been appointed.

Forced Evictions and Property Rights

The authorities in the capital, Dushanbe, continue to forcibly and sometimes violently evict people living in the city center and resettle them on the city outskirts, sometimes in unsafe buildings. The hundreds of victims include people whose homes will be demolished to make way for planned urban renewal, whose owner-ship title or purchase agreements were declared illegal, and residents of dormito-ries that were owned, and then privatized, by enterprises. Victims lack adequate information, are not consulted properly about planned evictions, are inadequate-ly compensated for their property, and lack effective legal remedies. In some cases police and marshals intimidate and beat persons resisting eviction.

Attempts by some to impede or challenge the evictions led to conflicts with law enforcement bodies, and in most cases were not successful. In February 2008 a Dushanbe court sentenced Bobodzhon Amirov to six years' imprisonment for obstructing law enforcement officials evicting his family; the sentence was reduced by half on appeal. On April 15, a group of more than 20 women approached the presidential administration building to hold a small protest to express grievances about evictions. Police arrested the demonstrators, beating and insulting some of them. The women were fined and released the same day.

Religious Freedom

At this writing, the government had not yet sent to parliament a controversial draft law on religion that had been sharply criticized in 2007. Under the draft law, all religious groups must reregister and meet such onerous conditions as provid-ing the address of any person who, at any point during the past 10 years, has been a member. The draft also prohibits foreigners from chairing religious organi-zations.

According to Forum 18, an independent, international religious freedom group, on September 29, 2008, a Dushanbe court reaffirmed the ban on activities of Jehovah's Witnesses imposed in 2007. A large consignment of Jehovah's Witness literature seized by customs in 2007 remains impounded. Two registered Christian groups that were suspended in 2007 could not operate as the govern-ment raised objections to their charters.

The Dushanbe synagogue was bulldozed in June, two months after a court ruled that its architecture was inconsistent with that of the presidential palace under construction nearby. The government did not compensate the Jewish community or provide it with an alternate location for worship. At this writing, the Protestant church Grace Sunmin was about to lose its building for worship in Dushanbe, pursuant to a ruling that the church's 1997 purchase of the building was illegal.

Actions in the Name of Countering Terrorism and Extremism

Following a recommendation by the prosecutor general, the Supreme Court of Tajikistan designated Hizb ut-Tahrir, a group that supports the reestablishment of the Caliphate, or Islamic state, by peaceful means, an "extremist" organization. The government continued to arrest alleged Hizb ut-Tahrir members and convict them either of sedition or incitement to racial, ethnic, or religious hatred, often simply for possessing the organization's leaflets.

Civil Society

The government continues to prohibit unregistered NGOs from operating and to use burdensome registration requirements to unduly interfere with the activities of local and international NGOs. More than a year after the new NGO law entered into force, a Ministry of Justice official reported in April that of 3,130 NGOs registered in previous years, only 1,390 had been reregistered, as had 116 of 145 previously registered international organizations. It is not known how many NGO registration applications were denied as opposed to how many NGOs did not have the human or financial resources to apply for reregistration (local NGOs complained that reregistration was a time-consuming and demanding process).

The National Democratic Institute, a US NGO, closed its Dushanbe office in May 2008, after the Justice Ministry denied for the third time in four months the organization's registration application. Also in May, the ministry imposed a three-month ban on Orphans, Refugees and Aid International, a Germany-based nondenominational Christian relief organization, for allegedly proselytizing.

Freedom of Assembly and Expression

While several small, unsanctioned peaceful demonstrations protesting social and economic problems took place in 2008, in April local authorities prohibited the opposition Social Democratic Party from holding a demonstration in Khorog, the capital of the Gorno-Badakhshan autonomous province. The authorities claimed that the issues to be protested—including the transfer of 98 hectares of land to China, the legal status of Gorno Badakhshan, and local police actions—were "beyond the competence of municipal authorities."

Libel and slander continue to be criminal offenses in Tajikistan, and at least two highly worrisome criminal cases are pending at this writing. In 2007 journalist Tursunali Aliev was charged with libel for publishing an article alleging illegal privatizations in Sugd province. The criminal case against him was closed after the preliminary investigation but reopened in August 2008. In September the prosecutor's office started a criminal investigation against Dodojon Avotulloev, founder of *Charogi Ruz* (an opposition newspaper published in exile) and leader of the opposition movement Vatandor. Avotulloev, who had been living in exile in Moscow, is facing charges of sedition and libel and slander of the president of Tajikistan. Fearing extradition, Avotulloev left Russia for a third country.

Torture and Deaths in Custody

Tajikistan's definition of torture does not comply fully with the UN Committee Against Torture's recommendations to the country in December 2006. In a positive move, in March 2008 the Criminal Procedure Code was amended to make evidence obtained under torture inadmissible in court proceedings.

Experts agree that in most cases there is impunity for rampant torture in Tajikistan. In one of the few cases that reached the courts, two policemen in Khatlon province were convicted in August 2008 for ill-treating minors; one of the two received a four-year prison sentence, and the other a suspended sentence.

NGOs and local media reported at least three deaths in custody in 2008, including the death from cancer of the ex-deputy chair of the Party of Islamic Revival Shamsiddin Shamsiddinov. The party alleged his arrest in 2003 was politically motivated and claimed that his life could have been saved had he been allowed to undergo surgery.

In an April 1, 2008 decision (Rakhmatov et al. v. Tajikistan) the UN Human Rights Committee found that Tajikistan violated the rights, including freedom from torture, of five applicants, two of them minors when they were arrested. Tajikistan failed to cooperate with the committee's consideration of the complaint. Similar violations were established in an October 30, 2008 decision (Khuseynov and Butaev v. Tajikistan).

Women's Rights

Women and girls in Tajikistan continue to confront gender-based discrimination and violence. Surveys indicate between one-third and one-half of women experience domestic violence, of whom most have little access to redress.
The parliament has yet to pass a pending bill on domestic violence first drafted in 2006. The UN special rapporteur on violence against women visited Tajikistan in May 2008. In her statement concluding the visit, she highlighted that women in Tajikistan "are caught within a web of poverty, patriarchy, and a weak protective infrastructure, resulting in increased vulnerability to violence and discrimination inside and outside their homes." She supported Tajikistan's draft domestic violence law and urged "other measures ... to enhance women's access to justice" and effective services to victims.

Key International Actors

On June 3, 2008, the chairman-in-office of the Organization for Security and Co-operation in Europe (OSCE) met with Tajikistan's president and foreign minister in Dushanbe. The three discussed a new "comprehensive mandate" for the OSCE Office in Tajikistan. The chairman-in-office also raised such problems as lack of prison access for the International Committee of the Red Cross, child labor, and government interference with media freedom.

TURKEY

A grave political crisis in 2008 halted progress in human rights reforms in Turkey for much of the year. The ruling Justice and Development Party (AKP) narrowly escaped closure in July, with the Constitutional Court instead fining it for anti-secular activities. The government failed to honor its post-election pledge to engage in meaningful consultation on a new constitution, needed to strengthen respect for rights.

With reform stalled, the protection of human rights continues to be eroded. Human rights defenders and journalists critical of the state face prosecution, although they continue to raise their voices loudly. Police abuse increased, with particular concern for excessive use of force at public demonstrations and fatal shootings of civilians. Widespread impunity for abuses by the police and other security forces remains.

Freedom of Expression, Association, and Assembly

Turkey's chief prosecutor launched a case in March to close down the ruling party on the grounds that it engaged in unconstitutional anti-secular activities, citing statements by the AKP leadership and the government's attempt in February, by parliamentary vote, to lift the constitutional ban on wearing the headscarf at university campuses.

The European Union and Council of Europe warned that closure of the party on the basis of the evidence presented would be a major blow to democracy. It would also have violated freedom of expression, association, and the right to political participation. The court ruled on July 30 that the AKP had engaged in anti-secular activity, but fell one vote short of closing the party; the penalty imposed instead was to cut its treasury funding.

The pro-Kurdish Democratic Society Party also faced possible closure by the Constitutional Court for activities and speeches deemed by the prosecutor to constitute separatism. The court's January 2008 ruling against the closure of the pro-Kurdish Rights and Freedoms Party set a precedent: statements about the Kurdish problem fall within the boundaries of free speech.

"We Need a Law for Liberation"

Gender, Sexuality, and Human Rights in a Changing Turkey

HUMAN
RIGHTS
WATCH

Critical and open debate increased, even as restrictions on free speech continue. In May the government made what amount to cosmetic amendments to article 301 of the 2005 Penal Code criminalizing statements that "publicly denigrate Turkishness" or state institutions, following intense pressure from the European Union. While the Ministry of Justice must now grant permission for investigations under article 301, in a number of cases it did so in 2008.

Prosecutors used other articles of the penal code, press law, and anti-terror law to prosecute speech in 2008, and hundreds of journalists, writers, publishers, academics, human rights defenders, and officials of Kurdish political parties and associations were tried and sometimes convicted, in some cases at the initiative of the government. The courts restricted access to numerous websites—including YouTube—during 2008.

The manner in which the government chose to address the issue of women wearing headscarves at university, and the ensuing political and constitutional confrontation, had the effect of failing to ameliorate the situation of thousands of women. The Constitutional Court on June 5 overturned February's parliamentary decision allowing headscarves at university.

Human Rights Defenders

The trial continued of 19 people accused of the January 2007 murder of Turkish-Armenian journalist and human rights defender Hrant Dink. At this writing, there has yet to be a breakthrough in uncovering a conspiracy behind the killing. Reports by the Parliamentary Human Rights Investigative Commission in July, and by the Prime Ministry Inspectorate in November point to multiple failures by state authorities to act on intelligence reports about plans to murder Dink, and support the Dink family lawyers' demand for criminal investigation of the Trabzon and Istanbul police. At this writing, the trial of two junior Trabzon gendarmerie members is ongoing, and permission has been granted for criminal investigation of six other gendarmerie members.

Most convictions of human rights defenders for speech-related offenses or under the anti-terror law result in fines and suspended sentences, making the prosecution of two members of the Human Rights Association (HRA) stand out. Ethem

TURKEY

Closing Ranks
Against Accountability

Barriers to Tackling Police Violence in Turkey

HUMAN
RIGHTS
WATCH

Açıkalın, chair of HRA's Adana branch, spent six months in pretrial detention following his arrest in January for "aiding and abetting an illegal organization" after attending a press conference organized by a legal political group. His prior 30-month sentence for speech-related offenses is under appeal at this writing. Rıdvan Kızgın, former chair of HRA's Bingol branch, is currently serving two-and-a-half years for "concealing evidence" in the 2003 killing by unknown perpetrators of five villagers. A related five-year sentence against him for "aiding and abetting an illegal organization" is currently under appeal.

The decision by an Istanbul court in May 2008 to close Lambda Istanbul, a group working on behalf of lesbian, gay, bisexual, and transgender people, highlighted the hostile environment for the LGBT community in Turkey. The case was initiated by the Istanbul governor's office, which claimed the group's aims were "against law and morality," a view the court supported. Lambda has appealed.

Torture, Ill-Treatment, and Killings by Security Forces

Police torture and ill-treatment is on the rise since 2007. It occurs during arrest, outside places of official detention, and during demonstrations, as well as in detention centers. There were continuing reports of ill-treatment and cruel, inhuman, and degrading conditions in prisons, and of fatal shootings of civilians by police officers. Engin Ceber, age 29, died in a hospital in Istanbul on October 10 after being beaten in police custody and in prison.

During banned Newroz (Kurdish new year) celebrations in March, police used excessive force, including indiscriminate beatings, against demonstrators and children; and two people in Van and one in Yüksekova were shot dead. Police beat demonstrators indiscriminately at a May Day protest in Istanbul, and used excessive force to disperse all peaceful assembly in and around the offices of the trade union confederation DİSK. The absence of a meaningful domestic investigation into the violence precipitated DİSK to apply in August to the European Court of Human Rights. The application was pending at this writing.

Impunity

Turkish courts continued to show excessive leniency toward police and other members of the security forces charged with abuse or misconduct, contributing to impunity, the persistence of torture, and the unwarranted resort to lethal force.

There was no progress in bringing to justice members of security forces responsible for the deaths of 30 prisoners during a series of prison transfers in December 2000. Two soldiers also died during the operation. In June 2008 the trial of soldiers for ill-treatment and of guards for misconduct during transfer from Bayrampaşa prison, where 12 of the prisoners died, exceeded the statute of limitations and collapsed. The main investigation into the deaths in that prison has yet to be concluded.

The retrial of two gendarmerie officers previously convicted for the deadly November 2005 bombing of a bookshop in Şemdinli continued in the Van military court. The officers were released on bail at the first hearing of the retrial in December 2007 and, according to media reports, returned to active service in the gendarmerie.

On October 20, 2008, the "Ergenekon" trial began. Over 100 defendants—including retired military and gendarmerie personnel, figures associated with organized crime, journalists, and academics—are charged with participating in an ultranationalist conspiracy to foster a military coup through civil disturbance, violent attacks, and planned assassinations. The criminal investigation was triggered by the June 2007 discovery of hand grenades in the Istanbul house of a retired army officer. Related grenades had been used in two attacks on the newspaper *Cumhuriyet* in May 2006, perpetrated by the same gang responsible for the April 2006 attack on the Council of State that killed a judge. While there are doubts that the criminal justice system is sufficiently empowered or independent to deal effectively with the case, it provides an unprecedented opportunity for Turkey to confront the negative role in political life played by elements of the military and state.

Attacks on Civilians

Against a background of escalating armed clashes between the military and the Kurdistan Workers' Party (PKK), attacks on civilians continued. Attacks included a suspected PKK bombing in Diyarbakır on January 3, killing six (four of them children); bombings on July 27 in Istanbul, killing 17; and on July 9 outside the US consulate in Ankara, killing six. In the latter two cases the identities of the perpetrators remain unclear.

Key International Actors

The European Union remains the most important international actor with the potential to foster respect for human rights in Turkey. The public hostility of some EU member states, notably France and Germany, to eventual EU membership for Turkey—even if those countries did not block Turkey-EU negotiations—lessened the EU's leverage. The European Commission commented on the continuing lack of progress on human rights in its annual progress report published in November.

At this writing, the European Court of Human Rights has issued 210 judgments against Turkey in 2008 for torture, extrajudicial execution, unfair trial, and other violations. In the November Grand Chamber judgment in *Demir and Baykara v. Turkey*—of major significance for furthering workers' rights in Turkey and across Europe—the court held that interference in the right of municipal civil servants to unionize and the cancellation of a collective bargaining agreement violated the rights of freedom of assembly and association under the European Convention. In a September interim resolution about the implementation of European Court judgments, the Committee of Ministers of the Council of Europe called on Turkey "to ensure effective investigations into members of security forces alleged to have committed violations."

TURKMENISTAN

In the two years since the death of Turkmenistan's president-for-life Saparmurad Niazov, the government under President Gurbanguly Berdymukhamedov has abolished aspects of his cult of personality, adopted a new constitution, and has begun to reverse some of Niazov's most ruinous social policies. The government ended the country's self-imposed isolation and has attracted unprecedented international interest in the country's hydrocarbon wealth.

But Turkmenistan remains one of the most repressive and authoritarian countries in the world because the government has not altered the institutions of repression that characterized Niazov's rule. Hundreds of people, perhaps more, languish in Turkmen prisons following unfair trials on what would appear to be politically motivated charges. Draconian restrictions on freedom of expression, association, movement, and religion remain in place. Teaching of the *Ruhnama*, Niazov's "book of the soul," has been cut back, but is still part of the state education curriculum.

There is no possibility to establish and operate an independent NGO or media outlet, and independent activists and journalists face government threats and harassment. The severity of those restrictions, in particular, make it impossible to assess a series of violent clashes in September 2008 that brought special forces and armored vehicles to the streets of a neighborhood in Ashgabat, the capital. The government stated that the clashes arose when law enforcement bodies sought to disarm drug dealers. Independent sources blame law enforcement for mishandling the situation, and put casualties at around a dozen dead and a similar number wounded. Little is known about the clashes' aftermath.

Constitutional Reform

The new constitution, adopted on September 26, 2008, dissolved the 2,507-member People's Council (Halk Maslakhaty), the supreme government body that had mixed legislative and executive powers and had been used by Niazov to rubberstamp his decisions. But the constitutional reform otherwise strengthened the already dominant institution of the presidency. The president appoints and dismisses judges without parliamentary review, forms the central election commission, and has the right to issue edicts that are mandatory. There are no presidential term limits. Political parties can be created, but a residency requirement would automatically prevent all members of Turkmen opposition movements who have been driven into exile from running for office. The constitution does not provide for a constitutional court or ombudsman.

Civil Society and Media Freedom

Independent activists and journalists in Turkmenistan and in exile are under constant threat of government reprisal for their work. Security services warned activists in Turkmenistan not to meet with European Union and other officials who visited the country, including the United Nations special rapporteur on freedom of religion or belief. Government proxies tried to pressure at least two exiled human rights activists to stop their work, and one exiled political activist, Annadyurdy Khajiev, received death threats by phone in August 2008.

Sazak Durdymuradov, an unpaid contributor to Radio Free Europe/Radio Liberty, was seized in his home in June 2008, detained, and transferred to a psychiatric clinic, where he was held for two weeks and beaten.

No independent organization has been permitted to carry out research on human rights abuses inside the country, and no international agency—governmental or nongovernmental—has had access to detention facilities. The utter vacuum of human rights monitoring in Turkmenistan was highlighted by a June 2008 European Court of Human Rights decision *(Ryabikin v. Russia),* which held that a Turkmen businessman living in Russia could not be extradited to Turkmenistan, in part because the authorities systematically refused international observers access to the country.

Political Prisoners, Government Purges, and Enforced Disappearances

The harsh repression that prevents civic activism impedes determining the number of political prisoners. Only one individual believed to be imprisoned for political reasons was released in 2008, having served his full prison term. None benefited from any of the three presidential pardons granting release to about 3,700 inmates. Well-known Niazov-era political prisoners, including Mukhmetkuli Aimuradov, Annakurban Amanklychev, and Sapardurdy Khajiev remain behind bars, the latter two in incommunicado detention.

Moreover, at least two persons were arrested in 2008 on politically motivated grounds. Civil activist Valery Pal was arrested in February and sentenced in May to 12 years' imprisonment on bogus embezzlement charges. In September Pal suffered a stroke in prison. Gulgeldy Annaniazov, a former dissident who had refugee status in Norway, returned to Ashgabat in June and was promptly arrested and charged with illegal border crossing. On October 7, he was sentenced to 11 years' imprisonment, the exact charges are unknown.

Still imprisoned are Ovezgeldy Ataev, the constitutionally designated successor to Niazov, and his wife. The fate of about 50 prisoners implicated in the alleged November 2002 attack on Niazov's life remains unknown, as do the whereabouts of imprisoned former foreign minister Boris Shikhmuradov, his brother Konstantin Shikhmuradov, and the former ambassador to the Organization for Security and Co-operation in Europe (OSCE), Batyr Berdiev.

In a July 2008 decision (*Komarovski v. Turkmenistan*), the UN Human Rights Committee found that in the aftermath of the alleged November 2002 attack the authorities flagrantly abused the justice process and failed to investigate and prosecute torture and arbitrary detention of suspects. The government so far has taken no action to implement the decision. The utter lack of a system to prevent torture and ill-treatment in Turkmenistan prompted the European Court of Human Rights to issue a ruling in October 2008 (*Soldatenko v. Ukraine*) amounting to a de facto ban on extraditions to the country.

Freedom of Movement

While some individuals have been permitted to travel abroad, the system of arbitrary restrictions on foreign travel remains in place. For example, after spending several months trying to clarify his status, Andrei Zatoka, an environmental activist, in July 2008 received a letter from the Prosecutor General's Office stating that he is still prohibited from travelling abroad. No explanation was provided.

Rashid Ruzimatov and Irina Kakabaeva, relatives of an exiled former government official, have been banned from travel abroad since 2003. Svetlana Orazova, sister of opposition leader Khudaiberdy Orazov, and her husband Ovez Annaev cannot travel abroad despite numerous attempts to challenge their travel ban in court, most recently in April 2008. In October the daughter of Gulgeldy Annaniazov and her family were not allowed to leave Turkmenistan.

Freedom of Religion

Following her September 2008 trip to Turkmenistan, the UN special rapporteur on freedom of religion or belief noted that religious freedom has improved since 2007. But she raised concerns about vague or excessive legislation regulating religion and its arbitrary implementation, prohibition of the activities of unregistered religious communities, and continued restrictions on places of worship and on importing religious material.

Key International Actors

Turkmenistan has hosted an unprecedented number of international delegations and conferences, some of which have included policy discussions with the government on human rights and the rule of law. The Turkmen government has misrepresented these occasions as unequivocal support for government policies.

In February 2008 the European Parliament upheld the human rights benchmarks previously adopted by its international trade committee. The Turkmen government must fulfill the benchmarks before the European Union can proceed with an Interim Trade Agreement with the country. These benchmarks include the release of political prisoners, abolishing the impediments to travel abroad, realigning the educational system with international standards, allowing free access for NGOs, and permitting UN bodies to operate freely. Under the EU's Central Asia Strategy the EU will guarantee loans by the European Investment Bank for projects in the region. A European Parliament resolution adopted in September would impose human rights conditionality on the lending, although at this writing the conditionality mechanism has not been elaborated.

In June the EU held a structured human rights dialogue with Turkmenistan, as part of its Central Asia strategy. But it failed publicly to comment on the numerous serious problems marring the Turkmen government's human rights record, including the arrests of Durdymuradov and Annaniazov, which coincided with the talks.

The United States' interest in Turkmenistan's energy wealth prompted active engagement with the Turkmen government and a reluctance to prioritize human rights. President Bush met President Berdymukhamedov on the sidelines of the April 2008 NATO summit.

The UN special rapporteur on religious freedom became the first UN special mandate holder to gain access to the country. Nine other UN special procedures remain barred from Turkmenistan as a result of the government's failure to extend these monitors the required invitations for country visits. Turkmenistan appears to treat its reporting obligation to various UN human rights bodies as a mere formality. In its report for the UN Human Right's Council's Universal Periodic Review due in December 2008, the Turkmen government did not recognize any serious problems in meeting its human rights obligations. In September Turkmenistan was also reviewed by the Human Rights Council's confidential complaint procedure, a body which considers "consistent patterns of gross and reliably attested violations of all human rights." While the council did not appoint a special rapporteur on Turkmenistan, it requested that the government respond to the numerous individual complaints received and agreed to reexamine the situation during its March 2009 session.

UKRAINE

2008 proved to be another year of political turmoil in Ukraine. The longtime conflict between President Viktor Yushchenko and parliament continued, despite the
appointment of Yulia Timoshenko as prime minister in late 2007 and the creation
of a coalition government with her party. During August's armed conflict in
Georgia and its breakaway region South Ossetia the political situation deteriorated, and in September the coalition government collapsed, as the president and
prime minister could not agree on the proper response to Russia's use of military
force in the conflict. In October Yushchenko issued a decree dissolving parliament. When their dispute went to the courts, both sides attempted to interfere in
the judicial process: Yushchenko abolished a court that ruled in favor of a
Timoshenko challenge to his decree calling early parliamentary elections, and
parliamentarians from Timoshenko's party physically disrupted a subsequent
hearing of Yushchenko's appeal against that ruling.

Despite adoption of some important legislation, Ukraine's human rights record
continued to be poor, with torture and ill-treatment in detention remaining commonplace. Employment discrimination against women, hostility to asylum seekers, hate attacks on ethnic minorities, and human rights abuses fueling Ukraine's
staggering HIV/AIDS epidemic are all problems that the Ukrainian government
still fails to address effectively.

Criminal Justice System

A significant victory for Ukraine's human rights community was the adoption of
the Criminal Justice and Law Enforcement Authorities reform, signed by President
Yushchenko on April 8, 2008. The reform was designed to bring the cumbersome
criminal justice system into line with international law. In particular, it aimed to
improve pretrial investigation procedures, strengthen protections for victims'
rights, humanize the conditions and procedures of criminal punishment, and end
corruption in the judicial process.

Torture and ill-treatment in detention persist, however, as well as a myriad of abusive conditions for detainees: overcrowding in jails and prisons, lack of adequate
sanitation, and too little light, food, water, and medical care.

Media Freedom

In March 2008 three former Interior Ministry police were convicted of the 2000 murder of journalist Georgy Gongadze. But there appeared to be no progress in the search for those who ordered the murder. Media activists continue to demand that this be meaningfully investigated.

Maxim Birovash, a correspondent for *Business* magazine, was assaulted in the elevator of his apartment building on December 7, 2007. Two men knocked him to the ground and stole his bag, which contained internal correspondence of the Ministry of Internal Affairs, as well as other documents related to Birovash's investigation into corruption in the issuance of passports. One assailant was detained, tried, and sentenced to five years in prison. The second man was not found, and the stolen documents were not recovered.

Employment Discrimination against Women

Although Ukraine has adopted legislation to ensure gender equality in employment, including the Law on Equal Rights and Opportunities for Men and Women and amendments to the Labor Code prohibiting gender discrimination in employment and pay, research shows that women do not enjoy equal access to employment opportunities. Both public and private employers regularly specify preferences for men, and discriminate on the basis of age or the physical appearance of potential female candidates during recruitment. Women are very often forced into the low-paying, unregulated informal economy, and are disproportionately affected by unemployment.

Treatment of Asylum Seekers and Migrants

The worrisome practice of removing refugees and asylum seekers continued in 2008. With no clear migration policy, Ukraine continues to deny asylum seekers protection and often refuses to grant refugee status on murky procedural grounds. Many migrants face deportation back to countries where they face torture or ill-treatment. In March 2008 the Ukrainian government forcibly returned 11 ethnic Tamil refugees to Sri Lanka, despite the fact that all 11 were registered with the Kyiv office of the United Nations High Commissioner for Refugees (UNHCR).

Oleg Kuznetsov, a Russian national, was arrested on July 19, 2007, and held for a year pending extradition. In March 2008 the State Committee on Nationalities and Religion granted him refugee status. On July 21 the district administrative court of Kyiv turned down the prosecutor's appeal against the decision to grant Kuznetsov asylum. Nevertheless, he was extradited to Russia a week later by order of the prosecutor general, despite his refugee status and in violation of Ukrainian refugee law.

Migrants and asylum seekers in detention commonly suffer violations of their fundamental rights to legal counsel, to be informed of their rights, to inform a third party of their detention, and to a fair trial.

Hate Crimes and Discrimination against Ethnic Minorities

Ukrainian human rights organizations note that nationalistic informal groups of young people have been on the rise since 2005, carrying out physical assaults and attacks on immigrants, refugees, asylum seekers, foreign students, and people of non-Slavic appearance including Roma. In the first four months of 2008 the Ministry of Internal Affairs reported 160 crimes against foreign nationals, including seven murders. In response, the government created special criminal investigation units for fighting racially motivated crimes, which have being operating in several Ukrainian cities.

Crimean Tatars continue to endure discrimination, including unequal allocation of land, unequal employment opportunities, unequal access to places of worship, and unavailability of education in their native language.

Human Rights Abuses Fueling the HIV/AIDS Epidemic

The Ukrainian National AIDS Center reported nearly 11,000 newly registered cases of HIV infection in the first seven months of 2008; 47 percent of newly registered cases are among injection drug users. NGOs report continuing police interference with the delivery of HIV prevention information and services. Those at highest risk of HIV/AIDS, including drug users and sex workers, are particularly vulnerable to police harassment and are frequently driven away from lifesaving services.

The government has taken important steps to increase access for drug users to medication-assisted treatment (MAT) with methadone and buprenorphine, which are widely recognized as among the most effective means to treat opiate dependence. In December 2007 the government lifted restrictions on methadone imports, and as of October 2008 more than 1,700 people received methadone or buprenorphine in 51 healthcare institutions in 24 regions of Ukraine. There is no MAT in prison, however, which means that drug users on MAT are forced to suffer abrupt withdrawal when taken into state custody.

The Ministry of Health has taken measures to expand provision of antiretroviral therapy for people living with HIV, although not on a scale sufficient to address the need for it. When selecting candidates for antiretroviral therapy, medical institutions frequently discriminate against drug users on the unfounded assumption that they will not adhere to a rigorous course of treatment.

Key International Actors

In January 2008, then European Union Trade Commissioner Peter Mandelson and Ukrainian Vice Prime Minister Hryhory Nemyrya signed an agreement outlining final terms for Ukraine's World Trade Organization membership. At the twelfth EU-Ukraine Cooperation Council, the EU complimented Ukraine on its parliamentary elections in September 2007, calling them "a lively campaign and genuine political competition." At the EU-Ukraine summit in Paris in September 2008 EU officials underlined their support for Ukraine's efforts to carry out vital political and economic reforms.

The sharpening presidential-parliamentary conflict and ongoing problematic human rights conditions were factors in NATO's deferring a decision to offer membership to Ukraine in April 2008.

Ukraine was reviewed under the UN Human Rights Council's Universal Periodic Review mechanism in May 2008. The outcome of this review was a set of recommendations related to discrimination and hate crimes, ending torture, investigating violence against journalists, and creating a more orderly process for refugees and asylum seekers in accordance with UNHCR guidelines.

The Legal Affairs Committee of the Parliamentary Assembly of the Council of Europe (PACE) called for a proper investigation to bring to justice those responsible for ordering the murder of journalist Georgy Gongadze. After a fact-finding mission in 2007, PACE officials called on Ukraine to finally launch reforms of the judicial and penal systems.

The number of individual applications to the European Court of Human Rights against Ukraine has been steadily increasing over the years; in 2007 there were 4,502 applications allocated to a decision body, and a further 4,144 in the first 10 months of 2008. The court handed down 109 judgments against Ukraine in 2007, mostly concerning torture and discrimination. Between January and November 1, 2008, the court found against Ukraine in 77 cases, mainly involving fair trial and property rights.

Uzbekistan

The Uzbek government's human rights record remains abysmal. In 2008 the authorities continued to suppress independent civil society activism and religious worship, and to deny accountability for the 2005 Andijan massacre, touting their own version of the events to foreign government representatives. Yet international pressure on the Uzbek government declined with the suspension and subsequent partial lifting of European Union sanctions.

Uzbekistan held presidential elections on December 23, 2007. According to the official tally, President Islam Karimov won reelection to a third term with 88.1 percent of the vote, but the elections lacked any competitiveness and failed to meet international standards. The legality of Karimov's third term was in question as he had already served the maximum two consecutive terms allowed by the constitution.

The lack of rule of law continues to be a fundamental, structural problem. The judiciary lacks independence and the weak parliament does not effectively check executive power. A deeply entrenched culture of impunity for abuses persists. Local media outlets are not free and the government refuses to accredit foreign journalists, while also blocking access to many websites offering independent information on Uzbekistan and on topics deemed sensitive by the government. Forced child labor in the cotton fields remains a key rights concern.

Human Rights Defenders and Independent Journalists

The Uzbek government continues to crack down on civil society, detaining and threatening rights defenders, journalists, and others with prosecution for their peaceful activism. Uzbekistan continues to hold at least 11 human rights defenders and independent journalists in prison on politically-motivated charges, and at least two new arrests occurred in 2008. These activists languish in prison following sham trials, serving lengthy sentences solely because of their legitimate human rights or civic activism. Among them is Jamshid Karimov, an independent journalist, who has been confined in a closed psychiatric ward since September 2006.

On October 10, 2008, a court in Nukus sentenced Solijon Abdurakhmanov, an independent journalist known for his critical reporting, especially on corruption, to 10 years in prison for selling drugs. Abdurakhmanov denies the charges and his lawyer believes that the police planted the drugs. Police investigators failed to carry out basic investigative steps such as fingerprinting the drugs despite the lawyer's repeated requests.

On October 23, a court in Manget sentenced Akzam Turgunov, head of the human rights organization Mazlum, to 10 years in prison on fabricated extortion charges. He had been arrested on July 11, and three days later, while in a police investigator's office writing a statement, someone poured boiling water down Turgunov's neck and back, severely scalding him and causing him to lose consciousness. The authorities refused to investigate the abuse until Turgunov removed his shirt to reveal his burn scars during a court hearing on September 16.

Uzbek authorities continue to imprison other independent civic activists for politically-motivated reasons. One such case is that of Yusuf Juma, a poet and dissident sentenced to five years in a penal colony after calling during a picket for President Karimov's resignation. Two of Juma's sons, Bobur and Mashrab, have also been imprisoned on trumped-up charges apparently in retaliation for their father's activism.

In January-February 2008 the government released seven human rights defenders, and another two in October, apparently as a gesture toward the European Union. However, nearly all of them were required to sign pledges agreeing to restrict their activities as a condition of release, and after release were subjected to close surveillance and harassment. The authorities prevented the released defenders from meeting with foreign visitors and generally from pursuing their human rights work. Two fled the country, fearing for their safety.

The few international NGOs that remain in Uzbekistan operate in a climate of government pressure and harassment. The government refused to allow any of the previously expelled foreign NGOs to return, although at least two of them attempted to do so. Human Rights Watch was forced to suspend its operations in the country in July after the government denied work accreditation to, and then outright banned its researcher from entering Uzbekistan.

The Andijan Massacre and the Situation of Refugees

The Uzbek government has adamantly rejected numerous and repeated calls for an independent international inquiry into the May 2005 Andijan massacre, when government forces killed hundreds of protestors, most of them unarmed. The circumstances surrounding the massacre have not been clarified, and those responsible for the killings have not been held accountable. The government continues to persecute anyone whom it deems to have any connection to or information about the Andijan events.

Refugees, who fled Uzbekistan in the immediate aftermath of the massacre and later returned to the country, as well as their families, have been a particular target of government pressure. They have been subjected to interrogations, constant surveillance, ostracism, and in some cases overt threats to life, which has triggered a new wave of refugees.

Refugees in neighboring countries fear for their security because Uzbek security forces operate in some areas across the border, such as Osh, Kyrgyzstan. The Uzbek government pressured Kyrgyz authorities to return the more than 200 Uzbek refugees in Kyrgyzstan. In 2008 several Uzbek refugees and asylum seekers were forcibly returned to Uzbekistan under suspicious circumstances. For example, on May 13 prison authorities in Osh handed Erkin Holikov to Uzbek police despite his asylum case being pending with a court. On September 19, an Uzbek refugee, Hayotjon Juraboev, disappeared after being stopped in Bishkek by unknown individuals whom witnesses said introduced themselves as security officials, and was forcibly returned to Uzbekistan.

Freedom of Religion

Uzbek authorities continue their unrelenting, multi-year campaign of unlawful arrest, torture, and imprisonment of Muslims who practice their faith outside state controls or who belong to unregistered religious organizations, with at least 6,000 currently incarcerated for nonviolent religious offenses. Peaceful religious believers are often branded "religious extremists." Dozens were arrested or convicted in 2008 on charges related to religious "extremism." Human Rights Watch documented allegations of ill-treatment in several of these cases.

Many religious prisoners had their sentences extended without due process for alleged violations of internal prison regulations or for alleged new crimes, as a means of keeping them in prison.

Criminal Justice, Torture, and Ill-Treatment

Abolition of the death penalty took effect in January 2008 and many death row inmates were given fixed-term sentences. The government also introduced habeas corpus that month. However, in the absence of an independent judiciary this did not provide meaningful protection against arbitrary detention or abuses in pretrial detention.

The United Nations Committee Against Torture, reviewing Uzbekistan in November 2007, concluded that torture and ill-treatment remained "routine" and issued urgent recommendations. The Uzbek authorities failed to implement these measures and Human Rights Watch continued to receive credible, serious allegations of torture, indicating that torture remained a widespread practice within a prevailing law enforcement and judicial culture of impunity.

Child Labor

Although a new law on children's rights took effect in January 2008 and the government in March ratified the International Labour Organization's Conventions on the Elimination of the Worst Forms of Child Labour and on the Minimum Age of Employment, forced child labor in the cotton harvest remains a key concern in Uzbekistan. Following the broadcast internationally of footage on forced child labor, several retailers and clothing companies in the United States and United Kingdom have taken measures to exclude the use of Uzbek cotton.

Human rights monitors who reported on forced child labor found themselves often harassed by the police. For example, on October 2, police in Gulistan briefly detained and assaulted Karim Bozorboyev, one of the seven human rights defenders released at the start of the year, after he video recorded children in Jizzakh being taken to the cotton fields to work.

Key International Actors

The Uzbek government persisted in its refusal to grant access to United Nations special rapporteurs with longstanding requests for invitation, including those on torture and human rights defenders, and failed to take meaningful action to address concerns and recommendations by a range of UN bodies. Uzbekistan was due to be reviewed under the Universal Periodic Review mechanism of the UN Human Rights Council in December 2008.

In a hugely disappointing move on October 13, EU foreign ministers decided to lift the visa ban on eight former and current Uzbek government officials thought to have been responsible for the Andijan massacre, while retaining the purely symbolic embargo on arms trade with Uzbekistan. The EU pledged to keep the situation under review and called on the Uzbek authorities to release all imprisoned human rights defenders, cease their harassment, cooperate with UN monitors, and end interference with NGO operations including Human Rights Watch. The EU cited progress in human rights as a justification for easing the sanctions, an assessment that bordered on the absurd when contrasted with the prevailing reality on the ground. Among the positive developments highlighted by the EU was a joint EU-Uzbek government-organized seminar on "Liberalization of the Media," held in Tashkent on October 2-3. Many civil society participants from the EU side had made clear that this seminar should not be considered evidence of progress in the context of the impending sanctions review. The EU also welcomed the structured human rights dialogue it had embarked on with Uzbekistan, without recognition that such dialogue alone could not constitute progress.

The United States Congress at long last adopted legislation in December 2007 establishing specific human rights benchmarks the Uzbek government must fulfill. In light of Uzbekistan's failure to meet these benchmarks, sanctions, which largely mirror those of the EU, were imposed in late June 2008.

Both the US and the EU issued calls for the release of Turgunov and Abdurakhmanov.

SAUDI ARABIA

The Ismailis of Najran

Second-class Saudi Citizens

HUMAN
RIGHTS
WATCH

WORLD REPORT
2009

MIDDLE EAST
AND NORTH AFRICA

ALGERIA

As the Algerian economy benefited from the worldwide surge in oil prices, Algerians continued to suffer restrictions on civil liberties, under a state of emergency imposed in 1992, and the government continued impunity for past and present abuses. While political violence is down considerably since the mid-1990s, the country confronted a new wave of bombings claimed by the al Qaeda Organization of the Islamic Maghreb. On November 12, 2008, parliament approved, without debate, and by a vote of 500 in favor, 21 against, and 8 abstentions, a constitutional amendment ending presidential term limits. This allows Abdelaziz Bouteflika to run for a third five-year term in the spring of 2009.

Freedom of Expression and Assembly

The broadcast media are state-controlled and air almost no critical coverage of, or dissent on, government policies, but they do provide live telecasts of parliamentary sessions. Privately-owned newspapers enjoy a considerably freer scope, but repressive press laws, dependence on revenues from public-sector advertising, and other factors limit their freedom to criticize the government, the military, and the powerful.

The press law imposes prison terms along with fines for defamation and for insulting government officials and state institutions. On March 4, 2008, an appeals court in Jijel upheld the defamation conviction of Ali Chawki Amari, a columnist for the independent *al-Watan* daily, and Omar Belhouchet, its director, for accusing a governor of buying his mistress a car with public funds. The court imposed sentences on the pair of two months in prison and a fine of 1 million dinars (US$15,000) each.

In June 2008 the government stripped the Agence France-Presse bureau chief and an Algiers-based Reuters correspondent of their press credentials, accusing the former of overstating the number of casualties caused by a terrorist bombing that month, and the latter of reporting a bombing that never happened. As of November, the Reuters correspondent was still without credentials and thus unable to report for any foreign media.

Pan-Arab television stations are popular among Algerian viewers. However, since 2004 the government has banned the most popular, Al Jazeera, from operating a news bureau inside the country.

A court in Sidi M'hamed convicted human rights lawyer Amine Sidhoum on April 13, 2008, of having, in a press interview, disparaged a court ruling and insulted state institutions. The court sentenced the Kubba-based lawyer to six months in prison and a fine. Sidhoum remained free pending an appeal hearing, which at this writing had not taken place.

Authorities used state of emergency powers to ban most public demonstrations and many gatherings. On October 5, authorities prevented a panel discussion in Algiers from taking place, organized by the Algerian League for the Defense of Human Rights on the riots that shook major Algerian cities in October 1988.

Religious Freedom

Religious freedom declined for Algeria's tiny non-Muslim minority in 2008, with increased enforcement of Ordinance 06-03. The 2006 law provides prison terms for proselytizing by non-Muslims and forbids them from gathering to worship except in state-approved locations. Authorities have refused numerous applications submitted by Protestant Christian groups to use buildings for worship, putting their members at risk of prosecution for worship in unauthorized places.

A court in the southwestern city of Tissemsilt on July 2, 2008, sentenced Protestants Rachid Mohammed Seghir and Jammal Dahmani to six-month suspended sentences and a fine of 100,000 dinars (US$1,500) on charges of distributing Christian publications that "aimed to weaken the faith of Muslims." Authorities applied the law also against members of the long-established Roman Catholic community. On January 30, 2008, in Maghnia, a court sentenced priest Pierre Wallez to one year in prison for ministering to clandestine sub-Saharan immigrants in an "unauthorized" location, a sentence that an appeals court later reduced to a two-month term, suspended.

In September a court in Biskra sentenced six Muslim men to four years in prison and a fine for eating during the fasting hours of Ramadan, under article 144bis (2) of the penal code, which criminalizes acts that are offensive to Islam. An appeals court overturned the verdict.

Impunity for Past Abuses

Over 100,000 Algerians died during the political strife of the 1990s. Thousands more were "disappeared" by security forces or abducted by armed groups fighting the government and have never been located, dead or alive. Perpetrators of atrocities during this era continue to enjoy impunity. The legal framework for that impunity is the 2006 Law on Peace and National Reconciliation, which provides an amnesty to security force members for the actions they took in the name of combating terrorism, and to armed group members not implicated in the most heinous acts.

The law promises compensation for families of "disappeared" persons but at the same time makes it a crime to denigrate state institutions or security forces for the way they conducted themselves during the period of political strife. Authorities have repeatedly harassed associations representing families of the "disappeared" who protest state policies by continuing to demand justice for the perpetrators or at least that the state provide information about the fate of their missing relatives. For example, a Constantine court on March 26, 2008, convicted Louisa Saker, Rabah Boulagheb, and Sofiane Mehamlia, all relatives of "disappeared," for their role in a demonstration related to the issue. The court convicted Saker of participation in an unauthorized demonstration, while Boulagheb and Mehamlia were convicted in absentia of that charge in addition to charges of violence, theft, and undermining the authority of public officials. Their appeals trial was in progress as of November.

Torture, Incommunicado Detention, and the Death Penalty

Algeria amended its penal code in 2004 to make torture an explicit crime. Nevertheless, Amnesty International "continues to regularly receive reports of incommunicado detention of suspects in unofficial places of detention and torture by the DRS [Department for Information and Security]." The International Committee of the Red Cross regularly visits ordinary prisons in Algeria but not DRS-run places of detention.

The UN Committee Against Torture, in its May 2008 examination of Algeria's report to the committee, expressed concern about reports that the legal limit of 12 days in pre-charge detention in terrorism cases "can, in practice, be extended repeatedly" and that "the law does not guarantee the right to counsel during the period of remand in custody, and that the right of a person in custody to have access to a doctor and to communicate with his or her family is not always respected."

Algerian courts pronounced scores of death sentences during 2008, many of them against defendants in terrorism cases and most of them in absentia. Despite pronouncing hundreds of death sentences in recent years, Algeria has observed a de facto moratorium on carrying out the death penalty since 1993.

Terrorism and Counterterrorism

From January to September 2008 at least 265 people were reported killed in more than 21 bombings claimed mostly by the al Qaida Organization of the Islamic Maghreb. The largest of them, a car bomb outside a police academy in Issers on August 19, reportedly killed 44 people and injured 45. On December 11, 2007, two bombs exploded a few minutes apart in Algiers, one targeting the United Nations office and the other going off in front of the Constitutional Council. The blasts killed 41 and injured over 177, according to news agencies. The Algerian government said the bombs killed 26.

Security forces, presumably the DRS, immediately took into custody two Algerians whom the United States transferred from Guantanamo Bay in July 2008, held them incommunicado for 12 days, and charged them with membership in a terrorist organization and use of false travel documents. The court then granted their pretrial release. A court filed the same charges against, and then granted pretrial release to, two other Algerians whom the United States sent from Guantanamo in August.

The penal code definition of terrorism is so broad that it can be used to prosecute the nonviolent exercise of civil liberties. The definition includes, for example, "any action that targets state security ... via actions whose purpose is to ... attack the symbols of the Nation and the Republic ... or obstruct the functioning of public institutions ... or the application of laws and regulations." The code also pro-vides up to 10 years' imprisonment for encouraging or justifying terrorist acts.

Polisario-Run Refugee Camps in Algeria for Sahrawis

The Polisario Front has since the late 1970s governed camps in remote southwest Algeria for Sahrawi refugees who fled from Western Sahara, just across the bor-der. The Polisario Front allows camp residents to criticize its management of day-to-day issues, but marginalizes those who openly challenge its rule or general political orientation. There were, however, no confirmed reports that the Polisario had detained anyone for political reasons during 2007 or the first half of 2008. In 2008 refugees were largely free to leave the camps if they wished, via Mauritania.

The government of Algeria did not, to Human Rights Watch's knowledge, explicitly recognize its responsibility for safeguarding the human rights of Sahrawis living in Polisario-run camps on Algerian soil.

Key International Actors

Despite serving on the UN Human Rights Council in 2006-2007, Algeria continued during 2008 its non-compliance with longstanding requests for country visits by the UN special rapporteurs on torture; on the promotion and protection of human rights while countering terrorism; and on extrajudicial, summary and arbitrary executions. Algeria was amongst the first group of countries reviewed under the Universal Periodic Review mechanism of the UN Human Rights Council in April 2008.

The United States provides almost no financial aid to oil-rich Algeria but the two countries have grown closer, notably as allies in counterterrorism. In the year's highest-level meeting between the two countries, US Secretary of State Condoleezza Rice visited President Bouteflika in Algiers on September 6, affirm-ing "ties of friendship" and counterterrorism cooperation. Rice made no public statement on human rights but on September 19, Ambassador-at-Large for International Religious Freedom John Hanford criticized Algeria's worsening treat-ment of religious minorities when he presented the State Department's 2008 International Religious Freedom report.

Bahrain

Human rights conditions in Bahrain deteriorated in 2008. Despite the important reforms that the king, Shaikh Hamad bin `Isa al-Khalifa, adopted in 2001-02, the government has done little to institutionalize human rights protections in law. The government continues to subject freedom of expression, assembly, and association to arbitrary restrictions. People detained after demonstrators and security forces clashed in Manama in December 2007 alleged they were tortured.

Opposition political societies that boycotted the first National Assembly elections in 2002 participated in 2006 elections, but some groups have since boycotted the Assembly, protesting what they regard as the absence of real legislative authority for the elected representatives.

In June 2008 the government executed a Bangladeshi man convicted of murder, the third execution in two years. Except for a single execution in 1996, a time of great political turmoil, Bahrain had not executed anyone since 1977.

Freedom of Expression and Information

Authorities continue to use the press law (Law 47/2002) to restrict coverage of controversial matters, including official corruption. In May 2008 the government announced a new draft press law that would remove criminal penalties for most journalistic infractions but appeared to retain the option of criminal penalties for certain types of written or spoken comment, including those found to harm national unity. The draft was awaiting approval by the National Assembly as of November 2008.

In July the independent Bahrain Center for Human Rights (BCHR) reported that six journalists from publications affiliated with opposition political movements had been detained briefly and faced charges of inciting sectarian strife.

The country's sole residential internet service provider, Batelco, is government-owned. The BCHR in October estimated that the authorities were blocking at least 22 discussion forums and other websites, including its own.

449

Freedom of Assembly

Law 32 of 2006 requires the organizers of any public meeting to notify the head of Public Security at least three days in advance, and authorizes that official to determine whether a meeting warrants police presence on the basis of "its subject … or any other circumstance." The law stipulates that meeting organizers are responsible for "forbidding any speech or discussion infringing on public order or morals," but leaves "public order or morals" undefined.

In December 2007 security forces and protesters clashed in and around Manama following the death of a protester in an earlier confrontation with security forces. Several demonstrators affiliated with opposition political movements subsequently faced charges, including those of illegal assembly, attacking security forces, and arson relating to the torching of a police vehicle during the clashes. Relatives of the detainees and several men detained briefly in connection with the clashes told Human Rights Watch that interrogators had tortured detainees and sexually assaulted at least one. Several detainees said interrogators abused them to elicit confessions. A court-ordered medical inquiry in April 2008 concluded that the men may have had injuries consistent with the abuses they described, but that delayed medical examinations made it impossible to verify claims of torture. In July Bahrain's High Criminal Court sentenced 11 of the detainees to jail terms ranging from one to seven years. Several of those convicted were subsequently pardoned; five were appealing their sentences as of November 2008.

Impunity

Decree 56/2002, which confers immunity from investigation or prosecution on government officials alleged to be responsible for torture and other serious human rights abuses committed prior to 2001, remains on the books. Despite the efforts of local human rights groups to establish a means for addressing such violations, the government insists that the matter is closed. In its submission to the United Nations Human Rights Council's Universal Periodic Review (UPR) mechanism in April 2008, Bahrain stated "there are no cases of torture in the kingdom."

Freedom of Association and Civil Society

The government continues to deny legal status to the Bahrain Center for Human Rights, which it ordered to be dissolved in 2004 after the BCHR's president publicly criticized the prime minister. Several other groups, including the National Committee for the Unemployed and the Bahrain Youth Human Rights Society, attempted in 2005 to register with the Ministry of Social Development, as required by law, but at this writing had received no response to their applications.

In 2007 the Ministry of Social Development drafted new legislation on civil society organizations, but at this writing the ministry had not submitted the draft to the parliament. The draft law contains some improvements over the existing Law 21/1989, but includes numerous provisions incompatible with international standards and best practices regarding freedom of association. For example, a version of the draft law circulated in November 2007 authorizes the Ministry of Social Development to close any organization for up to 60 days without a court order if it deems the organization to have violated any Bahraini law. It also appears to leave open the possibility of criminal penalties by stipulating that all Bahraini law applies to violations of the associations law.

Bahrain has ratified some International Labour Organization conventions, but neither of the two core conventions governing freedom of association. Law 33/2002 permits workers to form and join unions, but the General Federation of Bahrain Trade Unions (GFBTU) filed a complaint with the ILO in June 2005 protesting what it said was the government's repeated refusal to register six trade unions in the public sector. In 2007 the GFBTU filed another complaint protesting a November 2006 edict by the prime minister prohibiting strikes in numerous sectors of the economy on the grounds that they provide essential services. In March 2008 the ILO's Committee on Freedom of Association called on Bahrain to amend its trade union law and the prime minister's ruling, including providing a more limited definition of "essential services." But in April Bahrain's UPR submission noted that "trade union pluralism can weaken and split the trade union movement," and "all States tend to place restrictions on pluralism and limit the number of trade unions and federations, placing them under the umbrella of a single entity so they can address economic challenges." In September six Bahraini rights groups said Bahrain's Ministry of Education circulated a warning that month to employees that they risk termination if they take part in unauthorized demonstrations or advocate strikes in vital industries.

Migrant Worker Rights

Migrant workers face the risk of exploitation, despite some formal protections under Bahraini law including the right to join unions. In practice, foreign workers' dependence on their employer's sponsorship for legal residence curtails their ability to pursue legal remedies in labor disputes. Existing labor law does not extend to domestic workers, over whom employers exercise inordinate power to withhold wages and passports. Bahrain's labor minister has vowed to abolish the sponsorship system by the end of 2008.

Women's Rights

Bahrain has no written personal status law. Instead, separate Sharia-based family courts for Sunni and Shia Muslims hear marriage, divorce, custody, and inheritance cases. Family court judges, who are generally conservative religious scholars with limited formal legal training, render judgments according to their individual reading of Islamic jurisprudence. They have consistently favored men in their rulings and are unapologetically adverse to women's equality. In October three Bahraini women with pending divorce and custody cases met with representatives of the Ministry of Justice and Islamic Affairs to urge them to establish a committee charged with reviewing the decisions of these courts. Women's rights organizations continue to call for a written unified personal status law.

Counterterrorism Measures

In August 2006 the king signed into law the "Protecting Society from Terrorist Acts" bill, despite concerns expressed by the UN special rapporteur on the promotion and protection of human rights while countering terrorism that it contained excessively broad definitions of terrorism and terrorist acts. Article 1 prohibits any act that would "damage national unity" or "obstruct public authorities from performing their duties." Article 6 prescribes the death penalty for acts that "disrupt the provisions of the Constitution or laws, or prevent state enterprises or public authorities from exercising their duties." The law also allows for extended periods of detention without charge or judicial review. A group of Bahraini and foreign defendants accused of preparing terrorist attacks, the first people tried under the law, were sentenced in early 2008 to jail terms of several months but then released on the basis of time served in pretrial custody.

Key International Actors

Bahrain hosts the headquarters of the United States Navy's Fifth Fleet and figures in logistical support for military operations in Iraq and Afghanistan. The United States designated Bahrain a major non-NATO ally in 2002.

Bahrain was the first country to undergo the UPR in April 2008. Its voluntary pledges to the Human Rights Council include the establishment of a national human rights institution, expected to be in place by January 2009. Bahrain won a seat on the HRC in May 2008. Local and international NGOs also urged its government to ratify treaties and instruments including the Optional Protocol to the Convention against Torture and ILO conventions including Nos. 87 and 98 on freedom of association and collective bargaining.

EGYPT

Egypt continued its relentless attacks on political dissent in 2008. The government renewed the Emergency Law (Law No. 162 of 1958) in May for an additional two years, providing a continued basis for arbitrary detention and unfair trials, and despite repeated promises not to do so by top officials, including President Hosni Mubarak. Egyptian human rights organizations estimate that up to 5,000 people remain detained without charge under the law, some for over a decade.

Security forces acting with impunity prevented strikes, violently dispersed demonstrations, and harassed and in some cases tortured rights activists. Journalists, activists, and hundreds of members of the Muslim Brotherhood—the banned organization that is the country's largest opposition group—were jailed. The government used lethal force against migrants and refugees seeking to cross into Israel, and forcibly returned asylum seekers and refugees to countries where they could face torture.

Political Violence and Torture

On April 6-7, 2008, security forces prevented workers from striking in the city of Mahalla al-Kobra, and violently dispersed protests against rising food costs, wounding more than 100 people and apparently killing a 15-year-old bystander. They arrested hundreds of protestors, journalists, and activists, and detained scores for months without charge or despite court orders for their release. State Security Investigations officers in Mahalla tortured detainees during interrogations, including Mohamed Marei, a translator for a US journalist covering the protests who was detained for 87 days without being informed of any charges against him. In July the government transferred 49 detainees' cases to the Supreme State Security Court, where procedures violate fair trial rights.

Migrants' and Refugees' Rights

Egyptian border guards reportedly killed 22 migrants trying to cross into Israel in 2008; as of November Egyptian forces had killed 34 migrants on the Sinai border since July 2007. At this writing, Egypt had not allowed officials of the United

EGYPT/ISRAEL

Sinai Perils

Risks to Migrants, Refugees, and Asylum Seekers
in Egypt and Israel

**HUMAN
RIGHTS
WATCH**

Nations High Commissioner for Refugees (UNHCR) access to a group of 91 Eritreans, Sudanese, and Somalis whom Israel returned in August 2008. Egypt denied UNHCR access to a prior group of 48 whom Israel returned in August 2007, and reportedly returned between five and twenty of them to Sudan in late 2007 or early 2008.

In April 2008 Egypt forcibly returned 49 Sudanese men and boys, including 11 refugees and asylum seekers, to southern Sudan, where authorities detained them for four months. In June Egypt forcibly returned at least 740 Eritreans, including women and children, without allowing UNHCR access to them. They are reportedly detained at a military jail and are at risk of torture and ill-treatment.

Freedom of Expression

In March a Cairo court convicted Ibrahim Issa, editor of *Al-Dustur* newspaper, on charges of "publishing false information and rumors" about President Mubarak's health; a Cairo appeals court upheld the conviction in September, sentencing Issa to two months' jail, but Mubarak pardoned him in October. Issa and three other newspaper editors appealed one-year jail sentences handed down in September 2007 for publishing "false news, statements or rumors likely to disturb public order." In August a Cairo court convicted Saad Eddin Ibrahim in absentia of harming Egypt's reputation and sentenced him to two years in prison for writing articles urging the US to condition aid to Egypt on human rights reforms.

In February the Arab League adopted "principles" introduced by Egypt and Saudi Arabia that call on member states to prohibit satellite television broadcasts that "negatively affect social peace, national unity, public order, and public morals," or "defame leaders, or national and religious symbols" of Arab states. Egypt's state-controlled Nilesat satellite subsequently dropped three channels, including al-Hiwar, which broadcast programs featuring government critics and human rights abuse victims. In April plainclothes police shut down the Cairo News Company (CNC) after it supposedly supplied Al Jazeera with images of anti-government protests; in October a Cairo court fined CNC's owner US$27,000 on charges of owning and operating unlicensed equipment. In early February an appeals court upheld the conviction of Al Jazeera reporter Huwaida Taha for harming "the dignity of the country" with a documentary about torture in Egyptian police stations.

The government issued regulations in May requiring internet café users to provide detailed personal information in order to access the web. In April Cairo security officers arrested Esraa Abd al Fattah and others who used the social-networking website Facebook to call for strikes; and in May security officers in New Cairo stripped and beat Ahmed Maher Ibrahim for the same activity. In July security forces in Alexandria arrested Maher and 13 other members of the "6 April Youth" group and jailed them for two weeks without charge after they sang patriotic songs and refused to disperse when ordered.

Freedom of Association

Egypt's law governing associations, Law 84/2002, provides criminal penalties that stifle legitimate NGO activities, including for "engaging in political or union activities." The law governing political parties, Law 40/1977, empowers a committee headed by the ruling party chair to suspend other parties' activities "in the national interest."

In an April 2008 hearing closed to defense lawyers and the public, a military tribunal sentenced Muslim Brotherhood Deputy Supreme Guide Khairat al-Shatir and 24 other civilians, seven of them in absentia, to prison terms of up to 10 years and ordered the seizure of millions of dollars in assets. A regular criminal court had acquitted 17 of the defendants in January 2007 but the next month President Mubarak transferred their cases, along with 23 others, to the military tribunal. In March 2008, prior to local and municipal council elections, security forces arrested and detained without charge more than 800 Muslim Brotherhood members, including at least 148 would-be independent candidates.

In a positive development, in June 2008 the government granted NGO status to the Center for Trade and Union Workers' Services (CTUWS), which offers legal aid to factory workers and reports on labor rights issues. In 2007 the government had forcibly shut down all three CTUWS branches, blaming it for a wave of labor unrest.

Women's and Children's Rights

The Egyptian government has failed to create a legal environment that protects women from violence, encourages victims to report attacks, or deters perpetrators from committing these abuses. A 2008 survey by the Egyptian Center for Women's Rights found that 83 percent of Egyptian women have experienced sexual harassment in their lifetime. In October a mob of men and boys sexually assaulted women in Cairo while they were celebrating the Eid holiday marking the end of Ramadan. Eight men are reported to have been arrested and face prosecution. These attacks mark a repeat of similar violence two years earlier when police officers were videotaped doing nothing to stop the mob attacks.

Extensive amendments to Egypt's Child Law in June 2008 included establishing a network of government child protection committees, criminal penalties for officials who detain children with adults, and expanded legal assistance for children facing investigation or trial. They also criminalize female genital mutilation. At this writing, the government has yet to issue implementing regulations for the new law.

Privacy and Personal Integrity Rights

Since October 2007 police in Cairo have arrested at least a dozen men on suspicion of being HIV-positive, forcibly tested them for HIV without consent, beat them, and charged them with the "habitual practice of debauchery"—interpreted in Egyptian law to include consensual sex between adult men; nine were convicted of this charge. Initially, the men who tested HIV-positive were chained to their hospital beds, and were unchained only after a domestic and international outcry. In April 2008 police in Alexandria arrested 12 men and subjected them to forcible anal examinations, HIV tests, and other abuse; these men were also convicted of the "habitual practice of debauchery." In June Egypt blocked the Egyptian Initiative for Personal Rights, an NGO that has been instrumental in calling international attention to this crackdown, from attending a UN high-level meeting on HIV/AIDS.

A provision of the new Child Law makes marriage registration contingent on medical tests showing both partners free of diseases that would affect their health or their future children's health. Its vague wording raises concerns that it violates individuals' right to privacy and to found a family.

Religious Intolerance and Discrimination against Religious Minorities

Although Egypt's constitution provides for equal rights without regard to religion, discrimination against Egyptian Christians and official intolerance of Baha'is and some Muslim sects continue, despite court rulings early in 2008 that ordered the government to provide identification documents to Baha'is and to allow Muslim converts from Christianity to convert back to Christianity without penalty.

Disputes between Muslim and Christian Egyptians flared into violent clashes on several occasions, resulting in deaths and injuries as well as destruction of property. In January and again in May, Muslims attacked the Abu Fana monastery in Minya province with firearms in a dispute over land ownership.

Key International Actors

The United States remains Egypt's largest donor, providing approximately US$1.3 billion in military aid and US$415 million in economic assistance in 2007. In January 2008 President Bush, during a brief visit, praised Egypt's "vibrant civil society"; the following day, security forces prevented demonstrators in Cairo from holding a peaceful protest, arbitrarily detaining 30 people. In March the US administration waived congressional restrictions conditioning US$100 million in aid to Egypt on improving human rights conditions. In October US Secretary of State Condoleezza Rice admitted to "setbacks" in Egypt, but affirmed that "championing freedom is a national security imperative."

In January the European Parliament passed a resolution criticizing rights abuses in Egypt. In March the European Union agreed to give €558 million in aid by 2010 under the terms of an EU-Egypt Action Plan that formally insists on respect for human rights.

IRAN

With the government of President Mahmoud Ahmadinejad continuing to invoke "national security" as a justification for silencing dissent, 2008 saw a dramatic rise in arrests of political activists, academics, and others for peacefully exercising their rights of free expression and association in Iran. There were numerous reports of the torture and mistreatment of such detainees. The Judiciary, accountable to Supreme Leader Ali Khamenei, and the Ministry of Intelligence continued to be responsible for many serious human rights violations. The number of executions also increased sharply in 2008.

Freedom of Expression and Assembly

Iranian authorities systematically suppress freedom of expression and opinion by imprisoning journalists and editors, and strictly controlling publishing and academic activity. Most journalists arrested in 2008 were targeted for covering ethnic minority issues and civil society activities, and the National Security Council has given newspapers formal and informal warnings against covering issues such as human rights violations and social protests. The few independent dailies that remain heavily self-censor.

Many writers and intellectuals who have evaded imprisonment have left the country or ceased to be critical. The government has fired dissident university professors or forced them into early retirement, a trend that intensified in 2008. State universities also recently began banning some politically active students from registering for their next semester, putting pressure on student associations and their supporters to not criticize the government.

In 2008 the authorities continued to target student and internet journalists. The government systematically blocks Iranian and foreign websites that carry political news and analysis.

The Ahmadinejad government shows no tolerance for peaceful protests and gatherings. Security forces arrested over a hundred student activists in 2008, often without informing their families of the arrests. According to some of the imprisoned students and their families, security forces subjected these students to mis-treatment and abuse during their detention.

Civil Society

The government has increased pressure on civil society organizations that call for human rights and freedom of speech by restricting their activities and barring activists from leaving the country. These include the Center for Defenders of Human Rights, led by 2003 Noble Peace Prize Laureate Shirin Ebadi, and the Association of Iranian Journalists. On October 2 Iran's official news agency warned Ebadi, a lawyer who publically criticizes the government and regularly defends political and human rights cases in court, not to "misuse the tolerance of the government." The Malaysian foreign ministry, under pressure from the Iranian government, forced the International Peace Foundation to cancel an October 2008 conference that Ebadi was due to attend. Earlier in the year Ebadi had received death threats. In response, she announced that the Iranian government would be held responsible for any harm to her. The authorities later promised to guarantee her safety.

Government intelligence officials forced Mohammad Sadigh Kaboudvand, a jour-nalist and human rights activist in the western province of Kurdistan, to shut down his NGO Defending the Human Rights in Kurdistan, and in July 2007 arrest-ed him. He was sentenced to 11 years' imprisonment in June 2008 for acting against national security and engaging in propaganda against the state.

Criminal Justice and the Juvenile Death Penalty

Iranian law allows death sentences for persons who have reached puberty, defined in law as age 9 for girls and 15 for boys. At this writing, Iran was the only country to have executed juvenile offenders in 2008, a total of six persons for crimes committed while under age 18. The country carried out 26 of the 32 known executions of juvenile offenders worldwide since January 2005. According to mul-tiple sources, at least 130 other juvenile offenders are on death row in Iran. In many cases these sentences followed unfair trials, and the executions them-selves sometimes violated Iranian national laws, such as the failure to notify fam-ilies and lawyers of the execution 48 hours in advance.

On August 4, 2008, the Judiciary cancelled the execution by stoning of four Iranians. The Judiciary spokesman said that it would review all pending stoning sentences. However, stoning remains a sentence permitted under the penal code.

Women's Rights

The government escalated its crackdown on women's rights activists in 2008, subjecting dozens of women to arbitrary detention, travel bans, and harassment. Eight women's rights activists were arrested in June as they were commemorating a 2006 meeting on women's rights that was broken up by police. In October an Iranian-American student researching women's rights in Iran, Esha Momeni, was arrested and held for some three weeks in Tehran's Evin prison. Security agents seized her computer and footage of interviews she had conducted with women's rights activists. Later that month, security agents blocked Sussan Tahmasebi, a leader of the One Million Signatures Campaign for Equality, from boarding a plane and confiscated her passport, without charging her with any crime. The Judiciary has also prosecuted women involved in peaceful activities on behalf of the campaign for "disturbing public opinion," "propaganda against the order," and "publishing lies via the publication of false news."

In September an appeals court in Tehran upheld prison and lashing sentences against two women's rights activists, Massoumeh Zia and Marzieh Mortazi Langrudi, for taking part in a 2006 demonstration demanding equal rights. Four women were also sentenced earlier in the year to six months in jail each for writing articles for feminist websites.

In January 2008 the authorities released Maryam Hosseinkhah and Jelveh Javaheri from Evin prison, where they were serving sentences for "disturbing public opinion" and "publishing lies." Two other activists, Ronak Safazadeh and Hana Abdi, remain in detention in Sanandaj on charges of "endangering national security." Prior to their arrest they were active members of the Azarmehr Association of the Women of Kurdistan, a group that organizes capacity-building workshops for women in Iranian Kurdistan.

Minorities

Iran's ethnic and religious minorities are subject to discrimination and, in some cases, persecution. In the northwestern provinces of Azerbaijan and Kurdistan, the government restricts cultural and political activities by the Azerbaijani and Kurdish populations, including the operation of NGOs that focus on social issues. The government also restricts the promotion of minority cultures and languages. On September 10, for example, plainclothes Intelligence Ministry agents arrested 19 prominent Azerbaijani cultural activists and academics during a private Ramadan celebration and detained them in Evin Prison. The Iranian government accuses them of siding with armed opposition groups and acting against national security.

On September 30, Molavi Abdolhamid, one of the most prominent Sunni clerics in Iran, said that if the government failed to address the problems of the Sunni community, including discrimination, its members would be unlikely to participate in the presidential election in 2009. The 2008 execution of two Sunni clerics in Zahedan, the assassination of two Sunni clerics in Kurdistan, the destruction of the Abu-Hanifeh Sunni religious school near Zahedan, and the arrest of 11 Sunni clerics who protested against this assault, coupled with systematic efforts to remove Sunni citizens from governmental positions, the army, and the police force, are among the major criticisms Abdolhamid leveled against the government.

The government continues to deny Iran's Baha'i community permission to worship publicly or pursue religious activities. On May 14, security forces arrested six leading Baha'i adherents and members of the Baha'i national coordination group, without informing them of the charges against them, and sent them to Evin prison. One associate of this group had already been arrested on March 5. At this writing, all seven remain in detention.

HIV/AIDS

In late June security forces detained without charge Arash and Kamyar Alaei, who are well known in Iran and internationally for their contributions to HIV/AIDS prevention and treatment programs; they remain in detention at this writing. For more than 20 years the Alaei brothers have been active in addressing problems relating to drug use, with a focus on the spread of HIV/AIDS, and have played key roles in putting these issues on the national healthcare agenda.

Key International Actors

In 2008 Iran's nuclear program again dominated discussions and policies in the international arena, overshadowing the urgency of discussing Iran's human rights violations. During Ahmadinejad's presidency, critical dialogue between the West and the Iranian government on human rights issues effectively stopped. The European Union has pledged to tie progress in broader cooperation with Iran to respect for human rights, but the pledge has had little impact. The United Nations Security Council has adopted three resolutions since 2007 to sanction Iran economically for its nuclear program.

In 2008 Iran continued to use what it calls "foreign threats" as grounds to suppress civil society and ignore widespread domestic and international objections to human rights violations. The authorities use the rhetorical support of Western countries, especially the United States, for dissidents and human rights activists as an excuse to restrict the freedom of expression and assembly within the country.

The Iranian government has not allowed the UN Human Rights Council's special rapporteurs to enter Iran and investigate violations of human rights alleged by activists, the media, and independent sources since 2005.

IRAQ

Human rights conditions in Iraq remain extremely poor. Security gains in 2008 did little to ease Iraq's crisis of displacement, with about 2.8 million Iraqis displaced within the country and another 2 million abroad, mainly in Syria and Jordan.

The government continues to rest on a narrow political and ethnic/sectarian base, though Tawafuq, a Sunni bloc, returned to its ranks in July after a year-long boycott. The government was to incorporate into state forces up to 100,000 mainly Sunni paramilitaries paid by US forces to provide local security, but government officials disputed their numbers and threatened to arrest some leaders, casting doubt over the plans.

Government-run detention facilities struggled to accommodate over 24,000 detainees, and tardy judicial review of cases exacerbated overcrowding. The US military said in October its detainee population had fallen to about 17,000 from a peak of approximately 26,000 in late 2007. Some detainees have spent years in custody without charge or trial.

As of mid-November 2008, Iraq's parliament was preparing to vote on a security agreement with the US to govern the presence of foreign troops when the UN Security Council mandate for the Multi-National Force-Iraq (MNF) expired at the end of 2008.

Political Developments

Iraq's parliament passed legislation in February intended to refine procedures for vetting former Baath Party members; the new law continues to focus on group affiliation rather than individual responsibility for past abuses. An amnesty law was passed at the same time aimed in part at easing overcrowding in the detention system, but had limited impact on the detainee population. In September parliament passed legislation needed to hold provincial elections, seen as crucial to redressing a 2005 polls boycott by Sunnis and loyalists of Shia cleric Muqtada al-Sadr; however, it deferred a decision on elections in ethnically divided Kirkuk.

MNF and Iraqi Government Military Operations

Military operations by the MNF continued against insurgents throughout the country, and continued also to cause civilian casualties. For example, on September 19, US troops backed by airstrikes killed seven Iraqis north of Baghdad; the MNF said it had targeted an al Qaeda bomb maker, but local officials said those killed were members of a displaced Baghdad family.

Iraq's military launched offensives against insurgent and militia forces in various parts of the country. The government launched military operations with US military backing against loyalists of Muqtada al-Sadr in Basra and Baghdad in April and May. April operations centered in Baghdad's Sadr City killed at least 595 people, nearly half of them civilians, according to UN figures.

Attacks on Civilians and Displacement

Civilians remained the targets of attacks by Sunni and Shia armed groups across the country, though the number of such attacks fell after the US and Iraqi security offensive ("surge") in 2007. In February 2008 Muqtada al-Sadr extended a freeze on the activities of his Jaysh al-Mahdi (Mahdi Army) militia; many Iraqis attributed the reduced level of violence in Iraq to the halt in the militia's armed activities in 2007 following bloody clashes with rival Shiite forces.

In Baghdad, twin bombings in a crowded commercial district on March 7, 2008, killed as many as 71 people, a June 18 truck bomb in a neighborhood where Sunnis have been displaced by Shiite militias killed as many as 63 people, a female suicide bomber targeting Shia pilgrims killed at least 32 people on July 28, and two separate waves of attacks before and during the Eid al-Fitr holiday in early October killed at least 48 people. A car bomb in Dujail, north of Baghdad, killed as many as 32 people on September 12. A second female suicide bomber on July 28 in Kirkuk killed about 25 people during a Kurdish protest over the provincial elections law.

Displacement born of sectarian violence continued, but economic pressures and difficulties maintaining legal status in Syria, Jordan, and Egypt induced some refugees to return, and Iraq's government periodically announced financial incentives for returnees. (For the situation of the largest Iraqi refugee population, and of Palestinians fleeing Iraq and stuck at the Syrian border, see Syria chapter.) In Baghdad, returnees were seldom able to reclaim their former homes, though a campaign launched by security forces to evict squatters from homes they occupy was aimed at paving the way for returns. In Baghdad and elsewhere, orders for squatters to vacate public properties threatened to compound displacement.

In August the office of the United Nations High Commissioner for Refugees (UNHCR) reported that only 10,000 of the 30,000 Iraqis it had referred for settlement in the US since early 2007 had departed, though the pace accelerated in mid-2008. In September the US State Department said it had reached its goal of admitting 12,000 refugees in fiscal year 2008 (up from 1,600 in 2007), and had a target of 17,000 admissions in fiscal year 2009. The European Union for the first time also promised to take more Iraqi refugees.

Detention and Torture by Iraqi Forces

Reports of widespread torture and other abuse of detainees in detention facilities run by Iraq's defense and interior ministries and police continue to emerge. Detainees interviewed by Human Rights Watch at Iraq's Central Criminal Court in May recounted abuse by police and military personnel in initial detention; the United Nations Assistance Mission for Iraq (UNAMI) previously reported widespread allegations of abuse in pretrial detention. Iraq's presidency council in August ratified parliament's approval for Iraq to become a party to the UN Convention against Torture.

The number of detainees in Iraqi government custody (excluding the northern Kurdish region) stood at approximately 24,000 in August, according to a Human Rights Ministry official. Judicial authorities reported in August over 100,000 approved amnesty applications but as of September diplomats tracking amnesty implementation estimated releases stood at only 5,000-8,000; estimates from Iraqi officials in October suggested a lower figure. The United Nations Children's Fund (UNICEF) in August reported some easing of overcrowding at al-Tobchi juvenile detention facility—where detainees had told UNAMI of sexual abuse in custody in 2007—following the release of hundreds of detainees under the amnesty.

MNF Detention

As of early October 2008 the US military said it was holding about 17,000 detainees in Iraq; the previous month it said it had released approximately 13,000 since the beginning of 2008. Reviews of cases were limited to administrative hearings that fall short of internationally recognized due process norms. MNF officials estimated in May that no more than a tenth of detainees would be referred for criminal proceedings in Iraqi courts. In June the US Supreme Court issued a disappointing decision regarding two US citizens, Shawqi Omar and Mohammad Munaf, detained by the US in Iraq. While the Court upheld federal court jurisdiction over the men's cases, it paid little heed to the men's substantive claims that they would be tortured if turned over to Iraqi custody, stating that such assessments were for the political branches of government to make.

The number of children in MNF custody dropped during 2008 from a high of nearly 900 in December 2007 to approximately 170 as of mid-September 2008. The sharp decrease appears to reflect faster MNF processing of children's cases, transfers to Iraqi custody for trial, and a shift from arrests by the MNF to arrests by Iraqi forces. Juvenile detainees in MNF custody continue to lack access to independent legal counsel to challenge detention.

Accountability for Past Crimes

In May the Iraqi High Tribunal (IHT) began trying former foreign minister and deputy prime minister Tariq Aziz, along with seven other defendants, for the former government's execution of merchants accused of profiteering while Iraq was under sanctions in 1992. Previous trials in the IHT, including that of former president Saddam Hussein for crimes against humanity, were marred by failure to disclose key evidence, government conduct undermining the independence and impartiality of the court, and violations of defendants' right to confront witnesses.

Gender-Based Violence

Violence against women and girls in Iraq continues to be a serious problem, with members of insurgent groups and militias, soldiers, and police among the perpetrators. Even in high-profile cases involving police or security forces, prosecutions are rare. Insurgent groups operating in Basra and Baghdad have specifically targeted women who are politicians, civil servants, journalists, and women's rights activists. They have also attacked women on the street for what they consider "immoral" or "un-Islamic" behavior including not wearing a headscarf. The threat of these attacks keeps many Iraqi women at home. "Honor" killing by family members also remains a prevalent physical threat to Iraqi women and girls. While dozens of cases were reported in 2008, few resulted in convictions.

Lesbian, gay, bisexual, and transgender people are also vulnerable to attacks from state and non-state actors.

Key International Actors

As of September 2008, the United States had approximately 146,000 troops in Iraq (down from 160,000-170,000 at the height of the 2007 "surge"). The United Kingdom, the only other country with a significant number of personnel in Iraq, had approximately 4,000. Most other countries with forces in Iraq were expected to withdraw them ahead of the lapse of the MNF's mandate in December 2008.

Prime Minister Nouri al-Maliki's government in November approved a security agreement with the US that would entail the withdrawal of all US forces by the beginning of 2012. Drafts of the agreement indicated that Iraqi-US committees would determine whether Iraqi legal jurisdiction could apply in instances where US troops were accused of committing crimes while outside specified military installations.

In August the UN Security Council voted to extend the mission of UNAMI for one year. The UNAMI Human Rights Office monitors, reports, and follows up on human rights violations as part of a plan aimed at developing Iraqi mechanisms for addressing past and current abuses.

Israel/Occupied Palestinian Territories (OPT)

Israel's blockade of Gaza and restrictions on movement to protect illegal West Bank settlements, along with indiscriminate Palestinian rocket attacks on Israeli towns and serious abuses by Fatah and Hamas against each other's supporters, were major components of the human rights crisis in the Israeli-occupied Palestinian territories in 2008.

Palestinian civilians accounted for around half of those killed in Israeli military operations in Gaza prior to a June ceasefire between Hamas and Israel. More Palestinians were killed in Gaza by the Israel Defense Forces (IDF) in the first half of the year than in all of 2007 in both the West Bank and Gaza.

Israel's blockade of Gaza has exacerbated the humanitarian crisis affecting Gaza's 1.5 million residents. In the West Bank, Israel maintains onerous restrictions on freedom of movement for Palestinians.

Palestinian armed groups fired rockets and mortars indiscriminately into Israeli towns, particularly Sderot, killing four civilians and wounding others. Fatah and Hamas, the dominant Palestinian parties in the West Bank and Gaza, respectively, were responsible for extensive human rights violations as they sought to impose their authority, and retaliated for each other's violations.

Palestinian armed groups in Gaza continued to hold as hostage Israeli soldier Gilad Shalit, captured in June 2006.

Israel

Gaza Strip

Israel's comprehensive blockade of the Gaza Strip has severe humanitarian and economic consequences for the civilian population. Even after the June ceasefire, continued restrictions reduced the availability of basic goods and the provision of essential services. Imports in September represented 30 percent of what Israel allowed into Gaza in December 2005. Exports remained completely barred.

Israel is Gaza's major source of electricity and sole source of fuel, so its restrictions on their supply cripple transportation as well as water-pumping, sewage, and sanitation facilities.

Israel also continues to restrict the movement of Palestinians out of Gaza. The restrictions rely on Egypt's cooperation along its border with Gaza, in particular at the Rafah crossing.

In the first half of the year, Israel permitted only a small number of persons with medical emergencies to leave. In July a handful of students with foreign scholarships left Gaza. In August and September Israel eased some restrictions and allowed more emergency medical cases to exit. In September over four thousand Palestinians, including 1,100 pilgrims, entered Egypt via Rafah, but Egyptian authorities prevented some 800 students from leaving to study abroad. The vast majority of Palestinians remain unable to travel outside the territory. Foreign Minister Tzipi Livni wrote in July that this policy was due to a September 2007 security cabinet decision declaring Gaza to be a "hostile entity."

Israel reintroduced a complete blockade in November in retaliation for a wave of Palestinian rocket attacks. The complete closure by Israel cut off food and medical aid, as well as fuel supplies, halted the United Nations' food distribution to 750,000 people, and caused widespread power cuts.

Palestinian Deaths and Israeli Impunity

Between January and June 2008, Israeli forces conducting military operations killed 388 Palestinian fighters and civilians in Gaza, about half of whom were civilians; 59 of the dead were children. Israeli forces killed 41 Palestinians in the West Bank between January and the end of October, of whom at least 15 were civilians. The largest Israeli military operation, between February 27 and March 3 in Gaza, killed 107 Palestinians, more than half of them civilians. Human Rights Watch examined one area occupied by Israeli troops during the operation and found strong evidence in four incidents that Israeli forces deliberately fired at and killed five civilians, medical personnel, and incapacitated fighters. In other attacks, Israeli forces did not appear to take all feasible precautions to ensure targets were military and not civilian.

As of November 2008, Israeli Military Police launched only one formal investigation into suspicious killings of civilians.

On August 12, Judge Advocate General Brig.-Gen. Avishai Mandelblit informed the Reuters news agency that the decision by an Israeli tank crew to target a Reuters cameraman in Gaza on April 16 was "sound." The attack killed the cameraman and eight other civilians, including six children. Mandelblit said the crew acted properly even though, he acknowledged, they could not identify the cameraman as a combatant.

Freedom of Movement

Israel increased its extensive, often arbitrary restrictions on freedom of movement for Palestinians in the West Bank and East Jerusalem. From September 4, 2007, through September 1, 2008, "closure obstacles" in the West Bank increased from 572 to 630. These restrictions make it difficult or impossible for many Palestinians to access jobs, education, and health services, as well as to visit family and friends.

Settlements and the Wall

The route of the "separation barrier" or wall, more than 80 percent of which extends into the West Bank, further restricts the ability of thousands of Palestinian residents to access their land, essential services such as education and healthcare, and water.

As of mid-2008, more than 600 buildings were under construction in illegal West Bank settlements (not including East Jerusalem) and tenders had been issued for more than 2,400 others. In July government approval of Maskiot marked the first official recognition of a settlement in almost nine years.

The Israeli human rights organization B'Tselem, in October, reported 429 cases of settler violence against Palestinians and their property in 2008, a 75 percent increase over 2007. These included physical assaults with firearms, beatings, and destruction of crops and other property. Israeli authorities seldom apprehend or prosecute perpetrators. In September a bomb placed outside his home injured

ISRAEL

Off the Map

Land and Housing Rights Violations
in Israel's Unrecognized Bedouin Villages

HUMAN
RIGHTS
WATCH

77-year-old Hebrew University professor Zeev Sternhall, a prominent critic of the settlement movement.

Discriminatory Legislation

Israel continues to apply laws and policies that discriminate on the basis of ethnic or national origin. Since 2002 Israel has prohibited Palestinians from the OPT who are spouses of Israeli citizens from joining their partners in Israel. In 2007 the Knesset extended the ban through 2008 and expanded its scope to include citizens of Iran, Iraq, Syria, and Lebanon married to Israelis from living with their spouses in Israel.

In a positive development, since October 2007 Israel approved nearly 32,000 family unification requests in the West Bank and Gaza Strip, the first exceptions to a freeze on family unifications put in place in September 2000. Some 90,000 family reunification requests remain pending.

Israeli laws and practices continue to force tens of thousands of Bedouins in the Negev region to live in "unrecognized" shanty towns. The state deliberately excludes Bedouin villages from its national planning process, thus denying them legal status. Israeli authorities demolished dozens of Bedouin dwellings in 2008. An official commission headed by retired Supreme Court Justice Eliezer Goldberg held public hearings to examine the land ownership issues in early 2008, but as of November had not issued any findings or recommendations.

Expulsion of Asylum Seekers

Between August 23 and 29, the IDF forcibly returned to Egyptian custody 91 Eritreans, Sudanese, and Somalis who illegally crossed the border along the Sinai. (Egypt has not notified the UN High Commissioner for Refugees of their whereabouts, and reportedly deported to Sudan some of the 50 Sudanese whom Israel had forcibly returned in August 2007.)

The Palestinian Authority (PA) and Hamas

Attacks on Israeli Civilians

Palestinian armed groups in Gaza indiscriminately fired locally-made rockets into the Israeli border town of Sderot and other civilian areas throughout the first half of 2008. The rocket fire killed four Israeli civilians and wounded others in 2008, prior to the June ceasefire. Palestinian armed groups, excluding Hamas, continued to fire small numbers of rockets after the ceasefire came into effect. According to media reports, Hamas authorities temporarily detained several Islamic Jihad members for planning or carrying out rocket attacks. In early November Hamas and other Palestinian armed groups fired over 80 rockets at targets inside Israel, including civilian populated areas in response to an Israeli military operation that killed six fighters. As in previous rocket attacks, Palestinian authorities in Gaza took no action to prosecute any of the individuals involved.

On February 4, a Palestinian suicide bomber killed a 73-year-old woman and injured 11 other civilians in the southern Israeli town of Dimona. The Al-Aqsa Martyrs Brigades and Popular Front for the Liberation of Palestine claimed joint responsibility in a Gaza press conference. Neither of the groups or individuals who claimed responsibility were arrested by Palestinians authorities in Gaza or charged with any offense.

On March 3, a Palestinian with an assault rifle killed eight Israeli civilians, four of them under age 18, in a Jerusalem yeshiva, or seminary. The gunman, who was apparently acting independently, wounded 10 other students. Senior Hamas spokesmen appeared to give their support to the attack as well as to four others in 2008 in which Palestinians targeted Israeli civilians in Jerusalem.

Intra-Palestinian Fighting and Lawlessness

Hamas forces in Gaza and Fatah-dominated Palestinian Authority forces in the West Bank have carried out arbitrary arrests of each other's supporters, tortured prisoners in their custody, and closed down scores of charities, political societies, and other organizations. The PA prosecuted defendants before military courts, circumventing due process safeguards.

These abuses occurred throughout the period since Hamas took control of Gaza in June 2007, peaking in July 2008 after a bombing in a Gaza City beach café killed a four-year-old girl and five members of Hamas's armed wing, the Izzedin al-Qassam Brigades. Qassam Brigades members, who have no law enforcement powers, arbitrarily arrested over 200 people. In the West Bank, PA security forces responded by arbitrarily arresting over 100 people considered sympathetic to Hamas.

Palestinian security forces tortured detainees during interrogation, sometimes leading to their deaths. On February 14, the General Intelligence Services (GIS), which reports to PA President Mahmud Abbas, arrested Majid al-Barghuti, leader of a mosque in a village outside Ramallah. Eight days later al-Barghuti was dead, almost certainly as a result of injuries sustained from torture. On April 13, in Gaza, armed men arrested Sami `Atiya Khattab, a former GIS captain; 36 hours later he was dead, his body bearing what a Palestinian human rights defender called "obvious signs of torture."

In early August Hamas forces assaulted a Gaza City area controlled by the Hillis family, whom Hamas accused of sheltering the perpetrator of the beach café bombing. Of the 12 Hillis members killed, two were reportedly executed, and eye-witnesses said some of those wounded had been shot after they had surrendered.

In mid-September Hamas forces used excessive force in an attempt to arrest members of the Dugmush clan in Gaza City. Eleven family members were killed in the clashes, including three children, and 43 people were injured. Two policemen were also killed.

Despite the gravity of these violations, the Palestinian Authority took no steps to investigate them or hold anyone to account. Hamas authorities claimed in early June that they had punished 35 officers for "violating human rights" but did not provide details.

The struggle between Hamas and Fatah also contributed to Gaza's humanitarian crisis. In August Hamas authorities interrupted regular diesel shipments to the Coastal Municipalities Water Utility, an agency controlled by the PA in Ramallah.

Death Penalty

A military court in Gaza handed down a death sentence in January and another in July. In the West Bank a military court in Jenin handed down death sentences in April and July; a military court in Hebron also sentenced a man to death in April. A civil court in Gaza handed down death sentences in October to four men, including to a 22-year-old who was a juvenile at the time of the alleged offense. A military court in Bethlehem sentenced a 24-year-old man to death in November.

Key International Actors

Israel is the largest recipient of aid from the United States, receiving US$2.38 billion in military aid in 2008. Washington has not made any funds conditional on Israel improving its adherence to international human rights and humanitarian law. The US trained and equipped Palestinian security forces, which took over some security functions in Jenin and Hebron.

The current European Union-Israel Action Plan only briefly and vaguely mentions human rights concerns, in contrast to similar plans between the EU and other countries in the region. As talks commenced in late 2008 about an "upgraded" relationship with Israel, the EU said any new agreement would include a formal subcommittee on human rights.

The Quartet (the EU, US, Russia, and UN) provided limited humanitarian aid to Gaza; the US and EU continued their economic sanctions against the de facto Hamas government there.

Israel was reviewed under the Universal Periodic Review mechanism of the UN Human Rights Council in May 2008.

JORDAN

In 2008 Jordan promised human rights reform, but failed to implement it in most areas. In a missed opportunity for reform, Jordan's revision of an old, restrictive NGO law resulted in a new, more restrictive law. A new law on assembly remained incongruent with international human rights standards, despite changes. Attempts to extend trade union membership to non-Jordanian workers in a new labor law failed in parliament, but provisions to include domestic workers under labor protections succeeded. An ambitious prison reform program and legal amendments failed to tackle widespread torture. Jordan continues to observe an unofficial moratorium on carrying out the death penalty, in force since May 2006.

Arbitrary Detention, Administrative Detention, and Torture

The General Intelligence Department (GID) released 'Isam Barqawi (Abu Muhammad al-Maqdisi) after three years of arbitrary detention and denial of due process. Jordan also freed national security suspects 'Adnan Abu Nujila and Samir al-Barq, after the GID first arrested them but then prosecutors did not bring them to trial for two to three years.

A Penal Code amendment in October 2007 made torture a criminal offense for the first time. But Jordan has no effective mechanisms to bring perpetrators of torture to justice. A deficient complaint mechanism, lacklustre investigations and prosecutions, and lenient sentences at the Police Court, which is not independent, allow torture in prisons to remain routine and widespread and to take place with near total impunity. Riots occurred in February in Birain prison and in April in Muwaqqar and Swaqa prisons. Reasons included ill-treatment, nighttime strip searches, and a badly implemented plan to separate convicted from untried prisoners. In Muwaqqar a senior guard tortured several inmates in April by beating and suspending them from iron grates; two of those inmates died in a fire at the prison on April 14, which the authorities failed to quickly control.

In the first 10 months of 2007, provincial governors administratively detained 12,178 persons, more than in 2006, without proof of criminal conduct or to circumvent the obligation to present suspects to the prosecutor within 24 hours. Jordanian law allows governors to detain persons administratively under the

Crime Prevention Law. Administrative detainees must meet a financial bail guarantee to gain release, but indigent detainees frequently resort to hunger strikes instead.

Freedom of Expression, Association, and Assembly

Criticisms of the king, government officials, and the intelligence forces are strictly taboo and carry heavy penalties. Prosecutors also rely on the penal code to criminalize speech diminishing the prestige of the state, and harming relations with other states. In December 2007 police arrested Omar Matar of the Arab Organization for Human Rights for alleged remarks he made on King Abdullah's genealogy to a colleague in a private dispute. The State Security Court in December 2007 found him guilty and sentenced him to one year in prison, but an appeals court overturned the verdict and freed him in February 2008. In September a prosecutor charged a professor with *lèse majesté* for prohibiting colleagues from hanging the king's portrait in their offices, Agence France-Presse reported. A prosecutor in June summoned Danish journalists to Jordan for insulting the religious feelings of Jordanians by republishing cartoons about the Prophet Muhammad, and one journalist said he was prepared to go to Jordan to defend himself.

In July parliament passed an amended Law on Public Gatherings (Assembly Law) and a Law of Charitable Societies (Nongovernmental Organizations Law), both of which failed to fulfill promises Prime Minister Nader Dahabi had made in January following NGO protests on earlier drafts. The Assembly Law maintains a governor's power to deny, without justification, permission, to hold any meeting discussing public affairs. The NGO Law maintained provisions giving the government discretion to license an NGO and to shut it down without judicial process, in addition to broad powers to replace an NGO's management with government officials, and to reject an NGO's internal decisions. The law adds to these old restrictions new ones, such as prime ministerial approval for every donation or financial grant from foreigners to domestic NGOs, and from Jordanians to foreign NGOs. Dahabi promised in September 2008 to revise the law yet again.

JORDAN

Torture and Impunity in Jordan's Prisons

Reforms Fail to Tackle Widespread Abuse

HUMAN
RIGHTS
WATCH

Situation of Refugees Fleeing Iraq

There are an estimated 500,000 Iraqis in Jordan, most of them de facto refugees (only Syria hosts a higher number of Iraqis). The majority of Iraqi refugees in Jordan arrived after 2003. After the Amman hotel bombings of November 2005, Jordan's traditional tolerance toward Iraqis eroded. Jordan's government, which does not have an established mechanism to determine refugee status, has practically shut its land borders and airport to fleeing Iraqis. Since May 2008 a new visa regime prevents Iraqis from entering Jordan without a visa, and thus reaching safety. The governments of Iraq and Jordan encouraged Iraqis to return in 2008, despite inadequate measures to ensure their safety. Jordan again admitted Iraqi children to public schools for the 2007-2008 school year.

Women's Rights

In 2008 Jordan released all women victims of violence or under threat of violence held in "protective custody" from the Juwaida prison, with most moving either to a government-run or an anonymous NGO-run shelter. Jordanian authorities, however, require a family member to agree to their transfer. Girls who are victims of violence or who at risk of abuse continue to be held in "protective custody" in the Khanza juvenile detention center for girls.

Jordanian courts continue to issue lenient verdicts for "honor killings" perpetrated by family members against women and girls they suspect of "immoral" behavior. These killings make up the majority of female murders in Jordan. In October a resident of Amman confessed to killing his unmarried niece whom he suspected of being involved in an "illicit affair." By November 2008, 16 women had been killed in Jordan under the guise of "family honor."

Migrant Worker Rights

New reports documented abuses of Southeast Asian migrants working in Jordan's Qualified Industrial Zones or as domestic workers, and of Arab migrants working in construction and agriculture. The government toughened a policy of inspections and conditions for rewards of mention on a "golden list" attesting to a company's absence of labor violations. A new labor law of July 2008 for the first time included domestic workers under its provisions, but an attempt to give non-Jordanians (non-voting) rights in Jordanian labor unions under the new law failed in parliament.

In January 2008 the Philippines stopped its citizens from going to Jordan as domestic workers, due to the increased number of complaints of abuse. In September Indonesia arrested 40 Jordanians on charges of trafficking in humans there. Jordan's Ministry of Interior reacted by promising a new law against trafficking. The new labor law stipulates penalties of up to 2,000 dinars (US$3,000) for employers who "use any worker in a forced way, or through threat, deception, or coercion, including by keeping his travel document," the Amman Center for Human Rights reported.

Abusive labor conditions include beatings, sexual harassment and attacks, long working hours, withholding of passports and paychecks, pay discrimination based on sex or nationality, preventing workers from leaving the worksite at any time, and denying medical care.

Key International Actors

The United States gave Jordan more than US$700 million in economic and security-related assistance in 2008 (compared to the European Union's €265 million for 2007-2010), concluding in September for the first time an agreement securing US$660 million in annual assistance to Jordan for five years in support of "security and stability in the region, ... economic development and political reform." In February, the US Embassy's website for the first time published a long list of conditions Jordan had to fulfill to qualify for funding. Human rights conditions were not among them. However, US policy in 2008 supported—although unsuccessfully—further revision to the NGO Law before it passed parliament in July.

The EU continued to publicly praise Jordan, but was more critical in reporting progress on political and human rights reform and also initiated a program of prison reform with the Public Security Directorate. Nevertheless, the EU has not found a unified voice to speak in support of human rights in Jordan.

The United Kingdom continues to try to return at least two Jordanians to Jordan, saying that it relies on a 2005 memorandum of understanding with Jordan to prevent torture, under which the government permits Adaleh (a Jordanian NGO with a very limited track record of investigating, publicizing, and preventing torture) to monitor the treatment of a returned detainee.

In a positive step, Jordan in March 2008 ratified the International Covenant on Rights of Persons with Disabilities. Jordan is due to be reviewed under the Universal Periodic Review mechanism of the UN Human Rights Council in February 2009.

Double Jeopardy

CIA Renditions to Jordan

HUMAN
RIGHTS
WATCH

LEBANON

In 2008 Lebanon pulled back from the brink of civil war. Enduring tensions between the Hezbollah-led opposition and pro-government groups broke out into full-scale fighting in May. But the various parties reached a political agreement in Qatar on May 21, paving the way for the election of a new president, the formation of a national unity government, and the resumption of parliamentary activity. However, the agreement failed to set the ground for real reforms, and political instability and sporadic fighting endures.

Impunity remains prevalent with armed gunmen rarely held accountable for attacks against civilians. Security forces use force to extract confessions, especially from security suspects. Palestinian refugees from the destroyed Nahr al-Bared refugee camp are living in dire circumstances while awaiting the reconstruction of their camp. Lebanese law continues to discriminate against women by, among other things, denying them the right to pass their nationality to their children or spouses. Migrant domestic workers face exploitation and abuse by their employers with little possibility of redress.

Despite pledges by the new government, the families of the estimated 17,000 who "disappeared" during and after Lebanon's deadly 1975-1990 civil war continue to wait for information on the fate of their loved ones.

Internal Fighting

Fighting broke out on May 7 between the Hezbollah-led opposition and pro-government groups, killing at least 71 people in two weeks. Both opposition and pro-government fighters committed violations of international humanitarian law, including attacks on civilians and civilian property. Members of the opposition groups—Hezbollah, Amal, and the Syrian Social Nationalist Party—militarily took over parts of Beirut. They also attacked and shut down media offices affiliated with the Future Movement. Supporters of the pro-government groups—the Future Movement and the Progressive Socialist Party—also resorted to violence in areas under their control, including the killing of captive opposition fighters in the northern town of Halba.

LEBANON

Flooding South Lebanon

Israel's Use of Cluster Munitions in Lebanon
in July and August 2006

**H U M A N
R I G H T S
W A T C H**

The political settlement reached on May 21 failed to address abuses committed during the fighting. Sporadic clashes continued for another three months in the Beka` and the north, leaving at least 40 dead in Tripoli. With very limited exceptions, Lebanese judicial authorities have failed to hold to account those responsible for attacks against civilians.

Legacy of Past Wars

More than two years after the end of the war between Israel and Hezbollah, neither the Israeli nor the Lebanese government has investigated the violations of the laws of war committed by the warring parties.

The estimated one million cluster submunition "duds" left behind by Israel's bombing campaign continue to harm civilians. According to the official Lebanon Mine Action Center, such duds killed two civilians and wounded 35 in 2008, raising the post-war casualty toll from clusters to 42 killed and 282 wounded. Israel continues in its refusal to turn over detailed information on the location of the areas it targeted with cluster attacks.

In July 2008 Israel and Hezbollah swapped the bodies of 200 Lebanese and Palestinian fighters who had died in the 1970s and 1980s and five living Lebanese prisoners, including Samir Kontar, for the bodies of two Israeli soldiers kidnapped by Hezbollah in July 2006.

The Lebanese government pledged in its ministerial declaration on August 4 to take steps to uncover the fate of the Lebanese and other nationals who "disappeared" during and after Lebanon's 1975-1990 civil war and to ratify the International Convention for the Protection of All Persons from Enforced Disappearance. However, the government took no practical steps to uncover mass graves or collect information on the disappeared.

The fates of Lebanese and other residents of Lebanon who disappeared at the hands of Syrian security forces remain unknown. Lebanese human rights groups have compiled a list of 640 victims of Syrian enforced disappearances in Lebanon. An official joint Syrian-Lebanese committee established in May 2005 to investigate such cases had not published any findings at this writing.

Torture, Ill-Treatment, and Prison Conditions

A number of detainees reported being beaten and tortured during interrogation in a number of detention facilities, including the Military Intelligence unit of the Ministry of Defense, the Information Branch of the Internal Security Forces, the Drug Repression Bureau detention facilities in Beirut and Zahle, as well as certain police stations. Lebanese law prohibits torture, but accountability for ill-treatment and torture in detention remains elusive.

Conditions in prison and detention facilities remain poor, with overcrowding and lack of proper medical care a perennial problem. At least 21 people died in custody in 2008. In August the Ministry of Interior opened an investigation into allegations of abuse inside Lebanese prisons, following public allegations of corruption and ill-treatment of prisoners. The outcome of the investigations had not been made public at writing.

On October 10 the justice minister presented a draft law to abolish the death penalty.

Palestinian Refugees

Palestinians remain subject to wide-ranging restrictions on housing and work despite limited efforts by the authorities to relax some of the labor restrictions. Palestinians from the Nahr al-Bared refugee camp—destroyed in the 2007 battle between the Lebanese army and the armed Fatah al-Islam group—are living in dire conditions while they wait for the camp to be rebuilt. The Lebanese government appealed in June to international donors for US$445 million for the reconstruction of the camp, but only US$113 million has been pledged at this writing.

In August the Lebanese authorities agreed to issue temporary identity cards to Palestinian refugees in Lebanon without any legal documentation. The decision should improve the legal status of at least 3,000 Palestinians in Lebanon who had previously lived in constant fear of arrest.

Iraqi Refugees

An estimated 50,000 Iraqis live in Lebanon. The United Nations High Commissioner for Refugees (UNHCR) recognizes all Iraqis from central and southern Iraq seeking asylum in Lebanon as refugees on a prima facie basis. However, Lebanon does not give legal effect to UNHCR's recognition of Iraqi refugees and generally treats the vast majority of them as illegal immigrants subject to arrest. The number of detained Iraqis in Lebanon decreased in 2008 following the release of more than 200 Iraqis between March and September as part of a regularization of foreign nationals in Lebanon.

Hariri Tribunal

The UN-appointed international commission continues its investigations into the killing of former prime minister Rafiq Hariri in 2005 and other politically motivated assassinations, but it has not named any official suspects. Its final report is due on December 2. The tribunal to try those responsible for the Hariri killing, established by the UN Security Council in June 2007, is expected to start operating in 2009.

Four former heads of Lebanese intelligence and security services—Gen. `Ali al-Hajj, Gen. Raymond Azar, Brigadier Gen. Jamil al-Sayyed, and Gen. Mustafa Hamdan—as well as two civilians—Ahmad and Mahmud Abdel-`Al—remain in detention without charge following their arrest in 2005 on suspicion of their involvement in Hariri's assassination. In March the UN Working Group on Arbitrary Detention called their continued detention without charge "arbitrary" and "unjust."

Another civilian, Ibrahim Jarjoura, is also in detention since January 2006 on the accusation of making false statements to the international commission.

Discrimination against Women

Despite women's active participation in all aspects of Lebanese society, discriminatory provisions continue to exist in personal status laws, nationality laws, and penal laws relating to violence in the family. Current Lebanese law does not allow

Lebanese women to confer nationality on either their spouses or children. As a result, thousands of children born to Lebanese mothers and foreign fathers are denied full access to education, healthcare, and residency.

Migrant domestic workers face exploitation and abuse by employers, including excessive hours of work, non-payment of wages, and restrictions on their liberty. Many women migrants suffer physical and sexual abuse at the hands of employers, in a climate of impunity for employers. At least 45 migrant domestic workers died in Lebanon in 2008, a majority of whom committed suicide or died while trying to escape.

Key International Actors

Multiple international and regional actors compete for influence in Lebanon.

France, the United States, and the European Union are key supporters of the Lebanese government and provide assistance for a wide range of programs, including armed forces training, torture prevention seminars, and civil society activities. However, these countries have not used their leverage to push Lebanon to adopt concrete measures to improve its human rights record, such as investigating specific allegations of torture or adopting laws that respect the rights of refugees or migrant workers.

Regionally, Syria, Iran, and Saudi Arabia maintain strong influences on Lebanese politics through their local allies. After three tense years, Lebanese-Syrian relations improved in 2008 and the two countries agreed on October 15 to establish diplomatic relations following French mediation. Qatar emerged as a new powerbroker after its successful mediation of the fighting in May.

The UN Security Council continues to follow up on the implementation of Resolution 1559, which calls among other things for the Lebanese government to extend its control over all Lebanese territory. UN peacekeepers are still present in large numbers at Lebanon's southern border.

LIBYA

Libya's international reintegration accelerated in 2008 despite the government's ongoing human rights violations. In September a US secretary of state visited the country for the first time since 1953. Driven by business interests and Libya's cooperation in combating terrorism and illegal migration, European governments also strengthened ties with Libya during the year. The Libyan government continues to imprison individuals for criticizing the country's political system or its leader, Mu`ammar al-Qadhafi, and maintains harsh restrictions on freedom of expression and assembly.

Political Prisoners

Libya continues to detain scores of individuals for engaging in peaceful political activity. Hundreds more have been "disappeared," some for decades. Many were imprisoned for violating Law 71, which bans any group activity opposed to the principles of the 1969 revolution that brought al-Qadhafi to power. Violators of Law 71 can be executed.

Fathi al-Jahmi remains Libya's most prominent political prisoner, imprisoned since March 2004 after calling for democratization and criticizing al-Qadhafi. In late 2005 a secret court deemed al-Jahmi mentally incompetent and in May 2006 ordered his detention at a psychiatric hospital. According to al-Jahmi, who suffers from diabetes, hypertension, and heart disease, the authorities denied him medical care at the hospital. In July 2007 he was transferred to the state-run Tripoli Medical Center.

In March 2008 the Qadhafi Development Foundation, run by al-Qadhafi's son Seif al-Islam al-Qadhafi, facilitated a visit to al-Jahmi by Human Rights Watch and Physicians for Human Rights. The groups' investigation showed that negligent care in detention had seriously degraded his health. To Human Rights Watch's knowledge, al-Jahmi remains under guard in the Tripoli Medical Center, unable to leave his room and with restricted family visits.

In February 2007 Libyan security agents arrested 14 organizers of a planned peaceful demonstration intended to commemorate the anniversary of a violent crackdown on demonstrators in Benghazi. On May 27, 2008, the authorities released one of the men, Jum`a Boufayed, who had been missing since his arrest. A second man, `Adil Humaid, was released on June 10. A third man, `Abd al-Rahman al-Qotaiwi, has remained "disappeared" since his arrest. On June 10 a state security court found the remaining 11 men guilty of planning to overthrow the government and meeting with an official from a foreign government, apparently a US embassy official. The court, located inside Tripoli's Abu Salim prison, sentenced the men to prison terms of between six and 25 years. The main organizer of the planned demonstration, Idris Boufayed, received a 25-year sentence, but was released from detention on medical grounds in October due to his advanced lung cancer. Another member of the group, Jamal al-Haji, a writer who holds Danish citizenship, was sentenced to 12 years of imprisonment. Libyan authorities have rebuffed Danish government requests to visit him.

Freedom of Association and Freedom of Expression

Libya has no independent nongovernmental organizations. Law 19, "On Associations," requires a political body to approve all such organizations and does not allow appeals against negative decisions. The government has refused to allow independent journalists' and lawyers' organizations.

Freedom of expression is severely curtailed. Article 178 of the penal code orders life imprisonment for the dissemination of information considered to "tarnish [the country's] reputation or undermine confidence in it abroad." Negative comments about al-Qadhafi are frequently punished, and self-censorship is rife. Uncensored news is available via satellite television and Libyan websites based abroad, which the government occasionally blocks. In April 2007 Libya's legislative body, the General People's Congress, created a committee to examine the state-controlled media. The government has announced no further information about the committee's work.

The exceptions to these rules are organizations run by Seif al-Qadhafi, including the Qadhafi Development Foundation. In August 2007 his al-Ghad company launched Libya's first private newspapers and television station, which leveled mild criticisms at the government.

Torture

Reports of torture continue to be of deep concern, affecting both Libyan citizens and foreigners—mostly sub-Saharan Africans—who are detained during immigration sweeps.

Libyan human rights groups abroad allege that Libyan authorities tortured Mohamed Adel Abu Ali, a Libyan citizen whom Sweden returned to Tripoli in May 2008 after rejecting his asylum claim. The Swedish Migration Board confirmed that Abu Ali died in Libyan custody; a relative says he was detained incommunicado. Sweden suspended deportations to Libya in July, pending an investigation into the death. It lifted the moratorium in August after the investigation failed to determine how Abu Ali had died.

Violence against Women and Girls

The government's position on violence against women remains one of denial, leaving victims unprotected and without remedies. Libya has no domestic violence law, and inadequate laws punishing sexual violence. The government prosecutes only the most violent rape cases, and judges have the authority to propose marriage between the rapist and the victim as a "social remedy" to the crime. Rape victims themselves risk prosecution for adultery or fornication if they attempt to press charges.

Police officers are not trained to handle cases of violence against women, and there are no women's or girls' shelters. Instead, the government detains dozens of victims, particularly rape victims, in "social rehabilitation" facilities. Many are denied the opportunity to challenge the legality of their detention. The authorities subject them to forced virginity examinations and punitive treatment, including solitary confinement. The only way out of these facilities is if a male relative takes custody of the woman or girl, or if she consents to marriage. In February 2006 the government said it had established a committee to study the facilities; the committee's work, if any, is unknown.

Abu Salim Prison

The government still has not released any findings on the large-scale killings in Tripoli's Abu Salim prison in June 1996. According to an ex-prisoner, Internal Security Agency forces killed as many as 1,200 inmates who had revolted over prison conditions. In October 2006 guards killed at least one prisoner and reportedly injured nine after another reported revolt.

Families of the 1996 victims have gone to court to demand information about the fate of their missing relatives. In June 2008 a Benghazi court ordered the state to reveal the identities of the dead and the circumstances in which they had died. To Human Rights Watch's knowledge, the state has not yet complied with the ruling, sparking protests from family members. In July Seif al-Qadhafi stated that the results of an initial investigation into the killings showed "excessive use of force and abuse of power" at the prison. He promised a public trial but gave no timetable.

Treatment of Foreigners

The government continues to forcibly deport foreigners who lack proper documentation, sometimes to countries where they could face persecution, including Eritrea. Foreigners reported arbitrary arrests, beatings, and other abuse during their detention and deportation.

Libya has no asylum law, has not signed the 1951 Refugee Convention, and has no formal working agreement with the United Nations High Commissioner for Refugees (UNHCR). However, the government reportedly grants UNHCR representatives regular access to detention facilities.

Promises of Reform

In 2008 the government continued, for the fourth year, to review proposals for a new penal code and code of criminal procedure. In 2005 the secretary of justice stated the new penal code would impose the death penalty only for the "most dangerous crimes" and for "terrorism." A 2004 draft of the new code suggests the government might accept a very broad definition of terrorism, which could be used to criminalize the expression of peaceful political views. The government has yet to present either draft code to the General People's Congress.

Key International Actors

In 2008 the United States and some European governments upgraded relations with Libya despite its human rights abuses. In August the US and Libya signed a claims settlement agreement, indemnifying each other against outstanding lawsuits for Libyan bombings and US airstrikes in the 1990s. In September US Secretary of State Condoleezza Rice visited Libya, saying she "respectfully" raised human rights concerns with al-Qadhafi. Italian Prime Minister Silvio Berlusconi also visited Libya in September, pledging US$5 billion in reparations for "the damage inflicted" during Italy's colonial rule. Berlusconi said Italy would receive increased access to Libyan oil and gas and "fewer clandestine immigrants." Russia's then-president Vladimir Putin signed multi-billion-dollar arms and energy deals during a visit in April, the first by a Russian president. Al-Qadhafi signed billions of dollars in contracts during visits to France and Spain in December 2007.

Libya reportedly continues to share intelligence on militant Islamists with Western governments. In 2006 and 2007 the US government returned two Libyan citizens, Mohamed al-Rimi and Sofian Hamoodah, after detaining them at Guantanamo Bay. In December 2007 US officials visited both men at Libyan state security offices and reported that they were being detained without knowledge of the charges against them and apparently without access to a lawyer.

European countries continue to cooperate with Libya to control illegal migration, often without adequate regard for the rights of African migrants or the need to protect refugees and others at risk of abuse on return to their home countries.

Morocco/Western Sahara

Morocco continues to present a mixed picture on human rights. It has made great strides in addressing past abuses, allowed considerable space for public dissent and protest, and reduced gender inequality in the family code. But authorities, aided by complaisant courts, continue to use repressive legislation to punish peaceful opponents, especially those who violate the taboos against criticizing the king or the monarchy, questioning the "Moroccanness" of Western Sahara, or "denigrating" Islam. The police continue to use excessive force to break up demonstrations.

There was sporadic unrest in 2008 over socioeconomic grievances, notably in the city of Sidi Ifni where security forces intervened on June 7 to lift a protesters' blockade of the port. The security forces used excessive force and committed other abuses in Sidi Ifni, according to numerous reports.

Controls are particularly tight in the restive and disputed Western Sahara region, which Morocco administers as if it were part of its national territory. A pro-independence movement known as the Polisario Front (Popular Front for the Liberation of the Saguía al-Hamra and Río de Oro) contests Moroccan sovereignty and demands a referendum on self-determination for the Sahrawi people. The Polisario rejected a Moroccan proposal, presented in April 2007, for enhanced autonomy for the region, mainly because that proposal nowhere mentions a referendum in which independence would be an option. (For human rights in Polisario-run refugee camps, see Algeria chapter.)

Terrorism and Counterterrorism

Hundreds of suspected Islamist extremists arrested in the aftermath of the Casablanca bombings of May 2003 continue to serve prison terms, despite a series of royal pardons that freed a few hundred of them. Many of those rounded up in 2003 were held that year in secret detention for days or weeks, subjected to mistreatment and sometimes torture while under interrogation, then convicted in unfair trials. Some of those convicted were sentenced to death, a punishment that Morocco has not abolished even though it has not carried it out since 1993. Since August 2006 police arrested hundreds more suspected Islamist militants, bringing the total to more than a thousand (by some estimates) as of September 2008.

Intelligence agencies continued to interrogate terrorism suspects at an unacknowledged detention center at Temara, near Rabat, according to numerous reports from detainees. Suspects allege that police tortured them under interrogation, while holding them in pre-charge custody for longer than the 12-day maximum the law provides for terrorism cases. For example, schoolteacher Abdelkrim Hakkou went missing from near his home in Ain Taouijdat on May 16, 2008. His family did not learn his whereabouts until July, when he was brought before a judge and charged with attempting to recruit jihadists to fight in Iraq. Hakkou told his family that police had held him during most of the six-week period in secret detention in Temara, where they tortured him. At this writing, Hakkou remained in pretrial detention. The authorities claim Hakkou was arrested only on July 1 and presented to the prosecutor July 11.

Over the past decade, those like Hakkou who "disappeared" turned up after some weeks in police custody, unlike hundreds of persons who had "disappeared" during the reign of the late King Hassan II and were never found again alive. The state acknowledged responsibility for this practice following the work of Morocco's Equity and Reconciliation Commission and its 2005 report. Beginning in 2007, the state paid the equivalent of around US$85 million in compensation to some 16,000 victims or to their survivors, and began providing other forms of assistance to individuals and to communities that suffered repression in past years.

The Justice System and Law Enforcement

Police are rarely held accountable for violating human rights. In cases with political overtones, courts rarely provide fair trials, ignoring requests for medical examinations lodged by defendants who claim to have been tortured, refusing to summon exculpatory witnesses, and convicting defendants on the basis of apparently coerced confessions. Police in Marrakesh arrested Sahrawi human rights activist Naâma Asfari on April 17, 2008, and charged him with drunk driving and assaulting a woman motorist. According to Asfari, the police beat him severely during an interrogation that focused mainly on his political activism, and then forced him to sign a confession. The court sentenced him to two months in prison.

After raucous anti-gay demonstrations in the city streets, a court in Ksar el-Kbir, under penal code article 487, sentenced six men to between four and 10 months in prison on December 10, 2007, for committing homosexual acts, even though the prosecution introduced no evidence that acts violating the article had occurred. An appeals court upheld the verdicts on January 15, 2008.

In another closely watched case, authorities in February announced the dismantling of a terrorist plot and arrested five political figures and a journalist whom they accused of complicity. The figures included members of three legally recognized parties, one of which, al-Badil al-Hadari (the Civilized Alternative), they promptly dissolved. The men remained in custody while awaiting the scheduled opening of their trial November 14.

Morocco is home to an estimated 10,000 sub-Saharan illegal immigrants, many of whom hope to gain entry to Europe. On April 29 a Moroccan naval ship intercepted an inflatable dinghy filled with would-be migrants in the Mediterranean Sea. According to interviews a Moroccan NGO conducted with survivors, when the dinghy's crew defied orders to return to shore, a crewman of the naval ship punctured the dinghy, causing a reported 29 passengers to drown. Morocco denied its agents played any role in the drowning but conducted no inquiry that was made public.

Freedom of Association and Assembly

Authorities generally tolerate the work of the many human rights organizations active in Rabat and Casablanca. They generally do not hamper foreign human rights organizations visiting Morocco, and often respond to their letters of concern. However, in Western Sahara surveillance is tighter and harassment of rights defenders more common. Authorities have refused to grant legal recognition to any Sahrawi organization dedicated to exposing Moroccan abuses. Authorities expelled on April 25 a delegation from France that had come to observe the trial of Naâma Asfari and that included members of pro-Sahrawi organizations.

Most types of public assembly require authorization from the Interior Ministry, which can refuse permission if it deems them liable to "disturb the public order." Although many of the frequent public protests in Rabat run their course undisturbed, baton-wielding police have brutally broken up others. For example, during a peaceful sit-in on July 1 in front of the Parliament in Rabat in solidarity with political prisoners, law enforcement officers used excessive force to disperse participants, injuring members of the Moroccan Human Rights Association.

Police systematically prevented or dispersed peaceful sit-ins or gatherings by groups that favor independence for Western Sahara. They often used excessive force in responding to incidents when Sahrawi demonstrators laid stones across streets or threw rocks or, very occasionally, threw Molotov cocktails. Sahrawi protester violence fatally injured a policeman for the first time, on February 26 in Tantan.

Freedom of Expression and the Media

Media criticism of the authorities is often quite blunt. It is nevertheless circumscribed by a press law that provides prison terms for "maliciously" spreading "false information" likely to disturb the public order or for speech that is defamatory, offensive to members of the royal family, or that undermines "Islam, the institution of the monarchy, or [Morocco's] territorial integrity."

On July 11, 2008, a Rabat court fined Hassan Rachidi, Al Jazeera television's Morocco bureau chief, for maliciously spreading "false news." The charge stemmed from an Al Jazeera report, citing human rights sources, that people had died when security forces clashed with protestors in Sidi Ifni. The court convicted Rachidi even though Al Jazeera had broadcast government denials of the fatalities. Authorities also suspended Rachidi's press accreditation. The same day, a Rabat court convicted on the same grounds the person who had provided Al Jazeera this information, Brahim Sab'alil of the Moroccan Center for Human Rights. The day before, a court sentenced Sab'alil to six months in prison and a fine for "insulting authorities by alleging fictional crimes" when he accused security forces at a June 26 press conference of "crimes against humanity" in connection with alleged deaths, rapes, and "disappearances" in Sidi Ifni. An appeals court upheld Sab'alil's six-month sentence.

A Casablanca court sentenced Fouad Mourtada on February 22 to a three-year prison term on a charge of "usurping an identity" for having created an unauthorized and spurious, but non-defamatory, Facebook profile of King Mohamed VI's brother. An Agadir court on September 8, handed a two-year prison term to Mohamed Erraji for "disrespecting the king" in an article he published at www.hespress.com criticizing the way that the monarch dispensed privileges and favors. After international outcry over the convictions, the king pardoned Mourtada on March 18, and an appeals court overturned Erraji's conviction on September 18.

In April a royal pardon freed seven members of the Moroccan Human Rights Association imprisoned nearly one year earlier for "attacking sacred values" by allegedly chanting slogans against the king during 2007 marches. But in February, wheel-chair-bound, 95-year-old Ahmed Nasser died in prison, five months into the three-year sentence he received for "attacking sacred values" for allegedly insulting the king during a street altercation.

In May 2008 authorities revoked Al Jazeera's license to broadcast its Maghreb news show from Rabat. They cited technical and legal reasons, but observers suspected the real reason to be dissatisfaction with the station's coverage of Morocco.

Family Law and Women's and Children's Rights

Reforms to the family law enacted in 2004 have raised the minimum age of marriage for women from 15 to 18, made the family the joint responsibility of both spouses, rescinded the wife's duty of obedience to her husband, expanded access to divorce for women, and placed the practice of polygamy under strict judicial control. In January 2007 Morocco reformed its nationality code to give women the right to pass their nationality to their children. Reaffirming the minimum legal age for marriage, authorities in September 2008 closed schools and a website run by a cleric who advocated marriage for girls as young as nine.

Morocco lacks a functioning child protection system, and government efforts to create a system of child protection units showed little progress in 2008. Unaccompanied children are at special risk of abuse while attempting to cross to

Spain (see European Union chapter) and upon return to Morocco, including police beatings and detention with adult criminal suspects.

Key International Actors

Morocco has sought privileged relations with the European Union, which is in turn eager for Morocco's cooperation in combating terrorism and illegal migration. The kingdom is the biggest beneficiary of the European Neighbourhood and Partnership Instrument, with €654 million in aid earmarked for 2007-2010. On October 13, the EU voted to give Morocco "advanced status," placing it a notch above other members of the EU's "neighbourhood policy." While noting progress in many areas of human rights, the EU also "renew[ed] its appeal … that Morocco ensure respect for freedom of expression and … reform again the Press Code and the Penal Code by decriminalizing offenses of opinion." The EU also invited Morocco "to safeguard freedom of association and assembly, notably in the territory of Western Sahara," and called upon "the forces of authority [sic] to show restraint in the recourse to force."

Presenting its request that the United States grant Morocco a total of US$29 million in aid in 2009, the State Department called Morocco "one of the United States' oldest and closest allies in the region.… [A] moderate, stable, democratizing Arab Muslim nation, an important actor in the war on terrorism and a constructive force in the pursuit of Middle East peace." In 2007 the US government-backed Millennium Challenge Corporation approved a five-year US$697.5 million economic aid package to Morocco to fight poverty and promote economic growth.

The US State Department has stated that it supports autonomy for Western Sahara under Moroccan sovereignty. While supporting this basic Moroccan position, US officials held meetings with Sahrawi human rights activists, and publicly criticized Moroccan abuses in Western Sahara. In addition, a law took effect in December 2007 conditioning US$1 million in US military aid to Morocco on human rights progress, particularly in the realm of freedom of expression on the Western Sahara issue.

France is Morocco's leading trade partner and the leading source of public development aid and private investment. It also endorses Morocco's autonomy plan for Western Sahara.

The UN Security Council in April 2008 renewed for one year the MINURSO peacekeeping force in Western Sahara but once again declined to extend its mandate to include human rights observation and protection. Morocco opposes giving MINURSO such a mandate, whereas the Polisario says it supports it.

Morocco was examined under the UN Human Rights Council's Universal Periodic Review in April 2008. The review did not cover the situation in Western Sahara.

SAUDI ARABIA

Human rights conditions remain poor in Saudi Arabia. International and domestic pressure to improve human rights practices remained feeble, and the government undertook no major reforms in 2008. The government systematically suppressed the rights of 14 million Saudi women and an estimated 2 to 3 million members of minority Shia communities, and failed to protect the rights of foreign workers. Thousands of people received unfair trials or were subject to arbitrary detention. Curbs on freedom of association, expression, and movement, as well as a lack of official accountability, remain serious concerns.

The government-approved National Society for Human Rights failed to issue its second annual report in 2008. The governmental Human Rights Commission opened a women's branch, but its board remained all-male.

Women's Rights

The government continues to treat women as legal minors, denying them a host of fundamental human rights. The government requires women to obtain permission from a male guardian to work, study, marry, travel, and even receive a national identification card. The Ministry of Interior did not implement a cabinet recommendation from July to abolish the requirement for a guardian's permission to issue IDs to women.

In addition, the government neither set a minimum age for marriage nor adopted any comprehensive policies to combat forced and early marriages. Marriages of Saudi girls as young as 10 to much older men were reported in 2008, although the Human Rights Commission intervened in one such case to delay the marriage for five years.

Strictly enforced sex segregation hinders a Saudi woman's ability to participate fully in public life. Women are prohibited from working in offices or entering government buildings that lack female sections, or pursuing degrees in disciplines not taught in women's colleges. The Ministry of Labor replaced its prohibition on mixed workplaces with vaguely worded obligations to respect Islamic law on the matter, and so the current workplace environment remains highly segregated. The

Saudi Arabia

Perpetual Minors

Human Rights Abuses Stemming from Male Guardianship
and Sex Segregation in Saudi Arabia

HUMAN
RIGHTS
WATCH

Ministry of Justice denies women the right to be judges or prosecutors, or to practice law. In February 2008 religious police arrested a 36-year-old Saudi business-
woman for "illegal mingling" while meeting with a male colleague in a Starbucks
in Riyadh.

Migrant Worker Rights

An estimated 8 million foreign workers, primarily from India, Indonesia, the
Philippines, and Sri Lanka, fill jobs in the construction, domestic service, health,
and business sectors. Many suffer a range of abuses and labor exploitation,
sometimes rising to slavery-like conditions.

Despite renewed announcements in July, the Ministry of Labor did not implement
its commitment to end the restrictive *kafala* (sponsorship) system. This policy ties
migrant workers' residency permits to their employers, fueling abuses such as
employers confiscating passports, withholding wages, and forcing migrants to
work for months or years against their will.

The government also failed to enact an amendment, first proposed in 2005, to
extend labor law protections to the 1.5 million migrant domestic workers in the
country. Asian embassies report thousands of complaints each year from domestic workers who are forced to work 15-20 hours a day, seven days a week, and
denied their wages. Many endure a range of abuses including forced confinement
in the workplace, food deprivation, and psychological, physical, and sexual
abuse.

Migrants encountering the criminal justice system sometimes face severe delays
and lack access to interpreters, legal aid, or their consulates. Migrants pursuing
criminal cases against abusive employers have little hope of redress. In May
2008 a Riyadh court dropped charges against the Saudi employer who abused
Indonesian domestic worker Nour Miyati so severely she needed her toes and fin-
gers amputated.

SAUDI ARABIA

"As If I Am Not Human"

Abuses against Asian Domestic Workers in Saudi Arabia

HUMAN
RIGHTS
WATCH

Arbitrary Detention and Unfair Trials

Detainees, including children, are commonly the victims of systematic and multiple violations of due process and fair trial rights, including arbitrary arrest and torture and ill-treatment in detention. Saudi judges routinely sentence defendants to thousands of lashes, often carried out in public. In 2008 the kingdom carried out 88 executions as of mid-November (compared to 150 over the equivalent period in 2007), including for drug offenses.

Saudi Arabia has no law setting an age below which a child should not be tried as an adult, and judges have discretion regarding the bases for arrest and length of detention for children. In July 2008 an appeals court ordered the retrial in adult court of Sultan Kohail, whom a juvenile court had earlier sentenced to one year in prison and 200 lashes for his involvement when he was 16 in a schoolyard brawl that resulted in a young man's death. If convicted, Kohail faces the death penalty. A 2006 announcement raising the age of criminal responsibility for boys—there is none for girls—from seven to 12 years is not fully observed.

Saudi Arabia has made no progress in implementing the Judiciary Law adopted in October 2007 that sets up specialized courts, and has yet to write a penal code or ensure that law enforcement officials adhere to its criminal procedure code. Authorities rarely inform suspects of the crime with which they are charged, or the evidence supporting the accusation. In the absence of a penal code, prosecutors and judges have discretion to decide what constitutes a criminal offense. Detainees do not have access to a lawyer during interrogation, face excessive pretrial delays, and at trial often cannot examine witnesses or evidence or present a defense.

The Human Rights Commission was unable to resolve the arbitrary detention of Yondje Obed, a Cameroonian arrested in 2006 on frivolous charges whose trial has yet to begin. The commission protested the 2006 conviction of Fawza Falih for "witchcraft" only four months after being apprised of the case. At this writing, Falih remains on death row.

Secret police (*mabahith*) in 2008 detained or continued to detain without trial or access to lawyers—in many cases for years—around 2,000 persons suspected of sympathies with or involvement in terrorism. In October the government

SAUDI ARABIA

Precarious Justice

Arbitrary Detention and Unfair Trials in the Deficient
Criminal Justice System of Saudi Arabia

**HUMAN
RIGHTS
WATCH**

announced it would bring 991 domestic terrorism suspects to trial for the first time. The United States in late 2007 returned more Saudis from Guantanamo Bay, leaving only about a dozen Saudi detainees in US military custody there (out of a group originally comprising more than 130). The returnees faced detention without charge, usually for several months, and involuntary participation in rehabilitation programs.

Freedom of Expression

Freedom of expression in Saudi Arabia deteriorated in 2008. The government did not respond publicly when chief judge Salih al-Luhaidan in September endorsed the idea that owners of TV stations that broadcast allegedly lewd shows during Ramadan deserved to be killed. Nor did the government sanction prominent cleric Abd al-Rahman al-Barrak in March after he called for the killing of journalists Abdullah Bajad Utaibi and Yusif Aba al-Khair for articles criticizing extremist interpretations of Islam.

Official tolerance for incitement to violence contrasted with intolerance toward dissident opinions. Intelligence officials detained blogger Fu'ad Farhan without charge from December 2007 until April 2008 after he criticized the arbitrary arrest of other peaceful critics. Prosecutors in May charged Ra'if al-Badawi, a self-proclaimed "liberal" who challenges the views of the religious establishment, with "setting up an electronic [web]site that insults Islam," a charge that carries a five-year prison sentence under a 2007 Law to Combat Crimes of Information; the trial was set to begin in November. Also in May, secret police arrested Matrook al-Faleh, a prominent reform activist and university professor. As of November, he remained in solitary confinement without charge. The Human Rights Commission secured visitation rights for al-Faleh's wife, but did not address the underlying issue of his arbitrary detention.

Freedom of Religion and Religious Discrimination

Saudi Arabia systematically discriminates against its religious minorities—in particular, the Twelver Shia in the Eastern Province and around Medina, and the Ismailis, a distinct branch of Shiism, in Najran, in the southwest of the country. Official discrimination against Shia (including Ismailis) encompasses government employment, religious practices, education, and the justice system. Government officials exclude Ismailis from decision making and publicly disparage their faith. In 2006 and 2007, Judge al-Luhaidan and the Senior Council for Religious Scholars called Ismailis "infidels," a position reflected in official textbooks stating that the Ismaili faith constitutes the sin of "major polytheism."

In Najran, only one of the 35 department heads of local government is Ismaili; there are almost no Ismailis in senior security jobs or working as teachers of religion. Ismailis face difficulties obtaining building permits for their privately financed mosques, while the state funds Sunni mosques and pays the imams. After Ismaili leader Shaikh Ahmad bin Turki Al Sa'b met with King Abdullah in April 2008 to complain against official treatment of Ismailis, Saudi intelligence arrested him, and continued to detain him as of November. On November 4, the king accepted the resignation of Prince Mish'al, the governor of Najran.

Key International Actors

Saudi Arabia is a key ally of the United States and the United Kingdom. US pressure for human rights improvements was imperceptible in a year that saw visits by President Bush, Vice-President Cheney, and Secretary of State Rice. UK efforts through the Two Kingdoms Dialogue to promote human rights had no tangible effect, if such efforts were made at all.

Saudi Arabia is due to be reviewed under the Universal Periodic Review mechanism of the UN Human Rights Council in February 2009.

SYRIA

Syria emerged from its international isolation in 2008, but its human rights record remains very poor. The authorities arrested political and human rights activists, censored websites, detained bloggers, and imposed travel bans. Emergency rule, imposed in 1963, remains in effect and Syria's multiple security agencies continue to detain people without arrest warrants.

The Supreme State Security Court (SSSC), an exceptional court with almost no procedural guarantees, sentenced 75 people in 2008, mostly Islamists, to long prison terms. Syrian Kurds, the country's largest ethnic minority, continue to protest their treatment as second-class citizens. Months after military police shot and killed rioting inmates at Sednaya military prison, no information has been disclosed about casualties.

Political Activists on Trial

Starting in December 2007, the Syrian security services detained over 40 political activists who attended a meeting of the National Council of the Damascus Declaration, comprising a number of opposition groups. While most were released within 48 hours, the authorities referred 12, including former member of parliament Riad Seif, to the Damascus Criminal Court, which sentenced them on October 29, 2008, to 30 months in prison on charges of "weakening national sentiment," and "spreading false news affecting the country's morale." On May 7, 2008, security services detained writer and political analyst Habib Saleh for articles critical of the government and in defense of opposition figure Riad al-Turk. He is awaiting trial on multiple charges, including "weakening national sentiment."

The SSSC sentenced over 75 people in 2008 on various grounds, including membership in the banned Muslim Brotherhood, Kurdish activism, membership in unauthorized political groups, and independent criticism of the government.

On April 23 the Military Court in Damascus sentenced Kamal al-Labwani, a physician and founder of the Democratic Liberal Gathering, to a three-year prison term for reportedly "insulting the authorities" while in prison, in addition to the 12-year term he received in 2007 for having advocated peaceful reform while visiting the United States and Europe.

In a welcome move, on August 7 authorities released economics professor Dr. `Arif Dalila, a proponent of political liberalization who was serving a 10-year sentence for "attempting to change the constitution by illegal means."

Freedom of Expression

Syrian authorities continue to restrict freedom of expression, and an independent press remains nonexistent. The government has extended to online outlets restrictions it applies to other media, detaining journalists for posting information online. Syrian internet censorship extends to popular websites such as Google's blogging engine, Blogspot, as well as Facebook and YouTube.

On April 7 the SSSC sentenced writer and poet Firas Sa`ad to four years in jail for "weakening national sentiment" after he published articles on the website www.ahewar.org in which he defended a call for improved relations between Lebanon and Syria and criticized the Syrian army's role in the July 2006 war between Israel and Hezbollah. On May 11 the SSSC sentenced to three years in prison blogger Tarek Biasi, 23, whom the government detained in July 2007 for "insulting security services" and "weakening national sentiment." At this writing, Karim `Arbaji, 29, moderator of popular online youth forum www.akhawia.net, is on trial for "spreading false information that may weaken national sentiment."

Arbitrary Detention, Torture, and "Disappearances"

Syria's multiple security services continue to detain people without arrest warrants and frequently refuse to disclose their whereabouts for weeks and sometimes months, in effect forcibly disappearing them. On August 15 Syrian security services detained Mash`al al-Temmo, spokesperson for the Kurdish Future Current in Syria, an unauthorized political party, while he was driving alone at night, and held him incommunicado for 11 days. The security services are also believed to hold a small number of detainees who were arrested in Pakistan in recent years and held for a time in secret CIA custody.

Human Rights Watch received numerous reports of ill-treatment and torture by security agencies. In January, eight of the 12 detainees of the National Council of the Damascus Declaration reported that State Security officers beat them during interrogation, including prominent writer `Ali al-Abdullah who suffered ear injuries. A Kurdish activist showed Human Rights Watch photos of bruises he said Political Security officers inflicted on him in July 2008 during interrogation. At least 11 of the 75 people sentenced in 2008 by the SSSC had told the court that security agencies tortured them.

On July 5 military police opened fire on rioting inmates in Sednaya prison. A number of inmates and prison guards were reportedly killed, but authorities have released no information on the number or names of those killed and wounded.

As in previous years, the government failed to acknowledge security force involvement in the "disappearances" of an estimated 17,000 persons, mostly Muslim Brotherhood members and other Syrian activists detained by the government in the late 1970s and early 1980s as well as hundreds of Lebanese and Palestinians detained in Syria or abducted from Lebanon. The vast majority remains unaccounted for and many are believed to have been killed.

Human Rights Defenders

Human rights activists continue to be targets of government harassment and arrest. On April 22 a military court sentenced Ahmad al-Hajji al-Khalaf, a board member of the Arab Organization for Human Rights in Syria, to five days in jail for criticizing appointments at the Ministry of Education. Similarly, on June 23 a military court sentenced Mazen Darwish, president of the Syrian Center for Media and Freedom of Expression, to five days in jail for reporting on violent clashes in the Damascus suburb of `Adra. On June 29 a military court sentenced Muhammad Badi` Dek al-Bab, a member of the National Organization for Human Rights, to six months in jail for articles in which he criticized the government for detaining intellectuals.

The government continues to prevent activists from traveling abroad, and in some cases, their families also. The number of activists banned from traveling is estimated to be in the hundreds.

All Syrian human rights groups remain unlicensed, as officials consistently deny their requests for registration.

Discrimination and Repression against Kurds

Kurds, Syria's largest non-Arab ethnic minority, comprise about 10 percent of the population of 19 million. They remain subject to systematic discrimination, including the arbitrary denial of citizenship to an estimated 300,000 Syria-born Kurds.

Authorities suppress expressions of Kurdish identity, including the teaching of Kurdish in schools. On March 20, 2008, Syrian internal security forces opened fire on Kurds celebrating the Kurdish New Year in the town of Qamishli, leaving three dead.

On September 14 a military court sentenced 50 Kurds to six months in jail for demonstrating against the 2005 assassination of Kurdish leader Sheikh Ma`shuq al-Khaznawi. Security officials detained a number of Kurdish political activists, including Muhammad Musa, secretary of the Syrian Kurdish Left Party, and Mash`al al-Temmo and Omran al-Sayyid, leaders in the Kurdish Future Current in Syria. At this writing, all three face trial.

Women's Rights

Syria's constitution guarantees gender equality, and many women are active in public life, but personal status laws and the penal code contain provisions that discriminate against women and girls. The penal code allows a judge to suspend punishment for a rapist if the rapist chooses to marry his victim, and provides leniency for "honor" crimes. While the number of honor crimes is unknown, the Syrian Women's Observatory, an unlicensed group, documented at least 10 in 2008, including the killing in April of a 14-year-old by her brother because she had a relationship with another teenager.

According to media reports, a committee tasked with drafting a law against human trafficking submitted a draft to the Council of Ministers in July 2008. At this writing, the draft had not yet been made public or referred to Parliament.

Situation of Refugees Fleeing Iraq

Syria hosts the largest number of Iraqi refugees, estimated at 1 to 1.5 million, and provides them with access to public hospitals and schools but prohibits them from working. Since 2007 Syria has implemented increasingly restrictive visa and entry requirements for Iraqi refugees. Combined with the lack of employment in Syria and a relative improvement in the security situation in Iraq, this led thousands of Iraqi refugees to return to Iraq in early 2008: in May the United Nations High Commissioner for Refugees estimated that only slightly more Iraqis entered Syria each day than left for Iraq. Syria continues to refuse entry to Palestinians fleeing Iraq. At this writing, several hundred remain at makeshift camps in the no-man's-land between Iraqi and Syrian border checkpoints; with thousands more in camps on the Iraqi side close to the border.

Key International Actors

Syria emerged from its international isolation in 2008, with French President Sarkozy and other high-level foreign dignitaries visiting Damascus. However, the renewed ties have had little impact on Syria's human rights record. During 2008 the European Union issued public statements expressing concern over the human rights situation in Syria and calling for the release of all political prisoners, although in September Javier Solana, the EU foreign policy chief, indicated that the EU might be willing to resume talks on an Association Agreement, which were frozen following the assassination of Lebanese Prime Minister Hariri in February 2005.

Iran continues to be Syria's main regional ally, and the two countries increased their cooperation in the military and economic spheres. Saudi Arabia and Syria exchanged sharp criticism over regional roles, highlighting tensions between the two countries.

TUNISIA

President Zine al-Abidine Ben Ali and the ruling party, the Constitutional Democratic Assembly, dominate political life in Tunisia. The government uses the threat of terrorism and religious extremism as a pretext to crack down on peaceful dissent. There are continuous and credible reports of torture and ill-treatment being used to obtain statements from suspects in custody.

In office since 1987, Ben Ali announced he will seek a fifth term in 2009. The authorities keep the country's few legal opposition parties weak and marginalized through repressive measures and denying them media coverage.

On November 5, 2008, the president conditionally released the last 21 imprisoned members of the banned Islamist party al-Nahdha, who had been in prison since a military court convicted 265 party members and sympathizers in a tainted trial in 1992 on charges of plotting to topple the state. However, the overall number of political prisoners has grown in recent years as authorities have convicted scores of young men under the 2003 anti-terror law. The authorities make life difficult for released political prisoners, monitoring them closely, denying them passports and most jobs, and threatening to rearrest some who have spoken out on human rights or politics.

Human Rights Defenders

Authorities have refused to grant legal recognition to every truly independent human rights organization that has applied over the past decade. They then invoke the organization's "illegal" status to hamper its activities.

The independent Tunisian Human Rights League (LTDH), a legally recognized group, continues to face lawsuits filed by dissident members. The broader context showed these supposedly private suits to be part of a pattern of repression: the courts ruled systematically in favor of the plaintiffs, providing a legal veneer for large-scale police operations to prevent most League meetings at its branches around the country.

Human rights defenders and dissidents face surveillance, arbitrary travel bans, dismissal from work, interruptions in phone service, and physical assaults. Police arrested Bizerte-based Mohamed Ben Saïd of the LTDH on July 28, 2008, on a dubious charge of failing to obey a traffic policeman, a charge that earned him two months in prison after an unfair trial. Authorities on September 28 jailed Tarek Soussi, also of Bizerte, two days after he accused security forces of "abductions" on Al Jazeera television because of the way they had allegedly flouted legal arrest procedures. A court charged Soussi, a member of the unrecognized, Tunis-based International Association in Support of Political Prisoners, with "maliciously spreading false information capable of disturbing the public order" and on September 25 released him provisionally pending trial.

The Justice System

In cases that have a political character, courts fail to guarantee defendants a fair trial. Prosecutors and judges usually turn a blind eye to torture allegations, even when defense lawyers formally demand an investigation. Trial judges convict defendants solely or predominantly on the basis of coerced confessions, or on the testimony of witnesses whom the defendant does not have the opportunity to confront in court.

During consideration of Tunisia in March 2008 by the UN Human Rights Committee, Tunisian authorities announced they would grant Human Rights Watch's longstanding request to visit the country's prisons; the Justice Ministry and Human Rights Watch were negotiating the terms of the visits at this writing. If carried through, the arrangement will be the first time since 1991 Tunisia has opened its prisons to an independent human rights organization. The International Committee of the Red Cross visits Tunisian prisons but, in accordance with its mandate, reports its findings only to the government and not to the public.

According to human rights lawyers and organizations, the most common forms of torture and ill-treatment during police interrogation are sleep deprivation; threats to rape the detainee or female family members; beatings, especially on the soles of the feet (falaka); and tying and suspending detainees from the ceiling or from a rod in the "roast chicken" position.

Tunisia has ratified the Convention against Torture and enacted strong legislation criminalizing acts of torture. However, despite the submission of formal complaints by lawyers on behalf of defendants in hundreds of cases in recent years, no case has come to public attention of authorities holding a state agent accountable for torturing persons held for politically motivated offenses.

Media Freedom

None of the domestic print and broadcast media offers critical coverage of government policies, apart from a few low-circulation magazines such as *al-Mawkif*, an opposition party organ, that are subject to occasional confiscation. Tunisia has privately-owned radio and television stations, but private ownership is not synonymous with editorial independence. The government blocks access to certain domestic and international political or human rights websites featuring critical coverage of Tunisia, including www.kalimatunisie.com, whose print edition authorities have refused to legalize.

Journalist Slim Boukhdir of Sfax wrote online essays critical of the president and his relatives for nepotism. On November 26, 2007, police ordered him out of a taxi and placed him under arrest. A court convicted him one month later of insulting the police officer who stopped him, refusing to hand over his identification, and violating "public decency," accusations Boukhdir denied. Authorities insisted his case had nothing to do with free expression, but it was hardly the first time that they imprisoned critics on common criminal charges that appeared unfounded. They provisionally released Boukhdir on July 21, 2008, but continued to refuse him a passport, a situation he has faced since 2003.

Counterterrorism Measures

Since 1991 there has been one deadly terrorist attack in Tunisia: an April 2002 truck bomb that targeted a synagogue on the island of Djerba, for which al Qaeda claimed responsibility. In addition, security forces have clashed once with armed militants, in December 2006 and January 2007, outside the capital.

The 2003 Law in Support of "International Efforts to Fight Terrorism and the Repression of Money Laundering" contains a broad definition of terrorism that the

JN Human Rights Committee criticized on March 28, 2008, for its "lack of precision." The definition encompasses "acts of incitement to racial or religious hatred or fanaticism regardless of the means employed." Authorities have charged many hundreds of men, and some minors, under the law. Nearly all of those convicted stood accused of planning to join jihadist groups abroad or inciting others to join, rather than of having planned or committed specific acts of violence.

Suspects arrested in the context of the counterterrorism law commonly face a range of procedural abuses that includes the failure by authorities to notify their kin promptly, in violation of Tunisian law, extension of pre-arraignment detention beyond the legal six-day limit, and the refusal of judges and prosecutors to act on requests that the suspect undergo a medical examination, a means of detecting signs of torture.

Socioeconomic Unrest

Sporadic protests over corruption, joblessness, and high prices erupted in January 2008 in the depressed mining region surrounding the southern town of Redhayef, and simmered throughout the year. Authorities deployed large numbers of security forces to suppress the protests, round up their leaders, and seal off the region from journalists and others trying to reach it. On June 21, they arrested the spokesman of the protest movement, trade unionist Adnane Hajji, and charged him with founding a "criminal enterprise" and other offenses. Hajji remained in pretrial detention at this writing. Courts imposed prison terms of several months on dozens of others for their role in the protests. For example, authorities on July 27 arrested human rights and opposition party activist Zakia Dhifaoui and six others who had marched peacefully that day in Redhayef to demand the release of those arrested during the ongoing protests. An appeals court on September 15 sentenced Dhifaoui to four-and-a-half months in prison and the six others to three months. President Ben Ali conditionally released her in early November, along with about 20 others convicted for their role in the protests.

Key International Actors

In 2008 Tunisia announced it would accept visits by the UN special rapporteurs on torture and on the promotion and protection of human rights while countering terrorism, but neither had conducted a mission at this writing.

France is Tunisia's leading trade partner and its fourth largest foreign investor. In April 2008 President Sarkozy, on his second official visit to Tunisia, declared at a state dinner hosted by President Ben Ali, "Today, the sphere of liberties [in Tunisia] is progressing.... I have complete confidence in your will to continue to enlarge the space of freedom in Tunisia." Neither Sarkozy, nor his minister of state for human rights, Rama Yade, who accompanied him on this trip, offered any public human rights criticism, but the French presidency did announce during the visit Tunisair's purchase of several Airbus jets.

The United States enjoys good relations with Tunisia and praises it as a counter-terrorism ally, while urging human rights progress there more vocally than it does in most other countries in the region. In her first visit to Tunisia as US secretary of state, Condoleezza Rice met with Ben Ali on September 6 and told reporters later that despite some political reforms, "we have been very clear that we would hope that Tunisia would do more." She said she wished that "media access, freedom of the internet, access to the television for the opposition will really be enshrined" in the lead-up to the 2009 election.

While the US gives minimal financial aid to Tunisia, the Department of Defense provides counterterrorism training and exchange programs for the military.

United Arab Emirates (UAE)

While the economy of the UAE continues to grow, human rights progress remains scant. Authorities censor and harass human rights activists, impeding independent reporting that could help curb abuses. Other forms of governmental accountability are minimal. Only 6,600 UAE citizens, chosen by the rulers of the emirates out of a population of roughly 900,000 citizens (and 4.7 million foreigners), can vote or stand for the 20 elected seats in the 40-seat Federal National Council, an advisory body to the president.

Freedom of Association and Expression

The only legally recognized human rights organization, the Emirates Human Rights Association, took up the cause of cancer patients facing workplace discrimination, but did little to address persistent human rights abuses by the government. As of October 2008 the Ministry of Labor and Social Welfare had not responded to applications from 2004 and 2005 to establish other human rights organizations.

Human rights defenders and government critics face harassment, including criminal charges. According to Muhammad al-Mansoori, former president of the Jurists Association, charges against him from 2006 for allegedly "insulting the public prosecutor" were dropped, but revived in October 2007. Al-Mansoori sought to fight the charges in court but says the public prosecutor refuses to bring the case to trial. Al-Mansoori claims that officials warned him to cease his human rights advocacy, and have refused to renew his passport since March 2008.

In June 2005 authorities accused Hassan al-Diqqi, the founder of the unrecognized Emirates People's Rights Organization, of raping a housekeeper. The charges aroused suspicion, coming two months after al-Diqqi established the "PRO Emirates" website. Al-Diqqi went into hiding and was sentenced to death in absentia in a 2005 trial in which forensic evidence did not support the charge, according to a local rights activist and lawyer who saw the evidence. Sharjah police arrested al-Diqqi in July 2008 on the old rape charge. On August 5 a court ordered his release, and the next day an appeals court affirmed the release order, but then without explanation the first instance court rescinded its initial release decision. Al-Diqqi says authorities are harassing him because of his human rights activism.

Authorities arrested Salem Abdullah al-Dousari, a professor of religious education, on May 6 without explanation. According to the Geneva-based human rights organization Alkarama, he was detained in a psychiatric facility for three months without charge before being released.

In May the United Nations Working Group on Arbitrary Detention concluded that Sabihat Abdullah Sultan al-Alili was arbitrarily detained in February 2007 for exercising his right to freedom of expression. In October 2007 the Federal Supreme Court sentenced him to three years in prison for revealing state secrets. The Working Group noted that, at his trial, al-Alili was not allowed to speak, his lawyer was not allowed to plead, and a coerced confession was used against him.

According to lawyer and independent human rights activist Muhammad al-Roken, the government returned his passport in May 2007 but in 2008 the Ministry of Justice threatened to cancel his law license. Al-Roken received a three-month suspended sentence after being charged with sex out of wedlock in a politically motivated case in 2007.

Although Prime Minister Shaikh Muhammad decreed in 2007 that journalists should not face prison "for reasons related to their work," a 1980 law still in force provides for the imprisonment of journalists and suspension of publication for publishing "materials that cause confusion among the public." The government monitors press content, and journalists routinely exercise self-censorship. In July 2008, for example, *Al-Khaleej* newspaper refused to publish a column by `Abd al-Khaliq Abdullah on the growing demographic imbalance between foreign workers and Emiratis.

The government has targeted educators suspected of Islamist sympathies. In June, 83 teachers staged a protest 11 months after being removed from their positions, without explanation, because of what the government said were their Islamist views. In July authorities without explanation banned law professors Ahmed Salah al-Hamadi and Seif al-Shamsi from resuming their teaching positions at the national university in al-Ain.

Prisons and Ill-Treatment

In a positive development, a former Dubai prison director and six jail wardens were sentenced to six-month prison terms for beating prisoners during an inspection for contraband in August 2007. Another 18 jail wardens involved in the abuse were sentenced to three-months.

Migrant Workers' Rights

Foreigners account for up to 85 percent of UAE residents and nearly 99 percent of the private-sector workforce. Immigration sponsorship laws grant employers extraordinary power over the lives of migrant workers. Laws in force, as well as a draft revised labor law made public in 2007 but not yet implemented, fail to protect workers' rights to organize and to bargain collectively, provide punishments for striking workers, and exclude from coverage domestic workers employed in private households. Although the Labor Law of 1980 calls for a minimum wage, in June 2008 the Ministry of Labor stated it had no plans to adopt such a measure.

Women domestic workers are at risk of unpaid wages, food deprivation, forced confinement, and physical or sexual abuse. In October 2008 two Filipina domestic workers tried to leave their employers' household, complaining of physical abuse and non-payment of wages. Their employers returned them to their recruitment agency, Al Doukhi Labour Supply Company, which detained them in a small kitchen "for days" before they escaped.

The standard contract for domestic workers introduced in April 2007 provides some protections and calls for unspecified "adequate breaks," but does not limit working hours or provide for a rest day, overtime pay, or workers' compensation. The government announced plans in late 2007 to draft a law protecting domestic workers, but this has yet to be finalized.

Exploitation of migrant construction workers is also severe. Abuses include non-payment of wages, extended working hours without overtime compensation, unsafe working environments leading to deaths or illness, squalid living conditions in labor camps, and withholding of passports and travel documents.

In March, 1,500 workers with engineering contractor Drake and Scull went on a violent strike at a labor camp in Sharjah, destroying company offices, cars, and buses. Workers told local media they were protesting unpaid wages. In July police in Ras al-Khaima arrested more than 3,000 workers employed by the Al Hamra construction company after a riot reportedly sparked by anger at the poor quality of company-supplied food. Authorities detained most of those involved for 13 days, and the Labor Ministry ordered some "instigators" expelled from the country. Also in July, Sharjah police arrested 625 construction workers who blocked a road after they were denied promised housing and forced to sleep on construction sites. In October more than 3,000 workers of the ETA Contracting Company in Abu Dhabi went on strike to protest delayed payments and demand wage increases needed to meet food costs after the company banned workers from cooking their own meals.

The Labor Ministry mandated an afternoon break for workers on outdoor construction sites from 12:30 to 3 p.m. during July and August, when temperatures often exceed 43 degrees Celsius. In July 2005 the ministry had directed companies to give workers a four-hour break, but reduced it to two-and-a-half hours due to company lobbying. Heat exhaustion cases have reportedly decreased overall, although in August 2008 a hospital in Dubai reported receiving an increased number of construction workers suffering heat exhaustion during the mandated break period, suggesting some companies violated the law.

In August 2008 public health authorities in Dubai stated that 40 percent of that emirate's 1,093 labor camps violated minimum health and fire safety standards.

That same month, 11 construction workers died when the 30-room Dubai residence where 500 workers were illegally housed caught fire; some had to jump out of windows due to blocked exits. In June a chickenpox outbreak in a Sharjah labor camp was linked to unhygienic conditions and workers' inability to afford vaccines.

Workers died on the job due to apparently unsafe working conditions. In June three Indian employees of Seidco General Contracting were killed when a basement ceiling collapsed at a hotel construction site in Ajman; a police chief said the scaffolding was unable to take the weight of the concrete. In September Abu

Dhabi police blamed "lax safety procedures" for the deaths of two Pakistani workers when a well they were digging collapsed.

The UAE has not ratified core International Labour Organization conventions protecting freedom of association and the right to organize, which includes the right to strike and the right to collective bargaining.

In May the UAE released its first annual report on trafficking, dedicated substantial funds to counter-trafficking efforts, and publicly acknowledged that trafficking takes place. In its 2008 annual report on human trafficking the United States State Department listed the UAE as a Tier 2 country, taking it off its Watch List. The UAE government has yet to take crucial measures to fight trafficking and forced labor, however, such as major reform of inadequate labor and immigration laws, stronger monitoring of recruitment agencies, screening for trafficking, and prosecutions for trafficking into forced labor.

Key International Actors

The UAE cooperates with the United States on security matters. The US Navy routinely uses the Dubai port of Jebel Ali. In December 2007 the Bush administration notified the US Congress of the possible sale to the UAE of several air defense missile systems as well as various munitions. On July 28, 2008, the US returned to the UAE Abdullah al-Hamiri, a UAE national who had been detained at Guantanamo Bay.

In a bid to increase the UAE's food security, the Abu Dhabi Development Fund announced plans to buy and develop farmland in several countries, including tens of thousands of hectares in Sudan, and possible projects in Uzbekistan, Vietnam, and Cambodia.

The UAE was reviewed under the Universal Periodic Review mechanism of the UN Human Rights Council in December 2008.

YEMEN

The human rights situation in Yemen has deteriorated markedly over the past several years. Yemen had previously made advances in the rule of law, setting out rights in the constitution, the penal code, and criminal procedure code. However, these have been eroded by hundreds of arbitrary arrests and several dozen enforced disappearances, mainly in the context of armed clashes in the north, but also relating to the government's domestic counterterrorism efforts and crackdown on social and political unrest in the south of the country.

Yemen is one of only five countries known since January 2005 to have executed persons for crimes committed while under age 18.

Arbitrary Arrests and Enforced Disappearances

Conflict in Sa'da governorate between government forces, abetted by tribal allies, and a rebel group known as the Huthis, first erupted in 2004. A fifth round of fighting that broke out in May 2008 ended on July 17. In the context of this recurring armed conflict, Yemen's security forces carried out hundreds of arbitrary arrests and enforced disappearances of civilians. Since 2007, and especially in the first half of 2008, the extent of arbitrary arrests and "disappearances" expanded, with the authorities broadening the targets of such arrests and detentions to include persons reporting on the war's impact on civilians.

On August 17, a month after the fifth round of fighting ended, President Ali Abdullah Saleh announced some prisoner releases, but dozens, and possibly hundreds, of persons remain arbitrarily detained, and new arrests have taken place. Estimates of the numbers of persons "disappeared" vary. Yemeni rights organizations have documented dozens of cases of persons who have "disappeared," most of whom eventually reappeared at the facilities of the Political Security Organization, the security and intelligence agency directly linked to the office of President Saleh. In August 2008 officials stated that there were approximately 1,200 political prisoners still detained, with plans to release 130 of these. The government has taken no steps to investigate or hold accountable those responsible for enforced disappearances.

Denial of Humanitarian Access to Conflict Areas

Since June 2004 the armed conflict in northern Yemen has displaced up to 130,000 people, a great many of whom remained out of the reach of humanitarian agencies as of November 2008. Particularly since 2007, when international aid agencies sought access to all parts of Sa'da governorate, Yemeni authorities have severely restricted these agencies from reaching tens of thousands of civilians in need. After fighting erupted again in May 2008, the government blocked the movement of commercial goods in Sa'da, including basic foods and fuel, an act that appears to constitute collective punishment.

When President Saleh declared an end to the fighting in July, 60,000 displaced persons had found refuge in Sa'da town, where they received limited assistance. However, tens of thousands of others—possibly as many as 70,000 persons—had been displaced in remote areas or other urban areas, where government restrictions on movement largely prevented aid agencies from providing them with the assistance they needed. Since August the government has told international humanitarian agencies that they have unrestricted access to the whole of Sa'da governorate, but the reality is different. Many agencies are told they must apply for and be granted a separate Interior Ministry permission for each and every trip, an almost impossible operational requirement. At this writing the access of humanitarian agencies was insufficient to reach many of those who have long been without assistance and remain at risk.

Freedom of Information

Also distinguishing the conflict in 2008 was the extent of government control over information. Officials prevented journalists and humanitarian workers from going to the conflict zone, threatened journalists with reprisal if they reported on the conflict, and prosecuted at least one journalist, opposition website editor Abd al-Karim al-Khaiwani, before a State Security Court. In June 2008 the court sentenced him to a six-year prison term. President Saleh pardoned him on September 25. The authorities also had disconnected all but a select number of mobile telephone numbers in the conflict area.

YEMEN

Disappearances and Arbitrary Arrests in the Armed Conflict with Huthi Rebels in Yemen

H U M A N
R I G H T S
W A T C H

Terrorism and Counterterrorism

Terrorism resurged in Yemen in 2008. Al Qaeda in Yemen also launched an online magazine, *Sada al-Malahim* (Echoes of Battles), urging jihadists to kidnap Western tourists to secure the release of jailed members. In response, the United States has been pressuring the government to enact sweeping counterterrorism measures that local human rights groups fear would repress dissent and increase arbitrary arrests and detentions.

In September 2008 a sophisticated attack involving coordinated car bombs directed at the gates of the US Embassy in the Yemeni capital, San'a, killed six Yemeni security personnel, four civilians, and the six attackers. In March 2008 unknown perpetrators fired mortars toward the embassy, hitting a nearby school. In January 2008 gunmen killed two Belgian tourists and their two Yemeni drivers. Yemeni officials blamed insurgents linked to al Qaeda for all three attacks.

Yemeni authorities have released some arrested security suspects, including Jamal al-Badawi, a Yemeni convicted of organizing the October 2000 attack on the USS Cole, in return for their pledges to cooperate with security forces.

Of approximately 255 prisoners still in US military detention at Guantanamo Bay, more than 100 are Yemenis, the largest group by nationality. Two of the three Guantanamo detainees convicted by controversial US military commissions are Yemenis; both were convicted in 2008.

Criminal Justice and the Juvenile Death Penalty

Yemen retains the death penalty for a wide variety of offenses, among them murder of a Muslim, arson or explosion, endangering transport and communications, apostasy, robbery, prostitution, adultery, and homosexuality.

In 1994 Yemen amended its Penal Code to require reduced sentences for crimes committed by persons under 18, including a maximum penalty of 10 years' imprisonment for those who commit capital offenses. However, implementation of this provision and a similar provision in the Juvenile Act has been hampered by Yemen's very low birth registration rate and weak juvenile justice system, which make it difficult for many juvenile offenders to prove their age at the time of the

offense. While Yemeni law provides for age determinations conducted by an "expert," it does not clarify how the determinations should be conducted, nor require that defendants receive the benefit of the doubt if the expert finds that the defendant could have been younger than 18. According to NGOs working on juvenile justice in Yemen, the country lacks adequate forensic facilities with staff trained in conducting age determinations, and judges do not routinely question young defendants about their age at the time of the alleged offense to help ensure that juvenile offenders are not mistakenly tried as adults.

In February 2007 Yemen executed Adil Muhammad Saif al-Ma'amari for a crime allegedly committed when he was 16. According to Penal Reform International, at least 18 other juvenile offenders are believed to be on death row.

Early and Forced Marriage

Yemen's Personal Status Law sets no minimum age for marriage of girls, stating instead that a girl "is not to be wed until she is ready for sex, even if she exceeds 15 years." In addition, the Penal Code does not criminalize marital rape and girls and women in forced marriages have little recourse against abuse. Early marriage is widespread in Yemen and linked to elevated rates of maternal mortality, domestic violence, and school dropout. A 2005 survey in al-Hodeidah and Hadhramaut governorates by Sana'a University's Gender Development Research and Studies Center found 52 percent of girls were married by age 18, with some girls marrying as young as eight. In April 2008 parliamentary committees rejected provisions in a proposed Safe Motherhood Law, introduced in 2005, that would have raised the minimum age of marriage to 18 and banned female genital mutilation. The governmental Women's National Committee had called for the amendments following public outcry over the case of a nine-year-old girl who sought divorce after her forced marriage to a much older man who raped her. The Ministry of Health said it planned to reintroduce the draft law with a provision setting the minimum marriage age at 15.

Key International Actors

Saudi Arabia, Qatar, and other Persian Gulf states provide substantial amounts of assistance to Yemen, but for the most part do not make figures public. Many

Yemenis believe that this, along with substantial amounts of aid to private actors, including tribal leaders and religious institutions, make Saudi Arabia Yemen's largest donor.

Nine European Union states also provide aid to Yemen. The United Kingdom is the largest Western donor; the UK Department for International Development states that it will have provided £117 million (US$189 million) between 2007 and 2011.

Because of the presence of many Yemeni and other Arab veterans of wars in Afghanistan, counterterrorism has been the key issue in Yemen's relations with the United States. For the fiscal year 2008 the Bush administration estimates it spent US$17.5 million in military and other assistance to Yemen, including US$2 million specifically for counterterrorism measures. However, the US suspended a planned additional grant of US$20.6 million to the Yemeni government to protest the release of Jamal al-Badawi.

All donor states were reluctant in 2008 to press the government on its conduct in the Sa'da conflict, apparently out of concern about the government's political stability.

Numerous United Nations agencies have a presence in Yemen, including the World Food Program, UN Children's Fund, the UN Development Programme, and UN High Commissioner for Refugees, although the Office of the High Commissioner for Human Rights has no staff there. Security concerns have placed all UN staff in the country on heightened alert and agencies have operated in only two towns in Sa'da governorate.

Yemen is due to be reviewed under the Universal Periodic Review mechanism of the UN Human Rights Council in May 2009.

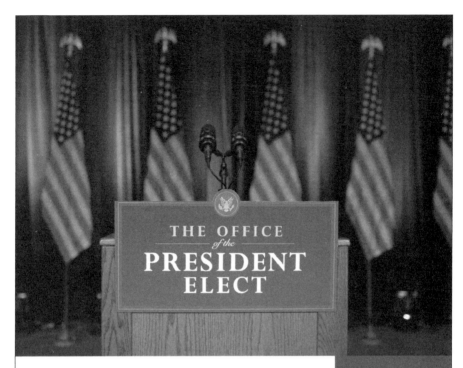

UNITED STATES

Fighting Terrorism
Fairly and Effectively

Recommendations for President-Elect Barack Obama

**HUMAN
RIGHTS
WATCH**

WORLD REPORT

2009

UNITED STATES

UNITED STATES

US criminal justice policy continues to raise serious human rights concerns. 2008 saw the resumption of executions after a seven-month hiatus and continued growth of the US prison population, already the world's largest. Also in 2008, Human Rights Watch confirmed that there are more than 2,500 US prisoners serving sentences of life without possibility of parole for crimes committed when they were under 18; no other country imposes this penalty on juvenile offenders.

In positive developments, the US Supreme Court struck down a law that barred Guantanamo detainees from challenging the legality of their detention, and the Department of Justice brought its first prosecution under a 1994 law allowing courts to try torture committed abroad by US citizens or anyone present in the United States.

Death Penalty

From September 2007 until May 2008 there were no executions in the United States while the Supreme Court considered whether lethal injection—the method used by all US death penalty jurisdictions—constitutes cruel and unusual punishment. In April 2008 the Court ruled in *Baze v. Rees* that it does not, and executions quickly resumed. Between May and October 2008 there were 30 executions, half of which were in Texas.

Nevertheless, courts and legislatures continue to narrow the scope of capital punishment. In December 2007 New Jersey abolished the death penalty, becoming the first state in more than 40 years to do so. In June 2008 in *Kennedy v. Louisiana* the US Supreme Court ruled that the death penalty may not be imposed for any crime against another person that does not result in death. US courts pronounced 110 new death sentences in 2007, the lowest number since capital punishment was reinstated in 1976.

Between January and October 2008, four prisoners were exonerated and released from death row, bringing to 130 the number of death-sentenced prisoners released since 1973 due to evidence of their innocence.

Targeting Blacks

Drug Law Enforcement and Race in the United States

**HUMAN
RIGHTS
WATCH**

2008 saw a step backward for non-citizens sentenced to death without being allowed to contact their consular officials as required by the Vienna Convention on Consular Relations. On August 5, Texas executed Mexican national José Medellin despite an International Court of Justice (ICJ) decision directing the United States to reexamine such cases, and a directive from President George W. Bush that state courts comply with the ICJ ruling.

Juvenile Life without Parole

In 2008 Human Rights Watch revised upward to 2,502 our estimate of the number of persons in the United States sentenced to life without the possibility of parole for crimes committed when they were under age 18. We also verified that there are no juvenile offenders serving this sentence anywhere else in the world.

Efforts to end juvenile life without parole in the United States continue with reform legislation pending in Congress and in state legislatures in California, Florida, Louisiana, Michigan, and Nebraska. In 2008 the United Nations Committee on the Elimination of Racial Discrimination recommended that the United States, "in light of the disproportionate imposition" of the sentence on racial minorities, discontinue its use for crimes committed by individuals under 18 and review the status of people already serving such sentences.

Incarceration

A June 2008 report by the US Justice Department's Bureau of Justice Statistics found that the incarcerated population had reached an all-time high of 2.3 million, or 762 per 100,000 residents. The United States continues to have both the largest incarcerated population and the highest per capita incarceration rate in the world.

The burden of incarceration falls disproportionately on members of racial and ethnic minorities. Black men are incarcerated at six times the rate of white men, and 10.7 percent of *all* black males age 30 to 34 are behind bars on any given day. A 2008 Human Rights Watch report, "Targeting Blacks," found that racial disparities are even worse for drug offenders, with a black man almost 12 times more likely

When I Die, They'll Send Me Home

Youth Sentenced to Life without Parole in California

HUMAN
RIGHTS
WATCH

than a white man to enter prison with a new drug conviction, despite similar rates of drug use among blacks and whites.

In March 2008 the United Nations Committee on the Elimination of Racial Discrimination expressed "concern with regard to the persistent racial disparities in the criminal justice system ... including the disproportionate number of persons belonging to racial, ethnic and national minorities in the prison population," and urged the United States to "take all necessary steps to guarantee the right of everyone to equal treatment before tribunals and all other organs administering justice."

One out of five state prisoners in the United States is incarcerated for a drug-related offense. Many prisoners, particularly those convicted of drug possession or property crimes, have histories of substance use and addiction. The prevalence of diseases related to injection drug use such as HIV/AIDS and hepatitis C is significantly greater among prisoners than in the general population. Yet US prisons and jails remain resistant, even hostile, to evidence-based practices such as condom distribution or methadone therapy, which have proven to reduce transmission of HIV, hepatitis C, and sexually transmitted diseases and to treat drug addiction.

The Prison Litigation Reform Act (PLRA) of 1996 creates a variety of obstacles for prisoners seeking to vindicate their rights in court. These restrictions—which apply only to prisoners—have resulted in dismissal of lawsuits alleging sexual abuse and other significant injuries. In November 2007 a bill was introduced in the House of Representatives to amend or repeal some provisions of the PLRA.

Corporal Punishment in Public Schools

According to the US Department of Education, more than 200,000 public school students received corporal punishment at least once during the 2006-2007 school year. Corporal punishment—which typically takes the form of one or more blows on the buttocks with a wooden paddle—is legal in public schools in 21 states. A 2008 Human Rights Watch report, "A Violent Education," focuses on corporal punishment in Texas and Mississippi, two of the states where it is most prevalent. The report found that corporal punishment can result in serious injury

UNITED STATES

A Violent Education
Corporal Punishment of Children in US Public Schools

HUMAN
RIGHTS
WATCH

and is used disproportionately against black students and special education students.

Women's Rights

Struggles to achieve pay equity for women continued in 2008, with members of Congress working to overturn a 2007 Supreme Court decision that narrowly construed the statute of limitations for pay discrimination lawsuits against employers. Despite widespread mobilization by women's rights groups, the Lilly Ledbetter Fair Pay Act died in the Senate after passing the House of Representatives. Nonetheless, the gender pay gap narrowed to its smallest size in history, with women earning 78 cents for every dollar earned by men.

US international aid remains laden with restrictions that undermine the sexual and reproductive rights of women. Congress in 2008 reauthorized the President's Emergency Plan for AIDS Relief for another five years, but continued to direct funding toward abstinence-only programs and retained the requirement that organizations pledge their opposition to sex work before receiving US funds. Similarly, the "global gag rule" continues to prohibit foreign organizations receiving US funding from providing abortions, counseling women about abortion, or engaging in advocacy for abortion rights, even if no US funds would be used in those efforts.

Sexual Violence

In the United States, the crime of rape has one of the lowest arrest, prosecution, and conviction rates among serious violent crimes. In 2008 Human Rights Watch began an investigation into the failure of law enforcement authorities to preserve and test evidence in rape cases. When reporting a sexually violent crime, a victim is asked to submit to a four- to six-hour exam to collect DNA evidence that, if tested, may aid in the criminal investigation. But the Justice Department estimates that up to 500,000 of these rape kits sit untested in crime labs and police storage facilities across the United States. In Los Angeles alone there are over 7,300 untested rape kits, with the backlog growing by about 30 a month.

Discrimination Based on Sexual Orientation and Gender Identity

US law continues to offer no national protections against discrimination based on sexual orientation or gender identity, in employment or other areas of life. The Defense of Marriage Act, which prohibits the federal government from recognizing the relationships formed by same-sex couples, remains in force. In 2008 the California and Connecticut supreme courts ruled in favor of equal access to marriage for same-sex couples in those states, but a statewide referendum in November overturned the California ruling. The Uniting American Families Act, which would allow same-sex relationships between a US citizen and a foreign national to be recognized for immigration purposes, did not advance in Congress.

Rights of Non-Citizens

There are some 38 million non-citizens living in the United States, of whom nearly 12 million are undocumented. In 2008 this population faced human rights problems largely similar to those in previous years.

As documented in our 2007 report, "Forced Apart," legal immigrants who have lived in the United States for decades, including lawful permanent residents, are summarily deported under laws passed in 1996 if they have been convicted of a crime, even a non-violent offense such as shoplifting or low-level drug possession. During the deportation proceedings, judges are not permitted to balance the seriousness of a non-citizen's crime against his lawful presence in the US, family relationships (including with a US citizen spouse and minor children), business ownership, tax payments, service in the US military, or likelihood of persecution after deportation. In 2006, the most recent year for which data are available, the number of non-citizens deported increased yet again, to 95,752 from 90,426 in 2005, bringing the total number of persons deported under these laws to 768,345.

In 2008 US Immigration and Customs Enforcement continued a pattern begun in 2007 of large-scale workplace raids in search of undocumented workers. In August 2008, in the largest such raid in US history; nearly 600 non-citizens were arrested in Laurel, Mississippi.

Similarly, in May 2008 immigration agents rounded up 389 undocumented workers at a meatpacking plant in Postville, Iowa. After the raids, Iowa's attorney general filed more than 9,300 criminal misdemeanor charges against the plant's owners and managers for labor law violations including child labor and long shifts without overtime pay. Prosecutors, however, also threatened to charge workers— some of whom had used false IDs to obtain work—with aggravated identity theft, a charge that carries severe penalties and is aimed at persons committing theft by fraud rather than undocumented immigrants seeking jobs.

The United States detains approximately 300,000 non-citizens each year at an annual cost of US$1.8 billion, according to Immigration and Customs Enforcement (ICE). Non-citizens are held in some 300 detention facilities: about two dozen are directly under the control of ICE, although some are operated by private companies, and the remainder are state and local prisons and jails that contract with ICE to provide bed space for ICE detainees.

The large number of detained non-citizens in the United States raises multiple human rights concerns. In a December 2007 report, "Chronic Indifference," we found that ICE fails to monitor adequately the medical care of detainees with HIV, and does not comply with international or national guidelines for appropriate HIV treatment. Research by Human Rights Watch into medical care for women in immigration detention facilities similarly found inadequate provision of routine gynecological care, cervical and breast cancer screenings and diagnosis, family planning services, pre- and post-natal care, and services for survivors of sexual and gender-based violence.

A series of articles published in the *Washington Post* in May 2008 revealed that 30 non-citizens died in detention between 2003 and 2008 as a result of actions taken or not taken by medical staff.

In a positive step, Congress repealed the 15-year-old law barring HIV-positive non-citizens from entering the United States. Although President Bush has signed the bill, at this writing the administration had not yet passed regulations to fully implement repeal of the travel ban.

UNITED STATES

Mixed Results

US Policy and International Standards on the Rights
and Interests of Victims of Crime

H U M A N
R I G H T S
W A T C H

Guantanamo Bay, Indefinite Detention, and Military Commissions

Although President Bush said he would like to see the detention facility at Guantanamo Bay closed, 255 men remained there at this writing, and no steps to close the facility were expected before the end of the administration. The vast majority of these detainees have been held for nearly seven years without charge. More than half are held in high-security facilities where they spend 22 hours a day in small cells with no natural light or fresh air and few diversions.

In June 2008 the Supreme Court in *Boumediene v. Bush* struck down a law that denied Guantanamo detainees the right to bring federal habeas corpus challenges to the legality of their detention. Nearly all of the detainees filed habeas petitions, but these cases have been delayed by a host of procedural and legal questions such as whether hearings can be conducted in secret.

More than two dozen detainees who were cleared for release cannot be returned to their home countries due to the likelihood that they would face torture upon return. In October 2008 a federal court ruled that the United States must release 17 Chinese Uighurs detained at Guantanamo into the United States. The US government had acknowledged that the men posed no threat but could not be returned to China because they face persecution there. A federal appeals court issued a stay of that order, and the fate of these men remained undecided at this writing.

The United States has continued to repatriate other Guantanamo detainees without meaningful or independent assessment of the risk of torture or abuse they faced upon return. While some detainees obtained court orders requiring advance notice of any transfer, many detainees do not have such orders in place. The United States has claimed that "diplomatic assurances"—promises of humane treatment—from the receiving governments are sufficient protection against abuse, despite compelling evidence to the contrary.

The US government continues to detain Qatari citizen Ali Saheh Kahlah al-Marri in the United States as an "enemy combatant" without charge or trial. Al-Marri was first declared an enemy combatant in 2003, just weeks before his scheduled trial for financial fraud and giving false statements. In 2007 a federal appeals court

UNITED STATES/COUNTERTERRORISM

Locked Up Alone

Detention Conditions and Mental Health at Guantanamo

HUMAN RIGHTS WATCH

panel ruled that al-Marri's detention was unlawful, but the full court overturned the decision. Al-Marri has appealed that ruling to the US Supreme Court.

Meanwhile, the administration continues to prosecute Guantanamo detainees before military commissions that lack fundamental due process guarantees. In May 2008 the US government filed military commission charges seeking the death penalty against Khalid Sheikh Mohammed and four other detainees accused of responsibility for the September 11 attacks. All five were held in secret CIA prisons before they were brought to Guantanamo, and were reportedly subject to years of torture and other abuse. No trial date has been set. The United States is also pursuing cases against 15 other detainees, including Omar Khadr and Mohammed Jawad, who were juveniles when they were first brought to Guantanamo nearly seven years ago.

Only three detainees had been convicted by military commissions at this writing. Australian David Hicks was convicted by plea agreement in March 2007 and is now free in Australia. The first military commission trial took place in July 2008 against Salim Ahmed Hamdan, Osama bin Laden's former driver. Hamdan was acquitted of conspiracy and convicted of providing material support to terrorism, and sentenced to five-and-a-half years with credit for five years' time served. As it has said with respect to all Guantanamo detainees, the Bush administration contends that Hamdan can be detained even after his sentence is completed. In November 2008 Ali Hamza al Bahlul was convicted on terrorism charges and sentenced to life in prison.

Torture Policy

Over the past three years Congress and the courts have repudiated the Bush administration's reliance on torture as an interrogation technique. In September 2006 the Pentagon announced new rules applicable to all US military interrogations and disavowed abusive techniques, such as waterboarding, forced nudity, and induced hypothermia. In February 2008 Congress passed legislation mandating that the CIA adhere to these same rules, but it was vetoed by President Bush.

Secret CIA Prisons

In April 2008 the Department of Defense announced the transfer to Guantanamo of a detainee previously held in CIA custody, indicating that the CIA's secret prisons were still operational as of that time. Two to three dozen former CIA detainees remain "disappeared," their whereabouts unknown. Many of them are believed to have been unlawfully rendered to countries such as Syria, Libya, Pakistan, and Algeria.

Denial of Refugee Protection

US law allows authorities to deny refugee protection to persons believed to have associated with or provided "material support" to certain armed groups. The broad terms of the law have led authorities to bar persons who qualify as refugees under international law, including rape victims forced into domestic servitude by rebel groups. In January 2008 Congress passed legislation that gave the administration the power to waive these bars in deserving cases, but the exercise of this discretion has been painstakingly slow.

Domestic Prosecution of Torture Abroad

In a positive development, the Department of Justice brought its first case under a 1994 law allowing courts to try torture committed abroad by US citizens or anyone present in the US. A Miami jury in October 2008 convicted Charles "Chuckie" Taylor, Jr., the son of the former Liberian president and a US citizen, on several counts of torture for crimes committed by the elite military unit he headed in Liberia from 1997 to 2003.

Key International Actors

At the conclusion of his June 2008 visit, the UN special rapporteur on extrajudicial, summary or arbitrary executions called on the United States to improve its military justice system and to ensure that the death penalty is applied fairly and without racial discrimination. The special rapporteur on contemporary forms of racism, racial discrimination, xenophobia and related intolerance expressed concern about residential racial segregation and the poor state of public education after his visit in mid-2008.

Although the European Union has called on the United States to close the Guantanamo detention facility, it has not publicly criticized the military commissions or made concrete proposals regarding trial or release of Guantanamo detainees. By contrast, the EU and member states have intervened and attempted to halt executions in a number of US death penalty cases.

Courting History
The Landmark International Criminal Court's First Years

H U M A N
RIGHTS
WATCH

2008
HUMAN RIGHTS WATCH
PUBLICATIONS

BY COUNTRY

Afghanistan
"Troops in Contact": Airstrikes and Civilian Deaths in Afghanistan, September 2008, 43pp.

Bangladesh
The Torture of Tasneem Khalil: How the Bangladesh Military Abuses Its Power Under the State of Emergency, February 2008, 44pp.

Bosnia and Herzegovina
Still Waiting: Bringing Justice for War Crimes, Crimes against Humanity, and Genocide in Bosnia and Herzegovina's Cantonal and District Courts, July 2008, 74pp.

Burma
Vote to Nowhere: The May 2008 Constitutional Referendum in Burma, May 2008, 65pp.

Crackdown: Repression of the 2007 Popular Protests in Burma, December 2007, 131pp.

Burundi
"Every Morning They Beat Me": Police Abuses in Burundi, April 2008, 41pp.

China
China's Forbidden Zones: Shutting the Media out of Tibet and Other "Sensitive" Stories, July 2008, 79pp.

"Walking on Thin Ice": Control, Intimidation and Harassment of Lawyers in China, April 2008, 146pp.

Denied Status, Denied Education: Children of North Korean Women in China, April 2008, 24pp.

"One Year of My Blood": Exploitation of Migrant Construction Workers in Beijing, March 2008, 59pp.

Colombia
Breaking the Grip?: Obstacles to Justice for Paramilitary Mafias in Colombia, October 2008, 140pp.

Côte d'Ivoire
"The Best School": Student Violence, Impunity, and the Crisis in Côte d'Ivoire,
May 2008, 102pp.

Democratic Republic of Congo
"We Will Crush You": The Restriction of Political Space in the Democratic Republic of Congo,
November 2008, 96pp.

Egypt
Sinai Perils: Risks to Migrants, Refugees, and Asylum Seekers in Egypt and Israel,
November 2008, 94pp.

Anatomy of a State Security Case: The "Victorious Sect" Arrests, December 2007, 87pp.

Ethiopia
"Why Am I Still Here?": The 2007 Horn of Africa Renditions and the Fate of Those Still Missing,
October 2008, 58pp.

Collective Punishment: War Crimes and Crimes against Humanity in the Ogaden area of
Ethiopia's Somali Region, June 2008, 136pp.

European Union
Benchmarks, Consultations, and Transparency: Making the EU Central Asia Strategy
an Effective Tool for Human Rights Improvements, April 2008, 15pp.

France
Preempting Justice: Counterterrorism Laws and Procedures in France, July 2008, 88pp.

Georgia
Crossing the Line: Georgia's Violent Dispersal of Protestors and Raid on Imedi Television,
December 2007, 102pp.

Greece
Stuck in a Revolving Door: Iraqis and Other Asylum Seekers and Migrants at the Greece/Turkey
Entrance to the European Union, November 2008, 135pp.

India

"These Fellows Must Be Eliminated": Relentless Violence and Impunity in Manipur, September 2008, 80pp.

Dangerous Duty: Children and the Chhattisgarh Conflict, September 2008, 62pp.

Getting Away with Murder: 50 Years of the Armed Forces (Special Powers) Act, August 2008, 20pp.

"Being Neutral is Our Biggest Crime": Government, Vigilante, and Naxalite Abuses in India's Chhattisgarh State, July 2008, 182pp.

Iran

Rights Crisis Escalates: Faces and Cases from Ahmadinejad's Crackdown, September 2008, 9pp.

The Last Holdouts: Ending the Juvenile Death Penalty in Iran, Saudi Arabia, Sudan, Pakistan, and Yemen, September 2008, 23pp.

"You Can Detain Anyone for Anything": Iran's Broadening Clampdown on Independent Activism, January 2008, 53pp.

Iraq

Stuck in a Revolving Door: Iraqis and Other Asylum Seekers and Migrants at the Greece/Turkey Entrance to the European Union, November 2008, 135pp.

Israel

Sinai Perils: Risks to Migrants, Refugees, and Asylum Seekers in Egypt and Israel, November 2008, 94pp.

Off the Map: Land and Housing Rights Violations in Israel's Unrecognized Bedouin Villages, March 2008, 128pp.

Flooding South Lebanon: Israel's Use of Cluster Munitions in Lebanon in July and August 2006, February 2008, 137pp.

Jordan

Torture and Impunity in Jordan's Prisons: Reforms Fail to Tackle Widespread Abuse, October 2008, 95pp.

Double Jeopardy: CIA Renditions to Jordan, April 2008, 39pp.

Shutting Out the Critics: Restrictive Laws Used to Repress Civil Society in Jordan, December 2007, 42pp.

Kenya
"Why Am I Still Here?": The 2007 Horn of Africa Renditions and the Fate of Those Still Missing, October 2008, 58pp.

"All the Men Have Gone": War Crimes in Kenya's Mt. Elgon Conflict, July 2008, 57pp.

Ballots to Bullets: Organized Political Violence and Kenya's Crisis of Governance, March 2008, 81pp.

Lebanon
Flooding South Lebanon: Israel's Use of Cluster Munitions in Lebanon in July and August 2006, February 2008, 137pp.

Rot Here or Die There: Bleak Choices for Iraqi Refugees in Lebanon, December 2007, 68pp.

Lesotho
A Testing Challenge: The Experience of Lesotho's Universal HIV Counseling and Testing Campaign, November 2008, 65pp.

Libya
Libya: Rights at Risk, September 2008, 10pp.

Mexico
Mexico's National Human Rights Commission: A Critical Assessment, February 2008, 130pp.

Nepal
Waiting for Justice: Unpunished Crimes from Nepal's Armed Conflict, September 2008, 122pp.

Appeasing China: Restricting the Rights of Tibetans in Nepal, July 2008, 64pp.

Netherlands
Discrimination in the Name of Integration: Migrants' Rights under the Integration Abroad Act, May 2008, 45pp.

Nigeria
Politics as War: The Human Rights Impact and Causes of Post-Election Violence in Rivers State, Nigeria, March 2008, 55pp.

North Korea
Denied Status, Denied Education: Children of North Korean Women in China, April 2008, 24pp.

Pakistan
The Last Holdouts: Ending the Juvenile Death Penalty in Iran, Saudi Arabia, Sudan, Pakistan, and Yemen, September 2008, 23pp.

Destroying Legality: Pakistan's Crackdown on Lawyers and Judges, December 2007, 86pp.

Palestinian Territories
Internal Fight: Palestinian Abuses in Gaza and the West Bank, July 2008, 113pp.

Peru
My Rights, and My Right to Know: Lack of Access to Therapeutic Abortion in Peru, July 2008, 53pp.

Russia
"As If They Fell From the Sky": Counterinsurgency, Rights Violations, and Rampant Impunity in Ingushetia, June 2008, 110pp.

Choking on Bureaucracy: State Curbs on Independent Civil Society Activism, February 2008, 74pp.

Rwanda
Law and Reality: Progress in Judicial Reform in Rwanda, July 2008, 113pp.

Saudi Arabia
The Ismailis of Najran: Second-class Saudi Citizens, September 2008, 89pp.

The Last Holdouts: Ending the Juvenile Death Penalty in Iran, Saudi Arabia, Sudan, Pakistan, and Yemen, September 2008, 23pp.

"As If I Am Not Human": Abuses against Asian Domestic Workers in Saudi Arabia, July 2008, 137pp.

Perpetual Minors: Human Rights Abuses Stemming from Male Guardianship and Sex Segregation in Saudi Arabia, April 2008, 59pp.

Precarious Justice: Arbitrary Detention and Unfair Trials in the Deficient Criminal Justice System of Saudi Arabia, March 2008, 146pp.

Adults Before Their Time: Children in Saudi Arabia's Criminal Justice System, March 2008, 82pp.

Serbia

Hostages of Tension: Intimidation and Harassment of Ethnic Albanians in Serbia after Kosovo's Declaration of Independence, November 2008, 78pp.

Kosovo Criminal Justice Scorecard, March 2008, 33pp.

Somalia

"Why Am I Still Here?": The 2007 Horn of Africa Renditions and the Fate of Those Still Missing, October 2008, 58pp.

South Africa

Neighbors In Need: Zimbabweans Seeking Refuge in South Africa, June 2008, 119pp.

Spain

Returns at Any Cost: Spain's Push to Repatriate Unaccompanied Children in the Absence of Safeguards, October 2008, 26pp.

Sri Lanka

Recurring Nightmare: State Responsibility for "Disappearances" and Abductions in Sri Lanka, March 2008, 241pp.

Sudan

The Last Holdouts: Ending the Juvenile Death Penalty in Iran, Saudi Arabia, Sudan, Pakistan, and Yemen, September 2008, 23pp.

Abandoning Abyei: Destruction and Displacement in May 2008, July 2008, 32pp.

Crackdown in Khartoum: Mass Arrests, Torture, and Disappearances since the May 10 Attack, June 2008, 31pp.

"They Shot at Us as We Fled": Government Attacks on Civilians in West Darfur in February 2008, May 2008, 38pp.

Five Years On: No Justice for Sexual Violence in Darfur, April 2008, 48pp.

Turkey

Stuck in a Revolving Door: Iraqis and Other Asylum Seekers and Migrants at the Greece/Turkey Entrance to the European Union, November 2008, 135pp.

"We Need a Law for Liberation": Gender, Sexuality, and Human Rights in a Changing Turkey, May 2008, 127pp.

United Kingdom

Not the Way Forward: The UK's Dangerous Reliance on Diplomatic Assurances, October 2008, 36pp.

United States

Fighting Terrorism Fairly and Effectively: Recommendations for the Next Administration, November 2008, 27pp.

A Way Forward for Workers' Rights in US Free Trade Accords, October 2008, 39pp.

Mixed Results: US Policy and International Standards on the Rights and Interests of Victims of Crime, September 2008, 45pp.

A Violent Education: Corporal Punishment of Children in US Public Schools, August 2008, 132pp.

Locked Up Alone: Detention Conditions and Mental Health at Guantanamo, June 2008, 57pp.

Targeting Blacks: Drug Law Enforcement and Race in the United States, June 2008, 69pp.

Double Jeopardy: CIA Renditions to Jordan, April 2008, 39pp.

"When I Die, They'll Send Me Home": Youth Sentenced to Life without Parole in California, January 2008, 102pp.

Chronic Indifference: HIV/AIDS Services for Immigrants Detained by the United States, December 2007, 498pp.

Uzbekistan

"Saving its Secrets": Government Repression in Andijan, May 2008, 49pp.

Venezuela

A Decade Under Chávez: Political Intolerance and Lost Opportunities for Advancing Human Rights in Venezuela, September 2008, 236pp.

Yemen

Invisible Civilians: The Challenge of Humanitarian Access in Yemen's Forgotten War, November 2008, 50pp.

Disappearances and Arbitrary Arrests in the Armed Conflict with Huthi Rebels in Yemen, October 2008, 49pp.

The Last Holdouts: Ending the Juvenile Death Penalty in Iran, Saudi Arabia, Sudan, Pakistan, and Yemen, September 2008, 23pp.

Zambia

Hidden in the Mealie Meal: Gender-Based Abuses and Women's HIV Treatment in Zambia, December 2007, 98pp.

Zimbabwe

"Our Hands Are Tied": Erosion of the Rule of Law in Zimbabwe, November 2008, 51pp.

"They Beat Me like a Dog": Political Persecution of Opposition Activists and Supporters in Zimbabwe, August 2008, 22pp.

Neighbors In Need: Zimbabweans Seeking Refuge in South Africa, June 2008, 119pp.

"Bullets for Each of You": State-Sponsored Violence since Zimbabwe's March 29 Elections, June 2008, 72pp.

All Over Again: Human Rights Abuses and Flawed Electoral Conditions in Zimbabwe's Coming General Elections, March 2008, 48pp.

BY THEME

Arms Issues

"Troops in Contact": Airstrikes and Civilian Deaths in Afghanistan, September 2008, 43pp.

Flooding South Lebanon: Israel's Use of Cluster Munitions in Lebanon in July and August 2006, February 2008, 137pp.

Business and Human Rights Issues

A Way Forward for Workers' Rights in US Free Trade Accords, October 2008, 39pp.

On the Margins of Profit: Rights at Risk in the Global Economy, February 2008, 54pp.

Terrorism and Counterterrorism Issues

Fighting Terrorism Fairly and Effectively: Recommendations for the Next Administration, November 2008, 27pp.

Not the Way Forward: The UK's Dangerous Reliance on Diplomatic Assurances, October 2008, 36pp.

"Why Am I Still Here?": The 2007 Horn of Africa Renditions and the Fate of Those Still Missing, October 2008, 58pp.

Preempting Justice: Counterterrorism Laws and Procedures in France, July 2008, 88pp.

Locked Up Alone: Detention Conditions and Mental Health at Guantanamo, June 2008, 57pp.

Double Jeopardy: CIA Renditions to Jordan, April 2008, 39pp.

Anatomy of a State Security Case: The "Victorious Sect" Arrests in Egypt, December 2007, 87pp.

Children's Rights Issues

Returns at Any Cost: Spain's Push to Repatriate Unaccompanied Children in the Absence of Safeguards, October 2008, 26pp.

Dangerous Duty: Children and the Chhattisgarh Conflict in India, September 2008, 62pp.

A Violent Education: Corporal Punishment of Children in US Public Schools, August 2008, 132pp.

Coercion and Intimidation of Child Soldiers to Participate in Violence, April 2008, 16pp.

Denied Status, Denied Education: Children of North Korean Women in China, April 2008, 24pp.

Adults Before Their Time: Children in Saudi Arabia's Criminal Justice System, March 2008, 82pp.

"When I Die, They'll Send Me Home": Youth Sentenced to Life without Parole in California, January 2008, 102pp.

HIV/AIDS Issues
A Testing Challenge: The Experience of Lesotho's Universal HIV Counseling and Testing Campaign, November 2008, 65pp.

Neighbors In Need: Zimbabweans Seeking Refuge in South Africa, June 2008, 119pp.

Hidden in the Mealie Meal: Gender-Based Abuses and Women's HIV Treatment in Zambia, December 2007, 98pp.

Chronic Indifference: HIV/AIDS Services for Immigrants Detained by the United States, December 2007, 498pp.

International Justice Issues
The Last Holdouts: Ending the Juvenile Death Penalty in Iran, Saudi Arabia, Sudan, Pakistan, and Yemen, September 2008, 23pp.

Courting History: The Landmark International Criminal Court's First Years, July 2008, 250pp.

Still Waiting: Bringing Justice for War Crimes, Crimes against Humanity, and Genocide in Bosnia and Herzegovina's Cantonal and District Courts, July 2008, 74pp.

Kosovo Criminal Justice Scorecard, March 2008, 34pp.

Lesbian, Gay, Bisexual, and Transgender Issues
"We Need a Law for Liberation": Gender, Sexuality, and Human Rights in a Changing Turkey, May 2008, 127pp.

Refugees/Displaced Persons Issues
Stuck in a Revolving Door: Iraqis and Other Asylum Seekers and Migrants at the Greece/Turkey Entrance to the European Union, November 2008, 135pp.

Sinai Perils: Risks to Migrants, Refugees, and Asylum Seekers in Egypt and Israel, November 2008, 94pp.

Returns at Any Cost: Spain's Push to Repatriate Unaccompanied Children in the Absence of Safeguards, October 2008, 26pp.

Neighbors In Need: Zimbabweans Seeking Refuge in South Africa, June 2008, 119pp.

Discrimination in the Name of Integration: Migrants' Rights under the Integration Abroad Act in the Netherlands, May 2008, 45pp.

Denied Status, Denied Education: Children of North Korean Women in China, April 2008, 24pp.

Rot Here or Die There: Bleak Choices for Iraqi Refugees in Lebanon, December 2007, 68pp.

Women's Rights Issues

My Rights, and My Right to Know: Lack of Access to Therapeutic Abortion in Peru, July 2008, 53pp.

Perpetual Minors: Human Rights Abuses Stemming from Male Guardianship and Sex Segregation in Saudi Arabia, April 2008, 59pp.

Five Years On: No Justice for Sexual Violence in Darfur, April 2008, 48pp.

Hidden in the Mealie Meal: Gender-Based Abuses and Women's HIV Treatment in Zambia, December 2007, 98pp.

All reports can be accessed online and ordered at www.hrw.org/en/publications.

ARCHBISHOP ALEMANY LIBRARY
DOMINICAN UNIVERSITY
SAN RAFAEL, CALIFORNIA 94901